2018

Changes | An Insider's View

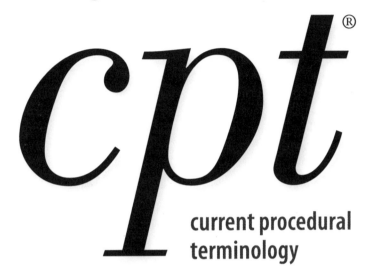

cpt®

current procedural
terminology

D1261901

AMA
AMERICAN MEDICAL
ASSOCIATION

Executive Vice President, Chief Executive Officer: James L. Madara, MD

Chief Operating Officer: Bernard L. Hengesbaugh

Senior Vice President, Health Solutions: Laurie A.S. McGraw

Vice President, Coding and Reimbursement Policy and Strategy: Jay Ahlman

Director, CPT Coding and Regulatory Services: Marie Mindeman

Director, Global Terminology & Data Operations: Corey Smith

Director, Global Terminology Content Development: Monique M. van Berkum, MD

Manager, CPT Editorial Panel Processes: Desiree Rozell

Coding Specialists and/or CPT Editorial Panel Coordinator: Thilani Attale; Martha Espronceda;
 Desiree Evans; Dehandro Hayden; Lianne Stancik

Manager, CPT Content Management and Development: Karen E. O'Hara

Coding and/or Content Management Specialists: Jennifer Bell; Angela Boudreau; Keisha Sutton

Business Operations Coordinator: Michael Pellegrino

Vice President, Operations: Denise Foy

Manager, Book and Product Development and Production: Nancy Baker

Senior Developmental Editor: Lisa Chin-Johnson

Production Specialist: Mary Ann Albanese

Vice President, Sales: Lisa Manoogian

Director, Channel Sales: Erin Kalitowski

Executive, Key Account Manager: Mark Daniels

Vice President, Marketing and Strategic Initiatives: Dave Sosnow

Director, Print and Digital Products: Richard W. Newman

Product Manager, Print and Digital Products: Carol Brockman

Marketing Manager: Vanessa Prieto

Director, CPT Data Products: Matt Menning

Copyright © 2017 by the American Medical Association. All rights reserved.
CPT® is a registered trademark of the American Medical Association

Printed in the United States of America. 17 18 19 20 / BD-WE / 9 8 7 6 5 4 3 2 1
Additional copies of this book may be ordered by calling 800-621-8335 or visit the AMA Store
at amastore.com. Refer to product number OP512918.

No part of this publication may be reproduced, stored in a retrieval system, transmitted in any form,
or by any means, electronic, mechanical, photocopying, recording, or otherwise, without prior written
permission of the publisher.

Current Procedural Terminology (CPT®) is copyright 1966, 1970, 1973, 1977, 1981, 1983–2017 by the
American Medical Association. All rights reserved.

The AMA does not directly or indirectly practice medicine or dispense medical services. This publication does not replace the AMA's *Current Procedural Terminology* codebook or other appropriate coding
authority. The coding information in this publication should be used only as a guide.

Internet address: www.ama-assn.org

To request a license for distribution of products containing or reprinting CPT codes and/or guidelines,
please see our website at www.ama-assn.org/go/cpt, or contact the American Medical Association
CPT/DBP Intellectual Property Services, 330 North Wabash Avenue, Suite 39300, Chicago, IL 60611,
312 464-5022.

ISBN: 978-1-62202-602-9
AC34: 11/17

Contents

Contents

Foreword

The American Medical Association (AMA) is pleased to offer *CPT® Changes 2018: An Insider's View (CPT Changes)*. Since this book was first published in 2000, it has served as the definitive text on additions, revisions, and deletions to the CPT code set.

In developing this book, it was our intention to provide CPT users with a glimpse of the logic, rationale, and proposed function of the changes in the CPT code set that resulted from the decisions of the CPT Editorial Panel and the yearly update process. The AMA staff members have the unique perspective of being both participants in the CPT editorial process and users of the CPT code set.

CPT Changes is intended to bridge understanding between clinical decisions made by the CPT Editorial Panel regarding appropriate service or procedure descriptions with functional interpretations of coding guidelines, code intent, and code combinations, which are necessary for users of the CPT code set. A new edition of this book, like the codebook, is published annually.

To assist CPT users in applying the new and revised CPT codes, this book includes clinical examples that describe the typical patient who might undergo the procedure and detailed descriptions of the procedure. Both of these are required as a part of the CPT code change proposal process, which are used by the CPT Editorial Panel in crafting language, guidelines, and parenthetical notes associated with the new or revised codes. In addition, many of the clinical examples and descriptions of the procedures are used in the AMA/Specialty Society Relative Value Scale (RVS) Update (RUC) process to conduct surveys on physician work and to develop work relative value recommendations to the Centers for Medicare and Medicaid Services (CMS) as part of the Medicare Physician Fee Schedule (MPFS).

We are confident that the information provided in *CPT Changes* will prove to be a valuable resource to CPT users, not only as they apply changes for the year of publication, but also as a resource for frequent reference as they continue their education in CPT coding. The AMA makes every effort to be a voice of clarity and consistency in an otherwise confusing system of health care claims and payment, and *CPT Changes 2018: An Insider's View* demonstrates our continued commitment to assist users of the CPT code set.

Using This Book

This book is designed to serve as a reference guide to understanding the changes contained in the Current Procedural Terminology (CPT®) 2018 code set and is not intended to replace the CPT codebook. Every effort is made to ensure accuracy, however, if differences exist, you should always defer to the information in the *CPT 2018* codebook.

The Symbols

This book uses the same coding conventions as those used in the CPT nomenclature.

● Indicates a new procedure number was added to the CPT nomenclature

▲ Indicates a code revision has resulted in a substantially altered procedure descriptor

+ Indicates a CPT add-on code

⊘ Indicates a code that is exempt from the use of modifier 51 but is not designated as a CPT add-on procedure or service

►◄ Indicates revised guidelines, cross-references, and/or explanatory text

✗ Indicates a code for a vaccine that is pending FDA approval

\# Indicates a resequenced code. Note that rather than deleting and renumbering, resequencing allows existing codes to be relocated to an appropriate location for the code concept, regardless of the numeric sequence. Numerically placed references (ie, Code is out of numerical sequence. See...) are used as navigational alerts in the CPT codebook to direct the user to the location of an out-of-sequence code. Therefore, remember to refer to the CPT codebook for these references.

★ Indicates a telemedicine code

Whenever possible, complete segments of text from the CPT codebook are provided; however, in some instances, only pertinent text is included.

The Rationale

After listing each change or series of changes from the CPT codebook, a rationale is provided. The rationale is intended to provide a brief clarification and explanation of the changes. Nevertheless, it is important to note that they may not address every question that may arise as a result of the changes.

Reading the Clinical Examples

The clinical examples and their procedural descriptions, which reflect typical clinical situations found in the health-care setting, are included in this text with many of the codes to provide practical situations for which the new and/or revised codes in the CPT 2018 code set would be appropriately reported. It is important to note that these examples do not suggest limiting the use of a code; instead, they are meant to represent the typical patient and service or procedure, as previously stated. In addition, they do not describe the universe of patients for whom the service or procedure would be appropriate. It is important to also note that third-party payer reporting policies may differ.

Summary of Additions, Deletions, and Revisions and Indexes

A **summary of additions, deletions, and revisions** for the section is presented in a tabular format at the beginning of each section. This table provides readers with the ability to quickly search and have an overview of all of the new, revised, and deleted codes for 2018. In addition to the tabular review of changes, the coding index individually lists all of the new, revised, and deleted codes with each code's status (new, revised, deleted) in parentheses. For more information about these indexes, please read the **Instructions for the Use of the Changes Indexes** on page 227.

CPT Codebook Conventions and Styles

Similar to the CPT codebook, the guidelines and revised and new CPT code descriptors and parenthetical notes in *CPT Changes 2018* are set in green type. Any revised text, guidelines, and/or headings are indicated with the ▶ ◀ symbols. To match the style used in the codebook, the revised or new text symbol is placed at the beginning and end of a paragraph or section that contains revisions, and the use of green text visually indicates new and/or revised content. Similarly, each section's and subsections' (Surgery) complete code range are listed in the tabs, regardless if these codes are discussed in this book. In addition, all of the different level of headings in the codebook are also picked up, as appropiate, and set in the same style and color. Besides matching the convention and style used in the CPT codebook, the Rationales are placed within a shaded box to distinguish them from the rest of the content for quick and easy reference.

Evaluation and Management

Numerous changes have been made to the Evaluation and Management (E/M) section. Some of the changes include editorial revisions to the hospital observation services codes (99217-99220) to include "outpatient hospital." These revisions affect only the site of service descriptor.

The Anticoagulation Management subsection and codes 99363 and 99364 have been deleted. A new cross-reference directs users to the new appropriate codes and subsection for home international normalized ratio management, now located in the Medicine section. Guidelines and parentheticals have been revised in other subsections within the E/M section to reflect this change.

The following three new subsections have been added: Cognitive Assessment and Care Plan Services, Psychiatric Collaborative Care Management Services, and General Behavioral Health Integration Care Management. The Cognitive Assessment and Care Plan Services subsection contains new guidelines, new code (99483), and a parenthetical note to report assessments and care plan services for patients with cognitive impairments. The Psychiatric Collaborative Care Management Services subsection contains three new codes (99492, 99493, 99494), along with new guidelines, definitions, and a coding tip on reporting collaborative care for psychiatric management services. The new subsection, General Behavioral Health Integration Care Management, contains guidelines, parenthetical notes, new code (99484), and a coding tip to report care management services for behavioral health conditions.

Guidelines in the Critical Care Services and Pediatric Critical Care Patient Transport subsections have been revised with the addition of new chest X-ray codes (71045, 71046). In addition, the inpatient neonatal and pediatric critical care guidelines have been revised to clarify reporting of services when time-based critical care services are reported by multiple individuals.

Summary of Additions, Deletions, and Revisions

The summary of changes shows the actual changes that have been made to the code descriptors.

New codes appear with a bullet (•) and are indicated as "Code added." Revised codes are preceded with a triangle (▲). Within revised codes, the deleted language appears with a ~~strikethrough~~, while new text appears underlined.

The ✗ symbol is used to identify codes for vaccines that are pending FDA approval. The # symbol is used to identify codes that have been resequenced. CPT add-on codes are annotated by the + symbol. The ⊘ symbol is used to identify codes that are exempt from the use of modifier 51. The ★ symbol is used to identify codes that may be used for reporting telemedicine services.

Code	Description
▲99217	**Observation care discharge** day management (This code is to be utilized to report all services provided to a patient on discharge from <u>outpatient hospital</u> "observation status" if the discharge is on other than the initial date of "observation status." To report services to a patient designated as "observation status" or "inpatient status" and discharged on the same date, use the codes for Observation or Inpatient Care Services [including Admission and Discharge Services, 99234-99236 as appropriate]).

Evaluation / Management 99201-99499

Code	Description
▲99218	**Initial observation care,** per day, for the evaluation and management of a patient which requires these 3 key components: • **A detailed or comprehensive history;** • **A detailed or comprehensive examination; and** • **Medical decision making that is straightforward or of low complexity.** Counseling and/or coordination of care with other physicians, other qualified health care professionals, or agencies are provided consistent with the nature of the problem(s) and the patient's and/or family's needs. Usually, the problem(s) requiring admission to <u>outpatient hospital</u> "observation status" are of low severity. Typically, 30 minutes are spent at the bedside and on the patient's hospital floor or unit.
▲99219	**Initial observation care,** per day, for the evaluation and management of a patient, which requires these 3 key components: • **A comprehensive history;** • **A comprehensive examination; and** • **Medical decision making of moderate complexity.** Counseling and/or coordination of care with other physicians, other qualified health care professionals, or agencies are provided consistent with the nature of the problem(s) and the patient's and/or family's needs. Usually, the problem(s) requiring admission to <u>outpatient hospital</u> "observation status" are of moderate severity. Typically, 50 minutes are spent at the bedside and on the patient's hospital floor or unit.
▲99220	**Initial observation care,** per day, for the evaluation and management of a patient, which requires these 3 key components: • **A comprehensive history;** • **A comprehensive examination; and** • **Medical decision making of high complexity.** Counseling and/or coordination of care with other physicians, other qualified health care professionals, or agencies are provided consistent with the nature of the problem(s) and the patient's and/or family's needs. Usually, the problem(s) requiring admission to <u>outpatient hospital</u> "observation status" are of high severity. Typically, 70 minutes are spent at the bedside and on the patient's hospital floor or unit.
99363	~~Anticoagulant management for an outpatient taking warfarin, physician review and interpretation of International Normalized Ratio (INR) testing, patient instructions, dosage adjustment (as needed), and ordering of additional tests; initial 90 days of therapy (must include a minimum of 8 INR measurements)~~
99364	~~each subsequent 90 days of therapy (must include a minimum of 3 INR measurements)~~
●99483	Code added
●99492	Code added
●99493	Code added
+●99494	Code added
#●99484	Code added

★ = Telemedicine   ✚ = Add-on code   ✐ = FDA approval pending   # = Resequenced code

Evaluation and Management

Hospital Observation Services

Observation Care Discharge Services

▲ **99217** **Observation care discharge** day management (This code is to be utilized to report all services provided to a patient on discharge from outpatient hospital "observation status" if the discharge is on other than the initial date of "observation status." To report services to a patient designated as "observation status" or "inpatient status" and discharged on the same date, use the codes for Observation or Inpatient Care Services [including Admission and Discharge Services, 99234-99236 as appropriate.])

Initial Observation Care

New or Established Patient

▶The following codes are used to report the encounter(s) by the supervising physician or other qualified health care professional with the patient when designated as outpatient hospital "observation status." This refers to the initiation of observation status, supervision of the care plan for observation and performance of periodic reassessments. For observation encounters by other physicians, see office or other outpatient consultation codes (99241-99245) or subsequent observation care codes (99224-99226) as appropriate.◀

▲ **99218** **Initial observation care,** per day, for the evaluation and management of a patient which requires these 3 key components:

- **A detailed or comprehensive history;**
- **A detailed or comprehensive examination; and**
- **Medical decision making that is straightforward or of low complexity.**

Counseling and/or coordination of care with other physicians, other qualified health care professionals, or agencies are provided consistent with the nature of the problem(s) and the patient's and/or family's needs.

Usually, the problem(s) requiring admission to outpatient hospital "observation status" are of low severity. Typically, 30 minutes are spent at the bedside and on the patient's hospital floor or unit.

▲ **99219** **Initial observation care,** per day, for the evaluation and management of a patient, which requires these 3 key components:

- **A comprehensive history;**
- **A comprehensive examination; and**
- **Medical decision making of moderate complexity.**

Counseling and/or coordination of care with other physicians, other qualified health care professionals, or agencies are provided consistent with the nature of the problem(s) and the patient's and/or family's needs.

Usually, the problem(s) requiring admission to outpatient hospital "observation status" are of moderate severity. Typically, 50 minutes are spent at the bedside and on the patient's hospital floor or unit.

▲ **99220** **Initial observation care,** per day, for the evaluation and management of a patient, which requires these 3 key components:

- **A comprehensive history;**
- **A comprehensive examination; and**
- **Medical decision making of high complexity.**

Counseling and/or coordination of care with other physicians, other qualified health care professionals, or agencies are provided consistent with the nature of the problem(s) and the patient's and/or family's needs.

Usually, the problem(s) requiring admission to outpatient hospital "observation status" are of high severity. Typically, 70 minutes are spent at the bedside and on the patient's hospital floor or unit.

Rationale

Codes 99217, 99218, 99219, and 99220 have been editorially revised by adding the term "outpatient hospital" in front of "observation status" in the code descriptor, in order to better align the CPT code set with other nomenclatures. This revision affects only the description of the site of service, therefore, it does not affect how these codes are used or reported because no service changes have been made to the code descriptor.

Critical Care Services

Critical care is the direct delivery by a physician(s) or other qualified health care professional of medical care for a critically ill or critically injured patient. A critical illness or injury acutely impairs one or more vital organ systems such that there is a high probability of imminent or life threatening deterioration in the patient's condition. Critical care involves high complexity decision making to assess, manipulate, and support vital system function(s) to treat single or multiple vital organ system failure and/or to prevent further life threatening deterioration of the patient's condition. Examples of vital organ system failure include, but are not limited to: central nervous system failure, circulatory failure, shock, renal, hepatic, metabolic, and/or respiratory failure. Although critical care typically requires interpretation of multiple physiologic parameters and/or application of advanced technology(s), critical care may be provided in life threatening situations when these elements are not present. Critical care may be provided on multiple days, even if no changes are made in the treatment rendered to the patient, provided that the patient's condition continues to require the level of attention described above.

Providing medical care to a critically ill, injured, or post-operative patient qualifies as a critical care service only if both the illness or injury and the treatment being provided meet the above requirements. Critical care is usually, but not always, given in a critical care area, such as the coronary care unit, intensive care unit, pediatric intensive care unit, respiratory care unit, or the emergency care facility.

Inpatient critical care services provided to infants 29 days through 71 months of age are reported with pediatric critical care codes 99471-99476. The pediatric critical care codes are reported as long as the infant/young child qualifies for critical care services during the hospital stay through 71 months of age. Inpatient critical care services provided to neonates (28 days of age or younger) are reported with the neonatal critical care codes 99468 and 99469. The neonatal critical care codes are reported as long as the neonate qualifies for critical care services during the hospital stay through the 28th postnatal day. The reporting of the pediatric and neonatal critical care services is not based on time or the type of unit (eg, pediatric or neonatal critical care unit) and it is not dependent upon the type of physician or other qualified health care professional delivering the care. To report critical care services provided in the outpatient setting (eg, emergency department or office), for neonates and pediatric patients up through 71 months of age, see the critical care codes 99291, 99292. If the same individual provides critical care services for a neonatal or pediatric patient in both the outpatient and inpatient settings on the same day, report only the appropriate neonatal or pediatric critical care code 99468-99472 for all critical care services provided on that day. Also report 99291-99292 for neonatal or pediatric critical care services provided by the individual providing critical care at one facility but transferring the patient to another facility. Critical care services provided by a second individual of a different specialty not reporting a per day neonatal or pediatric critical care code can be reported with codes 99291, 99292. For additional instructions on reporting these services, see the Neonatal and Pediatric Critical Care section and codes 99468-99476.

Services for a patient who is not critically ill but happens to be in a critical care unit are reported using other appropriate E/M codes.

Critical care and other E/M services may be provided to the same patient on the same date by the same individual.

▶For reporting by professionals, the following services are included in critical care when performed during the critical period by the physician(s) providing critical care: the interpretation of cardiac output measurements (93561, 93562), chest X rays (71045, 71046), pulse oximetry (94760, 94761, 94762), blood gases, and information data stored in computers (eg, ECGs, blood pressures, hematologic data [99090]); gastric intubation (43752, 43753); temporary transcutaneous pacing (92953); ventilatory management (94002-94004, 94660, 94662); and vascular access procedures (36000, 36410, 36415, 36591, 36600). Any services performed that are not included in this listing should be reported separately. Facilities may report the above services separately.◀

99291   **Critical care, evaluation and management** of the critically ill or critically injured patient; first 30-74 minutes

+ **99292**   each additional 30 minutes (List separately in addition to code for primary service)

(Use 99292 in conjunction with 99291)

Rationale

In support of the establishment of new codes to report chest X ray, codes 71010, 71015, and 71020 have been deleted. Therefore, these deleted codes that were in the Critical Care Services section guidelines and the Coding Tip (after code 99292) have been replaced with new codes 71045 and 71046.

Refer to the codebook and the Rationale for codes 71045-71048 for a full discussion of the changes.

Domiciliary, Rest Home (eg, Boarding Home), or Custodial Care Services

▶The following codes are used to report evaluation and management services in a facility which provides room, board and other personal assistance services, generally on a long-term basis. These codes include evaluation and management services provided in an assisted living facility, group home, custodial care, and intermediate care facilities.◀

★ =Telemedicine   ✚ =Add-on code   ✐ =FDA approval pending   # =Resequenced code

New Patient

99324 Domiciliary or rest home visit for the evaluation and management of a new patient, which requires these 3 key components:

- **A problem focused history;**
- **A problem focused examination; and**
- **Straightforward medical decision making.**

Counseling and/or coordination of care with other physicians, other qualified health care professionals, or agencies are provided consistent with the nature of the problem(s) and the patient's and/or family's needs.

Usually, the presenting problem(s) are of low severity. Typically, 20 minutes are spent with the patient and/or family or caregiver.

99325 Domiciliary or rest home visit for the evaluation and management of a new patient, which requires these 3 key components:

- **An expanded problem focused history;**
- **An expanded problem focused examination; and**
- **Medical decision making of low complexity.**

Counseling and/or coordination of care with other physicians, other qualified health care professionals, or agencies are provided consistent with the nature of the problem(s) and the patient's and/or family's needs.

Usually, the presenting problem(s) are of moderate severity. Typically, 30 minutes are spent with the patient and/or family or caregiver.

99326 Domiciliary or rest home visit for the evaluation and management of a new patient, which requires these 3 key components:

- **A detailed history;**
- **A detailed examination; and**
- **Medical decision making of moderate complexity.**

Counseling and/or coordination of care with other physicians, other qualified health care professionals, or agencies are provided consistent with the nature of the problem(s) and the patient's and/or family's needs.

Usually, the presenting problem(s) are of moderate to high severity. Typically, 45 minutes are spent with the patient and/or family or caregiver.

Rationale

The Domiciliary, Rest Home (eg, Boarding Home), or Custodial Care Services guidelines have been editorially revised to include "group home, custodial care, and intermediate care facilities." The addition of these terms within the guidelines ensures that the CPT code set is aligned and synchronized with other nomenclatures.

Prolonged Services

Prolonged Service With Direct Patient Contact

►Codes 99354-99357 are used when a physician or other qualified health care professional provides prolonged service(s) involving direct patient contact that is provided beyond the usual service in either the inpatient or outpatient setting. Direct patient contact is face-to-face and includes additional non-face-to-face services on the patient's floor or unit in the hospital or nursing facility during the same session. This service is reported in addition to the primary procedure (ie, the designated evaluation and management services at any level, code 90837, *Psychotherapy, 60 minutes with patient*, 90847, *Family psychotherapy [conjoint psychotherapy] [with patient present], 50 minutes*), and any other services provided at the same session. Appropriate codes should be selected for supplies provided or other procedures performed in the care of the patient during this period.◄

Codes 99354-99355 are used to report the total duration of face-to-face time spent by a physician or other qualified health care professional on a given date providing prolonged service in the office or other outpatient setting, even if the time spent by the physician or other qualified health care professional on that date is not continuous. Codes 99356-99357 are used to report the total duration of time spent by a physician or other qualified health care professional at the bedside and on the patient's floor or unit in the hospital or nursing facility on a given date providing prolonged service to a patient, even if the time spent by the physician or other qualified health care professional on that date is not continuous.

Time spent performing separately reported services other than the E/M or psychotherapy service is not counted toward the prolonged services time.

★+ **99354** Prolonged evaluation and management or psychotherapy service(s) (beyond the typical service time of the primary procedure) in the office or other outpatient setting requiring direct patient contact beyond the usual service; first hour (List separately in addition to code for office or other outpatient **Evaluation and Management** or psychotherapy service)

▶(Use 99354 in conjunction with 90837, 90847, 99201-99215, 99241-99245, 99324-99337, 99341-99350, 99483)◀

(Do not report 99354 in conjunction with 99415, 99416)

★+ **99355** each additional 30 minutes (List separately in addition to code for prolonged service)

(Use 99355 in conjunction with 99354)

(Do not report 99355 in conjunction with 99415, 99416)

+ **99356** Prolonged service in the inpatient or observation setting, requiring unit/floor time beyond the usual service; first hour (List separately in addition to code for inpatient **Evaluation and Management** service)

(Use 99356 in conjunction with 90837, 99218-99220, 99221-99223, 99224-99226, 99231-99233, 99234-99236, 99251-99255, 99304-99310)

+ **99357** each additional 30 minutes (List separately in addition to code for prolonged service)

(Use 99357 in conjunction with 99356)

Rationale

The Prolonged Services guidelines have been editorially revised to allow the reporting of family psychotherapy code 90847 with codes 99354-99357 since 90847 is now a time-based code.

The parenthetical note that follows code 99354 has also been revised. This was done in accordance with the addition of the cognitive assessment and care plan services code 99483.

Refer to the codebook and the Rationale for code 99483 for a full discussion of the changes.

Prolonged Service Without Direct Patient Contact

Codes 99358 and 99359 are used when a prolonged service is provided that is neither face-to-face time in the office or outpatient setting, nor additional unit/floor time in the hospital or nursing facility setting during the same session of an evaluation and management service and is beyond the usual physician or other qualified health care professional service time.

This service is to be reported in relation to other physician or other qualified health care professional services, including evaluation and management services at any level. This prolonged service may be reported on a different date than the primary service to which it is related. For example, extensive record review may relate to a previous evaluation and management service performed earlier and commences upon receipt of past

records. However, it must relate to a service or patient where (face-to-face) patient care has occurred or will occur and relate to ongoing patient management. A typical time for the primary service need not be established within the CPT code set.

Codes 99358 and 99359 are used to report the total duration of non-face-to-face time spent by a physician or other qualified health care professional on a given date providing prolonged service, even if the time spent by the physician or other qualified health care professional on that date is not continuous. Code 99358 is used to report the first hour of prolonged service on a given date regardless of the place of service. It should be used only once per date.

Prolonged service of less than 30 minutes total duration on a given date is not separately reported.

Code 99359 is used to report each additional 30 minutes beyond the first hour regardless of the place of service. It may also be used to report the final 15 to 30 minutes of prolonged service on a given date.

Prolonged service of less than 15 minutes beyond the first hour or less than 15 minutes beyond the final 30 minutes is not reported separately.

▶Do not report 99358, 99359 for time spent in care plan oversight services (99339, 99340, 99374-99380), home and outpatient INR monitoring (93792, 93793), medical team conferences (99366-99368), on-line medical evaluations (99444), or other non-face-to-face services that have more specific codes and no upper time limit in the CPT code set. Codes 99358, 99359 may be reported when related to other non-face-to-face services codes that have a published maximum time (eg, telephone services).◀

99358 **Prolonged evaluation and management service** before and/or after direct patient care; first hour

+ **99359** each additional 30 minutes (List separately in addition to code for prolonged service)

Rationale

In support of the establishment of new codes to report home international normalization ratio (INR) management, the guidelines included in the Prolonged Services Without Direct Patient Contact section have been revised. References to anticoagulation management services (99363 and 99364) have been deleted and replaced with the new home and outpatient INR monitoring services codes (93792 and 93793).

Refer to the codebook and the Rationale for codes 93792 and 93793 for a full discussion of the changes.

★ = Telemedicine   + = Add-on code   ✗ = FDA approval pending   # = Resequenced code

Case Management Services

Case management is a process in which a physician or another qualified health care professional is responsible for direct care of a patient and, additionally, for coordinating, managing access to, initiating, and/or supervising other health care services needed by the patient.

Anticoagulant Management

▶(99363, 99364 have been deleted. To report, see 93792, 93793)◀

Rationale

In support of the establishment of new codes to report home INR management, the Anticoagulant Management subsection and codes 99363 and 99364 have been deleted. A cross-reference parenthetical note replaces this content and directs users to the appropriate codes to report anticoagulation management services.

Refer to the codebook and the Rationale for codes 93792 and 93793 for a full discussion of the changes.

Non-Face-to-Face Services

Telephone Services

99441 Telephone evaluation and management service by a physician or other qualified health care professional who may report evaluation and management services provided to an established patient, parent, or guardian not originating from a related E/M service provided within the previous 7 days nor leading to an E/M service or procedure within the next 24 hours or soonest available appointment; 5-10 minutes of medical discussion

99442 11-20 minutes of medical discussion

99443 21-30 minutes of medical discussion

(Do not report 99441-99443 when using 99339-99340, 99374-99380 for the same call[s])

▶(Do not report 99441-99443 for home and outpatient INR monitoring when reporting 93792, 93793)◀

(Do not report 99441-99443 during the same month with 99487-99489)

(Do not report 99441-99443 when performed during the service time of codes 99495 or 99496)

Rationale

In support of the establishment of new codes to report home INR management, an exclusionary parenthetical note that follows code 99443 in the Telephone Services subsection has been revised. References to anticoagulation management services have been deleted and replaced with home and outpatient INR monitoring services codes 93792 and 93793.

Refer to the codebook and the Rationale for codes 93792 and 93793 for a full discussion of the changes.

On-Line Medical Evaluation

99444 Online evaluation and management service provided by a physician or other qualified health care professional who may report evaluation and management services provided to an established patient or guardian, not originating from a related E/M service provided within the previous 7 days, using the Internet or similar electronic communications network

(Do not report 99444 when using 99339, 99340, 99374-99380 for the same communication[s])

▶(Do not report 99444 for home and outpatient INR monitoring when reporting 93792, 93793)◀

(Do not report 99444 during the same month with 99487-99489)

(Do not report 99444 when performed during the service time of codes 99495 or 99496)

Rationale

In support of the establishment of new codes to report home INR management, an exclusionary parenthetical note that follows code 99444 in the On-Line Medical Evaluation subsection has been revised. References to anticoagulation management services have been deleted and replaced with home and outpatient INR monitoring services codes 93792 and 93793.

Refer to the codebook and the Rationale for codes 93792 and 93793 for a full discussion of the changes.

Evaluation / Management   99201-99499

Inpatient Neonatal Intensive Care Services and Pediatric and Neonatal Critical Care Services

Pediatric Critical Care Patient Transport

Codes 99466, 99467 are used to report the physical attendance and direct face-to-face care by a physician during the interfacility transport of a critically ill or critically injured pediatric patient 24 months of age or younger. Codes 99485, 99486 are used to report the control physician's non-face-to-face supervision of interfacility transport of a critically ill or critically injured pediatric patient 24 months of age or younger. These codes are not reported together for the same patient by the same physician. For the purpose of reporting 99466 and 99467, face-to-face care begins when the physician assumes primary responsibility of the pediatric patient at the referring facility, and ends when the receiving facility accepts responsibility for the pediatric patient's care. Only the time the physician spends in direct face-to-face contact with the patient during the transport should be reported. Pediatric patient transport services involving less than 30 minutes of face-to-face physician care should not be reported using 99466, 99467. Procedure(s) or service(s) performed by other members of the transporting team may not be reported by the supervising physician.

Codes 99485, 99486 may be used to report control physician's non-face-to-face supervision of interfacility pediatric critical care transport, which includes all two-way communication between the control physician and the specialized transport team prior to transport, at the referring facility and during transport of the patient back to the receiving facility. The "control" physician is the physician directing transport services. These codes do not include pretransport communication between the control physician and the referring facility before or following patient transport. These codes may only be reported for patients 24 months of age or younger who are critically ill or critically injured. The control physician provides treatment advice to a specialized transport team who are present and delivering the hands-on patient care. The control physician does not report any services provided by the specialized transport team. The control physician's non-face-to-face time

begins with the first contact by the control physician with the specialized transport team and ends when the patient's care is handed over to the receiving facility team. Refer to 99466 and 99467 for face-to-face transport care of the critically ill/injured patient. Time spent with the individual patient's transport team and reviewing data submissions should be recorded. Code 99485 is used to report the first 16-45 minutes of direction on a given date and should only be used once even if time spent by the physician is discontinuous. Do not report services of 15 minutes or less or any time when another physician is reporting 99466, 99467. Do not report 99485 or 99486 in conjunction with 99466, 99467 when performed by the same physician.

For the definition of the critically injured pediatric patient, see the **Neonatal and Pediatric Critical Care Services** section.

The non-face-to-face direction of emergency care to a patient's transporting staff by a physician located in a hospital or other facility by two-way communication is not considered direct face-to-face care and should not be reported with 99466, 99467. Physician-directed non-face-to-face emergency care through outside voice communication to transporting staff personnel is reported with 99288 or 99485, 99486 based upon the age and clinical condition of the patient.

Emergency department services (99281-99285), initial hospital care (99221-99223), critical care (99291, 99292), initial date neonatal intensive (99477) or critical care (99468) may only be reported after the patient has been admitted to the emergency department, the inpatient floor, or the critical care unit of the receiving facility. If inpatient critical care services are reported in the referring facility prior to transfer to the receiving hospital, use the critical care codes (99291, 99292).

▶The following services are included when performed during the pediatric patient transport by the physician providing critical care and may not be reported separately: routine monitoring evaluations (eg, heart rate, respiratory rate, blood pressure, and pulse oximetry), the interpretation of cardiac output measurements (93562), chest X rays (71045, 71046), pulse oximetry (94760, 94761, 94762), blood gases and information data stored in computers (eg, ECGs, blood pressures, hematologic data) (99090), gastric intubation (43752, 43753), temporary transcutaneous pacing (92953), ventilatory management (94002, 94003, 94660, 94662), and vascular access procedures (36000, 36400, 36405, 36406, 36415, 36591, 36600). Any services performed which are not listed above should be reported separately.◀

Rationale

In support of the establishment of new codes to report chest X ray, codes 71010, 71015, and 71020 have been deleted. Therefore, these deleted codes that were in the Pediatric Critical Care Patient Transport guidelines have been replaced with new codes 71045 and 71046.

Refer to the codebook and the Rationale for codes 71045-71048 for a full discussion of the changes.

Inpatient Neonatal and Pediatric Critical Care

The same definitions for critical care services apply for the adult, child, and neonate.

Codes 99468, 99469 may be used to report the services of directing the inpatient care of a critically ill neonate or infant 28 days of age or younger. They represent care starting with the date of admission (99468) for critical care services and all subsequent day(s) (99469) that the neonate remains in critical care. These codes may be reported only by a single individual and only once per calendar day, per patient. Initial inpatient neonatal critical care (99468) may only be reported once per hospital admission. If readmitted for neonatal critical care services during the same hospital stay, then report the subsequent inpatient neonatal critical care code (99469) for the first day of readmission to critical care, and 99469 for each day of critical care following readmission.

The initial inpatient neonatal critical care code (99468) can be used in addition to 99464 or 99465 as appropriate, when the physician or other qualified health care professional is present for the delivery (99464) or resuscitation (99465) is required. Other procedures performed as a necessary part of the resuscitation (eg, endotracheal intubation [31500]) may also be reported separately, when performed as part of the pre-admission delivery room care. In order to report these procedures separately, they must be performed as a necessary component of the resuscitation and not simply as a convenience before admission to the neonatal intensive care unit.

When a neonate, infant, or child requires initial critical care services on the same day the patient already has received hospital care or intensive care services by the same individual or group, only the initial critical care service code (99468, 99471, 99475) is reported.

▶Time-based critical care services (99291, 99292) are not reportable by the same individual or different individual of the same specialty and same group, when neonatal or pediatric critical care services (99468-99476) may be reported for the same patient on the same day. Time-based critical care services (99291, 99292) may be reported by an individual of a different specialty from either the same or different group on the same day that neonatal or pediatric critical care services are reported. Critical care interfacility transport face-to-face (99466, 99467) or supervisory (99485, 99486) services may be reported by the same or different individual of the same specialty and same group, when neonatal or pediatric critical care services (99468-99476) are reported for the same patient on the same day.◀

Rationale

The guidelines included in the Inpatient Neonatal and Pediatric Critical Care section have been revised to clarify how these services should be reported when these time-based services are reported by multiple individuals. Time-based critical care services (99291 and 99292) may be reported by an individual of a different specialty whether that individual is of the same group or from a group that is different from the one that is providing the neonatal or pediatric critical care services. The guidelines also explain that critical care interfacility transport services (performed face to face or supervisory) may be reported when the services are provided by the same or different individual of the same specialty and same group practice as another individual who provides critical care services (99468-99476) on the same day.

The previous language in the guidelines restricted users from reporting critical care services provided by individuals of the same group. Because different services may be required by individuals of different specialties, changes have been made to reflect the effort required by individuals of a different specialty in providing care, regardless of the group to which they belong. Different services may be required when critical care is provided during an interfacility transport service (99466 and 99467) or during supervision (99485 and 99486) of transport care to a critically ill or critically injured patient who receives neonatal or pediatric critical care services (99468-99476) on the same day. As a result, the instruction directs users to separately report these services under these circumstances.

▸Cognitive Assessment and Care Plan Services◂

▸Cognitive assessment and care plan services are provided when a comprehensive evaluation of a new or existing patient, who exhibits signs and/or symptoms of cognitive impairment, is required to establish or confirm a diagnosis, etiology and severity for the condition. This service includes a thorough evaluation of medical and psychosocial factors, potentially contributing to increased morbidity. Do not report cognitive assessment and care plan services if any of the required elements are not performed or are deemed unnecessary for the patient's condition. For these services, see the appropriate evaluation and management code. A single physician or other qualified health care professional should not report 99483 more than once every 180 days.

Services for cognitive assessment and care plan include a cognition-relevant history, as well as an assessment of factors that could be contributing to cognitive impairment, including, but not limited to, psychoactive medication, chronic pain syndromes, infection, depression and other brain disease (eg, tumor, stroke, normal pressure hydrocephalus). Medical decision making includes current and likely progression of the disease, assessing the need for referral for rehabilitative, social, legal, financial, or community-based services, meal, transportation, and other personal assistance services.◂

● **99483**   Assessment of and care planning for a patient with cognitive impairment, requiring an independent historian, in the office or other outpatient, home or domiciliary or rest home, with all of the following required elements:

- Cognition-focused evaluation including a pertinent history and examination;

- Medical decision making of moderate or high complexity;

- Functional assessment (eg, basic and instrumental activities of daily living), including decision-making capacity;

- Use of standardized instruments for staging of dementia (eg, functional assessment staging test [FAST], clinical dementia rating [CDR]);

- Medication reconciliation and review for high-risk medications;

- Evaluation for neuropsychiatric and behavioral symptoms, including depression, including use of standardized screening instrument(s);

- Evaluation of safety (eg, home), including motor vehicle operation;

- Identification of caregiver(s), caregiver knowledge, caregiver needs, social supports, and the willingness of caregiver to take on caregiving tasks;

- Development, updating or revision, or review of an Advance Care Plan;

- Creation of a written care plan, including initial plans to address any neuropsychiatric symptoms, neurocognitive symptoms, functional limitations, and referral to community resources as needed (eg, rehabilitation services, adult day programs, support groups) shared with the patient and/or caregiver with initial education and support.

Typically, 50 minutes are spent face-to-face with the patient and/or family or caregiver.

▸(Do not report 99483 in conjunction with E/M services [99201, 99202, 99203, 99204, 99205, 99211, 99212, 99213, 99214, 99215, 99241, 99242, 99243, 99244, 99245, 99324, 99325, 99326, 99327, 99328, 99334, 99335, 99336, 99337, 99341, 99342, 99343, 99344, 99345, 99347, 99348, 99349, 99350, 99366, 99367, 99368, 99487, 99489, 99490, 99495, 99496, 99497, 99498]; psychiatric diagnostic procedures [90785, 90791, 90792]; psychological testing [96103]; neuropsychological testing [96120]; brief emotional/behavioral assessment [96127]; medication therapy management services [99605, 99606, 99607])◂

99484   Code is out of numerical sequence. See 99497-99499

Rationale

Cognitive Assessment and Care Plan Services is a new section, which includes new guidelines, a parenthetical note, and new code 99483, that has been established to report assessments and care-plan services for patients with cognitive impairments.

Currently, there is no specific CPT code to report cognitive assessment and care planning. The addition of code 99483 enables these services to be described, addresses the gaps in the provision of care, and promotes quality of care by listing required elements.

Code 99483 is used to report assessment and care planning for a patient with cognitive impairment in the office or other outpatient setting, in the home, or in a domiciliary or rest home. Ten elements, which are specified in the code, must be met in order to report this code. An exclusionary parenthetical note has been added to clarify the reporting of this service.

The new guidelines state that the appropriate evaluation and management services code should be reported if all of the required elements are not met or performed. In addition, a physician or other qualified health care professional should not report code 99483 more than once per 180 days.

★ = Telemedicine   ✚ = Add-on code   ✎ = FDA approval pending   # = Resequenced code

Clinical Example (99483)

An 83-year-old female with hypertension, diabetes, arthritis, and coronary artery disease presents with confusion, weight loss, and failure to maintain her house, where she lives alone.

Description of Procedure (99483)

A complete history, including a focus on the patient's decline, is obtained from the patient, family, and/or caregiver to include identification of potential symptoms that may indicate confounding underlying disease. A pertinent physical examination and assessment of affect, cognition, and functional status (basic activities of daily living and instrumental activities of daily living) are performed, including decision-making capacity, mobility, balance, vision, hearing, psychosocial function, and safety (ie, at home and/or driving). The patient is evaluated for neuropsychiatric and behavioral symptoms, including depression, mood instability, psychotic symptoms, aggression, apathy, and other behavioral disturbance. The stage of dementia is assessed using standardized instruments. A medication reconciliation is completed, and a review for high-risk medications that may affect cognition (separate from rating scales noted in preservice) is performed. The values and preferences of the patient and caregiver for care and goals of care (eg, quality of life, advance care planning) are discussed. The caregiver's relationship to the patient, availability, knowledge, general capability (eg, any physical limitation), and ability and willingness to implement a care plan are evaluated and discussed. Relevant data, options, and risks are considered. A diagnosis is formulated, and a care plan (moderate to high-complexity medical decision making) is developed. A meeting with the clinical care team is held to review findings and develop a care plan. Based on medication reconciliation, a prescription(s) is written, and arrangements for diagnostic testing or referral are made, as necessary. The written care plan is created, and a copy is provided to the patient and/or family or caregiver. Findings and the care plan are reviewed with the patient and/or family or caregiver, to include the etiology and severity of the cognitive impairment, goals of treatment, changes in medication, and recommendations for physical and/or occupational therapy. Safety issues are addressed, caregiving issues are discussed, and recommendations for appropriate community services (eg, rehabilitation services, adult day programs, support groups) are made.

Care Management Services

Care management services are management and support services provided by clinical staff, under the direction of a physician or other qualified health care professional, to a patient residing at home or in a domiciliary, rest home, or assisted living facility. Services may include establishing, implementing, revising, or monitoring the care plan, coordinating the care of other professionals and agencies, and educating the patient or caregiver about the patient's condition, care plan, and prognosis. The physician or other qualified health care professional provides or oversees the management and/or coordination of services, as needed, for all medical conditions, psychosocial needs, and activities of daily living.

A plan of care must be documented and shared with the patient and/or caregiver. A care plan is based on a physical, mental, cognitive, social, functional, and environmental assessment. It is a comprehensive plan of care for all health problems. It typically includes, but is not limited to, the following elements: problem list, expected outcome and prognosis, measurable treatment goals, symptom management, planned interventions, medication management, community/social services ordered, how the services of agencies and specialists unconnected to the practice will be directed/coordinated, identification of the individuals responsible for each intervention, requirements for periodic review, and, when applicable, revision of the care plan.

Codes 99487, 99489, 99490 are reported only once per calendar month and may only be reported by the single physician or other qualified health care professional who assumes the care management role with a particular patient for the calendar month.

The face-to-face and non-face-to-face time spent by the clinical staff in communicating with the patient and/or family, caregivers, other professionals, and agencies; revising, documenting, and implementing the care plan; or teaching self-management is used in determining the care management clinical staff time for the month. Only the time of the clinical staff of the reporting professional is counted. Only count the time of one clinical staff member when two or more clinical staff members are meeting about the patient. **Note:** Do not count any clinical staff time on a day when the physician or qualified health care professional reports an E/M service (office or other outpatient services 99201, 99202, 99203, 99204, 99205, 99211, 99212, 99213, 99214, 99215, domiciliary, rest home services 99324, 99325, 99326, 99327, 99328, 99334, 99335, 99336, 99337, home services 99341, 99342, 99343, 99344, 99345, 99347, 99348, 99349, 99350).

Care management activities performed by clinical staff typically include:

- communication and engagement with patient, family members, guardian or caretaker, surrogate decision makers, and/or other professionals regarding aspects of care;

- communication with home health agencies and other community services utilized by the patient;

- collection of health outcomes data and registry documentation;

- patient and/or family/caregiver education to support self-management, independent living, and activities of daily living;

- assessment and support for treatment regimen adherence and medication management;

- identification of available community and health resources;

- facilitating access to care and services needed by the patient and/or family;

- management of care transitions not reported as part of transitional care management (99495, 99496);

- ongoing review of patient status, including review of laboratory and other studies not reported as part of an E/M service, noted above;

- development, communication, and maintenance of a comprehensive care plan.

The care management office/practice must have the following capabilities:

- provide 24/7 access to physicians or other qualified health care professionals or clinical staff including providing patients/caregivers with a means to make contact with health care professionals in the practice to address urgent needs regardless of the time of day or day of week;

- provide continuity of care with a designated member of the care team with whom the patient is able to schedule successive routine appointments;

- provide timely access and management for follow-up after an emergency department visit or facility discharge;

- utilize an electronic health record system so that care providers have timely access to clinical information;

- use a standardized methodology to identify patients who require care management services;

- have an internal care management process/function whereby a patient identified as meeting the requirements for these services starts receiving them in a timely manner;

- use a form and format in the medical record that is standardized within the practice;

- be able to engage and educate patients and caregivers as well as coordinate care among all service professionals, as appropriate for each patient.

▶E/M services may be reported separately by the same physician or other qualified health care professional during the same calendar month. Care management services include care plan oversight services (99339, 99340, 99374-99380), prolonged services without direct patient contact (99358, 99359), home and outpatient INR monitoring (93792, 93793), medical team conferences (99366, 99367, 99368), education and training (98960, 98961, 98962, 99071, 99078), telephone services (99366, 99367, 99368, 99441, 99442, 99443), on-line medical evaluation (98969, 99444), preparation of special reports (99080), analysis of data (99090, 99091), transitional care management services (99495, 99496), medication therapy management services (99605, 99606, 99607) and, if performed, these services may not be reported separately during the month for which 99487, 99489, 99490 are reported. All other services may be reported. Do not report 99487, 99489, 99490 if reporting ESRD services (90951-90970) during the same month. If the care management services are performed within the postoperative period of a reported surgery, the same individual may not report 99487, 99489, 99490.◀

Care management may be reported in any calendar month during which the clinical staff time requirements are met. If care management resumes after a discharge during a new month, start a new period or report transitional care management services (99495, 99496) as appropriate. If discharge occurs in the same month, continue the reporting period or report Transitional Care Management Services. Do not report 99487, 99489, 99490 for any post-discharge care management services for any days within 30 days of discharge, if reporting 99495, 99496.

Rationale

The guidelines included in the Care Management Services section have been revised. References to anticoagulation management services have been deleted and replaced with home and outpatient INR monitoring services codes 93792 and 93793.

Refer to the codebook and the Rationale for codes 93792 and 93793 for a full discussion of the changes.

►For psychiatric collaborative care management services, see 99492, 99493, 99494.◄

Rationale

In accordance with the establishment of codes 99492, 99493, and 99494, a cross-reference parenthetical note has been added after the Care Management Services guidelines. This note directs users to the new Psychiatric Collaborative Care Management Services codes.

Refer to the codebook and the Rationale for codes 99492, 99493, and 99494 for a full discussion of the changes.

Complex Chronic Care Management Services

Complex chronic care management services are provided during a calendar month that includes criteria for chronic care management services as well as establishment or substantial revision of a comprehensive care plan; medical, functional, and/or psychosocial problems requiring medical decision making of moderate or high complexity; and clinical staff care management services for at least 60 minutes, under the direction of a physician or other qualified health care professional. Physicians or other qualified health care professionals may not report complex chronic care management services if the care plan is unchanged or requires minimal change (eg, only a medication is changed or an adjustment in a treatment modality is ordered). Medical decision making as defined in the Evaluation and Management (E/M) guidelines is determined by the problems addressed by the reporting individual during the month.

Patients who require complex chronic care management services may be identified by practice-specific or other published algorithms that recognize multiple illnesses, multiple medication use, inability to perform activities of daily living, requirement for a caregiver, and/or repeat admissions or emergency department visits. Typical adult patients who receive complex chronic care management services are treated with three or more prescription medications and may be receiving other types of therapeutic interventions (eg, physical therapy, occupational therapy). Typical pediatric patients receive three or more therapeutic interventions (eg, medications, nutritional support, respiratory therapy). All patients have two or more chronic continuous or episodic health conditions that are expected to last at least 12 months, or until the death of the patient, and that place the patient at significant risk of death, acute exacerbation/

decompensation, or functional decline. Typical patients have complex diseases and morbidities and, as a result, demonstrate one or more of the following:

- need for the coordination of a number of specialties and services;
- inability to perform activities of daily living and/or cognitive impairment resulting in poor adherence to the treatment plan without substantial assistance from a caregiver;
- psychiatric and other medical comorbidities (eg, dementia and chronic obstructive pulmonary disease or substance abuse and diabetes) that complicate their care; and/or
- social support requirements or difficulty with access to care.

99487 Complex chronic care management services, with the following required elements:

- multiple (two or more) chronic conditions expected to last at least 12 months, or until the death of the patient,
- chronic conditions place the patient at significant risk of death, acute exacerbation/decompensation, or functional decline,
- establishment or substantial revision of a comprehensive care plan,
- moderate or high complexity medical decision making;
- 60 minutes of clinical staff time directed by a physician or other qualified health care professional, per calendar month.

(Complex chronic care management services of less than 60 minutes duration, in a calendar month, are not reported separately)

(99488 has been deleted. To report one or more face-to-face visits by the physician or other qualified health care professional that are performed in the same month as 99487, use the appropriate E/M code[s])

+ 99489 each additional 30 minutes of clinical staff time directed by a physician or other qualified health care professional, per calendar month (List separately in addition to code for primary procedure)

(Report 99489 in conjunction with 99487)

(Do not report 99489 for care management services of less than 30 minutes additional to the first 60 minutes of complex chronic care management services during a calendar month)

►(Do not report 99487, 99489, 99490 during the same month with 90951-90970, 93792, 93793, 98960-98962, 98966-98969, 99071, 99078, 99080, 99090, 99091, 99339, 99340, 99358, 99359, 99366-99368, 99374-99380, 99441-99444, 99495, 99496, 99605-99607)◄

Rationale

A parenthetical note that follows code 99489 in the Complex Chronic Care Management Services section has been revised. Reference to codes 99363 and 99364 has been deleted, and codes 93792 and 93793 have been added.

Refer to the codebook and the Rationale for codes 93792 and 93793 for a full discussion of the changes.

▶Psychiatric Collaborative Care Management Services◀

▶Psychiatric collaborative care services are provided under the direction of a treating physician or other qualified health care professional (see definitions below) during a calendar month. These services are provided when a patient has a diagnosed psychiatric disorder that requires a behavioral health care assessment; establishing, implementing, revising, or monitoring a care plan; and provision of brief interventions. These services are reported by the treating physician or other qualified health care professional and include the services of the treating physician or other qualified health care professional, the behavioral health care manager (see definition below), and the psychiatric consultant (see definition below), who has contracted directly with the treating physician or other qualified health care professional, to provide consultation.

Patients directed to the behavioral health care manager typically have newly diagnosed conditions, may need help in engaging in treatment, have not responded to standard care delivered in a nonpsychiatric setting, or require further assessment and engagement, prior to consideration of referral to a psychiatric care setting. The following definitions apply to this section:

Definitions

Episode of care patients are treated for an episode of care, which is defined as beginning when the patient is directed by the treating physician or other qualified health care professional to the behavioral health care manager and ending with:

- the attainment of targeted treatment goals, which typically results in the discontinuation of care management services and continuation of usual follow-up with the treating physician or other qualified healthcare professional; or

- failure to attain targeted treatment goals culminating in referral to a psychiatric care provider for ongoing treatment; or

- lack of continued engagement with no psychiatric collaborative care management services provided over a consecutive six month calendar period (break in episode).

A new episode of care starts after a break in episode of six calendar months or more.

Health care professionals refers to the treating physician or other qualified health care professional who directs the behavioral health care manager and continues to oversee the patient's care, including prescribing medications, providing treatments for medical conditions, and making referrals to specialty care when needed. Evaluation and management (E/M) and other services may be reported separately by the same physician or other qualified health care professional during the same calendar month.

Behavioral health care manager refers to clinical staff with a masters-/doctoral-level education or specialized training in behavioral health who provides care management services as well as an assessment of needs, including the administration of validated rating scales, the development of a care plan, provision of brief interventions, ongoing collaboration with the treating physician or other qualified health care professional, maintenance of a registry, all in consultation with a psychiatric consultant. Services are provided both face-to-face and non-face-to-face and psychiatric consultation is provided minimally on a weekly basis, typically non-face-to-face.

The behavioral health care manager providing other services in the same calendar month, such as psychiatric evaluation (90791, 90792), psychotherapy (90832, 90833, 90834, 90836, 90837, 90838), psychotherapy for crisis (90839, 90840), family psychotherapy (90846, 90847), multiple family group psychotherapy (90849), group psychotherapy (90853), smoking and tobacco use cessation counseling (99406, 99407), and alcohol and/or substance abuse structured screening and brief intervention services (99408, 99409), may report these services separately. Activities for services reported separately are not included in the time applied to 99492, 99493, 99494.

Psychiatric consultant refers to a medical professional, who is trained in psychiatry or behavioral health, and qualified to prescribe the full range of medications. The psychiatric consultant advises and makes recommendations, as needed, for psychiatric and other medical care, including psychiatric and other medical differential diagnosis, treatment strategies regarding appropriate therapies, medication management, medical management of complications associated with treatment

Type of Service	Total Duration of Collaborative Care Management Over Calendar Month	Code(s)
Initial - 70 minutes	Less than 36 minutes	Not reported separately
	36-85 minutes	99492
	(36 minutes - 1 hr. 25 minutes)	
Initial plus each additional increment up to 30 minutes	86-115 minutes	99492 X 1 AND 99494 X 1
	(1 hr. 26 minutes - 1 hr. 55 minutes)	
Subsequent - 60 minutes	Less than 31 minutes	Not reported separately
	31-75 minutes	99493
	(31 minutes - 1 hr. 15 minutes)	
Subsequent plus each additional increment up to 30 minutes	76-105 minutes	99493 X 1 AND 99494 X 1
	(1 hr. 16 minutes - 1 hr. 45 minutes)	

of psychiatric disorders, and referral for specialty services, which are typically communicated to the treating physician or other qualified health care professional through the behavioral health care manager. The psychiatric consultant typically does not see the patient or prescribe medications, except in rare circumstances.

The psychiatric consultant may provide services in the calendar month described by other codes, such as evaluation and management (E/M) services and psychiatric evaluation (90791, 90792). These services may be reported separately by the psychiatric consultant. Activities for services reported separately are not included in the services reported using 99492, 99493, 99494.

Do not report 99492 and 99493 in the same calendar month.◄

● **99492** **Initial psychiatric collaborative care management,** first 70 minutes in the first calendar month of behavioral health care manager activities, in consultation with a psychiatric consultant, and directed by the treating physician or other qualified health care professional, with the following required elements:

■ outreach to and engagement in treatment of a patient directed by the treating physician or other qualified health care professional;

■ initial assessment of the patient, including administration of validated rating scales, with the development of an individualized treatment plan;

■ review by the psychiatric consultant with modifications of the plan if recommended;

■ entering patient in a registry and tracking patient follow-up and progress using the registry, with appropriate documentation, and participation in weekly caseload consultation with the psychiatric consultant; and

■ provision of brief interventions using evidence-based techniques such as behavioral activation, motivational interviewing, and other focused treatment strategies.

● **99493** **Subsequent psychiatric collaborative care management,** first 60 minutes in a subsequent month of behavioral health care manager activities, in consultation with a psychiatric consultant, and directed by the treating physician or other qualified health care professional, with the following required elements:

■ tracking patient follow-up and progress using the registry, with appropriate documentation;

■ participation in weekly caseload consultation with the psychiatric consultant;

■ ongoing collaboration with and coordination of the patient's mental health care with the treating physician or other qualified health care professional and any other treating mental health providers;

■ additional review of progress and recommendations for changes in treatment, as indicated, including medications, based on recommendations provided by the psychiatric consultant;

■ provision of brief interventions using evidence-based techniques such as behavioral activation, motivational interviewing, and other focused treatment strategies;

■ monitoring of patient outcomes using validated rating scales; and

■ relapse prevention planning with patients as they achieve remission of symptoms and/or other treatment goals and are prepared for discharge from active treatment.

+● **99494** **Initial or subsequent psychiatric collaborative care management,** each additional 30 minutes in a calendar month of behavioral health care manager activities, in consultation with a psychiatric consultant, and directed by the treating physician or other qualified health care professional (List separately in addition to code for primary procedure)

►(Use 99494 in conjunction with 99492, 99493)◄

Evaluation / Management 99201-99499

—— *Coding Tip* ——————

If the treating physician or other qualified health care professional personally performs behavioral health care manager activities and those activities are not used to meet criteria for a separately reported code, his or her time may be counted toward the required behavioral health care manager time to meet the elements of 99492, 99493, 99494.

Behavioral health care manager time spent coordinating care with the emergency department may be reported using 99492, 99493, 99494, but time spent while the patient is inpatient or admitted to observation status may not be reported using 99492, 99493, 99494.

Rationale

Three new codes (99492, 99493, and 99494), and new guidelines, definitions, and a coding tip have been established in the Care Management Services subsection to report collaborative care for psychiatric management services.

The changes were initiated under the development of a collaborative care model that provides psychiatric care for the most common psychiatric disorders managed in the primary care setting by a team. The addition of these codes allows reporting of psychiatric collaborative services provided under the direction of a treating physician or other qualified health care professional during a calendar month and includes the services of the behavioral health care manager and psychiatric consultant.

These codes are used for patients with common psychiatric conditions who can be treated in a primary care setting by a care manager and psychiatric consultant (usually a psychiatrist), who work with the primary care provider. These conditions include, but are not limited to, depression, anxiety disorders, attention deficit disorder, post-traumatic stress disorder, and substance use disorders. Patients with these conditions are identified and referred by their primary care physician to a psychiatric collaborative care manager.

These codes are reported by the treating physician or other qualified health care professional for a calendar month and include the services of the treating health care professional, behavioral health care manager, and psychiatric consultant. Code 99492 should be reported for the first 70 minutes of initial psychiatric collaborative care management in the first calendar month of behavioral care management activities. Code 99493 should be reported for the first 60 minutes of subsequent psychiatric collaborative care management in a subsequent month.

Code 99494 may be used to report each additional 30 minutes of psychiatric collaborative care management in an initial or subsequent calendar month. See the specific CPT code descriptors for the required elements associated with codes 99492 and 99493.

Because code 99494 is an add-on code, it is not intended to be reported as a stand-alone code. Therefore, instructional parenthetical notes have been added to identify the primary codes that should be reported when this service is performed. The table, **Total Duration of Collaborative Care Management Over a Calendar Month,** may be used to assist with the correct reporting of the psychiatric collaborative care management codes.

Clinical Example (99492)

Adult: A 55-year-old female, who is separated from her husband and has no children at home, has been feeling more fatigued, not sleeping well, and not taking her medicine for hypertension and diabetes. She also worries a lot about her future. The patient is diagnosed as having a behavioral health disorder. The primary care physician (PCP) recommends that the patient be enrolled in the psychiatric collaborative care management services program.

Child/Adolescent: A 15-year-old child is brought in by a parent because of concerns about social withdrawal, anxiety, diminished school performance, and substance abuse. The patient is diagnosed as having a behavioral health disorder. The PCP recommends that the patient be enrolled in the psychiatric collaborative care management services program.

Description of Procedure (99492)

PCP/Treating Physician: General supervision of the behavioral healthcare manager (BHCM) is directed and provided by the physician, who continues to provide or oversee the management and/or coordination of services, as needed, for all medical conditions, psychosocial needs, and activities of daily living. Treatment recommendations from the psychiatric consultant are reviewed with the BHCM by the physician and recommendations are implemented, as appropriate. The physician ensures services are documented appropriately.

Psychiatric Consultant: Information from the BHCM, including history of present illness, past psychiatric/chemical dependency history, family history, social history, and treatments, as well as medical history, review of systems, and focused questions related to safety, lethality, aggression, and/or competence, as indicated, are received and reviewed by the consultant. The recommended treatment plan from the PCP is reviewed by the consultant and any additional treatment recommendations, as indicated, are formulated. Recommendations and associated rationale are communicated by the consultant to the BHCM who, in turn, communicates those to the PCP/treating physician to consider for implementation.

Clinical Example (99493)

Adult: A 55-year-old female, who is separated from her husband and has no children at home, has been feeling more fatigued, not sleeping well, and not taking her medicine for hypertension and diabetes. She also worries a lot about her future. The patient is diagnosed as having a behavioral health disorder. She is enrolled in the psychiatric collaborative care management services program but continues to have symptoms.

Child/Adolescent: A 15-year-old child is brought in by a parent because of concerns about social withdrawal, anxiety, diminished school performance, and substance abuse. The patient is diagnosed as having a behavioral health disorder. The patient is enrolled in the psychiatric collaborative care management services program but continues to have symptoms.

Description of Procedure (99493)

PCP/Treating Physician: General supervision of the BHCM is directed and provided by the physician, who will continue to provide or oversee the management and/or coordination of services, as needed, for all medical conditions, psychosocial needs, and activities of daily living. Treatment recommendations from the psychiatric consultant are reviewed with the BHCM by the physician and recommendations are implemented, as appropriate. The physician ensures services are documented appropriately.

Psychiatric Consultant: Patient progress is reviewed by the consultant with the BHCM, and information provided by the BHCM and/or included in the patient record are solicited and analyzed. Ongoing advice and treatment recommendations, as needed (based on the data), for psychiatric and other medical care, including treatment strategies such as appropriate therapies, medication management, medical management of complications associated with treatment of psychiatric disorders, and referral for specialty care services are provided by the consultant, which are communicated to the PCP/treating physician through the BHCM.

Clinical Example (99494)

Adult: A 50-year-old male has been feeling fatigued and lacks interest in his life after suffering a heart attack six months ago. He is accompanied by his wife who reports that he has been drinking more alcohol during this time. The patient is diagnosed as having a behavioral health disorder. The PCP recommends that the patient be enrolled in or continue with the psychiatric collaborative care management services program. (Use 99494 in conjunction with 99492, 99493.)

Child/Adolescent: A 12-year-old child is brought in by a parent who states that the child was found with marijuana in her room, has been truant from school, and has refused to take her insulin on several occasions. The mother believes she may be sexually active. Her parents separated six months ago. The patient is diagnosed as having a behavioral health disorder. The PCP recommends that the patient be enrolled in or continue with the psychiatric collaborative care management services program. (Use 99494 in conjunction with 99492, 99493.)

Description of Procedure (99494)

PCP/Treating Physician: General supervision of the BHCM is directed and provided by the physician, who will continue to provide or oversee the management and/or coordination of services, as needed, for all medical conditions, psychosocial needs, and activities of daily living. Treatment recommendations from the psychiatric consultant are reviewed with the BHCM by the physician and recommendations are implemented, as appropriate. The physician ensures services are documented appropriately.

Psychiatric Consultant: New patient information or established patient progress is reviewed by the consultant with the BHCM, and clinical information provided by the BHCM and/or located in the patient record are solicited and analyzed. Ongoing advice and treatment recommendations, as needed (based on the data), for psychiatric and other medical care, including treatment strategies such as appropriate therapies, medication management, medical management of complications associated with treatment of psychiatric disorders, and referral for specialty care services are provided by the consultant, which are communicated to the PCP/treating physician through the BHCM.

Transitional Care Management Services

Codes 99495 and 99496 are used to report transitional care management services (TCM). These services are for a new or established patient whose medical and/or psychosocial problems require moderate or high complexity medical decision making during transitions in care from an inpatient hospital setting (including acute hospital, rehabilitation hospital, long-term acute care hospital), partial hospital, observation status in a hospital, or skilled nursing facility/nursing facility to the patient's community setting (home, domiciliary, rest home, or assisted living). TCM commences upon the date of discharge and continues for the next 29 days.

▶A physician or other qualified health care professional who reports codes 99495, 99496 may not report care plan oversight services (99339, 99340, 99374-99380), prolonged services without direct patient contact (99358, 99359), home and outpatient INR monitoring (93792, 93793), medical team conferences (99366-99368), education and training (98960-98962, 99071, 99078), telephone services (98966-98968, 99441-99443), end stage renal disease services (90951-90970), online medical evaluation services (98969, 99444), preparation of special reports (99080), analysis of data (99090, 99091), complex chronic care coordination services (99487-99489), medication therapy management services (99605-99607), during the time period covered by the transitional care management services codes.◀

★ 99495   **Transitional Care Management Services** with the following required elements:

- Communication (direct contact, telephone, electronic) with the patient and/or caregiver within 2 business days of discharge

- Medical decision making of at least moderate complexity during the service period

- Face-to-face visit, within 14 calendar days of discharge

★ 99496   **Transitional Care Management Services** with the following required elements:

- Communication (direct contact, telephone, electronic) with the patient and/or caregiver within 2 business days of discharge

- Medical decision making of high complexity during the service period

- Face-to-face visit, within 7 calendar days of discharge

▶(Do not report 99495, 99496 in conjunction with 93792, 93793)◀

▶(Do not report 90951-90970, 98960-98962, 98966-98969, 99071, 99078, 99080, 99090, 99091, 99339, 99340, 99358, 99359, 99366-99368, 99374-99380, 99441-99444, 99487-99489, 99605-99607 when performed during the service time of codes 99495 or 99496)◀

Rationale

Guidelines in the Transitional Care Management section have been revised. References to anticoagulation management services have been deleted and replaced with home and outpatient INR monitoring services codes 93792 and 93793. A parenthetical note has been added after code 99496 to restrict reporting of this code in conjunction with anticoagulation management (home and outpatient INR monitoring services). A separate parenthetical note has also been revised with the deletion of codes 99363 and 99364.

Refer to the codebook and the Rationale for codes 93792 and 93793 for a full discussion of the changes.

Advance Care Planning

99497   Advance care planning including the explanation and discussion of advance directives such as standard forms (with completion of such forms, when performed), by the physician or other qualified health care professional; first 30 minutes, face-to-face with the patient, family member(s), and/or surrogate

+ 99498   each additional 30 minutes (List separately in addition to code for primary procedure)

(Use 99498 in conjunction with 99497)

▶(Do not report 99497 and 99498 on the same date of service as 99291, 99292, 99468, 99469, 99471, 99472, 99475, 99476, 99477, 99478, 99479, 99480, 99483)◀

Rationale

In accordance with the addition of the cognitive assessment and care plan services code 99483, the parenthetical note that follows code 99498 has been revised.

Refer to the codebook and the Rationale for code 99483 for a full discussion of the changes.

▶General Behavioral Health Integration Care Management ◀

▶General behavioral health integration care management services (99484) are reported by the supervising physician or other qualified health care professional. The services are performed by clinical staff for a patient with a behavioral health (including substance use) condition that requires care management services (face-to-face or non-face-to-face) of 20 or more minutes in a calendar month. A treatment plan as well as the specified elements of the service description is required. The assessment and treatment plan is not required to be comprehensive and the office/practice is not required to have all the functions of chronic care management (99487, 99489, 99490). Code 99484 may be used in any outpatient setting, as long as the reporting professional has an ongoing relationship with the patient and clinical staff and as long as the clinical staff is available for face-to-face services with the patient.

The reporting professional must be able to perform the evaluation and management (E/M) services of an initiating visit. General behavioral integration care management (99484) and chronic care management services may be reported by the same professional in the same month, as long as distinct care management services are performed. Behavioral health integration care management (99484) and psychiatric collaborative care management (99492, 99493, 99494) may not be reported by the same professional in the same month. Behavioral health care integration clinical staff are not required to have qualifications that would permit them to separately report services (eg, psychotherapy), but, if qualified and they perform such services, they may report such services separately, as long as the time of the service is not used in reporting 99484.◄

#● **99484**   Care management services for behavioral health conditions, at least 20 minutes of clinical staff time, directed by a physician or other qualified health care professional, per calendar month, with the following required elements:

- initial assessment or follow-up monitoring, including the use of applicable validated rating scales;

- behavioral health care planning in relation to behavioral/psychiatric health problems, including revision for patients who are not progressing or whose status changes;

- facilitating and coordinating treatment such as psychotherapy, pharmacotherapy, counseling and/or psychiatric consultation; and

- continuity of care with a designated member of the care team.

   ▶(Do not report 99484 in conjunction with 99492, 99493, 99494 in the same calendar month)◄

▶(E/M services, including care management services [99487, 99489, 99490, 99495, 99496], and psychiatric services [90785-90899] may be reported separately by the same physician or other qualified health care professional on the same day or during the same calendar month, but activities used to meet criteria for another reported service do not count toward meeting criteria for 99484)◄

—— *Coding Tip* ——

If the treating physician or other qualified health care professional personally performs behavioral health care manager activities and those activities are not used to meet the criteria for a separately reported code, his or her time may be counted toward the required behavioral health care manager time to meet the elements of 99484, 99492, 99493, 99494.

Behavioral health care manager time spent coordinating care with the emergency department may be reported using 99484, 99492, 99493, 99494, but time spent while the patient is inpatient or admitted to observation status may not be reported using 99484, 99492, 99493, 99494.

Clinical staff time spent coordinating care with the emergency department may be reported using 99484, but time spent while the patient is inpatient or admitted to observation status may not be reported using 99484.

Rationale

General Behavioral Health Integration Care Management is a new subsection that has been added, which includes the addition of a new code (99484), new guidelines, parenthetical notes, and coding tips, to report care management services for behavioral health conditions.

Code 99484 uses a 20-minute threshold to report clinical staff time directed by a physician or other qualified health care professional for management/oversight of behavioral health issues. In contrast to new code 99484, the chronic care management and complex chronic care management codes (99487-99490) allow for a range of diagnoses. Code 99484 details a different set of assessment, monitoring, and management requirements that are integral to behavioral health and psychiatric diagnoses.

The exclusionary parenthetical note that follows code 99484 specifies that this code may not be reported in conjunction with the psychiatric collaborative care management services codes (99492, 99493, and 99494). However, as stated in the Coding Tip, if the treating physician or other qualified health care professional personally performs behavioral health care manager activities and those activities are not used to meet the criteria for a separately reported code, his or her time may be counted toward the required behavioral health care manager time to meet the elements of codes 99484, 99492, 99493, and 99494.

Clinical Example (99484)

Adult: A 50-year-old female established patient presents with complaints of fatigue and sleep disturbance following the recent loss of her spouse. The primary care physician diagnoses the patient with a behavioral health disorder and recommends that the patient receive behavioral health care management as part of the treatment.

Child/Adolescent: A 15-year-old child presents to the primary care physician with vague complaints of stomachaches, fatigue, excessive sleep, and atypically poor grades. The primary care physician diagnoses the patient with a behavioral health disorder and recommends that the patient receive behavioral health care management as part of the treatment plan.

Description of Procedure (99484)

Direction and general supervision of care management services are provided for behavioral health conditions, which are generally provided by clinical staff. Management and/or coordination of services are provided and overseen, as needed, for all medical conditions, psychosocial needs, and activities of daily living.

Anesthesia

Five codes have been added to the Anesthesia section: 00731 and 00732 for anesthesia for upper gastrointestinal endoscopic procedures; 00811 and 00812 for anesthesia for lower intestinal endoscopic procedures; and 00813 for anesthesia for combined upper and lower gastrointestinal endoscopic procedures. In addition, five codes (00740, 00810, 01180, 01190, 01682) have been deleted, of which four of them (00810, 01180, 01190, and 01682) have been deleted due to extremely low utilization. With the deletion of code 01682, code 01680 was reformatted to appear as a stand-alone code.

Summary of Additions, Deletions, and Revisions

The summary of changes shows the actual changes that have been made to the code descriptors.

New codes appear with a bullet (•) and are indicated as "Code added." Revised codes are preceded with a triangle (▲). Within revised codes, the deleted language appears with a ~~strikethrough~~, while new text appears <u>underlined</u>.

The ✁ symbol is used to identify codes for vaccines that are pending FDA approval. The # symbol is used to identify codes that have been resequenced. CPT add-on codes are annotated by the ✛ symbol. The ⊘ symbol is used to identify codes that are exempt from the use of modifier 51. The ★ symbol is used to identify codes that may be used for reporting telemedicine services.

Code	Description
•00731	Code added
•00732	Code added
00740	~~Anesthesia for upper gastrointestinal endoscopic procedures, endoscope introduced proximal to duodenum~~
00810	~~Anesthesia for lower intestinal endoscopic procedures, endoscope introduced distal to duodenum~~
•00811	Code added
•00812	Code added
•00813	Code added
01180	~~Anesthesia for obturator neurectomy; extrapelvic~~
01190	~~intrapelvic~~
01682	~~shoulder spica~~

Anesthesia

Upper Abdomen

00730   Anesthesia for procedures on upper posterior abdominal wall

● **00731**   Anesthesia for upper gastrointestinal endoscopic procedures, endoscope introduced proximal to duodenum; not otherwise specified

● **00732**   endoscopic retrograde cholangiopancreatography (ERCP)

▶(For combined upper and lower gastrointestinal endoscopic procedures, use 00813)◀

▶(00740 has been deleted. To report, see 00731, 00732)◀

Lower Abdomen

00800   Anesthesia for procedures on lower anterior abdominal wall; not otherwise specified

00802   panniculectomy

▶(00810 has been deleted. To report, see 00811, 00812, 00813)◀

● **00811**   Anesthesia for lower intestinal endoscopic procedures, endoscope introduced distal to duodenum; not otherwise specified

● **00812**   screening colonoscopy

▶(Report 00812 to describe anesthesia for any screening colonoscopy regardless of ultimate findings)◀

● **00813**   Anesthesia for combined upper and lower gastrointestinal endoscopic procedures, endoscope introduced both proximal to and distal to the duodenum

Rationale

Codes 00731, 00732, 00811, 00812, and 00813 have been established to report anesthesia management of upper and lower endoscopic procedures. Codes 00740 and 00810, which were not granular enough to capture data for reporting purposes, have been deleted.

These changes have been made in response to a Centers for Medicare & Medicaid Services (CMS) analysis that indicated that codes 00740 and 00810 were potentially misvalued. In Medicare claims data, it was noted that a separate anesthesia service was being reported more than 50% of the time when several types of gastrointestinal endoscopic procedures were reported.

Given the significant change in the relative frequency with which anesthesia codes are reported with gastrointestinal endoscopic services, CMS believed that the base units of the anesthesia services should be re-examined.

Prior to these changes, only one code existed for anesthesia for upper gastrointestinal endoscopic procedures (00740), and one code existed for lower gastrointestinal endoscopic procedures (00810). The new family of five codes provides sufficient granularity to describe typical patients who undergo upper endoscopic procedures and to differentiate them from patients who undergo endoscopic retrograde cholangiopancreatography. These codes also differentiate patients who undergo screening colonoscopies from those who undergo diagnostic and/or therapeutic lower gastrointestinal endoscopic procedures.

This family of codes also specifically identifies patients who undergo both upper and lower gastrointestinal endoscopic procedures sequentially on the same day. Before the change, the additional anesthesia work performed during a combined procedure, such as repositioning the patient, responding to physiologic changes when the scope is reinserted into a different location, and other nonduplicative work involved in the additional procedure, was not being captured.

Clinical Example (00731)

A 63-year-old patient with abdominal pain and persistent dyspepsia undergoes an esophagogastroduodenoscopy (EGD). The upper gastrointestinal (GI) track is evaluated, and multiple biopsies are taken for histology and Helicobacter pylori rapid urease test.

Description of Procedure (00731)

A peripheral intravenous catheter is started, an anxiolytic is administered, and the patient is transported to the procedure room (operating room [OR] or GI suite). In the procedure room, placement of standard monitors (ECG, pulse oximetry, noninvasive blood pressure, end-tidal carbon dioxide) is confirmed. A presurgical review to confirm correct patient and procedure is performed. A nasal cannula or facemask is placed on the patient to provide supplemental oxygen during the procedure. Anesthesia care is induced or started. If medically indicated, an artificial airway (may range from oral or nasal airway to intubation) is placed to maintain ventilation. A GI bite block (mouth guard) is placed between the teeth to prevent the patient from biting on the endoscope. The patient is positioned in the left lateral position. During the procedure, it may be necessary to assist in positioning the patient in supine, right lateral, or prone as determined by the physician performing the procedure. If the patient is in the lateral position, protection of pressure points, such as behind the dependent shoulder, the dependent eye, and ear, is ensured. The resulting position along with the presence of the endoscope may compromise access to the airway should it be necessary to assist ventilation during the procedure. Anesthesia care is provided, medications are titrated, the patient is monitored and reassessed throughout the procedure. At the end of the procedure, the patient is "emerged" and transferred to the postanesthetic care unit. A postanesthetic report is provided to the recovery room nursing staff. During anesthesia care, anesthesia care is personally documented in the anesthesia record, including vital signs (at least every five minutes), positioning, anesthesia procedures, medications, and significant events.

Clinical Example (00732)

A 68-year-old patient presents with abdominal pain and abnormal laboratory tests (aspartate aminotransferase, alanine aminotransferase, alkaline phosphatase, total bilirubin, amylase). Imaging studies show an apparent retained common bile duct stone. Therapeutic endoscopic retrograde cholangiopancreatography with stone removal is performed.

Description of Procedure (00732)

A peripheral intravenous catheter is started, an anxiolytic is administered, and the patient is transported to the procedure room (OR, radiology suite or GI suite). In the procedure room, placement of standard monitors (ECG, pulse oximetry, noninvasive blood pressure, and end-tidal carbon dioxide) is confirmed. A presurgical review, confirming correct patient and correct procedure, is performed. The patient is preoxygenated and then induced and intubated. After the airway is secured, the GI bite block (mouth guard) is placed between the teeth to prevent patient from biting on the endoscope. The patient is placed in the prone position. A pillow is placed under the patient's right chest for slight tilt. Neck extension in the neutral position is ensured, with head toward right shoulder and pressure points padded (eg, head on foam or towel ring to prevent pressure on down orbit, nose, ear, or mouth). Because fluoroscopy is generally used during this procedure, it is necessary to confirm that necessary X-ray protection has been placed on the patient. Anesthesia care is provided, medications are titrated, and the patient is monitored and reassessed throughout the procedure. At the end of the procedure, the patient is turned supine, "emerged," and extubated when medically appropriate. The patient is transferred to the postanesthetic care unit. A postanesthetic report is provided to recovery room nursing staff. During anesthesia care, anesthesia care is personally documented in the anesthesia record,

including vital signs (at least every five minutes), positioning, anesthesia procedures, medications, and significant events.

Clinical Example (00811)

A 66-year-old patient presents with diarrhea, anemia, and intermittent rectal bleeding. Colonoscopy with biopsies of a lesion is performed.

Description of Procedure (00811)

A peripheral intravenous catheter is started, an anxiolytic is administered, and the patient is transported to the procedure room (OR or GI suite). Fluids to counteract volume changes as a result of bowel preparation, medications, and underlying comorbidities are administered. In the procedure room, placement of standard monitors (ECG, pulse oximetry, noninvasive blood pressure, end-tidal carbon dioxide) is confirmed. A presurgical review, confirming correct patient and procedure, is performed. A nasal cannula or facemask is placed on the patient to provide supplemental oxygen during the procedure. Anesthesia care is induced or started. If medically indicated, an artificial airway (may range from oral or nasal airway to intubation) is placed to maintain ventilation. The patient is initially placed in the left lateral position. During the procedure, it may be necessary to assist in positioning the patient in supine, right lateral, or prone as determined by the physician performing the procedure. If the patient is in the lateral position, protection of pressure points, such as behind the dependent shoulder, the dependent eye, and ear, is ensured. Anesthesia care is provided, medications are titrated, and the patient is monitored and reassessed throughout the procedure. Medications are administered to counter physiologic changes such as hypotension and tachycardia that may result from a combination of bowel preparation, medications, and underlying comorbidities. At the end of the procedure, the patient is "emerged" and transferred to the postanesthetic care unit. A postanesthetic report is provided to recovery room nursing staff. During the anesthesia care, anesthesia care is personally documented in the anesthesia record, including vital signs (at least every five minutes), positioning, anesthesia procedures, medications, and significant events.

Clinical Example (00812)

A 64-year-old patient is referred for colorectal cancer screening.

Description of Procedure (00812)

A peripheral intravenous catheter is started, an anxiolytic is administered, and the patient is transported to the procedure room (OR or GI suite). Fluids to counteract volume changes as a result of bowel preparation,

Anesthesia 00100–01999

medications, and underlying comorbidities are administered. In the procedure room, placement of standard monitors (ECG, pulse oximetry, noninvasive blood pressure, end-tidal carbon dioxide) is confirmed. A presurgical review, confirming correct patient and procedure is performed. A nasal cannula or facemask is placed on the patient to provide supplemental oxygen during the procedure. Anesthesia care is started or induced. If medically indicated, an artificial airway (may range from oral or nasal airway to intubation) is placed to maintain ventilation. The patient is initially placed in the left lateral position. During the procedure, it may be necessary to assist in positioning the patient in supine, right lateral, or prone as determined by the physician performing the procedure. If the patient is in the lateral position, protection of pressure points, such as behind the dependent shoulder, the dependent eye, and ear, is ensured. Anesthesia care is provided, medications are titrated, and the patient is monitored and reassessed throughout the procedure. Medications to counter physiologic changes such as hypotension and tachycardia that may result from a combination of bowel preparation, medications, and underlying comorbidities are administered. At the end of the procedure, the patient is "emerged" and then transferred to the postanesthetic care unit. A postanesthetic report is provided to recovery room nursing staff. During anesthesia care, anesthesia care is personally documented in the anesthesia record, including vital signs (at least every five minutes), positioning, anesthesia procedures, medications, and significant events.

Clinical Example (00813)

A 68-year-old patient with persistent abdominal pain, positive fecal blood tests, and mild anemia on laboratory exam presents for upper and lower GI endoscopic procedures to determine cause of occult bleeding.

Description of Procedure (00813)

A peripheral intravenous catheter is started, an anxiolytic is administered, and the patient is transported to the procedure room (OR or GI suite). Fluids to counteract volume changes as a result of bowel preparation, medications, and underlying comorbidities are administered. In the procedure room, placement of standard monitors (ECG, pulse oximetry, noninvasive blood pressure, end-tidal carbon dioxide) is confirmed. A presurgical review, confirming correct patient and procedure is performed. A nasal cannula or facemask is placed on the patient to provide supplemental oxygen during the procedure. Anesthesia care is induced or started. If medically indicated, an artificial airway (may range from oral or nasal airway to intubation) is placed to maintain ventilation. A GI bite block (mouth guard)

is placed between the teeth to prevent the patient from biting on the endoscope. The patient is initially placed in the left lateral position. During the procedure, it may be necessary to assist in positioning the patient in supine, right lateral, or prone as determined by the physician performing the procedure. If the patient is in the lateral position, protection of pressure points, such as behind the dependent shoulder, the dependent eye, and ear, is ensured. The resulting position along with the presence of the endoscope may compromise access to the airway should it be necessary to assist ventilation during the procedure. Anesthesia care is provided, medications are titrated, and the patient is monitored and reassessed throughout the procedure. Medications to counter physiologic changes, such as hypotension and tachycardia, that may result from a combination of bowel preparation, medications, and underlying comorbidities are administered. At the end of the EGD procedure, the patient's stretcher is turned 180°. After turning the bed, the patient's ventilation is re-evaluated. Monitors and intravenous access are assessed. Although the initial position for the lower endoscopic procedure is the left lateral position, during the procedure, it may be necessary to assist in positioning the patient in supine, right lateral, or prone as determined by the physician performing the procedure. At the end of the procedure, the patient is "emerged" and transferred to the postanesthetic care unit. A postanesthetic report is provided to recovery room nursing staff. During anesthesia care, anesthesia care is personally documented in the anesthesia record, including vital signs (at least every five minutes), positioning, anesthesia procedures, medications, and significant events.

Pelvis (Except Hip)

01173 Anesthesia for open repair of fracture disruption of pelvis or column fracture involving acetabulum

▶(01180, 01190 have been deleted)◀

Rationale

Codes 01180 (anesthesia for obturator neurectomy; extrapelvic) and 01190 (anesthesia for obturator neurectomy; intrapelvic) have been deleted due to low utilization. This was done to ensure that the CPT code set reflects current clinical practice.

★ = Telemedicine   ✚ = Add-on code   ✔ = FDA approval pending   # = Resequenced code

Shoulder and Axilla

01670 Anesthesia for all procedures on veins of shoulder and axilla

01680 Anesthesia for shoulder cast application, removal or repair, not otherwise specified

▶(01682 has been deleted)◀

Rationale

Code 01682 (anesthesia for shoulder cast application, removal or repair; shoulder spica) has been deleted due to low utilization. This was done to ensure that the CPT code set reflects current clinical practice.

Notes

Surgery

In the Integumentary section, three new codes (15730, 15733, and 19294) have been added, one code deleted (15732), and one code (17250) has been revised. In addition, multiple parenthetical notes have been added and revised within this subsection.

In the Musculoskeletal System section, one new add-on code (20939) has been added for reporting bone marrow aspiration for bone grafting during spine surgery only and two codes (29582 and 29583) have been deleted due to low utilization and misreporting.

In the Sinus Endoscopy subsection of the Respiratory section, five new codes (31241, 31253, 31257, 31259, and 31298) have been added and three codes (31254, 31255, and 31276) have been revised. In the Larynx subsection, code 31320 has been deleted due to low utilization. Codes 31645 and 31646 in the Trachea and Bronchi subsection have been revised. In the Lungs and Pleura subsection, code 32994 has been added and code 32998 has been revised. In addition, new guidelines, new parenthetical notes, and revised parenthetical notes have been added to the Respiratory section.

In the Cardiovascular section, three new codes (33927, 33928, and 33929) have been added to the Heart/Lung Transplantation subsection for reporting artificial heart system procedures, replacing three deleted Category III codes (0051T, 0052T, and 0053T). The biggest changes in the Cardiovascular section are in the endovascular repair of abdominal aorta and/or iliac arteries codes. Codes 34800–34806, 34825, 34826, and 34900 have been deleted, and codes 34701-34713, 34714, 34715, and 34716 have been added along with numerous guidelines and parenthetical notes. The previously titled subsection of Endovascular Repair of Abdominal Aortic Aneurysm has been renamed to "Endovascular Repair of Abdominal Aorta and/or Iliac Arteries." Following the addition of the new codes, changes have also been made to the guidelines in the Fenestrated Endovascular Repair of the Visceral and Infrarenal Aorta, Endovascular Repair of Iliac Aneurysm, and Direct Repair of Aneurysm or Excision (Partial or Total) and Graft Insertion for Aneurysm, Pseudoaneurysm, Ruptured Aneurysm, and Associated Occlusive Disease subsections. In addition, code 34900 has been deleted. Changes in the Vascular Injection Procedures subsection include new and deleted guidelines, two deleted codes (36120 and 36515), six revised codes (36140, 36468, 36470, 36471, 36516, and 36908), and four new codes (36465, 36466, 36482, and 36483). Two codes (38220 and 38221) have been revised in the Bone Marrow or Stem Cell Services/Procedures subsection of the Hemic and Lymphatic Systems section, and one new code (38222) has been added. Parenthetical notes have been added, revised, and deleted in this subsection as well. In addition, code 38573 and an exclusionary parenthetical note have been added to the Lymph Nodes and Lymphatic Channels subsection.

In the Esophagus subsection of the Digestive System section, three new codes (43286, 43287, and 43288) have been added to identify esophagectomy performed with a scope and one code (43112) has been revised. Multiple parenthetical notes have been added and revised within this section as well.

In the Male Genital System section, code 55450 has been deleted due to low utilization, and code 55874 has been added for reporting peri-prostatic transperineal placement of biodegradable matter.

In the Female Genital System section, codes 57240, 57260, and 57265 have been revised to include cystourethroscopy, when performed. In addition, code 58575 has been added to the Corpus Uteri subsection.

Surgery 10021-69990

In the three subsections in the Spine and Spinal Cord of the Nervous System section, definitions have been added to provide clarity on the use of partial corpectomy. The Neurostimulators (Peripheral Nerve) subsection has new guidelines, one revised code (64550), and one deleted code (64565). The Neurorrhaphy With Nerve Graft, Vein Graft, or Conduit subsection contains two new codes (64912 and 64913) to describe new repair with nerve allograft.

In the Auditory System section, codes 69820 and 69840 have been deleted due to low utilization.

Summary of Additions, Deletions, and Revisions

The summary of changes shows the actual changes that have been made to the code descriptors.

New codes appear with a bullet (●) and are indicated as "Code added." Revised codes are preceded with a triangle (▲). Within revised codes, the deleted language appears with a ~~strikethrough~~, while new text appears <u>underlined</u>.

The ⟋ symbol is used to identify codes for vaccines that are pending FDA approval. The # symbol is used to identify codes that have been resequenced. CPT add-on codes are annotated by the ✚ symbol. The ⊘ symbol is used to identify codes that are exempt from the use of modifier 51. The ★ symbol is used to identify codes that may be used for reporting telemedicine services.

Code	Description
●**15730**	Code added
15732	~~Muscle, myocutaneous, or fasciocutaneous flap; head and neck (eg, temporalis, masseter muscle, sternocleidomastoid, levator scapulae)~~
●**15733**	Code added
▲**17250**	Chemical cauterization of granulation tissue (<u>ie,</u> proud flesh~~, sinus or fistula~~)
✚●**19294**	Code added
✚●**20939**	Code added
29582	~~thigh and leg, including ankle and foot, when performed~~
29583	~~upper arm and forearm~~
●**31241**	Code added
▲**31254**	Nasal/sinus endoscopy, surgical<u> with ethmoidectomy</u>; ~~with ethmoidectomy,~~ partial (anterior)
▲**31255**	~~with ethmoidectomy,~~ total (anterior and posterior)
#●**31253**	Code added
#●**31257**	Code added
#●**31259**	Code added
▲**31276**	Nasal/sinus endoscopy, surgical, with frontal sinus exploration, ~~with or without~~<u>including</u> removal of tissue from frontal sinus<u>, when performed</u>
●**31298**	Code added
31320	~~diagnostic~~

Code	Description
▲31645	with therapeutic aspiration of tracheobronchial tree, initial ~~(eg, drainage of lung abscess)~~
▲31646	with therapeutic aspiration of tracheobronchial tree, subsequent, <u>same hospital stay</u>
▲32998	Ablation therapy for reduction or eradication of 1 or more pulmonary tumor(s) including pleura or chest wall when involved by tumor extension, percutaneous, ~~radiofrequency~~<u>including imaging guidance when performed</u>, unilateral<u>;</u> <u>radiofrequency</u>
#●32994	Code added
●33927	Code added
●33928	Code added
+●33929	Code added
●34701	Code added
●34702	Code added
●34703	Code added
●34704	Code added
●34705	Code added
●34706	Code added
●34707	Code added
●34708	Code added
+●34709	Code added
●34710	Code added
+●34711	Code added
●34712	Code added
+●34713	Code added
#+▲34812	Open femoral artery exposure for delivery of endovascular prosthesis, by groin incision, unilateral <u>(List separately in addition to code for primary procedure)</u>
+●34714	Code added
#+▲34820	Open iliac artery exposure for delivery of endovascular prosthesis or iliac occlusion during endovascular therapy, by abdominal or retroperitoneal incision, unilateral <u>(List separately in addition to code for primary procedure)</u>
#+▲34833	Open iliac artery exposure with creation of conduit for delivery of ~~aortic or iliac~~ endovascular prosthesis <u>or for</u> <u>establishment of cardiopulmonary bypass</u>, by abdominal or retroperitoneal incision, unilateral <u>(List separately in addition to code for primary procedure)</u>
#+▲34834	Open brachial artery exposure ~~to assist in the deployment of aortic or iliac endovascular prosthesis by arm incision, unilateral~~<u>for delivery of endovascular prosthesis, unilateral (List separately in addition to code for primary procedure)</u>
+●34715	Code added
+●34716	Code added
34800	~~Endovascular repair of infrarenal abdominal aortic aneurysm or dissection; using aorto-aortic tube prosthesis~~

Surgery 10021-69990

Code	Description
34802	~~using modular bifurcated prosthesis (1 docking limb)~~
34803	~~using modular bifurcated prosthesis (2 docking limbs)~~
34804	~~using unibody bifurcated prosthesis~~
34805	~~using aorto-uniiliac or aorto-unifemoral prosthesis~~
34806	~~Transcatheter placement of wireless physiologic sensor in aneurysmal sac during endovascular repair, including radiological supervision and interpretation, instrument calibration, and collection of pressure data (List separately in addition to code for primary procedure)~~
34825	~~Placement of proximal or distal extension prosthesis for endovascular repair of infrarenal abdominal aortic or iliac aneurysm, false aneurysm, or dissection; initial vessel~~
34826	~~each additional vessel (List separately in addition to code for primary procedure)~~
34900	~~Endovascular repair of iliac artery (eg, aneurysm, pseudoaneurysm, arteriovenous malformation, trauma) using ilio-iliac tube endoprosthesis~~
36120	~~Introduction of needle or intracatheter; retrograde brachial artery~~
▲36140	Introduction of needle or intracatheter, upper or lower extremity artery ~~extremity artery~~
▲36468	~~Single or multiple injections~~Injection(s) of ~~sclerosing solutions,~~sclerosant for spider veins (telangiectasia), limb or trunk
▲36470	Injection of ~~sclerosing solution~~sclerosant; single incompetent vein (other than telangiectasia)
▲36471	multiple incompetent veins (other than telangiectasia), same leg
#●36465	Code added
#●36466	Code added
#●36482	Code added
#+●36483	Code added
36515	~~with extracorporeal immunoadsorption and plasma reinfusion~~
▲36516	with extracorporeal immunoadsorption, selective adsorption or selective filtration and plasma reinfusion
+▲36908	Transcatheter placement of intravascular stent(s), central dialysis segment, performed through dialysis circuit, including all imaging and radiological supervision and interpretation required to perform the stenting, and all angioplasty in the central dialysis segment (List separately in addition to code for primary procedure)
▲38220	~~Bone~~Diagnostic bone marrow; aspiration ~~only~~(s)
▲38221	biopsy, ~~needle or trocar~~(ies)
●38222	Code added
●38573	Code added
▲43112	Total or near total esophagectomy, with thoracotomy; with pharyngogastrostomy or cervical esophagogastrostomy, with or without pyloroplasty (ie, McKeown esophagectomy or tri-incisional esophagectomy)
●43286	Code added
●43287	Code added

★ = Telemedicine   ✚ = Add-on code   𝒩 = FDA approval pending   # = Resequenced code

Code	Description
●**43288**	Code added
55450	~~Ligation (percutaneous) of vas deferens, unilateral or bilateral (separate procedure)~~
●**55874**	Code added
▲**57240**	Anterior colporrhaphy, repair of cystocele with or without repair of urethrocele, including cystourethroscopy, when performed
▲**57260**	Combined anteroposterior colporrhaphy, including cystourethroscopy, when performed;
▲**57265**	with enterocele repair
●**58575**	Code added
▲**64550**	Application of surface (transcutaneous) neurostimulator (eg, TENS unit)
64565	~~neuromuscular~~
●**64912**	Code added
+●64913	Code added
69820	~~Fenestration semicircular canal~~
69840	~~Revision fenestration operation~~

Surgery

Integumentary System

Skin, Subcutaneous, and Accessory Structures

Debridement

+ **11008** Removal of prosthetic material or mesh, abdominal wall for infection (eg, for chronic or recurrent mesh infection or necrotizing soft tissue infection) (List separately in addition to code for primary procedure)

(Use 11008 in conjunction with 10180, 11004-11006)

(Report skin grafts or flaps separately when performed for closure at the same session as 11004-11008)

(When insertion of mesh is used for closure, use 49568)

Rationale

Changes have been made throughout the CPT code set (ie, within different subsections of the Surgery, Radiology, and Category III sections) to clarify the intended use for a number of codes that may be reported together if services referenced in the revised content are performed as distinct procedural services. The changes that have been made reflect intent to allow the reporting of the referenced services when they are performed during a different session; as a different procedure or surgery; performed on a different site; as part of a separate incision/excision; or when addressing a separate injury that is not ordinarily encountered or performed on the same day by the same individual undergoing the noted procedures. Affected subsections and their accompanying guidelines and parenthetical notes have been similarly revised to align with the changes made. In accordance with these changes, the exclusionary parenthetical note following code 11008 that precluded use with debridement codes 11000, 11001, 11010-11044 has been deleted. This was done to allow reporting of code 11008 in conjunction with debridement services, as noted in the deleted parenthetical note, during the same operative session, but not at the same site/wound. In these events, the codes could be reported with the appropriate modifier.

Excision—Benign Lesions

Excision (including simple closure) of benign lesions of skin (eg, neoplasm, cicatricial, fibrous, inflammatory, congenital, cystic lesions), includes local anesthesia. See appropriate size and area below. For shave removal, see 11300 et seq, and for electrosurgical and other methods see 17000 et seq.

Excision is defined as full-thickness (through the dermis) removal of a lesion, including margins, and includes simple (non-layered) closure when performed. Report separately each benign lesion excised. Code selection is determined by measuring the greatest clinical diameter of the apparent lesion plus that margin required for complete excision (lesion diameter plus the most narrow margins required equals the excised diameter). The margins refer to the most narrow margin required to adequately excise the lesion, based on individual judgment. The measurement of lesion plus margin is made prior to excision. The excised diameter is the same whether the surgical defect is repaired in a linear fashion, or reconstructed (eg, with a skin graft).

The closure of defects created by incision, excision, or trauma may require intermediate or complex closure. Repair by intermediate or complex closure should be reported separately. For excision of benign lesions requiring more than simple closure, ie, requiring intermediate or complex closure, report 11400-11446 in addition to appropriate intermediate (12031-12057) or complex closure (13100-13153) codes. For reconstructive closure, see 15002-15261, 15570-15770. For excision performed in conjunction with adjacent tissue transfer, report only the adjacent tissue transfer code (14000-14302). Excision of lesion (11400-11446) is not separately reportable with adjacent tissue transfer.

> ▶(For destruction [eg, laser surgery, electrosurgery, cryosurgery, chemosurgery, surgical curette] of benign lesions other than skin tags or cutaneous vascular proliferative lesions, see 17110, 17111; premalignant lesions, see 17000, 17003, 17004; cutaneous vascular proliferative lesions, see 17106, 17107, 17108; malignant lesions, see 17260-17286)◀

> ▶(For excision of cicatricial lesion[s] [eg, full thickness excision, through the dermis], see 11400-11446)◀

> ▶(For incisional removal of burn scar, see 16035, 16036)◀

> ▶(For fractional ablative laser fenestration for functional improvement of traumatic or burn scars, see 0479T, 0480T)◀

11400 Excision, benign lesion including margins, except skin tag (unless listed elsewhere), trunk, arms or legs; excised diameter 0.5 cm or less

Rationale

In support of the establishment of new Category III codes 0479T and 0480T, four cross-reference parenthetical notes have been added before code 11400 (benign lesion excision) to assist users in determining when to report other destruction, excision (eg, cicatricial lesion), and incisional (eg, incisional removal of burn scar) treatment codes.

Refer to the codebook and the Rationale for codes 0479T and 0480T for a full discussion of the changes.

Repair (Closure)

Flaps (Skin and/or Deep Tissues)

The regions listed refer to the recipient area (not the donor site) when a flap is being attached in a transfer or to a final site.

▶The regions listed refer to a donor site when a tube is formed for later transfer or when a "delay" of flap occurs prior to the transfer. Codes 15733-15738 are described by donor site of the muscle, myocutaneous, or fasciocutaneous flap.◀

Codes 15570-15738 do not include extensive immobilization (eg, large plaster casts and other immobilizing devices are considered additional separate procedures).

A repair of a donor site requiring a skin graft or local flaps is considered an additional separate procedure.

● **15730** Midface flap (ie, zygomaticofacial flap) with preservation of vascular pedicle(s)

15731 Forehead flap with preservation of vascular pedicle (eg, axial pattern flap, paramedian forehead flap)

▶(For muscle, myocutaneous, or fasciocutaneous flap of the head or neck, use 15733)◀

▶(15732 has been deleted. To report myocutaneous or fasciocutaneous flap, use 15733)◀

● **15733** Muscle, myocutaneous, or fasciocutaneous flap; head and neck with named vascular pedicle (ie, buccinators, genioglossus, temporalis, masseter, sternocleidomastoid, levator scapulae)

(For forehead flap with preservation of vascular pedicle, use 15731)

▶(For anterior pericranial flap on named vascular pedicle, for repair of extracranial defect, use 15731)◀

▶(For repair of head and neck defects using non-axial pattern advancement flaps [including lesion] and/or repair by adjacent tissue transfer or rearrangement [eg, Z-plasty, W-plasty, V-Y plasty, rotation flap, random island flap, advancement flap], see 14040, 14041, 14060, 14061, 14301, 14302)◀

15734 trunk

15736 upper extremity

15738 lower extremity

Rationale

Two new codes have been established (15730, 15733) and one code (15732) has been deleted to clarify reporting of myocutaneous and fasciocutaneous flap procedures of the head and neck. To coincide with these changes, a guideline revision has been made and instructional and deletion parenthetical notes have been established to provide guidance regarding appropriate reporting for the noted services.

Code 15730 has been added for reporting midface flap procedures, which differ from the procedure reported with code 15733, as these flaps are not based on a named vascular pedicle. In accordance with the establishment of code 15730, several parenthetical notes have been established to direct users to codes that are differentiated by the type of flaps used to accomplish the repair. The AMA RUC identified code 15732 during its review of high-level E/M services in the postoperative period. The review of utilization data showed a wide range of place of service for these procedures (inpatient vs outpatient). To improve code selection, differentiation was requested. As a result, code 15732 has been replaced with code 15733 to better identify the muscle myocutaneous or fasciocutaneous flap procedure.

Language that identifies the flaps used to accomplish that particular procedure has been added to the myocutaneous or fasciocutaneous flap procedure code (15733). (Note that this language is included only as part of code 15733 for head and neck myocutaneous or fasciocutaneous flaps.)

To accommodate the CPT convention for organization of the code structure (anatomical listing of codes when appropriate), code 15733, which is used to report head and neck procedures, has been established as the parent of existing codes 15734, 15736, and 15738, which are intended to be used to report the same flap procedures performed on the trunk, upper extremity, and lower extremity, respectively. This allows for continuity of the coding structure and facilitates the placement of these codes in appropriate location within the code set. In addition, because the list in the parenthesis uses "ie" in

Surgery / Integumentary System 10021-19499

the descriptor of code 15733, the identified pedicles are the only pedicles that are intended to be used for this code.

Per the concept of the permanence principle, which dictates that new code numbers be established if a revision alters the meaning of a code, code 15232 was deleted and replaced with code 15733 to acknowledge the significant changes included for this service. In addition, a deletion parenthetical note for code 15732 has been included to direct users to the appropriate code for reporting myocutaneous or fasciocutaneous flap development for repair/closure.

Clinical Example (15730)

A 62-year-old female has an inferiorly displaced lower eyelid and cicatricial lagophthalmos three months after excision of a carcinoma with primary rotational flap closure. A midface zygomaticofacial myocutaneous flap is performed to allow for adequate lid closure.

Description of Procedure (15730)

The fixed tissue defect is identified and a flap design marked based on surrounding eyelid and mid-facial tissue that can be mobilized and remains well vascularized by facial, infraorbital, and zygomaticofacial arteries. The facial nerve branches may be identified with a nerve stimulator and marked. A lateral canthotomy is extended along the zygomatic arch with inferior cantholysis to the orbital rim. A total subperiosteal release of the anterior malar face includes dissection of the anterior half of the zygomatic arch down to the premasseteric fascia laterally, deep to the gingival sulcus inferiorly, and to the nasal ala medially, with care to identify and preserve all neurovascular bundles and vascular pedicles. When the flap is adequately released, it is mobilized. A drain is placed and the flap is anchored to the deep temporalis fascia, with fixation screws to the orbital rim and lateral nasal wall.

Clinical Example (15733)

A 79-year-old male presents with a large defect in the upper cheek from excision of an invasive squamous cell carcinoma. In addition to the defect of the skin and subcutaneous tissue, there is exposed bone of malar eminence that cannot be covered with the adjacent skin.

Description of Procedure (15733)

After the ablative part of procedure has been completed, the appropriate measurements of defect and plan for size of flap are obtained. An incision is made over ipsilateral temporalis muscle. Dissection is carried down through the superficial temporal fascia, which is elevated off the muscle. The anterior, superior, and posterior borders of the muscle are exposed, muscle fascia attachments to the

skull are divided, and muscle from the skull down to the zygomatic arch is elevated. The location of facial nerve for flap planning is determined to avoid damaging the nerve. A subcutaneous tunnel is made between defect and incision overlying the temporalis muscle. A superficial level of dissection is maintained to prevent damage to frontal branch of the facial nerve. The size of the tunnel is adjusted to allow for passage of muscle flap without excessive pressure on the flap, and the flap is passed through the tunnel and into the cheek defect. The flap is inset into the edge of the defect with sutures. Drains are placed beneath the flap and in the donor defect and sutured into position. Muscle is assessed for venous congestion and the subcutaneous tunnel is adjusted as necessary. The donor site superficial temporal fascia is closed. The skin is closed in layers. A skin graft is performed, which is reported separately. Sterile dressings are applied to the flap.

Other Procedures

15830   Excision, excessive skin and subcutaneous tissue (includes lipectomy); abdomen, infraumbilical panniculectomy

►(Do not report 15830 in conjunction with 12031-12037, 13100-13102, 14000, 14001, 14302 for the same wound)◄

Rationale

The phrase "for the same wound" has been added to the exclusionary parenthetical note that follows code 15830. Codes 12031-12037, 13100-13102, 14000, 14001, and 14302 may be reported alone or in conjunction with codes for another procedure that is performed during the same operative session; however, they may not be reported for procedures performed on the same site or wound as excision of excessive skin and subcutaneous tissue of the abdomen (infraumbilical panniculectomy [15830]). In addition, if the excision of excessive skin and subcutaneous tissue of the abdomen is a distinct procedural service, modifier 59 or other appropriate modifier should be appended to the secondary service. Refer to the codebook and the Rationale for the deletion of the exclusionary parenthetical following code 11008 for a full discussion of the change.

15876   Suction assisted lipectomy; head and neck
15877   trunk
15878   upper extremity
15879   lower extremity

►(Do not report 15876, 15877, 15878, 15879 in conjunction with 0489T, 0490T)◄

►(For harvesting of adipose tissue for autologous adipose-derived regenerative cell therapy, see 0489T, 0490T)◄

Rationale

In support of the establishment of autologous adipose-derived regenerative cell therapy codes 0489T and 0490T, two parenthetical notes have been added after code 15879.

Refer to the codebook and the Rationale for codes 0489T and 0490T for a full discussion of the changes.

Burns, Local Treatment

Procedures 16000-16036 refer to local treatment of burned surface only. Codes 16020-16030 include the application of materials (eg, dressings) not described in codes 15100-15278.

List percentage of body surface involved and depth of burn.

For necessary related medical services (eg, hospital visits, detention) in management of burned patients, see appropriate services in **Evaluation and Management** and **Medicine** sections.

For the application of skin grafts or skin substitutes, see codes 15100-15777.

►(For fractional ablative laser fenestration for functional improvement of traumatic or burn scars, see 0479T, 0480T)◄

Rationale

In support of establishment of Category III codes 0479T and 0480T, a cross-reference parenthetical note has been added following the burns, local treatment guidelines in the Integumentary section to direct users to the new codes.

Refer to the codebook and the Rationale for codes 0479T and 0480T for a full discussion of the changes.

Destruction

Destruction means the ablation of benign, premalignant or malignant tissues by any method, with or without curettement, including local anesthesia, and not usually requiring closure.

Any method includes electrosurgery, cryosurgery, laser and chemical treatment. Lesions include condylomata, papillomata, molluscum contagiosum, herpetic lesions, warts (ie, common, plantar, flat), milia, or other benign, premalignant (eg, actinic keratoses), or malignant lesions.

(For destruction of lesion(s) in specific anatomic sites, see 40820, 46900-46917, 46924, 54050-54057, 54065, 56501, 56515, 57061, 57065, 67850, 68135)

(For laser treatment for inflammatory skin disease, see 96920-96922)

(For paring or cutting of benign hyperkeratotic lesions (eg, corns or calluses), see 11055-11057)

(For sharp removal or electrosurgical destruction of skin tags and fibrocutaneous tags, see 11200, 11201)

(For cryotherapy of acne, use 17340)

(For initiation or follow-up care of topical chemotherapy (eg, 5-FU or similar agents), see appropriate office visits)

(For shaving of epidermal or dermal lesions, see 11300-11313)

►(For excision of cicatricial lesion[s] [eg, full thickness excision, through the dermis], see 11400-11446)◄

►(For incisional removal of burn scar, see 16035, 16036)◄

►(For fractional ablative laser fenestration for functional improvement of traumatic or burn scars, see 0479T, 0480T)◄

Rationale

In support of establishment of Category III codes 0479T and 0480T, three cross-reference parenthetical notes have been added following the destruction guidelines in the Integumentary section to assist users in determining when to report other treatment codes.

Refer to the codebook and the Rationale for codes 0479T and 0480T for a full discussion of the changes.

Destruction, Benign or Premalignant Lesions

▲ **17250**   Chemical cauterization of granulation tissue (ie, proud flesh)

►(Do not report 17250 with removal or excision codes for the same lesion)◄

►(Do not report 17250 when chemical cauterization is used to achieve wound hemostasis)◄

►(Do not report 17250 in conjunction with 97597, 97598, 97602 for the same lesion)◄

Rationale

Code 17250 has been editorially revised to more appropriately identify its intended use. To accommodate this revision, an editorial revision has been made to the existing parenthetical note that follows code 17250, and two new parentheticals have been added to further clarify the intended use for this code.

The AMA RUC RAW had recommended a review of code 17250 for high-volume growth. As a result, a decision was made to revise the descriptor and provide coding guidance regarding appropriate reporting of this code for chemical cauterization procedures.

The following changes have been made: code 17250 has been revised to eliminate the phrase "sinus or fistula" from the instructional parenthetical note in the descriptor; language has been added to the existing parenthetical note to conform to CPT code convention for exclusionary parenthetical notes; and exclusionary parenthetical notes that instruct the appropriate reporting of this service have been added. The instructional parenthetical notes prohibit reporting code 17250 for chemical cauterization for wound hemostasis and from being reported in conjunction with active wound care management services (97597, 97598, 97602). To further clarify this, a reciprocal instructional parenthetical note has been placed in the active wound care management guidelines in the Medicine section to inform users that code 17250 (achieve wound hemostasis) is not separately reportable for the same lesion.

Breast

Excision

Excisional breast surgery includes certain biopsy procedures, the removal of cysts or other benign or malignant tumors or lesions, and the surgical treatment of breast and chest wall malignancies. Biopsy procedures may be percutaneous or open, and they involve the removal of differing amounts of tissue for diagnosis.

Breast biopsies, without image guidance are reported with 19100 and 19101. Image-guided breast biopsies, including the placement of localization devices when performed, are reported using codes 19081-19086. The image-guided placement of localization devices without image-guided biopsy are reported with 19281-19288. When more than one biopsy or localization device placement is performed using the same imaging modality, use an add-on code whether the additional service(s) is on the same or contra-lateral breast. If additional biopsies or localization device placements are performed using different imaging modalities, report

another primary code for each additional biopsy or localization device placement performed using a different image guidance modality. When an open incisional biopsy is performed after image-guided placement of a localization device, 19101 is reported and the appropriate image-guided localization device placement code is reported. The open excision of breast lesions (eg, lesions of the breast ducts, cysts, benign or malignant tumors), without specific attention to adequate surgical margins, with or without the preoperative placement of radiological markers, is reported using codes 19110-19126. Partial mastectomy procedures (eg, lumpectomy, tylectomy, quadrantectomy, or segmentectomy) describe open excisions of breast tissue with specific attention to adequate surgical margins.

▶Partial mastectomy procedures are reported using codes 19301 or 19302 as appropriate. Documentation for partial mastectomy procedures includes attention to the removal of adequate surgical margins surrounding the breast mass or lesion. Intraoperative placement of clip(s) is not separately reported.

Total mastectomy procedures include simple mastectomy, complete mastectomy, subcutaneous mastectomy, modified radical mastectomy, radical mastectomy, and more extended procedures (eg, Urban type operation). Total mastectomy procedures are reported using codes 19303-19307 as appropriate. Intraoperative placement of clip(s) is not separately reported.◀

Excisions or resections of chest wall tumors including ribs, with or without reconstruction, with or without mediastinal lymphadenectomy, are reported using codes 19260, 19271, or 19272. Codes 19260-19272 are not restricted to breast tumors and are used to report resections of chest wall tumors originating from any chest wall component. (For excision of lung or pleura, see 32310 et seq.)

When more than one breast biopsy is performed using the same imaging modality, use an add-on code whether the additional service(s) is on the same or contra-lateral breast. If additional biopsies are performed using different imaging modalities, report another primary code for each additional modality.

To report bilateral image-guided breast biopsies, report 19081, 19083, or 19085 for the initial biopsy. The contra-lateral and each additional breast image guided biopsy are then reported with code 19082, 19084 or 19086.

(To report bilateral procedures for codes 19100-19120, report modifier 50 with the procedure code)

19125 Excision of breast lesion identified by preoperative placement of radiological marker, open; single lesion

+ 19126   each additional lesion separately identified by a preoperative radiological marker (List separately in addition to code for primary procedure)

(Use 19126 in conjunction with 19125)

▶(Intraoperative placement of clip[s] is not separately reported)◀

Rationale

The guidelines in the Breast subsection of the Integumentary System section have been editorially revised to indicate that intraoperative placement of clip(s) is not separately reported. Instructional parenthetical notes have been added throughout the codes for mastectomy procedures to preclude reporting an intraoperative placement of clip(s) with these codes.

Previously, there was no parenthetical note in the Integumentary System section or in the guidelines to indicate that placement of clips was included in codes 19126 and 19301-19307, even though the intraservice work for these codes does include the placement of clips.

This editorial revision to the guidelines and the addition of parenthetical notes in the Breast Excision and Mastectomy Procedures subsections serve to clarify the inclusion of intraoperative placement of clip(s).

Introduction

Breast biopsies without image guidance are reported with 19100 and 19101. Image-guided breast biopsies, including the placement of localization devices when performed, are reported using 19081-19086. The image-guided placement of localization devices without image-guided biopsy are reported with 19281-19288. When more than one biopsy or localization device placement is performed using the same imaging modality, use an add-on code whether the additional service(s) is on the same or contra-lateral breast. If additional biopsies or localization device placements are performed using different imaging modalities, report another primary code for each additional biopsy or localization device placement performed using a different image guidance modality. When an open incisional biopsy is performed after image-guided placement of a localization device, 19101 is reported and the appropriate image-guided localization device placement code is reported.

When more than one breast localization device placement is performed using the same imaging modality, use an add-on code whether the additional service(s) is on the same or contra-lateral breast. If additional localization devices are placed using different imaging modalities, report another primary code for

each additional modality. When an open incisional biopsy is performed after image-guided placement of a localization device, 19101 is reported and the appropriate image-guided localization device placement code is reported.

To report bilateral image-guided placement of localization devices report 19281, 19283, 19285, or 19287 for the initial lesion localized. The contra-lateral and each additional breast image-guided localization device placement is reported with code 19282, 19284, 19286 or 19288.

▶Code 19294 is used to report the preparation of the tumor cavity with placement of an intraoperative radiation therapy applicator concurrent with partial mastectomy (19301, 19302).◀

+● 19294   Preparation of tumor cavity, with placement of a radiation therapy applicator for intraoperative radiation therapy (IORT) concurrent with partial mastectomy (List separately in addition to code for primary procedure)

▶(Use 19294 in conjunction with 19301, 19302)◀

19298   Placement of radiotherapy after loading brachytherapy catheters (multiple tube and button type) into the breast for interstitial radioelement application following (at the time of or subsequent to) partial mastectomy, includes imaging guidance

Rationale

Code 19294 is an add-on code that has been established to report the preparation of a tumor cavity with placement of an applicator for the delivery of intraoperative radiation therapy, which is the delivery of radiation directly to the tumor bed immediately after removal of a tumor, by a surgeon. Prior to 2018, no specific code existed in the CPT code set for this procedure. Code 19294 does not include the removal of the applicator, as that service is provided by the radiation oncologist, which may be reported with code 77469 (intraoperative radiation treatment management). Since 19294 is an add-on code, a parenthetical note has also been added to instruct the use of a partial mastectomy code (19301, 19302) in conjunction with code 19294.

Clinical Example (19294)

A 55-year-old female has been diagnosed with invasive ductal breast carcinoma. Immediately following a partial mastectomy (reported separately), the tumor cavity is prepared and an applicator to deliver intraoperative radiation therapy is placed at the treatment site. Following radiation delivery by the radiation oncologist, the tumor cavity is closed. (Note: This is an add-on code for the additional work related to preparing the tumor cavity with intraoperative placement of a radiation therapy applicator. The partial mastectomy, including closure, is reported separately as the primary procedure and not included in the work of this add-on code.)

Description of Procedure (19294)

Note that the patient remains under anesthesia and sterility is maintained throughout intraoperative radiation therapy (IORT). After the removal of the tumor and pathology assessment that tumor margins are clinically clear, the tumor cavity and remaining breast tissue are examined by the surgeon and radiation oncologist to ensure there is adequate tissue for the radiotherapy applicator to be safely and securely positioned. As appropriate, breast tissue is dissected off the underlying chest muscle for several inches to create a pocket into which an internal radiation barrier may be inserted. The posterior layers of the breast parenchyma are closed over this radiation barrier using sutures. The cavity size is measured by the surgeon. Dimensions are discussed with the radiation oncologist. An appropriately sized and shaped radiotherapy applicator is brought to the operative field. The surgeon places the applicator. (Separately reported by radiation oncologist: The position of the applicator is confirmed or manipulated, as needed, by the radiation oncologist.)

Multiple sutures are placed by the surgeon as required to ensure the surgical margins are aligned with the applicator surface. To minimize local skin radiation toxicity, the skin edges adjacent to the cavity are then dissected from the underlying breast parenchyma followed by placement of retraction device(s) or multiple retraction sutures to retract the skin edges away from the radiotherapy applicator. (Separately reported by radiation oncologist: Necessary additional work prior to radiation delivery [eg, additional shielding, adjustments to angles and measurements] and radiation delivery. The radiation treatment is planned and delivered under the supervision of the radiation oncologist.) Note that the surgeon must be available during the preradiation and radiation period in the event that additional surgical work is needed to retract skin or other tissues. After the radiation treatment is complete, the surgeon removes the conforming sutures. (Separately reported by radiation oncologist: The applicator and radiation ensemble are removed.) The surgeon removes the internal radiation barrier, if placed. After inspection of the wound, the surgeon closes the wound (closure is included in the partial mastectomy procedure).

Mastectomy Procedures

19300   Mastectomy for gynecomastia

19301   Mastectomy, partial (eg, lumpectomy, tylectomy, quadrantectomy, segmentectomy);

19302   with axillary lymphadenectomy

(For placement of radiotherapy afterloading balloon/brachytherapy catheters, see 19296-19298)

▶(Intraoperative placement of clip[s] is not separately reported)◀

▶(For the preparation of tumor cavity with placement of an intraoperative radiation therapy applicator concurrent with partial mastectomy, use 19294)◀

19303   Mastectomy, simple, complete

▶(Intraoperative placement of clip[s] is not separately reported)◀

(For immediate or delayed insertion of implant, see 19340, 19342)

(For gynecomastia, use 19300)

19304   Mastectomy, subcutaneous

▶(Intraoperative placement of clip[s] is not separately reported)◀

(For immediate or delayed insertion of implant, see 19340, 19342)

19305   Mastectomy, radical, including pectoral muscles, axillary lymph nodes

▶(Intraoperative placement of clip[s] is not separately reported)◀

(For immediate or delayed insertion of implant, see 19340, 19342)

19306   Mastectomy, radical, including pectoral muscles, axillary and internal mammary lymph nodes (Urban type operation)

▶(Intraoperative placement of clip[s] is not separately reported)◀

(For immediate or delayed insertion of implant, see 19340, 19342)

19307   Mastectomy, modified radical, including axillary lymph nodes, with or without pectoralis minor muscle, but excluding pectoralis major muscle

▶(Intraoperative placement of clip[s] is not separately reported)◀

(For immediate or delayed insertion of implant, see 19340, 19342)

Rationale

In accordance with the revisions to the guidelines in the Breast subsection of the Integumentary System section, parenthetical notes have been added following several mastectomy codes to preclude reporting intraoperative placement of clip(s) separately. In addition, in accordance with the addition of code 19294, a parenthetical note has been added following code 19302 directing users to this new code.

Refer to the codebook and the Rationale for the Breast Excision guidelines and code 19294 for a full discussion of these changes.

Musculoskeletal System

General

Excision

20150   Excision of epiphyseal bar, with or without autogenous soft tissue graft obtained through same fascial incision

20200   Biopsy, muscle; superficial

20205   deep

20220   Biopsy, bone, trocar, or needle; superficial (eg, ilium, sternum, spinous process, ribs)

20225   deep (eg, vertebral body, femur)

(Do not report 20225 in conjunction with 22510, 22511, 22512, 22513, 22514, 22515, 0200T, 0201T, when performed at the same level)

▶(For bone marrow biopsy[ies] and/or aspiration[s], see 38220, 38221, 38222)◀

(For radiologic supervision and interpretation, see 77002, 77012, 77021)

Rationale

A parenthetical note that follows code 20150 has been deleted, and an instructional parenthetical note that follows code 20225 has been revised to accommodate changes made in reporting diagnostic and therapeutic bone marrow aspiration procedures. The instructional parenthetical note that followed code 20150 directed users to report code 38220 for bone marrow aspiration. However, this code has been revised to reflect diagnostic marrow aspiration and that it is intended to be used only for that purpose. Other new codes (eg, 20939, 38222) now exist for reporting other diagnostic and therapeutic bone marrow aspiration and biopsy procedures.

In addition, the instructional parenthetical note that follows code 20225 has been revised to identify reporting multiple biopsies or aspiration procedures and to include codes 38220 and 38222.

Refer to the codebook and the Rationale for code 38222 for a full discussion of the changes.

Introduction or Removal

(For injection procedure for arthrography, see anatomical area)

▶(For injection of autologous adipose-derived regenerative cells, see 0489T, 0490T)◀

20500   Injection of sinus tract; therapeutic (separate procedure)

Rationale

In support of the establishment of the two new codes (0489T and 0490T) for autologous adipose-derived regenerative cell therapy, a parenthetical note has been added preceding code 20500 to direct users to these new codes.

Refer to the codebook and the Rationale for codes 0489T and 0490T for a full discussion of the changes.

20550   Injection(s); single tendon sheath, or ligament, aponeurosis (eg, plantar "fascia")

(For injection of Morton's neuroma, see 64455, 64632)

20551   single tendon origin/insertion

▶(Do not report 20550, 20551 in conjunction with 0232T, 0481T)◀

▶(For harvesting, preparation, and injection[s] of platelet-rich plasma, use 0232T)◀

Rationale

In support of the establishment of Category III code 0481T, the parenthetical notes that follow code 20551 have been updated.

Refer to the codebook and the Rationale for code 0481T for a full discussion of the changes.

20600   Arthrocentesis, aspiration and/or injection, small joint or bursa (eg, fingers, toes); without ultrasound guidance

20604   with ultrasound guidance, with permanent recording and reporting

▶(Do not report 20600, 20604 in conjunction with 76942, 0489T, 0490T)◀

Rationale

In support of the establishment of the two new codes (0489T and 0490T) for autologous adipose-derived regenerative cell therapy, the exclusionary parenthetical note that follows code 20604 has been updated to include these codes.

Refer to the codebook and the Rationale for codes 0489T and 0490T for a full discussion of the changes.

Grafts (or Implants)

▶Codes for obtaining autogenous bone, cartilage, tendon, fascia lata grafts, bone marrow, or other tissues through separate skin/fascial incisions should be reported separately, unless the code descriptor references the harvesting of the graft or implant (eg, includes obtaining graft).◀

20926   Tissue grafts, other (eg, paratenon, fat, dermis)

▶(Do not report 20926 in conjunction with 0489T, 0490T)◀

▶(For harvesting of adipose tissue for autologous adipose-derived regenerative cell therapy, see 0489T, 0490T)◀

▶(For injection of autologous adipose-derived regenerative cells, see 0489T, 0490T)◀

▶(For harvesting, preparation, and injection[s] of platelet-rich plasma, use 0232T)◀

Rationale

In support of the establishment of code 38222, the guidelines for the Grafts (or Implants) subsection in the Musculoskeletal section have been revised. Refer to the codebook and the Rationale for codes 38220, 38221, and 38222 for a full discussion of the changes.

In support of the establishment of the two new codes (0489T and 0490T) for autologous adipose-derived regenerative cell therapy, three parenthetical notes have been added after code 20926. Refer to the codebook and the Rationale for codes 0489T and 0490T for a full discussion of the changes.

In support of establishment of Category III code 0481T, a parenthetical note that follows code 20926 has been revised. Refer to the codebook and the Rationale for code 0481T for a full discussion of the changes.

+ 20936   Autograft for spine surgery only (includes harvesting the graft); local (eg, ribs, spinous process, or laminar fragments) obtained from same incision (List separately in addition to code for primary procedure)

(Use 20936 in conjunction with 22319, 22532, 22533, 22548-22558, 22590-22612, 22630, 22633, 22634, 22800-22812)

+ 20937   morselized (through separate skin or fascial incision) (List separately in addition to code for primary procedure)

(Use 20937 in conjunction with 22319, 22532, 22533, 22548-22558, 22590-22612, 22630, 22633, 22634, 22800-22812)

+ 20938   structural, bicortical or tricortical (through separate skin or fascial incision) (List separately in addition to code for primary procedure)

(Use 20938 in conjunction with 22319, 22532, 22533, 22548-22558, 22590-22612, 22630, 22633, 22634, 22800-22812)

▶(For aspiration of bone marrow for bone grafting, spine surgery only, use 20939)◀

+● 20939   Bone marrow aspiration for bone grafting, spine surgery only, through separate skin or fascial incision (List separately in addition to code for primary procedure)

▶(Use 20939 in conjunction with 22319, 22532, 22533, 22534, 22548, 22551, 22552, 22554, 22556, 22558, 22590, 22595, 22600, 22610, 22612, 22630, 22633, 22634, 22800, 22802, 22804, 22808, 22810, 22812)◀

▶(For bilateral procedure, use 20939 with modifier 50)◀

▶(For aspiration of bone marrow for the purpose of bone grafting, other than spine surgery and other therapeutic musculoskeletal applications, use 20999)◀

▶(For bone marrow aspiration[s] for platelet-rich stem cell injection, use 0232T)◀

▶(For diagnostic bone marrow aspiration[s], see 38220, 38222)◀

Rationale

In accordance with the revisions made in reporting diagnostic and therapeutic bone marrow aspiration procedures, code 20939 has been established to report therapeutic bone marrow aspiration procedures for spine surgery only. In addition, a number of parenthetical notes have been added and/or deleted to reflect this change. Refer to the codebook and the Rationale for codes 38220, 38221, and 38222 for a full discussion of the changes.

Clinical Example (20939)

A 50-year-old male undergoes a posterior cervical fusion of C5–C6 for degenerative disease. A posterior stab incision is made over the right iliac crest, and a trephine needle is placed into the bone. A syringe is used to aspirate 30 cc of bone marrow to mix with allograft. (Code 20939 is an add-on code that represents the additional work for harvesting of bone marrow aspirate. Arthrodesis and/or instrumentation would be reported separately using the appropriate code[s].)

★ =Telemedicine   + =Add-on code   ✐ =FDA approval pending   # =Resequenced code

Description of Procedure (20939)

Prior to surgery, the surgeon has a discussion with the patient and obtains consent for the separate incision and bone marrow aspiration. At surgery, the area of the separate skin or fascial incision is prepared and draped (eg, iliac crest). A stab incision is made, and a trephine needle is placed into the bone marrow space. A syringe is used to aspirate 30 cc of bone marrow. The trephine needle is then removed. A suture is placed to close the stab incision, and a dressing is placed. After surgery, the additional bone marrow aspiration procedure is documented as part of the primary procedure operative note.

Application of Casts and Strapping

The listed procedures apply when the cast application or strapping is a replacement procedure used during or after the period of follow-up care, or when the cast application or strapping is an initial service performed without a restorative treatment or procedure(s) to stabilize or protect a fracture, injury, or dislocation and/or to afford comfort to a patient. Restorative treatment or procedure(s) rendered by another individual following the application of the initial cast/splint/strap may be reported with a treatment of fracture and/or dislocation code.

An individual who applies the initial cast, strap, or splint and also assumes all of the subsequent fracture, dislocation, or injury care cannot use the application of casts and strapping codes as an initial service, since the first cast/splint or strap application is included in the treatment of fracture and/or dislocation codes. (See notes under Musculoskeletal System, page 108 [in the *CPT Professional* codebook].) A temporary cast/splint/strap is not considered to be part of the preoperative care, and the use of the modifier 56 is not applicable. Additional evaluation and management services are reportable only if significant identifiable further services are provided at the time of the cast application or strapping.

If cast application or strapping is provided as an initial service (eg, casting of a sprained ankle or knee) in which no other procedure or treatment (eg, surgical repair, reduction of a fracture, or joint dislocation) is performed or is expected to be performed by an individual rendering the initial care only, use the casting, strapping, and/or supply code (99070) in addition to an evaluation and management code as appropriate.

Listed procedures include removal of cast or strapping.

▶(For orthotics management and training, see 97760, 97761, 97763)◀

Rationale

In accordance with the deletion of code 97762, the parenthetical note that follows the application of casts and strapping guidelines has been revised with the removal of this code and replacement with new code 97763. Refer to the codebook and the Rationale for codes 97760, 97761, and 97763 for a full discussion of the changes.

Lower Extremity

Strapping—Any Age

29520   Strapping; hip

29540   ankle and/or foot

▶(Do not report 29540 in conjunction with 29581)◀

29580   Unna boot

▶(Do not report 29580 in conjunction with 29581)◀

29581   Application of multi-layer compression system; leg (below knee), including ankle and foot

▶(Do not report 29581 in conjunction with 29540, 29580, 36468, 36470, 36471, 36475, 36476, 36478, 36479)◀

▶(29582, 29583 have been deleted)◀

29584   upper arm, forearm, hand, and fingers

Rationale

Codes 29582 and 29583 for the application of a multilayer compression system on the thigh and leg, and upper arm and forearm have been deleted. As a result, references to these codes in the parenthetical notes throughout the code set have been updated to reflect these deletions.

To ensure that the CPT code set reflects current clinical practice, codes 29582 and 29583 have been deleted due to low utilization and misreporting. The exclusionary parenthetical note that follows code 29581 has been revised to reflect the deletions and to preclude the reporting this code with codes 36468 (single or multiple injections of sclerosing solutions, spider veins, limb, or trunk), 36470, and 36471 (injections of sclerosing solution single vein or multiple veins).

Surgery / Musculoskeletal System 20005-29999

Endoscopy/Arthroscopy

29888   Arthroscopically aided anterior cruciate ligament repair/augmentation or reconstruction

29889   Arthroscopically aided posterior cruciate ligament repair/augmentation or reconstruction

Rationale

A parenthetical note that followed code 29889 has been deleted. This change is an editorial revision made to allow reporting of codes 29888, 29889 for arthroscopically aided repair of cruciate ligament with codes 27427-27429 for open ligament repair/reconstruction. This is because both open and arthroscopic ligament repair/reconstruction procedures are commonly performed on a knee.

Respiratory System

Accessory Sinuses

Endoscopy

A surgical sinus endoscopy includes a sinusotomy (when appropriate) and diagnostic endoscopy.

▶Codes 31295-31298 describe dilation of sinus ostia by displacement of tissue, any method, and include fluoroscopy if performed.

Stereotactic computer-assisted navigation may be used to facilitate the performance of endoscopic sinus surgery, and may be reported with 61782.

Codes 31233-31298 are used to report unilateral procedures unless otherwise specified.

Codes 31231-31235 for diagnostic evaluation refer to employing a nasal/sinus endoscope to inspect the interior of the nasal cavity and the middle and superior meatus, the turbinates, and the spheno-ethmoid recess. Any time a diagnostic evaluation is performed all these areas would be inspected and a separate code is not reported for each area. To report these services when all of the elements are not fully examined (eg, judged not clinically pertinent), or because the clinical situation precludes such exam (eg, technically unable, altered anatomy), append modifier 52 if repeat examination is not planned, or modifier 53 if repeat examination is planned.◀

31237   Nasal/sinus endoscopy, surgical; with biopsy, polypectomy or debridement (separate procedure)

31238   with control of nasal hemorrhage

▶(Do not report 31238 in conjunction with 31241, when performed on the ipsilateral side)◀

31239   with dacryocystorhinostomy

31240   with concha bullosa resection

(For endoscopic osteomeatal complex [OMC] resection with antrostomy and/or anterior ethmoidectomy, with or without removal of polyp[s], use 31254 and 31256)

(For endoscopic osteomeatal complex [OMC] resection with antrostomy, removal of antral mucosal disease, and/or anterior ethmoidectomy, with or without removal of polyp[s], use 31254 and 31267)

(For endoscopic frontal sinus exploration, osteomeatal complex [OMC] resection and/or anterior ethmoidectomy, with or without removal of polyp[s], use 31254 and 31276)

(For endoscopic frontal sinus exploration, osteomeatal complex [OMC] resection, antrostomy, and/or anterior ethmoidectomy, with or without removal of polyp[s], use 31254, 31256, and 31276)

(For endoscopic nasal diagnostic endoscopy, see 31231-31235)

(For endoscopic osteomeatal complex [OMC] resection, frontal sinus exploration, antrostomy, removal of antral mucosal disease, and/or anterior ethmoidectomy, with or without removal of polyp[s], use 31254, 31267, and 31276)

● **31241**   with ligation of sphenopalatine artery

▶(Do not report 31241 in conjunction with 31238, when performed on the ipsilateral side)◀

31253   Code is out of numerical sequence. See 31254-31267

▲ **31254**   Nasal/sinus endoscopy, surgical with ethmoidectomy; partial (anterior)

▶(Do not report 31254 in conjunction with 31253, 31255, 31257, 31259, 0406T, 0407T, when performed on the ipsilateral side)◀

▲ **31255**   total (anterior and posterior)

▶(Do not report 31255 in conjunction with 31253, 31254, 31257, 31259, 31276, 31287, 31288, 0406T, 0407T, when performed on the ipsilateral side)◀

#● **31253**   total (anterior and posterior), including frontal sinus exploration, with removal of tissue from frontal sinus, when performed

▶(Do not report 31253 in conjunction with 31237, 31254, 31255, 31276, 31296, 31298, 0406T, 0407T, when performed on the ipsilateral side)◀

★ = Telemedicine   ✚ = Add-on code   ✎ = FDA approval pending   # = Resequenced code

Surgery / Respiratory System   30000-32999

#• **31257**   total (anterior and posterior), including sphenoidotomy

▶(Do not report 31257 in conjunction with 31235, 31237, 31254, 31255, 31259, 31287, 31288, 31297, 31298, 0406T, 0407T, when performed on the ipsilateral side)◀

#• **31259**   total (anterior and posterior), including sphenoidotomy, with removal of tissue from the sphenoid sinus

▶(Do not report 31259 in conjunction with 31235, 31237, 31254, 31255, 31257, 31287, 31288, 31297, 31298, 0406T, 0407T, when performed on the ipsilateral side)◀

31256   Nasal/sinus endoscopy, surgical, with maxillary antrostomy;

(For endoscopic anterior and posterior ethmoidectomy [APE] and antrostomy, with or without removal of polyp[s], use 31255 and 31256)

(For endoscopic anterior and posterior ethmoidectomy [APE], antrostomy and removal of antral mucosal disease, with or without removal of polyp[s], use 31255 and 31267)

(For endoscopic anterior and posterior ethmoidectomy [APE], and frontal sinus exploration, with or without removal of polyp[s], use 31255 and 31276)

31257   Code is out of numerical sequence. See 31254-31267

31259   Code is out of numerical sequence. See 31254-31267

31267   with removal of tissue from maxillary sinus

(Do not report 31256, 31267 in conjunction with 31295 when performed on the same sinus)

(For endoscopic anterior and posterior ethmoidectomy [APE], and frontal sinus exploration and antrostomy, with or without removal of polyp[s], use 31255, 31256, and 31276)

(For endoscopic anterior and posterior ethmoidectomy [APE], frontal sinus exploration, antrostomy, and removal of antral mucosal disease, with or without removal of polyp[s], use 31255, 31267, and 31276)

▲ **31276**   Nasal/sinus endoscopy, surgical, with frontal sinus exploration, including removal of tissue from frontal sinus, when performed

▶(Do not report 31276 in conjunction with 31253, 31255, 31296, 31298, when performed on the ipsilateral side)◀

(For endoscopic anterior and posterior ethmoidectomy and sphenoidotomy [APS], with or without removal of polyp[s], use 31255, 31287 or 31288)

(For endoscopic anterior and posterior ethmoidectomy and sphenoidotomy [APS], and antrostomy, with or without removal of polyp[s], use 31255, 31256, and 31287 or 31288)

(For endoscopic anterior and posterior ethmoidectomy and sphenoidotomy [APS], antrostomy and removal of antral mucosal disease, with or without removal of polyp[s], use 31255, 31267, and 31287 or 31288)

(For endoscopic anterior and posterior ethmoidectomy and sphenoidotomy [APS], and frontal sinus exploration with or without removal of polyp[s], use 31255, 31287 or 31288, and 31276)

(For endoscopic anterior and posterior ethmoidectomy and sphenoidotomy [APS], with or without removal of polyp[s], with frontal sinus exploration and antrostomy, use 31255, 31256, 31287 or 31288, and 31276)

(For unilateral endoscopy of 2 or more sinuses, see 31231-31235)

(For endoscopic anterior and posterior ethmoidectomy and sphenoidotomy [APS], frontal sinus exploration, antrostomy and removal of antral mucosal disease, with or without removal of polyp[s], see 31255, 31267, 31287 or 31288 and 31276)

31287   Nasal/sinus endoscopy, surgical, with sphenoidotomy;

▶(Do not report 31287 in conjunction with 31235, 31255, 31257, 31259, 31288, 31297, 31298, when performed on the ipsilateral side)◀

31288   with removal of tissue from the sphenoid sinus

▶(Do not report 31288 in conjunction with 31235, 31255, 31257, 31259, 31287, 31297, 31298, when performed on the ipsilateral side)◀

31295   Nasal/sinus endoscopy, surgical; with dilation of maxillary sinus ostium (eg, balloon dilation), transnasal or via canine fossa

▶(Do not report 31295 in conjunction with 31233, 31256, 31267, when performed on the ipsilateral side)◀

31296   with dilation of frontal sinus ostium (eg, balloon dilation)

▶(Do not report 31296 in conjunction with 31253, 31276, 31297, 31298, when performed on the ipsilateral side)◀

31297   with dilation of sphenoid sinus ostium (eg, balloon dilation)

▶(Do not report 31297 in conjunction with 31235, 31257, 31259, 31287, 31288, 31296, 31298, when performed on the ipsilateral side)◀

• **31298**   with dilation of frontal and sphenoid sinus ostia (eg, balloon dilation)

▶(Do not report 31298 in conjunction with 31235, 31237, 31253, 31257, 31259, 31276, 31287, 31288, 31296, 31297, when performed on the ipsilateral side)◀

Rationale

Codes 31241, 31253, 31257, 31259, and 31298 have been established; the guidelines in the Endoscopy subsection of the Respiratory System section have been revised; and codes 31254, 31255, and 31276 have been revised. In addition, parenthetical notes have been added and revised throughout the Respiratory section to conform with these changes.

These changes have been initiated because of a survey requested by the AMA RUC RAW, which identified the current code family as being potentially misvalued. It was determined that adding and revising these codes would provide a solution to the family of surgical endoscopic services.

As a result, code 31241 may be reported for a nasal/sinus endoscopy with ligation of sphenopalatine artery. Code 31254 has been revised to a parent code with four codes in its family. This new family of codes (31254, 31255, 31253, 31257, 31259) should be used to report surgical nasal endoscopies with ethmoidectomy (partial, anterior and posterior, including frontal sinus exploration; with sphenoidotomy; and sphenoidotomy, with removal of tissue from the sphenoid sinus).

In addition, the guidelines referencing codes 31231-31235 have been revised to provide instruction on the use of modifier 52 or modifier 53 depending on the circumstances of the examination.

Clinical Example (31241)

A 62-year-old male presents with left-sided epistaxis refractory to attempt to control. The patient undergoes left endoscopic ligation of the sphenopalatine artery.

Description of Procedure (31241)

Previously placed nasal packing and pledgets are removed, and attempts are made to isolate and slow down the bleeding to allow adequate visualization. Comprehensive nasal endoscopy is performed, and presurgical findings are confirmed. Topical decongestion is performed in the middle meatus. An intranasal anesthetic/vasoconstrictive agent is injected. The middle turbinate is medialized, and the posterior attachment is identified. Local anesthesia is infiltrated into the posterior attachment of the middle turbinate. An incision is made along the lateral nasal wall, and a mucoperiosteal flap is raised with identification of the crista ethmoidalis. The sphenopalatine foramen is identified, and the sphenopalatine artery is traced out. This takes place in the midst of active bleeding, which obscures visualization and requires repeated packing

with topical vasoconstrictors. There are often multiple branches of the sphenopalatine artery, and each one is traced out and dissected from surrounding tissues. An endoscopic clip applier is then used to clip each branch of the vessel in multiple spots, and the vessel is ligated. Hemostasis is then obtained using topical vaso-constrictors. The mucoperiosteal flap is replaced. Packing or a stent may be placed.

Clinical Example (31253)

A 48-year-old female presents with chronic right frontal and ipsilateral ethmoid sinusitis, with obstruction of the right frontal and anterior and posterior ethmoid sinuses. She has failed medical therapy. The patient undergoes right endoscopic frontal sinusotomy and right endoscopic total ethmoidectomy.

Description of Procedure (31253)

Previously placed pledgets are removed. Comprehensive nasal endoscopy is performed, and presurgical findings are confirmed. Topical decongestion is performed in the middle meatus. An intranasal anesthetic/vasoconstrictive agent is injected. The middle turbinate is medialized. The superior portion of the uncinate process is identified and resected. The bulla ethmoidalis is entered and its walls removed. Following identification of the orbital wall (lamina papyracea), all ethmoid lamella are removed posteriorly to the level of basal lamella and superiorly to the level of the ethmoid skull base. The anterior ethmoidal neurovascular bundle is identified and preserved. After completion of the anterior ethmoidectomy, the basal lamella is incised to gain access to the posterior ethmoid cells. The orbit is identified posterior to the basal lamella, and the superior turbinate is identified. All posterior ethmoid lamella are resected posteriorly to the anterior face of the sphenoid sinus, laterally to the orbit (lamina papyracea), and superiorly to the posterior ethmoid skull base. Using angled endoscopes and instruments, the agger nasi cell at the superior extent of the uncinate process is entered inferiorly, allowing access to the frontal recess. Cells within the frontal recess and superior to the bulla ethmoidalis are examined and sequentially resected laterally to the orbital wall (lamina papyracea), posteriorly to the anterior ethmoidal neurovascular bundle, and medially to the lateral lamella of the cribriform plate. After access to the frontal sinus is established, tissue may be removed from within the sinus. Care is taken to preserve mucosa on all surfaces of the frontal recess, as denuded mucosa will lead to scarring of the frontal ostium. Following completion of the procedure, hemostasis is ensured, and packing or a stent may be placed within the middle meatus.

Clinical Example (31254)

A 48-year-old female presents with chronic left ethmoid sinusitis, which has been refractory to medical management. Endoscopic examination reveals chronic ethmoiditis. A computed tomography (CT) scan demonstrated opacification of the osteomeatal complex and anterior ethmoid sinuses. A nasal/sinus endoscopy, with ethmoidectomy, partial (anterior) is performed.

Description of Procedure (31254)

Previously placed pledgets are removed. Comprehensive nasal endoscopy is performed, and pre-surgical findings are confirmed. Topical decongestion is performed in the middle meatus. An intranasal anesthetic/vasoconstrictive agent is injected. The middle turbinate is medialized. Bulla ethmoidalis is entered and its walls removed. Following identification of the orbital wall (lamina papyracea), all ethmoid lamella are removed posteriorly to the level of basal lamella and superiorly to the level of the ethmoid skull base. The anterior ethmoidal neurovascular bundle is identified and preserved. Following completion of the procedure, hemostasis is ensured, and packing or a stent may be placed within the middle meatus.

Clinical Example (31255)

A 48-year-old female presents with chronic left ethmoid sinusitis, which has been refractory to medical management. Endoscopic examination reveals chronic ethmoiditis. A CT scan demonstrated opacification of the osteomeatal complex and anterior and posterior ethmoid sinuses. A nasal/sinus endoscopy with ethmoidectomy, total (anterior and posterior), is performed.

Description of Procedure (31255)

Previously placed pledgets are removed. Comprehensive nasal endoscopy is performed, and presurgical findings are confirmed. Topical decongestion is performed in the middle meatus. An intranasal anesthetic/vasoconstrictive agent is injected. The middle turbinate is medialized. The bulla ethmoidalis is entered and its walls removed. Following identification of the orbital wall (lamina papyracea), all ethmoid lamella are removed posteriorly to the level of basal lamella and superiorly to the level of the ethmoid skull base. The anterior ethmoidal neurovascular bundle is identified and preserved. After completion of the anterior ethmoidectomy, the basal lamella is incised to gain access to the posterior ethmoid cells. The orbit is identified posterior to the basal lamella, and the superior turbinate is identified. All posterior ethmoid lamella are resected posteriorly to the anterior face of the sphenoid sinus, laterally to the orbit

(lamina papyracea), and superiorly to the posterior ethmoid skull base. Following completion of the procedure, hemostasis is ensured, and packing or a stent may be placed within the middle meatus.

Clinical Example (31257)

A 48-year-old female presents with chronic left ethmoid and ipsilateral sphenoid sinusitis, with obstruction of the left sphenoid and anterior and posterior ethmoid sinuses. She has failed medical therapy. The patient undergoes left endoscopic total ethmoidectomy and left endoscopic sphenoidotomy.

Description of Procedure (31257)

Previously placed pledgets are removed. Comprehensive nasal endoscopy is performed, and presurgical findings are confirmed. Topical decongestion is performed in the middle meatus. An intranasal anesthetic/vasoconstrictive agent is injected. The middle turbinate is medialized. The uncinate process is identified and resected. The bulla ethmoidalis is entered and its walls removed. Following identification of the orbital wall (lamina papyracea), all ethmoid lamella are removed posteriorly to the level of basal lamella and superiorly to the level of the ethmoid skull base. The anterior ethmoidal neurovascular bundle is identified and preserved. After completion of the anterior ethmoidectomy, the basal lamella is incised to gain access to the posterior ethmoid cells. The orbit is identified posterior to the basal lamella, and the superior turbinate is identified. All posterior ethmoid lamella are resected posteriorly to the anterior face of the sphenoid sinus, laterally to the orbit (lamina papyracea), and superiorly to the posterior ethmoid skull base. The superior turbinate is then identified. The natural ostium of the sphenoid sinus is identified and surgically enlarged. The anterior face of the sphenoid is resected superiorly to sphenoid planum (sphenoid skull base) and laterally to the level of the orbit. The sphenoid sinus is irrigated and/or suctioned. Following completion of the procedure, hemostasis is ensured, and packing or a stent may be placed within the middle meatus.

Clinical Example (31259)

A 46-year-old female presents with chronic left ethmoid and ipsilateral sphenoid sinusitis, with obstruction of the left sphenoid and anterior and posterior ethmoid sinuses. Significant diseased tissue is present within the sphenoid sinus. She has failed medical therapy. The patient undergoes left endoscopic total ethmoidectomy and sphenoidotomy with removal of tissue from the sphenoid sinus cavity.

Description of Procedure (31259)

Previously placed pledgets are removed. Comprehensive nasal endoscopy is performed, and presurgical findings are confirmed. Topical decongestion is performed in the middle meatus. An intranasal anesthetic/vasoconstrictive agent is injected. The middle turbinate is medialized. The uncinate process is identified and resected. The bulla ethmoidalis is entered and its walls removed. Following identification of the orbital wall (lamina papyracea), all ethmoid lamella are removed posteriorly to the level of basal lamella and superiorly to the level of the ethmoid skull base. The anterior ethmoidal neurovascular bundle is identified and preserved. After completion of the anterior ethmoidectomy, the basal lamella is incised to gain access to the posterior ethmoid cells. The orbit is identified posterior to the basal lamella, and the superior turbinate is identified. All posterior ethmoid lamella are resected posteriorly to the anterior face of the sphenoid sinus, laterally to the orbit (lamina papyracea), and superiorly to the posterior ethmoid skull base. The superior turbinate is identified. Inflammatory tissue extending into the sphenoethmoid recess and nasal cavity from the sphenoid sinus is removed to provide visualization. After hemostasis, the natural ostium of the sphenoid sinus is identified and surgically enlarged. The anterior face of the sphenoid is resected superiorly to the sphenoid planum (sphenoid skull base) and laterally to the level of the orbit. The sphenoid sinus is irrigated and/or suctioned. The sphenoid sinus is inspected, and inflammatory tissue and inspissated debris within the sinus are surgically removed. Following completion of the procedure, hemostasis is ensured, and packing or a stent may be placed within the middle meatus.

Clinical Example (31276)

A 48-year-old female presents with chronic right frontal sinusitis, which has been refractory to medical management. Endoscopic examination reveals edema and/or mucopurulence within the ipsilateral frontal recess. A CT scan demonstrates opacification of the right frontal sinus. A nasal/sinus endoscopy with frontal exploration is performed.

Description of Procedure (31276)

Previously placed pledgets are removed. Comprehensive nasal endoscopy is performed, and presurgical findings are confirmed. Topical decongestion is performed in the middle meatus. An intranasal anesthetic/vasoconstrictive agent is injected. The middle turbinate is medialized. The bulla ethmoidalis is identified and used to serve as the posterior limit of frontal recess dissection. The superior portion of the uncinate process is identified and

resected. Using angled endoscopes and instruments, the agger nasi cell at the superior extent of the uncinate process is entered inferiorly, allowing access to the frontal recess. Cells within the frontal recess and superior to the bulla ethmoidalis are examined and sequentially resected laterally to the orbital wall (lamina papyracea), posteriorly to the anterior ethmoidal neurovascular bundle, and medially to the lateral lamella of the cribriform plate. After access to the frontal sinus is established, tissue may be removed from within the sinus. Care is taken to preserve mucosa on all surfaces of the frontal recess as denuded mucosa will lead to scarring of the frontal ostium. Following completion of the procedure, hemostasis is ensured and packing or a stent may be placed within the middle meatus.

Clinical Example (31298)

A 48-year-old female presents with chronic right frontal and ipsilateral sphenoid sinusitis, with obstruction of the right sphenoid ostium and of the frontal recess. She has failed medical therapy. The patient undergoes balloon dilatation of the right frontal and sphenoid sinus ostia.

Description of Procedure (31298)

Previously placed pledgets are removed. Under endoscopic visualization, pledgets soaked in decongestant and anesthesia are placed in the middle meatus, followed by a wait time for them to take effect. Pledgets are then removed and an intranasal anesthetic/vasoconstrictive agent is injected into the middle turbinate and uncinate process, followed by a wait time for this to take effect. The middle turbinate is medialized. Pledgets soaked in decongestant and anesthesia are placed in the frontal recess, followed by a wait time for them to take effect. Under endoscopic visualization, a guidewire is introduced into the frontal recess via a transnasal approach. A deflated balloon catheter is threaded over the guidewire and introduced into the frontal ostium. Positioning of both the guidewire and the balloon are confirmed endoscopically and with transillumination during the course of the placement of each. The balloon is then inflated, resulting in dilation of the natural ostium of the sinus, displacing bone and mucosa. After dilation, the balloon is deflated and removed. In some cases, a separate catheter can be introduced over the guidewire for irrigation of the sinus. The middle turbinate is then lateralized, and pledgets soaked in decongestant and anesthesia are placed in the sphenoethmoid recess, followed by a wait time for this to take effect. Pledgets are then removed. Under endoscopic visualization, a guidewire is introduced into the sphenoid ostium via a transnasal approach. A deflated balloon catheter is threaded over the guidewire and introduced into the sphenoid ostium. Positioning of both the

★ = Telemedicine   ✚ = Add-on code   ✒ = FDA approval pending   # = Resequenced code

guidewire and the balloon are confirmed endoscopically during the course of the placement of each. The balloon is then inflated, resulting in dilation of the natural ostium of the sinus, displacing bone and mucosa. After dilation, the balloon is deflated and removed. In some cases, a separate catheter can be introduced over the guidewire for irrigation of the sinus.

Larynx

Excision

31300   Laryngotomy (thyrotomy, laryngofissure), with removal of tumor or laryngocele, cordectomy

▶(31320 has been deleted)◀

31360   Laryngectomy; total, without radical neck dissection

31365   total, with radical neck dissection

Rationale

Code 31320 (laryngotomy [thyrotomy, laryngofissure]; diagnostic) has been deleted due to low utilization and to ensure that the CPT code set reflects current clinical practice.

Trachea and Bronchi

Endoscopy

31622   Bronchoscopy, rigid or flexible, including fluoroscopic guidance, when performed; diagnostic, with cell washing, when performed (separate procedure)

31643   with placement of catheter(s) for intracavitary radioelement application

(For intracavitary radioelement application, see 77761-77763, 77770, 77771, 77772)

▲ **31645**   with therapeutic aspiration of tracheobronchial tree, initial

▲ **31646**   with therapeutic aspiration of tracheobronchial tree, subsequent, same hospital stay

▶(For catheter aspiration of tracheobronchial tree with fiberscope at bedside, use 31725)◀

+ **31654**   with transendoscopic endobronchial ultrasound (EBUS) during bronchoscopic diagnostic or therapeutic intervention(s) for peripheral lesion(s) (List separately in addition to code for primary procedure[s])

(Use 31654 in conjunction with 31622, 31623, 31624, 31625, 31626, 31628, 31629, 31640, 31643, 31645, 31646)

(For EBUS to access mediastinal or hilar lymph node station[s] or adjacent structure[s], see 31652, 31653)

(Report 31652, 31653, 31654 only once per session)

Rationale

Code 31645 has been revised with the removal of the example "(eg, drainage of lung abscess)." Similarly, code 31646 has been revised with the addition of the phrase "same hospital stay" to specify that the initial therapeutic aspiration of the tracheobronchial tree is performed at the same hospital stay. Code 31645 was identified by the AMA RAW as potentially misvalued.

The instructional parenthetical note that follows code 31646 has been revised to instruct users to refer to code 31725 when reporting catheter aspiration of the tracheobronchial tree with a fiberscope at the bedside. The phrase "with fiberscope" has been added to the parenthetical note because code 31725 was revised in 2017 to include the use of a fiberscope at the bedside.

Clinical Example (31645)

A 60-year-old male has been hospitalized for one week for respiratory failure. He has respiratory decompensation, oxygen requirements have increased, and a chest radiograph shows new lung atelectasis. Bronchoscopy is performed for the clearance of secretions that are obstructing bronchi.

Description of Procedure (31645)

The physician evaluates for the appropriate topical anesthesia and moderate sedation. O_2 is evaluated to maintain normal O_2 saturations throughout procedure. A flexible bronchoscope is inserted through the mouth or nostril to visualize the upper airways to the vocal cords. The vocal cords are observed for function. The bronchoscope is then advanced into the trachea. All airways are inspected. Secretions are identified and aspirated. All segments of the lung are visualized, and each segment is aspirated, as needed, to clear secretions. Sterile saline may be required to mobilize more viscous and distal secretions. The bronchoscope is removed, and the inner channel is flushed, as necessary, to clear more tenacious secretions. The bronchoscope is reinserted, as necessary, until the secretions are clear. The physician examines the patient immediately post-endoscopy to ascertain that no complication, such as desaturation or respiratory failure, has occurred.

Surgery / Respiratory System 30000-32999

Clinical Example (31646)

A 60-year-old male who previously underwent bronchoscopy for obstructing secretions during the current hospitalization, develops new or recurrent signs of respiratory compromise, retained secretions, and atelectasis. Bronchoscopy is performed again for the clearance of secretions.

Description of Procedure (31646)

The physician evaluates for the appropriate topical anesthesia and moderate sedation. O_2 is evaluated to maintain normal O_2 saturations throughout procedure. A flexible bronchoscope is inserted through the mouth or nostril to visualize the upper airways to the vocal cords. The vocal cords are observed for function. The bronchoscope is then advanced into the trachea. All airways are inspected. Secretions are identified and aspirated. All segments of the lung are visualized, and each segment is aspirated, as needed, to clear secretions. Sterile saline may be required to mobilize more viscous and distal secretions. The bronchoscope is removed, and the inner channel is flushed, as necessary, to clear more tenacious secretions. The bronchoscope is reinserted, as necessary, until the secretions are clear. The physician examines the patient immediately post-endoscopy to ascertain that no complication, such as desaturation or respiratory failure, has occurred.

Lungs and Pleura

Thoracoscopy (Video-assisted thoracic surgery [VATS])

32650   Thoracoscopy, surgical; with pleurodesis (eg, mechanical or chemical)

+ 32674   with mediastinal and regional lymphadenectomy (List separately in addition to code for primary procedure)

(On the right, mediastinal lymph nodes include the paratracheal, subcarinal, paraesophageal, and inferior pulmonary ligament)

(On the left, mediastinal lymph nodes include the aortopulmonary window, subcarinal, paraesophageal, and inferior pulmonary ligament)

▶(Report 32674 in conjunction with 19260, 31760, 31766, 31786, 32096-32200, 32220-32320, 32440-32491, 32503-32505, 32601-32663, 32666, 32669-32673, 32815, 33025, 33030, 33050-33130, 39200-39220, 39560, 39561, 43101, 43112, 43117, 43118, 43122, 43123, 43287, 43288, 43351, 60270, 60505)◀

(To report mediastinal and regional lymphadenectomy via thoracotomy, use 38746)

Rationale

The parenthetical note that follows code 32674 has been updated to include a list of the esophagectomy procedures that include a thoracoscopic component for the removal procedure.

Refer to the codebook and the Rationale for codes 43286-43288 for a full discussion of the changes.

Lung Transplantation

Lung allotransplantation involves three distinct components of physician work:

1. **Cadaver donor pneumonectomy(s),** which include(s) harvesting the allograft and cold preservation of the allograft (perfusing with cold preservation solution and cold maintenance) (use 32850).

2. **Backbench work:**

   Preparation of a cadaver donor single lung allograft prior to transplantation, including dissection of the allograft from surrounding soft tissues to prepare the pulmonary venous/atrial cuff, pulmonary artery, and bronchus unilaterally (use 32855).

   Preparation of a cadaver donor double lung allograft prior to transplantation, including dissection of the allograft from surrounding soft tissues to prepare the pulmonary venous/atrial cuff, pulmonary artery, and bronchus bilaterally (use 32856).

3. **Recipient lung allotransplantation,** which includes transplantation of a single or double lung allograft and care of the recipient (see 32851-32854).

   ▶(For ex-vivo assessment of marginal donor lung transplant, see 0494T, 0495T, 0496T)◀

Rationale

An instructional parenthetical note has been added to the Lung Transplantation guidelines to direct users to the appropriate codes when reporting ex-vivo assessment of marginal donor lung transplant. Refer to the codebook and the Rationale for codes 0494T, 0495T, and 0496T for a full discussion of the changes.

Other Procedures

32994   Code is out of numerical sequence. See 32997-32999

(For bronchoscopic bronchial alveolar lavage, use 31624)

▲ **32998**   Ablation therapy for reduction or eradication of 1 or more pulmonary tumor(s) including pleura or chest wall when involved by tumor extension, percutaneous, including imaging guidance when performed, unilateral; radiofrequency

#● **32994**   cryoablation

▶(For bilateral procedure, report 32994, 32998 with modifier 50)◀

Rationale

Code 0340T has been deleted from Category III codes and converted to Category I code 32994. In addition, code 32998 has been revised to accommodate the establishment of code 32994 to report ablation therapy of pulmonary tumors performed via cryoablation. An instructional parenthetical note regarding the appropriate reporting of this procedure has been included.

Code 32994 has been established to allow the appropriate reporting of ablation of pulmonary tumors using cryoablation. Code 32998 has been changed into a parent code; a semicolon has been appended so that the new code uses similar language in its descriptor. In addition, code 32998 has been revised by the addition of a phrase that identifies the use of imaging guidance when imaging is used for the procedure. Because these procedures are commonly performed unilaterally, the term "unilateral" has been added before the semicolon so that the term is part of the common language for both the new and revised codes. Because the procedure may be performed bilaterally, instruction has been provided to direct the use of either code with modifier 50 appended in order to identify the bilateral procedure when it is performed.

In an effort to provide further guidance regarding the intended use of these codes, instructions have been revised in other sections of the CPT code set to reflect the addition of the ablation code. This has been accomplished by listing the new and revised codes in parenthetical notes to include ablation as a procedure that may be reported when appropriate.

Clinical Example (32994)

A 68-year-old male presents with a history of large right renal cell carcinoma previously treated by a surgical partial nephrectomy. Several years later, a series of CT chest examinations reveal an enlarging pulmonary (lingular segment) nodule consistent with renal cell carcinoma metastasis. Imaging and clinical findings were reviewed in a multidisciplinary setting with thoracic surgery, interventional radiology, and medical oncology. Focal therapy was advised for the lingular nodule. Percutaneous cryoablation therapy was scheduled.

Description of Procedure (32994)

Using CT imaging guidance, a 19-gauge outer cannula of a coaxial system is placed at the anterior pleura for additional local anesthesia and localization. Using intermittent CT, a 17-gauge cryoablation needle is placed into the lingular nodule from an anterior approach. Two additional 17-gauge cryoablation needles are placed approximately 1.5 cm apart to allow for complete tumor ablation using the planned therapeutic ice ball. The cryoablation procedure is initiated with activation of the three cryoneedles simultaneously. Three freeze–thaw cycles are conducted under imaging guidance. The location and dimensions of the ice-ball coverage are monitored with noncontrast CT imaging approximately every two to five minutes throughout the freeze–thaw cycles. The cryoneedles are then removed following the final thaw cycle. The patient is assessed by physical exam and final postprocedure CT imaging for potential complications including pneumothorax or hemothorax. The patient wakes from anesthesia and is sent to the recovery room.

Clinical Example (32998)

A 54-year-old patient presents with nonoperable right upper lobe recurrent lung cancer. Recent positron emission tomography (PET)–CT scans (separately reportable) are reviewed. The most recent study shows a 2-cm right apical pulmonary mass with hypermetabolic activity consistent with recurrent lung cancer. Pulmonary percutaneous radiofrequency ablation therapy (RFA) is discussed as well as other treatment options. The patient, who is a good candidate for percutaneous pulmonary RFA therapy, wishes to proceed. The procedure is scheduled. Preoperative orders are written.

Description of Procedure (32998)

Using CT imaging guidance, a 19-gauge outer cannula of a coaxial system is placed at the anterior pleura for additional local anesthesia and localization. Using intermittent CT, a 17-gauge internally cooled radiofrequency (RF) needle electrode is placed into the center of the lesion to avoid healthy tissue and major blood vessels. CT confirms needle tip location. Two additional RFA probes are positioned 1.5 cm apart to ensure adequate tumor ablation with satisfactory margins. RF power is applied as many times as needed, until satisfactory core heating is achieved. The internal temperature of the tumor is monitored before and after each treatment (based on type of RFA probe used) to confirm the completion of treatment. The RF probe is withdrawn after satisfactory necrosis, with the probe tract cauterized to achieve hemostasis along the tract. The patient is assessed by physical exam and final postprocedure CT imaging for potential complications including pneumothorax or hemothorax. The patient wakes from anesthesia and is sent to the recovery room.

Cardiovascular System

Heart and Pericardium

Cardiac Valves

Aortic Valve

33361 Transcatheter aortic valve replacement (TAVR/TAVI) with prosthetic valve; percutaneous femoral artery approach

+ 33367 cardiopulmonary bypass support with percutaneous peripheral arterial and venous cannulation (eg, femoral vessels) (List separately in addition to code for primary procedure)

▶(Use 33367 in conjunction with 33361, 33362, 33363, 33364, 33365, 33366, 33418, 33477, 0483T, 0484T)◀

(Do not report 33367 in conjunction with 33368, 33369)

+ 33368 cardiopulmonary bypass support with open peripheral arterial and venous cannulation (eg, femoral, iliac, axillary vessels) (List separately in addition to code for primary procedure)

▶(Use 33368 in conjunction with 33361, 33362, 33363, 33364, 33365, 33366, 33418, 33477, 0483T, 0484T)◀

+ 33369 cardiopulmonary bypass support with central arterial and venous cannulation (eg, aorta, right atrium, pulmonary artery) (List separately in addition to code for primary procedure)

▶(Use 33369 in conjunction with 33361, 33362, 33363, 33364, 33365, 33366, 33418, 33477, 0483T, 0484T)◀

(Do not report 33369 in conjunction with 33367, 33368)

Mitral Valve

33418 Transcatheter mitral valve repair, percutaneous approach, including transseptal puncture when performed; initial prosthesis

(Do not report 33418 in conjunction with 93462 unless transapical puncture is performed)

+ 33419 additional prosthesis(es) during same session (List separately in addition to code for primary procedure)

(Use 33419 in conjunction with 33418)

▶(For transcatheter mitral valve repair, percutaneous approach via the coronary sinus, use 0345T)◀

▶(For transcatheter mitral valve implantation/replacement [TMVI], see 0483T, 0484T)◀

Rationale

The parenthetical notes that follow codes 33367-33369 have been revised to allow reporting of transcatheter mitral valve implantation/replacement (0483T, 0484T). In addition, the parenthetical notes that follow code 33419 have been revised to specify repair of a transcatheter mitral valve (0345T) and refer to the new codes for transcatheter mitral valve implantation/replacement (0483T, 0484T).

Refer to the codebook and the Rationale for codes 0483T and 0484T for a full discussion of the changes.

Endovascular Repair of Descending Thoracic Aorta

Codes 33880-33891 represent a family of procedures to report placement of an endovascular graft for repair of the descending thoracic aorta. These codes include all device introduction, manipulation, positioning, and deployment. All balloon angioplasty and/or stent deployment within the target treatment zone for the endoprosthesis, either before or after endograft deployment, are not separately reportable.

▶Open arterial exposure and associated closure of the arteriotomy sites (eg, 34714, 34715, 34716, 34812, 34820, 34833, 34834), introduction of guidewires and catheters (eg, 36140, 36200-36218), and extensive repair or replacement of an artery (eg, 35226, 35286) may be additionally reported. Transposition of subclavian artery to carotid, and carotid-carotid bypass performed in conjunction with endovascular repair of the descending thoracic aorta (eg, 33889, 33891) may be separately reported. The primary codes, 33880 and 33881, include placement of all distal extensions, if required, in the distal thoracic aorta, while proximal extensions, if needed, may be reported separately.◀

For fluoroscopic guidance in conjunction with endovascular repair of the thoracic aorta, see codes 75956-75959 as appropriate. Codes 75956 and 75957 include all angiography of the thoracic aorta and its branches for diagnostic imaging prior to deployment of the primary endovascular devices (including all routine components of modular devices), fluoroscopic guidance in the delivery of the endovascular components, and intraprocedural arterial angiography (eg, confirm position, detect endoleak, evaluate runoff). Code 75958 includes the analogous services for placement of each proximal thoracic endovascular extension. Code 75959 includes the analogous services for placement of a distal thoracic endovascular extension(s) placed during a procedure after the primary repair.

Other interventional procedures performed at the time of endovascular repair of the descending thoracic aorta should be additionally reported (eg, innominate, carotid, subclavian, visceral, or iliac artery transluminal angioplasty or stenting, arterial embolization, intravascular ultrasound) when performed before or after deployment of the aortic prostheses.

33880 Endovascular repair of descending thoracic aorta (eg, aneurysm, pseudoaneurysm, dissection, penetrating ulcer, intramural hematoma, or traumatic disruption); involving coverage of left subclavian artery origin, initial endoprosthesis plus descending thoracic aortic extension(s), if required, to level of celiac artery origin

Rationale

In support of the changes in reporting endovascular repair of abdominal aorta and/or iliac arteries procedures, codes 34714, 34715, and 34716 have been added to the guidelines regarding open arterial exposure in the Endovascular Repair of Descending Thoracic Aorta subsection.

Refer to the codebook and the Rationale for codes 34701-34713, 34714, 34715, and 34716 for a full discussion of these changes.

Heart/Lung Transplantation

3. ***Recipient heart with or without lung allotransplantation,*** which includes transplantation of allograft and care of the recipient (see 33935, 33945).

 ►(For implantation of a total replacement heart system [artificial heart] with recipient cardiectomy, use 33927)◄

● **33927** Implantation of a total replacement heart system (artificial heart) with recipient cardiectomy

 ►(For implantation of ventricular assist device, see 33975, 33976, 33979, 33990, 33991)◄

● **33928** Removal and replacement of total replacement heart system (artificial heart)

 ►(For revision or replacement of components only of a replacement heart system [artificial heart], use 33999)◄

+● **33929** Removal of a total replacement heart system (artificial heart) for heart transplantation (List separately in addition to code for primary procedure)

 ►(Use 33929 in conjunction with 33945)◄

33930 Donor cardiectomy-pneumonectomy (including cold preservation)

33935 Heart-lung transplant with recipient cardiectomy-pneumonectomy

33945 Heart transplant, with or without recipient cardiectomy

Rationale

Category III codes 0051T, 0052T, and 0053T, which were used for reporting artificial heart system procedures, have been deleted and replaced by Category I codes 33927, 33928, and 33929.

Category III code 0051T has been converted to Category I code 33927 to reflect standard practice.

Category III codes 0052T and 0053T have been deleted because they are not applicable in practice. Code 0052T was previously used to report repair or replacement of the thoracic unit of a total replacement heart system, and code 0053T was previously used to report replacement or repair of implantable components. These are no longer applicable because in current practice the entire heart system is most often replaced, rather than replacing or repairing the components. Therefore, codes 0052T and 0053T have been replaced with codes 33928 and 33929, which should be used to report removal and replacement procedures of a total replacement heart system. In accordance with the deletion of codes 0051T, 0052T, and 0053T, appropriate new cross-reference parenthetical notes for reporting these new procedures, as well as references to other procedures, have been added.

Clinical Example (33927)

A 50-year-old male presents for treatment of decompensated ischemic cardiomyopathy. The patient's history includes myocardial infarction and prior coronary artery bypass surgery with defibrillator implantation. Echocardiography shows global hypokinesis and an ejection fraction of 15%. After evaluation, the patient is listed in the United Network for Organ Sharing (UNOS) and is status 1A (urgent need) for heart transplantation. He continues to decline, despite multiple inotropes and placement of an intra-aortic balloon pump. The patient is at high risk for imminent death from irreversible biventricular cardiac failure. The patient is referred for implantation of a total artificial heart (TAH).

Description of Procedure (33927)

Median sternotomy is performed in the usual fashion. The pericardium is opened, and the heart is suspended in a pericardial cradle. The atrial quick connects are brought to the field and cut to appropriate length. Two stab wounds are made in the left upper quadrant, and the drivelines to the ventricle are tunneled

Surgery / Cardiovascular System 33010-39599

subcutaneously. A 20-Fr aortic cannula is inserted for cardiopulmonary bypass. Another cannula is placed in the superior vena cava (SVC). Tourniquets are placed on the SVC and inferior vena cava (IVC). The SVC venous line is connected to the femoral vein line. Another cannula for venous return is placed in the IVC and secured. Cardiopulmonary bypass is initiated. The tourniquets are placed on the SVC and IVC, and the aorta is cross clamped. A ventriculectomy is made below the atrioventricular groove circumferentially. The tricuspid valve is transected leaving about 1–2 mm of tissue in the tricuspid valve annulus. In a similar fashion, the ventricular septum is divided. The wires from the automated implantable cardioverter defibrillator (AICD) generator are removed. The mitral valve is excised leaving 1 or 2 mm of valve tissue. The aorta and the pulmonary artery are divided. The right ventricular outflow tract is excised, leaving the posterior aspect of the aorta and anterior leaflet of the mitral valve. The coronary sinus is closed. The first atrial quick-connect is anastomosed to the left atrium. The other atrial quick-connect is placed in the tricuspid valve and sutured in place. The artificial ventricles are brought into the field. The aortic and the pulmonary artery conduits are measured and cut to appropriate length. The pulmonary artery and aortic conduits are sewn in place. The artificial left ventricle is connected to the mitral quick-connect and to the aorta. The artificial right ventricle is connected to the tricuspid valve. The pulmonary artery conduit is connected to the prosthetic right ventricle. The patient is placed in the Trendelenburg position. The aorta is vented. The TAH is connected to the drivelines. Single shots are given in order to remove air. Echocardiography is used throughout the procedure, especially at the time of chest closure to ensure that the heart does not impinge on surrounding structures and to ensure that there is no evidence of air. The patient is weaned off cardiopulmonary bypass without any difficulty. Once the patient is hemodynamically stable, all cannulae are removed and protamine is given. Hemostatic control is obtained from all bleeding surfaces. The AICD generator is removed by incision, and the AICD pocket is closed in layers. The skin is closed. Two chest tubes are placed in the mediastinum. Once there is no evidence of bleeding, polytetrafluoroethylene surgical membranes are placed over and around the TAH. Blue bands are placed around the aorta, SVC, and IVC. The chest tubes and drivelines are secured to the skin. Sternal wires are placed with a polymeric silicone membrane that is placed between the wires and the sternum. The sternum is reapproximated. The subcutaneous tissues are closed in layers. The skin is closed. A sterile dressing is placed over all wounds. The patient is then transferred to the intensive care unit (ICU), intubated, and hemodynamically stable. (Note: The echocardiography procedure throughout the surgery is not performed by the surgeon who performs the heart transplant.)

Clinical Example (33928)

A 59-year-old female was implanted with a TAH while awaiting a compatible organ donor four years ago. The implanted TAH demonstrated signs of wear during routine device evaluations, the result of long-term continual use. The patient is scheduled to receive a replacement TAH system.

Description of Procedure (33928)

The patient is placed on the operating room table in the supine position, and general anesthesia is administered via endotracheal tube. The entire neck, chest, abdomen, and both legs circumferentially to the knees are prepared with povidone-iodine solution and draped in a sterile manner. The previous median sternotomy is opened with great care. Numerous adhesions are encountered and taken down. The membranes and blue bands are removed. Two stab wounds are made in the left upper quadrant, and the drivelines to the ventricle are tunneled subcutaneously.

A 20-French aortic cannula is inserted for cardiopulmonary bypass. Another cannula is placed in the SVC. Tourniquets are placed on the SVC and IVC. The SVC venous line is connected to the femoral vein line. Another cannula is placed in the inferior vena cava for venous return and secured. Cardiopulmonary bypass is initiated. The tourniquets are placed on the SVC and IVC, and the aorta is cross-clamped. Once on cardiopulmonary bypass, the artificial heart is turned off and the aorta is cross-clamped. The drive lines to the TAH are amputated. The prosthetic right ventricle is removed from the atrial quick-connect and the pulmonary artery (PA) conduit. The prosthetic left ventricle is removed in a similar fashion. The drive lines for the new TAH are tunneled subcutaneously. The new prosthetic left ventricle is connected to the left atrial quick-connect and the aortic conduit. The new prosthetic right ventricle is connected to the right-sided atrial quick-connect and PA conduit. The patient is placed in the Trendelenburg position. The aorta is unclamped. Air is removed from the ascending aorta. The TAH is connected to the drivelines. Single shots are given in order to remove air. Echocardiography is used throughout the procedure and especially at the time of chest closure to ensure that the heart does not impinge on surrounding structures and to ensure that there is no evidence of air. The patient is weaned off cardiopulmonary bypass without any difficulty.

Once the patient is hemodynamically stable, all cannulae are removed and protamine is given. Hemostatic control is obtained from all bleeding surfaces. The skin is closed. Two chest tubes are placed in the mediastinum. Once there is no evidence of bleeding, polytetrafluoroethylene surgical membranes are placed over and around the

TAH. Blue bands are placed around the aorta and SVC and IVC. The chest tubes and the drivelines are secured to the skin.

Sternal wires are placed with a polymeric silicone membrane that is placed between the wires and the sternum. The sternum is reapproximated. The subcutaneous tissues are closed in layers. The skin is closed. A sterile dressing is placed over all wounds. The patient is transferred to the ICU and intubated. The patient is hemodynamically stable.

Note: The echocardiography procedure throughout the surgery is not performed by the surgeon who performs the heart transplant.

Clinical Example (33929)

A 58-year-old female had dilated cardiomyopathy, heart failure, ventricular ectopy, prior pacemaker–cardioverter–defibrillator placement, atrial fibrillation, hypothyroidism, hypertension, hyperlipidemia, and diabetes. The patient presented with severely impaired biventricular cardiac function. However, end organ perfusion was adequate and no donors were available, so a decision was made to bridge the patient with a TAH. The patient rehabilitated physically and nutritionally. A compatible organ donor became available on post-implantation day 204.

Description of Procedure (33929)

The patient is taken to the operating room and placed on the operating table in the supine position. General anesthesia is given via endotracheal tube. Once the appropriate level of anesthesia is obtained, the entire neck, chest, abdomen, and both legs circumferentially to the knees are prepared with povidone-iodine solution and draped in a sterile manner.

The previous median sternotomy is opened with great care. The polymeric silicone membrane is removed and sent for culture. Adhesions on the anterior surface of the TAH are dissected. Dissection around the aorta and right atrium is performed. The blue bands are identified, and tourniquets are placed around the superior and inferior vena cava. Umbilical tape is placed around the aorta. Heparin is given. The ascending aorta and superior and inferior vena cava are cannulated for cardiopulmonary bypass. Once the donor heart is in the room, the blood type is verified. Cardiopulmonary bypass is initiated. The TAH is turned off. The aortic cross-clamp is placed. The tourniquets are cinched down. The right ventricle is amputated. The device is released from the pulmonary artery and right atrium. In a similar fashion, the driveline to the left ventricle is amputated, and the device is disconnected from the left atrium and the aorta. The aortic conduit is removed.

The PA conduit is amputated. The atrial quick-connects are removed. Dissection is carried down around the atrial edges. The donor heart is brought to the field.

Extracorporeal Membrane Oxygenation or Extracorporeal Life Support Services

33946   Extracorporeal membrane oxygenation (ECMO)/ extracorporeal life support (ECLS) provided by physician; initiation, veno-venous

33954   insertion of peripheral (arterial and/or venous) cannula(e), open, 6 years and older

▶(Do not report 33953, 33954 in conjunction with 34714, 34715, 34716, 34812, 34820, 34833, 34834)◀

(For maintenance of extracorporeal circulation, see 33946, 33947, 33948, 33949)

33958   reposition peripheral (arterial and/or venous) cannula(e), percutaneous, 6 years and older (includes fluoroscopic guidance, when performed)

▶(Do not report 33957, 33958 in conjunction with 34713)◀

33959   reposition peripheral (arterial and/or venous) cannula(e), open, birth through 5 years of age (includes fluoroscopic guidance, when performed)

 # 33962   reposition peripheral (arterial and/or venous) cannula(e), open, 6 years and older (includes fluoroscopic guidance, when performed)

▶(Do not report 33959, 33962 in conjunction with 34714, 34715, 34716, 34812, 34820, 34834)◀

 # 33969   removal of peripheral (arterial and/or venous) cannula(e), open, birth through 5 years of age

▶(Do not report 33969 in conjunction with 34714, 34715, 34716, 34812, 34820, 34834, 35201, 35206, 35211, 35226)◀

 # 33984   removal of peripheral (arterial and/or venous) cannula(e), open, 6 years and older

▶(Do not report 33984 in conjunction with 34714, 34715, 34716, 34812, 34820, 34834, 35201, 35206, 35211, 35226)◀

#+ 33987   Arterial exposure with creation of graft conduit (eg, chimney graft) to facilitate arterial perfusion for ECMO/ECLS (List separately in addition to code for primary procedure)

(Use 33987 in conjunction with 33953, 33954, 33955, 33956)

▶(Do not report 33987 in conjunction with 34714, 34716, 34833)◀

Rationale

In support of the changes in reporting endovascular repair of abdominal aorta and/or iliac arteries procedures, the exclusionary parenthetical notes that follow codes 33954, 33958, 33962, 33969, and 33984 (peripheral cannula services) and 33987 (arterial exposure with graft conduit creation) have been revised to include endovascular repair of abdominal aorta and/or iliac arteries codes, as appropriate, to clarify that these codes may not be reported together.

Refer to the codebook and the Rationale for codes 34701-34713, 34714, 34715, and 34716 for a full discussion of these changes.

Cardiac Assist

The insertion of a ventricular assist device (VAD) can be performed via percutaneous (33990, 33991) or transthoracic (33975, 33976, 33979) approach. The location of the ventricular assist device may be intracorporeal or extracorporeal.

▶Open arterial exposure when necessary to facilitate percutaneous ventricular assist device insertion (33990, 33991), may be reported separately (34714, 34715, 34716, 34812, 34820, 34833, 34834). Extensive repair or replacement of an artery may be additionally reported (eg, 35226 or 35286).◀

Removal of a ventricular assist device (33977, 33978, 33980, 33992) includes removal of the entire device, including the cannulas. Removal of a percutaneous ventricular assist device at the same session as insertion is not separately reportable. For removal of a percutaneous ventricular assist device at a separate and distinct session, but on the same day as insertion, report 33992 appended with modifier 59 indicating a distinct procedural service.

Repositioning of a percutaneous ventricular assist device at the same session as insertion is not separately reportable. Repositioning of percutaneous ventricular assist device not necessitating imaging guidance is not a reportable service. For repositioning of a percutaneous ventricular assist device necessitating imaging guidance at a separate and distinct session, but on the same day as insertion, report 33993 with modifier 59 indicating a distinct procedural service.

Replacement of a ventricular assist device pump (ie, 33981-33983) includes the removal of the pump and insertion of a new pump, connection, de-airing, and initiation of the new pump.

Replacement of the entire implantable ventricular assist device system, ie, pump(s) and cannulas, is reported using the insertion codes (ie, 33975, 33976, 33979). Removal (ie, 33977, 33978, 33980) of the ventricular

assist device system being replaced is not separately reported. Replacement of a percutaneous ventricular assist device is reported using implantation codes (ie, 33990, 33991). Removal (ie, 33992) is not reported separately.

33967   Insertion of intra-aortic balloon assist device, percutaneous

Rationale

In support of the changes in reporting endovascular repair of abdominal aorta and/or iliac arteries procedures, codes 34714, 34715, 34716, 34820, 34833, and 34834 have been added to the open arterial exposure guidelines in the Cardiac Assist section. Refer to the codebook and the Rationale for codes 34701-34713, 34714, 34715, and 34716 for a full discussion of these changes.

Arteries and Veins

▶Endovascular Repair of Abdominal Aorta and/or Iliac Arteries◀

▶Codes 34701, 34702, 34703, 34704, 34705, 34706 describe introduction, positioning, and deployment of an endograft for treatment of abdominal aortic pathology (with or without rupture), such as aneurysm, pseudoaneurysm, dissection, penetrating ulcer, or traumatic disruption in the infrarenal abdominal aorta with or without extension into the iliac artery(ies). The terms, endovascular graft, endoprosthesis, endograft, and stentgraft, refer to a covered stent. The infrarenal aortic endograft may be an aortic tube device, a bifurcated unibody device, a modular bifurcated docking system with docking limb(s), or an aorto-uni-iliac device. Codes 34707 and 34708 describe introduction, positioning, and deployment of an ilio-iliac endograft for treatment of isolated arterial pathology (with or without rupture), such as aneurysm, pseudoaneurysm, arteriovenous malformation, or trauma involving the iliac artery. For treatment of atherosclerotic occlusive disease in the iliac artery(ies) with a covered stent(s), see 37221, 37223. For covered stent placement for atherosclerotic occlusive disease in the aorta, see 37236, 37237.

Report 34705 or 34706 for simultaneous bilateral iliac artery aneurysm repairs with aorto-bi-iliac endograft. For isolated bilateral iliac artery repair, report 34707 or 34708 with modifier 50 appended.

Decompressive laparotomy for abdominal compartment syndrome after ruptured abdominal aortic and/or iliac artery aneurysm repair may be separately reported with 49000 in addition to 34702, 34704, 34706, or 34708.

The treatment zone for endograft procedures is defined by those vessels that contain an endograft(s) (main body, docking limb[s], and/or extension[s]) deployed during that operative session. Adjunctive procedures outside the treatment zone may be separately reported (eg, angioplasty, endovascular stent placement, embolization). For example, when an endograft terminates in the common iliac artery, any additional treatment performed in the external and/or internal iliac artery may be separately reportable. Placement of a docking limb is inherent to a modular endograft(s), and, therefore, 34709 may not be reported separately if the docking limb extends into the external iliac artery. In addition, any interventions (eg, angioplasty, stenting, additional stent graft extension[s]) in the external iliac artery where the docking limb terminates may not be reported separately. Any catheterization or treatment of the internal iliac artery, such as embolization, may be separately reported. For 34701 and 34702, the abdominal aortic treatment zone is defined as the infrarenal aorta. For 34703 and 34704, the abdominal aortic treatment zone is typically defined as the infrarenal aorta and ipsilateral common iliac artery. For 34705 and 34706, the abdominal aortic treatment zone is typically defined as the infrarenal aorta and both common iliac arteries. For 34707 and 34708, the treatment zone is defined as the portion of the iliac artery(ies) (eg, common, internal, external iliac arteries) that contains the endograft. For a bifurcated iliac branch device, use 0254T.

Codes 34702, 34704, 34706, 34708 are reported when endovascular repair is performed on ruptured aneurysm in the aorta or iliac artery(ies). Rupture is defined as clinical and/or radiographic evidence of acute hemorrhage for purposes of reporting these codes. A chronic, contained rupture is considered a pseudoaneurysm, and endovascular treatment of a chronic, contained rupture is reported with 34701, 34703, 34705, or 34707.

Code 34709 is reported for placement of extension prosthesis(es) that terminate(s) either in the internal iliac, external iliac, or common femoral artery(ies) or in the abdominal aorta proximal to the renal artery(ies) in conjunction with 34701, 34702, 34703, 34704, 34705, 34706, 34707, 34708. Code 34709 may only be reported once per vessel treated (ie, multiple endograft extensions placed in a single vessel may only be reported once). Endograft extension(s) that terminate(s) in the common iliac arteries are included in 34703, 34704, 34705, 34706, 34707, 34708 and are not separately reported. Treatment zone angioplasty/stenting, when performed, is included in 34709. In addition, proximal infrarenal abdominal aortic extension prosthesis(es) that terminate(s) in the aorta below the renal artery(ies) are also included in 34701, 34702, 34703, 34704, 34705, 34706 and are not separately reportable.

Codes 34710, 34711 are reported for delayed placement of distal or proximal extension prosthesis(es) for endovascular repair of infrarenal abdominal aortic or iliac aneurysm, false aneurysm, dissection, endoleak, or endograft migration. Pre-procedure sizing and device selection, all nonselective catheterization(s), all associated radiological supervision and interpretation, and treatment zone angioplasty/stenting, when performed, are included in 34710 and 34711. Codes 34710 and 34711 may only be reported once per vessel treated (ie, multiple endograft extensions placed in a single vessel may only be reported once).

Nonselective catheterization is included in 34701, 34702, 34703, 34704, 34705, 34706, 34707, 34708 and is not separately reported. However, selective catheterization of the hypogastric artery(ies), renal artery(ies), and/or arterial families outside the treatment zone of the endograft may be separately reported. Intravascular ultrasound (37252, 37253) performed during endovascular aneurysm repair may be separately reported. Balloon angioplasty and/or stenting within the treatment zone of the endograft, either before or after endograft deployment, is not separately reported. Fluoroscopic guidance and radiological supervision and interpretation in conjunction with endograft repair is not separately reported, and includes all intraprocedural imaging (eg, angiography, rotational CT) of the aorta and its branches prior to deployment of the endovascular device, fluoroscopic guidance and roadmapping used in the delivery of the endovascular components, and intraprocedural and completion angiography (eg, confirm position, detect endoleak, evaluate runoff) performed at the time of the endovascular infrarenal aorta and/or iliac repair.

Codes 34709, 34710, 34711 include nonselective introduction of guidewires and catheters into the treatment zone from peripheral artery access(es). However, selective catheterization of the hypogastric artery(ies), renal artery(ies), and/or arterial families outside the treatment zone may be separately reported. Codes 34709, 34710, 34711 also include balloon angioplasty and/or stenting within the treatment zone of the endograft extension, either before or after deployment of the endograft, fluoroscopic guidance, and all associated radiological supervision and interpretation performed in conjunction with endovascular endograft extension (eg, angiographic diagnostic imaging of the aorta and its branches prior to deployment of the endovascular device, fluoroscopic guidance in the delivery of the endovascular components, and intraprocedural and completion angiography to confirm endograft position, detect endoleak, and evaluate runoff).

Code 34712 describes transcatheter delivery of accessory-enhanced fixation devices to the endograft (eg, anchor, screw, tack), including all associated radiological supervision and interpretation. Code 34712 may only be reported once per operative session.

Vascular access requiring use of closure devices for large sheaths (ie, 12 French or larger) or access requiring open surgical arterial exposure may be separately reported (eg, 34713, 34714, 34715, 34716, 34812, 34820, 34833, 34834). Code 34713 describes percutaneous access and closure of a femoral arteriotomy for delivery of endovascular prosthesis through a large arterial sheath (ie, 12 French or larger). Ultrasound guidance (ie, 76937), when performed, is included in 34713. (Percutaneous access using a sheath smaller than 12 French is included in 34701-34712 and is not separately reported.)

Code 34812 describes open repair and closure of the femoral artery. Extensive repair of an artery (eg, 35226, 35286, 35371) may also be reported separately. Iliac exposure for device delivery through a retroperitoneal incision, open brachial exposure, or axillary or subclavian exposure through an infraclavicular, or supraclavicular or sternotomy incision during endovascular aneurysm repair may be separately reported (eg, 34715, 34812, 34820, 34834). Endovascular device delivery or establishment of cardiopulmonary bypass that requires creation of a prosthetic conduit utilizing a femoral artery, iliac artery with a retroperitoneal incision, or axillary or subclavian artery exposure through an infraclavicular, supraclavicular, or sternotomy incision (34714, 34716, 34833) and oversewing of the conduit at the time of procedure completion may be separately reported during endovascular aneurysm repair or cardiac procedures requiring cardiopulmonary bypass. If a conduit is converted to a bypass, report the bypass (eg, 35665) and not the arterial exposure with conduit (34714, 34716, 34833). Arterial embolization(s) of renal, lumbar, inferior mesenteric, hypogastric or external iliac arteries to facilitate complete endovascular aneurysm exclusion may be separately reported (eg, 37242).

Balloon angioplasty and/or stenting at the sealing zone(s) of an endograft is an integral part of the procedure and is not separately reported. However, balloon angioplasty and/or stent deployment in vessels that do not contain endograft (outside the treatment zone for the endograft), either before or after endograft deployment, may be separately reported (eg, 37220, 37221, 37222, 37223).

Other interventional procedures performed at the time of endovascular abdominal aortic aneurysm repair may be additionally reported (eg, renal transluminal angioplasty, arterial embolization, intravascular ultrasound, balloon angioplasty or stenting of native artery[s] outside the endograft treatment zone, when done before or after deployment of endograft).◄

(For fenestrated endovascular repair of the visceral aorta, see 34841-34844. For fenestrated endovascular repair of the visceral aorta and concomitant infrarenal abdominal aorta, see 34845-34848)

● 34701 Endovascular repair of infrarenal aorta by deployment of an aorto-aortic tube endograft including pre-procedure sizing and device selection, all nonselective catheterization(s), all associated radiological supervision and interpretation, all endograft extension(s) placed in the aorta from the level of the renal arteries to the aortic bifurcation, and all angioplasty/stenting performed from the level of the renal arteries to the aortic bifurcation; for other than rupture (eg, for aneurysm, pseudoaneurysm, dissection, penetrating ulcer)

► (For covered stent placement[s] for atherosclerotic occlusive disease isolated to the aorta, see 37236, 37237)◄

● 34702 for rupture including temporary aortic and/or iliac balloon occlusion, when performed (eg, for aneurysm, pseudoaneurysm, dissection, penetrating ulcer, traumatic disruption)

● 34703 Endovascular repair of infrarenal aorta and/or iliac artery(ies) by deployment of an aorto-uni-iliac endograft including pre-procedure sizing and device selection, all nonselective catheterization(s), all associated radiological supervision and interpretation, all endograft extension(s) placed in the aorta from the level of the renal arteries to the iliac bifurcation, and all angioplasty/stenting performed from the level of the renal arteries to the iliac bifurcation; for other than rupture (eg, for aneurysm, pseudoaneurysm, dissection, penetrating ulcer)

● 34704 for rupture including temporary aortic and/or iliac balloon occlusion, when performed (eg, for aneurysm, pseudoaneurysm, dissection, penetrating ulcer, traumatic disruption)

● 34705 Endovascular repair of infrarenal aorta and/or iliac artery(ies) by deployment of an aorto-bi-iliac endograft including pre-procedure sizing and device selection, all nonselective catheterization(s), all associated radiological supervision and interpretation, all endograft extension(s) placed in the aorta from the level of the renal arteries to the iliac bifurcation, and all angioplasty/stenting performed from the level of the renal arteries to the iliac bifurcation; for other than rupture (eg, for aneurysm, pseudoaneurysm, dissection, penetrating ulcer)

● 34706 for rupture including temporary aortic and/or iliac balloon occlusion, when performed (eg, for aneurysm, pseudoaneurysm, dissection, penetrating ulcer, traumatic disruption)

● **34707**   Endovascular repair of iliac artery by deployment of an ilio-iliac tube endograft including pre-procedure sizing and device selection, all nonselective catheterization(s), all associated radiological supervision and interpretation, and all endograft extension(s) proximally to the aortic bifurcation and distally to the iliac bifurcation, and treatment zone angioplasty/stenting, when performed, unilateral; for other than rupture (eg, for aneurysm, pseudoaneurysm, dissection, arteriovenous malformation)

▶(For covered stent placement[s] for atherosclerotic occlusive disease of the abdominal aorta, see 37236, 37237)◀

▶(For covered stent placement[s] for atherosclerotic occlusive disease of the iliac artery, see 37221, 37223)◀

● **34708**   for rupture including temporary aortic and/or iliac balloon occlusion, when performed (eg, for aneurysm, pseudoaneurysm, dissection, arteriovenous malformation, traumatic disruption)

+● **34709**   Placement of extension prosthesis(es) distal to the common iliac artery(ies) or proximal to the renal artery(ies) for endovascular repair of infrarenal abdominal aortic or iliac aneurysm, false aneurysm, dissection, penetrating ulcer, including pre-procedure sizing and device selection, all nonselective catheterization(s), all associated radiological supervision and interpretation, and treatment zone angioplasty/stenting, when performed, per vessel treated (List separately in addition to code for primary procedure)

▶(Use 34709 in conjunction with 34701, 34702, 34703, 34704, 34705, 34706, 34707, 34708)◀

▶(34709 may only be reported once per vessel treated [ie, multiple endograft extensions placed in a single vessel may only be reported once])◀

▶(Do not report 34709 for placement of a docking limb that extends into the external iliac artery)◀

▶(For endograft placement into a renal artery that is being covered by a proximal extension, see 37236, 37237)◀

● **34710**   Delayed placement of distal or proximal extension prosthesis for endovascular repair of infrarenal abdominal aortic or iliac aneurysm, false aneurysm, dissection, endoleak, or endograft migration, including pre-procedure sizing and device selection, all nonselective catheterization(s), all associated radiological supervision and interpretation, and treatment zone angioplasty/stenting, when performed; initial vessel treated

+● **34711**   each additional vessel treated (List separately in addition to code for primary procedure)

▶(Use 34711 in conjunction with 34710)◀

▶(34710, 34711 may each be reported only once per operative session [ie, multiple endograft extensions placed in a single vessel may only be reported with a single code])◀

▶(For decompressive laparotomy, use 49000 in conjunction with 34702, 34704, 34706, 34708, 34710)◀

▶(If the delayed revision is a transcatheter enhanced fixation device [eg, anchors, screws], report 34712)◀

▶(Do not report 34710, 34711 in conjunction with 34701, 34702, 34703, 34704, 34705, 34706, 34707, 34708, 34709)◀

▶(Do not report 34701-34711 in conjunction with 34841, 34842, 34843, 34844, 34845, 34846, 34847, 34848)◀

▶(For endovascular repair of iliac artery bifurcation [eg, aneurysm, pseudoaneurysm, arteriovenous malformation, trauma] using bifurcated endograft, use 0254T)◀

▶(Report 37252, 37253 for intravascular ultrasound when performed during endovascular aneurysm repair)◀

▶(For isolated bilateral iliac artery repair, report 34707 or 34708 with modifier 50)◀

▶(For open arterial exposure, report 34714, 34715, 34716, 34812, 34820, 34833, 34834 as appropriate, in conjunction with 34701, 34702, 34703, 34704, 34705, 34706, 34707, 34708, 34710)◀

▶(For percutaneous arterial closure, report 34713 as appropriate, in conjunction with 34701, 34702, 34703, 34704, 34705, 34706, 34707, 34708, 34710)◀

▶(For simultaneous bilateral iliac artery aneurysm repairs with aorto-biiliac endograft, see 34705, 34706, as appropriate)◀

● **34712**   Transcatheter delivery of enhanced fixation device(s) to the endograft (eg, anchor, screw, tack) and all associated radiological supervision and interpretation

▶(Report 34712 only once per operative session)◀

+● **34713**   Percutaneous access and closure of femoral artery for delivery of endograft through a large sheath (12 French or larger), including ultrasound guidance, when performed, unilateral (List separately in addition to code for primary procedure)

▶(Use 34713 in conjunction with 33880, 33881, 33883, 33884, 33886, 34701, 34702, 34703, 34704, 34705, 34706, 34707, 34708, 34841, 34842, 34843, 34844, 34845, 34846, 34847, 34848 as appropriate. However, do not report 34713 in conjunction with 33880, 33881, 33883, 33884, 33886, 34701, 34702, 34703, 34704, 34705, 34706, 34707, 34708, 34841, 34842, 34843, 34844, 34845, 34846, 34847, 34848 for percutaneous closure of femoral artery after delivery of endovascular prosthesis if a sheath smaller than 12 French was used)◀

▶(34713 may only be reported once per side. For bilateral procedure, report 34713 twice)◀

▶(Do not report ultrasound guidance [ie, 76937] for percutaneous vascular access in conjunction with 34713 for the same access)◀

Surgery / Cardiovascular System 33010-39599

►(Do not report 34713 for percutaneous access and closure of the femoral artery in conjunction with 37221, 37223, 37236, 37237)◄

►(Do not report 34713 in conjunction with 37221, 37223 for covered stent placement[s] for atherosclerotic occlusive disease of the iliac artery[ies])◄

#+▲ 34812   Open femoral artery exposure for delivery of endovascular prosthesis, by groin incision, unilateral (List separately in addition to code for primary procedure)

►(Use 34812 in conjunction with 33880, 33881, 33883, 33884, 33886, 33990, 33991, 34701, 34702, 34703, 34704, 34705, 34706, 34707, 34708, 34841, 34842, 34843, 34844, 34845, 34846, 34847, 34848, 0254T)◄

►(34812 may only be reported once per side. For bilateral procedure, report 34812 twice)◄

►(Do not report 34812 in conjunction with 33953, 33954, 33959, 33962, 33969, 33984, 33987)◄

+● 34714   Open femoral artery exposure with creation of conduit for delivery of endovascular prosthesis or for establishment of cardiopulmonary bypass, by groin incision, unilateral (List separately in addition to code for primary procedure)

►(Use 34714 in conjunction with 32852, 32854, 33031, 33120, 33251, 33256, 33259, 33261, 33305, 33315, 33322, 33335, 33390, 33391, 33404-33417, 33422, 33425, 33426, 33427, 33430, 33460, 33463, 33464, 33465, 33468, 33474, 33475, 33476, 33478, 33496, 33500, 33502, 33504, 33505, 33506, 33507, 33510, 33511, 33512, 33513, 33514, 33516, 33533, 33534, 33535, 33536, 33542, 33545, 33548, 33600-33688, 33692, 33694, 33697, 33702, 33710, 33720, 33722, 33724, 33726, 33730, 33732, 33736, 33750, 33755, 33762, 33764, 33766, 33767, 33770-33783, 33786, 33788, 33802, 33803, 33814, 33820, 33822, 33824, 33840, 33845, 33851, 33853, 33860, 33863, 33864, 33870, 33875, 33877, 33880, 33881, 33883, 33884, 33886, 33910, 33916, 33917, 33920, 33922, 33926, 33935, 33945, 33975, 33976, 33977, 33978, 33979, 33980, 33983, 33990, 33991, 34701, 34702, 34703, 34704, 34705, 34706, 34707, 34708, 34841, 34842, 34843, 34844, 34845, 34846, 34847, 34848, 0254T)◄

►(34714 may only be reported once per side. For bilateral procedure, report 34714 twice)◄

►(Do not report 34714 in conjunction with 33362, 33953, 33954, 33959, 33962, 33969, 33984, 34812 when performed on the same side)◄

#+▲ 34820   Open iliac artery exposure for delivery of endovascular prosthesis or iliac occlusion during endovascular therapy, by abdominal or retroperitoneal incision, unilateral (List separately in addition to code for primary procedure)

►(Use 34820 in conjunction with 33880, 33881, 33883, 33884, 33886, 33990, 33991, 34701, 34702, 34703, 34704, 34705, 34706, 34707, 34708, 34841, 34842, 34843, 34844, 34845, 34846, 34847, 34848, 0254T)◄

►(34820 may only be reported once per side. For bilateral procedure, report 34820 twice)◄

►(Do not report 34820 in conjunction with 33953, 33954, 33959, 33962, 33969, 33984)◄

#+▲ 34833   Open iliac artery exposure with creation of conduit for delivery of endovascular prosthesis or for establishment of cardiopulmonary bypass, by abdominal or retroperitoneal incision, unilateral (List separately in addition to code for primary procedure)

►(Use 34833 in conjunction with 32852, 32854, 33031, 33120, 33251, 33256, 33259, 33261, 33305, 33315, 33322, 33335, 33390, 33391, 33404-33417, 33422, 33425, 33426, 33427, 33430, 33460, 33463, 33464, 33465, 33468, 33474, 33475, 33476, 33478, 33496, 33500, 33502, 33504, 33505, 33506, 33507, 33510, 33511, 33512, 33513, 33514, 33516, 33533, 33534, 33535, 33536, 33542, 33545, 33548, 33600-33688, 33692, 33694, 33697, 33702, 33710, 33720, 33722, 33724, 33726, 33730, 33732, 33736, 33750, 33755, 33762, 33764, 33766, 33767, 33770-33783, 33786, 33788, 33802, 33803, 33814, 33820, 33822, 33824, 33840, 33845, 33851, 33853, 33860, 33863, 33864, 33870, 33875, 33877, 33880, 33881, 33883, 33884, 33886, 33910, 33916, 33917, 33920, 33922, 33926, 33935, 33945, 33975, 33976, 33977, 33978, 33979, 33980, 33983, 33990, 33991, 34701, 34702, 34703, 34704, 34705, 34706, 34707, 34708, 34841, 34842, 34843, 34844, 34845, 34846, 34847, 34848, 0254T)◄

►(34833 may only be reported once per side. For bilateral procedure, report 34833 twice)◄

►(Do not report 34833 in conjunction with 33364, 33953, 33954, 33959, 33962, 33969, 33984, 34820 when performed on the same side)◄

#+▲ 34834   Open brachial artery exposure for delivery of endovascular prosthesis, unilateral (List separately in addition to code for primary procedure)

►(Use 34834 in conjunction with 33880, 33881, 33883, 33884, 33886, 33990, 33991, 34701, 34702, 34703, 34704, 34705, 34706, 34707, 34708, 34841, 34842, 34843, 34844, 34845, 34846, 34847, 34848, 0254T)◄

►(34834 may only be reported once per side. For bilateral procedure, report 34834 twice)◄

►(Do not report 34834 in conjunction with 33953, 33954, 33959, 33962, 33969, 33984)◄

+● 34715   Open axillary/subclavian artery exposure for delivery of endovascular prosthesis by infraclavicular or supraclavicular incision, unilateral (List separately in addition to code for primary procedure)

►(Use 34715 in conjunction with 33880, 33881, 33883, 33884, 33886, 33990, 33991, 34701, 34702, 34703, 34704, 34705, 34706, 34707, 34708, 34841, 34842, 34843, 34844, 34845, 34846, 34847, 34848, 0254T)◄

►(34715 may only be reported once per side. For bilateral procedure, report 34715 twice)◄

►(Do not report 34715 in conjunction with 33363, 33953, 33954, 33959, 33962, 33969, 33984, 0451T, 0452T, 0455T, 0456T)◄

+• 34716 Open axillary/subclavian artery exposure with creation of conduit for delivery of endovascular prosthesis or for establishment of cardiopulmonary bypass, by infraclavicular or supraclavicular incision, unilateral (List separately in addition to code for primary procedure)

►(Use 34716 in conjunction with 32852, 32854, 33031, 33120, 33251, 33256, 33259-33261, 33305, 33315, 33322, 33335, 33390, 33391, 33404-33417, 33422, 33425, 33426, 33427, 33430, 33460, 33463, 33464, 33465, 33468, 33474, 33475, 33476, 33478, 33496, 33500, 33502, 33504, 33505, 33506, 33507, 33510, 33511, 33512, 33513, 33514, 33516, 33533, 33534, 33535, 33536, 33542, 33545, 33548, 33600-33688, 33692, 33694, 33697, 33702-33722, 33724, 33726, 33730, 33732, 33736, 33750, 33755, 33762, 33764, 33766, 33767, 33770-33783, 33786, 33788, 33802, 33803, 33814, 33820, 33822, 33824, 33840, 33845, 33851, 33853, 33860, 33863, 33864, 33870, 33875, 33877, 33880, 33881, 33883, 33884, 33886, 33910, 33916, 33917, 33920, 33922, 33926, 33935, 33945, 33975, 33976, 33977, 33978, 33979, 33980, 33983, 33990, 33991, 34701, 34702, 34703, 34704, 34705, 34706, 34707, 34708, 34841, 34842, 34843, 34844, 34845, 34846, 34847, 34848, 0254T)◄

►(34716 may only be reported once per side. For bilateral procedure, report 34716 twice)◄

►(Do not report 34716 in conjunction with 33953, 33954, 33959, 33962, 33969, 33984, 0451T, 0452T, 0455T, 0456T)◄

►(34800, 34802, 34803, 34804, 34805, 34806 have been deleted. To report, see 34701, 34702, 34703, 34704, 34705, 34706, 34707, 34708)◄

+ 34808 Endovascular placement of iliac artery occlusion device (List separately in addition to code for primary procedure)

►(Use 34808 in conjunction with 34701, 34702, 34707, 34708, 34709, 34710, 34813, 34841, 34842, 34843, 34844)◄

34812 Code is out of numerical sequence. See 34712-34716

+ 34813 Placement of femoral-femoral prosthetic graft during endovascular aortic aneurysm repair (List separately in addition to code for primary procedure)

(Use 34813 in conjunction with 34812)

(For femoral artery grafting, see 35521, 35533, 35539, 35540, 35556, 35558, 35566, 35621, 35646, 35654-35661, 35666, 35700)

34820 Code is out of numerical sequence. See 34712-34716

►(34825, 34826 have been deleted. To report, see 34709, 34710, 34711)◄

34830 Open repair of infrarenal aortic aneurysm or dissection, plus repair of associated arterial trauma, following unsuccessful endovascular repair; tube prosthesis

34831 aorto-bi-iliac prosthesis

34832 aorto-bifemoral prosthesis

34833 Code is out of numerical sequence. See 34712-34716

34834 Code is out of numerical sequence. See 34712-34716

Rationale

Endovascular abdominal aortic aneurysm repair codes 34800-34806, 34825, 34826, and 34900 have been deleted. Sixteen new codes (34701-34713, 34714, 34715, 34716) have been added and four related codes (34812, 34820, 34833, 34834) have been revised. A substantial number of new guidelines have been added, and parenthetical notes have been added, deleted, and/or revised to assist with correct reporting of these services. The Endovascular Repair of Abdominal Aortic Aneurysm subsection, which houses the codes, has been renamed as "Endovascular Repair of Abdominal Aorta and/or Iliac Arteries" in order to accurately reflect the vascular anatomy treated using these procedures and to avoid limiting the type of injury to aneurysms. These changes to the reporting were prompted by the identification of codes 34800-34806, 34825, and 34826 on the AMA RUC RAW screen for services that are frequently billed together. It was subsequently determined that the entire family of codes should be revised to reflect current practice and technology and to bundle services that are frequently performed together. The previous codes (34800-34805) described treatment of vascular injury and were structured based on the type of device used. For example, code 34800 described endovascular repair of an infrarenal abdominal aortic aneurysm or dissection using an aorto-aortic tube. Diagnostic imaging (ie, angiography) and imaging guidance, such as fluoroscopy, performed in conjunction with the repair was reported separately with codes 75952-75954 based on the type of imaging performed.

The new codes (34701-34708) include more detailed description of the vessels involved and what is included in the procedures. They are structured based on the vascular anatomy involved (ie, infrarenal aorta and/or iliac artery[ies]) and the type of endograft deployed. The new codes also distinguish between endovascular repair with rupture and for other than rupture. This distinction is based on evidence that repair of a ruptured vessel will involve more complexity, intensity, and work, including placement of a temporary aortic and/or iliac occlusion balloon, when necessary. This balloon would be inflated if the patient goes into hemorrhagic shock. Endovascular repair of ruptured vessels for which this additional work is performed is reported with codes 34702, 34704, 34706, and 34708. Endovascular repair of the infrarenal aorta and/or iliac arteries for other than rupture are reported with codes 34701, 34703, 34705, and 34707. The new guidelines address this distinction and should be reviewed carefully before a code is assigned.

Services that have been bundled into the new codes include angioplasty and stenting performed within the treatment zone; placement of endografts; placement of extensions in the aorta from the renal arteries to the iliac bifurcation; nonselective catheterization; and radiological supervision and interpretation. These bundled services are not reported separately. Prior to 2018, there was no definition of treatment zone in the guidelines. For 2018, the new guidelines include a definition. Treatment zone is defined as the vessel(s) in which an endograft(s), including the main body, docking limb(s), and/or extension(s), is deployed. Procedures performed outside of the treatment zone, such as angioplasty or embolization, may be reported separately. This means that when an endograft terminates in the common iliac artery, any additional treatment performed in that artery is not reported separately; however, treatment that is performed in the external or internal iliac artery may be reported separately. The new guidelines regarding the treatment zone provide clear instructions about when it is appropriate to report additional procedures, and these should be reviewed carefully when these procedures are reported. These procedures involve the time-intensive preoperative work of sizing the aneurysm and selecting the appropriate type of endograft to be deployed. However, the previous codes did not clarify that this work was included in the procedure, and it was unclear whether or how this work should be reported. Preprocedure sizing and device selection are part of the preservice work. For 2018, the new codes specify that this work is included.

Add-on code 34709 describes placement of an extension prosthesis(es) distal to the common iliac artery(ies) or proximal to the renal artery(ies), which should be reported in conjunction with codes 34701-34708, when performed. An endograft extension(s) that terminates within the common iliac arteries is included in codes 34703, 34704, 34705, 34706, 34707, and 34708 and is not reported separately. Codes 34710 and 34711 describe delayed placement of an extension prosthesis(es). Code 34711 is an add-on code and is reported with code 34710 for each additional vessel treated. Codes 34710 and 34711 should not be reported with code 34701, 34702, 34703, 34704, 34705, 34706, 34707, or 34708 or with code 34709 (extension prosthesis placement) because delayed placement of the extension prosthesis is not performed at the same operative session as these procedures. Code 34712 describes delivery of an enhanced fixation device(s) to an endograft, such as an anchor, screw, or tack. It is reported once per operative session, regardless of the number of fixation devices deployed, and it includes

radiological supervision and interpretation. Add-on code 34713 describes percutaneous access and closure of the femoral artery for delivery of an endograft through a sheath of 12-French or larger. Code 34713 may be reported with codes 33880-33886 (endovascular repair of the descending thoracic aorta), 34701-34708, and 34841-34848 (endovascular fenestrated repair of the visceral aorta/infrarenal abdominal aorta), as appropriate. Code 34713 is not reported separately, if a sheath smaller than 12-French is used.

Open arterial exposure is performed during endovascular repair of abdominal aorta and/or iliac arteries procedures when a vessel is too small in diameter to accommodate passage of the endograft. Changes have been made to the reporting of open arterial exposure performed for delivery of endovascular prostheses in these procedures. Prior to 2018, the existing open arterial exposure codes were stand-alone codes, and some limited the endovascular prosthesis to the aortic or iliac type. For 2018, the arterial exposure codes (34812, 34820, 34833, 34834) have been revised with the designation of add-on code and the removal of the restriction to the iliac or aortic type of endovascular prosthesis, where appropriate. Code 34833 has been further revised to describe arterial exposure for establishment of cardiopulmonary bypass. Codes 34714 and 34716 also describe exposure for establishment of cardiopulmonary bypass. In addition, new add-on codes have been established to describe open exposure of the femoral artery (34714) and axillary/subclavian artery (34715 and 34716).

Codes 34812, 34820, 34833, 34834, 34714, 34715, and 34716 should be used to report unilateral procedures. Prior to 2018, bilateral arterial exposure was reported by appending modifier 50 to the appropriate code. For 2018, this instruction has been replaced with the instruction to report the open exposure add-on code twice when it is performed bilaterally. It is important to review the guidelines and parenthetical notes carefully when reporting the open arterial exposure codes.

Clinical Example (34701)

A 75-year-old male with coronary artery disease (CAD) and chronic obstructive pulmonary disease (COPD) presents with an asymptomatic infrarenal abdominal aortic aneurysm (AAA). Endovascular repair is performed by deployment of an aorto-aortic tube endograft and all required infrarenal aortic extension(s), as necessary.

Description of Procedure (34701)

Although deployment of this prosthesis is accomplished from a single femoral or iliac access site, the requirement for accurate positioning typically means that

★ = Telemedicine   ✚ = Add-on code   ✔ = FDA approval pending   # = Resequenced code

intra-arterial catheterization is performed bilaterally. Catheter placement is bundled in this procedure. Under fluoroscopic guidance, an introducer needle is used to access the vessel. A series of graded guidewires, vascular sheaths, and catheters is introduced. Flush aortography is performed to confirm the location of the renal arteries and the aortoiliac anatomy. The patient is then systemically anticoagulated. A rigid wire is inserted over a catheter to provide secure tracking of the large introducer sheath for the endograft. The endograft is loaded onto the guidewire and advanced through the access vessel into the aorta. The endograft is positioned and deployed under fluoroscopic guidance with intermittent angiographic control imaging. A large compliant balloon is placed over the wire into the endograft to perform balloon dilation at the proximal and distal seal zones of the endograft. An aortogram is performed for adequacy of the graft position, patency of adjacent branch vessels (renals and hypogastrics), presence or absence of endoleaks, and type of endoleak, if present. The patency of collateral vessels (lumbar or inferior mesenteric arteries) that may contribute to persistent endoleaks is also assessed. Adjunctive balloon angioplasty is performed for endoleak treatment, as necessary. Extensions required to achieve fixation and seal from the lowest renal artery to the aortic bifurcation are deployed (and included in this service). When the graft is in the appropriate position and free of endoleaks on angiogram, the catheters and guidewires are removed.

Clinical Example (34702)

A 75-year-old male with CAD and COPD presents with a ruptured infrarenal AAA. Endovascular repair is performed by deployment of an aorto-aortic tube endograft and all required infrarenal aortic extension(s), as necessary.

Description of Procedure (34702)

Although deployment of this prosthesis is accomplished from a single femoral or iliac access site, the requirement for accurate positioning typically means that intra-arterial catheterization is performed bilaterally. Under fluoroscopic guidance, introducer needles are used to access the vessels. A series of graded guidewires, vascular sheaths, and catheters is introduced, and flush aortography is performed to confirm the location of the renal arteries and the aortoiliac anatomy. A large sheath is placed, as needed, in the suprarenal aorta for stabilization of an aortic occlusion balloon. At any time in this process, the aortic occlusion balloon may be inflated if the patient suffers hemorrhagic shock. The patient may be systemically anticoagulated. A rigid wire is inserted over a catheter to provide secure tracking of the large introducer sheath for the endograft. The endograft is loaded onto the guidewire and advanced through the access vessel into the aorta. The endograft is

positioned and deployed under fluoroscopic guidance with intermittent angiographic control imaging. A large compliant balloon is placed over the wire into the endograft to perform balloon dilation at the proximal and distal seal zones of the endograft. An aortogram is performed for adequacy of the graft position, patency of adjacent branch vessels (renals and hypogastrics), presence or absence of endoleaks, and type of endoleak, if present. The patency of collateral vessels (lumbar or inferior mesenteric arteries) that may contribute to persistent endoleaks is assessed. Adjunctive balloon angioplasty is performed for endoleak treatment, as necessary (not separately reportable). When the graft is in the appropriate position and free of endoleak on angiogram, the catheters and guidewires are removed.

Clinical Example (34703)

A 75-year-old male with CAD and COPD presents with asymptomatic infrarenal AAA. Endovascular repair is performed by deployment of an aorto-uni-iliac endograft and all required proximal infrarenal extension(s) and all distal extension(s) to the level of the iliac artery bifurcation, as necessary.

Description of Procedure (34703)

Although deployment of this prosthesis is accomplished from a single femoral or iliac access site, the requirement for accurate positioning typically means that intra-arterial catheterization is performed bilaterally. Performance of an aorto-uni-iliac graft requires additional considerations and steps related to treatment of the iliac artery that are not required for the aorto-aortic graft. Catheter placement is bundled in this procedure. Under fluoroscopic guidance, an introducer needle is used to access the vessel. A series of graded guidewires, vascular sheaths, and catheters is introduced. Flush aortography is performed to confirm the location of the renal arteries and the aortoiliac anatomy. The patient is then systemically anticoagulated. A rigid wire is inserted over a catheter to provide secure tracking of the large introducer sheath for the main body of the endograft. The endograft is loaded onto the guidewire and advanced through the access vessel into the aorta. The endograft is positioned and deployed under fluoroscopic guidance with intermittent angiographic control imaging. Additional limbs and extensions are implanted as required to obtain coverage of diseased aorta and common iliac. A large compliant balloon is placed over the wire into the endograft to perform balloon dilation at the proximal and distal seal zones of the endograft. An aortogram is performed for adequacy of the graft position, patency of adjacent branch vessels (renals and hypogastrics), presence or absence of endoleaks, and type of endoleak, if present. The patency of collateral vessels (lumbar or inferior mesenteric arteries) that may contribute to persistent endoleaks is

Surgery / Cardiovascular System 33010-39599

also assessed. Adjunctive balloon angioplasty is performed for endoleak treatment, as necessary. An extension is placed to achieve fixation and seal. When the graft is in the appropriate position and free of endoleaks on angiogram, the catheters and guidewires are removed.

Clinical Example (34704)

A 75-year-old male with CAD and COPD presents with a ruptured infrarenal AAA. Endovascular repair is performed by deployment of an aorto-uni-iliac endograft and all required proximal infrarenal extension(s) and all distal extension(s) to the level of the iliac artery bifurcation, as necessary.

Description of Procedure (34704)

Although deployment of this prosthesis is accomplished from a single femoral or iliac access site, the requirement for accurate positioning typically means that intra-arterial catheterization is performed bilaterally. Performance of an aorto-uni-iliac graft requires additional considerations and steps related to treatment of the iliac artery that are not required for the aorto-aortic graft. Under fluoroscopic guidance, introducer needles are used to access the vessels. A series of graded guidewires, vascular sheaths, and catheters is introduced, and flush aortography is performed to confirm the location of the renal arteries and the aortoiliac anatomy. A large sheath is placed, as needed, in the suprarenal aorta for stabilization of an aortic occlusion balloon. At any time in this process, the aortic occlusion balloon may be inflated if the patient suffers hemorrhagic shock. The patient may be systemically anticoagulated. A rigid wire is inserted over a catheter to provide secure tracking of the large introducer sheath for the endograft. The endograft is loaded onto the guidewire and advanced through the access vessel into the aorta. The endograft is positioned and deployed under fluoroscopic guidance with intermittent angiographic control imaging. Additional limbs and extensions are implanted as required to obtain coverage of diseased aorta and common iliac. A large compliant balloon is placed over the wire into the endograft to perform balloon dilation at the proximal and distal seal zones of the endograft. An aortogram is performed for adequacy of the graft position, patency of adjacent branch vessels (renals and hypogastrics), presence or absence of endoleaks, and type of endoleak, if present. The patency of collateral vessels (lumbar or inferior mesenteric arteries) that may contribute to persistent endoleaks is also assessed. Adjunctive balloon angioplasty is performed for endoleak treatment, as necessary (not separately reportable). When the graft is in the appropriate position and free of endoleak on angiogram, the catheters and guidewires are removed.

Clinical Example (34705)

A 75-year-old male with CAD and COPD presents with asymptomatic infrarenal AAA. Endovascular repair is performed by deployment of an aorto-bi-iliac endograft and all required proximal infrarenal extension(s) and all distal extension(s) to the level of the iliac artery bifurcation, as necessary.

Description of Procedure (34705)

Deployment of this prosthesis is accomplished from bilateral femoral or iliac access sites, and intra-arterial catheterization is performed from both sides. Performance of an aorto-bi-iliac graft requires additional considerations and steps related to treatment of both iliac arteries. This is more work, more steps, and more devices than required for the aorto-aortic endograft or the aorto-uni-iliac endograft. Catheter placement is bundled in this procedure. Under fluoroscopic guidance, an introducer needle is used to access the vessel. A series of graded guidewires, vascular sheaths, and catheters is introduced. Flush aortography is performed to confirm the location of the renal arteries and the aortoiliac anatomy. In a similar manner, catheterization of the aorta from the contralateral femoral or iliac artery is performed. The patient is then systemically anticoagulated. A rigid wire is inserted through catheters to provide secure tracking of the large introducer sheaths for the main body and limbs of the endograft. The first component of the endograft is loaded onto the guidewire and advanced through the access vessel into the aorta. The main body is positioned and deployed under fluoroscopic guidance with intermittent angiographic control imaging. Additional limbs and extensions are implanted as required to obtain coverage of diseased aorta and both common iliacs. A large compliant balloon is placed over the wire into the endograft to perform balloon dilation at the proximal and distal seal zones of the endograft. Both iliac limbs undergo balloon expansion. An aortogram is performed for adequacy of the graft position, patency of adjacent branch vessels (renals and hypogastrics), presence or absence of endoleaks, and type of endoleak, if present. The patency of collateral vessels (lumbar or inferior mesenteric arteries) that may contribute to persistent endoleaks is also assessed. Adjunctive balloon angioplasty is performed for endoleak treatment, as necessary. Extensions are placed to achieve fixation and seal, as required. When the graft is in the appropriate position and free of endoleaks on angiogram, the catheters and guidewires are removed.

Clinical Example (34706)

A 75-year-old male with CAD and COPD presents with a ruptured infrarenal AAA. Endovascular repair is performed by deployment of an aorto-bi-iliac endograft and all required proximal infrarenal extension(s) and all distal extension(s) to the level of the iliac artery bifurcation, as necessary.

Description of Procedure (34706)

The prosthesis is deployed through bilateral femoral or iliac access. An aorto-bi-iliac graft, which requires additional considerations and steps related to treatment of both iliac arteries above and beyond that required for an aorto-aortic endograft or an aorto-uni-iliac endograft, is performed. Under fluoroscopic guidance, introducer needles are used to access bilateral vessels. A series of graded guidewires, vascular sheaths, and catheters is introduced, and flush aortography is performed to confirm the location of the renal arteries and the aortoiliac anatomy. A large sheath is placed, as needed, in the suprarenal aorta for stabilization of an aortic occlusion balloon. At any time in this process, the aortic occlusion balloon may be inflated if the patient suffers hemorrhagic shock. The patient may be systemically anticoagulated. Rigid wires are inserted through bilateral catheters to provide secure tracking of the large introducer sheaths. The main body endograft is loaded onto a guidewire and advanced through the access vessel into the aorta. The main body is positioned and deployed under fluoroscopic guidance with intermittent angiographic control imaging. Additional limbs and extensions are implanted bilaterally, as needed, to obtain coverage of diseased aorta and common iliac arteries. A large compliant balloon is placed over the wire into the endograft to perform balloon dilation at the proximal and distal seal zones of the endograft. An aortogram is performed for adequacy of the graft position, patency of adjacent branch vessels (renals and hypogastrics), presence or absence of endoleaks, and type of endoleak, if present. The patency of collateral vessels (lumbar or inferior mesenteric arteries) that may contribute to persistent endoleaks is also assessed. Adjunctive balloon angioplasty is performed for endoleak treatment, as necessary (not separately reportable). When the graft is in the appropriate position and free of endoleak on angiogram, the catheters and guidewires are removed.

Clinical Example (34707)

A 75-year-old male with CAD and COPD presents with asymptomatic unilateral iliac artery aneurysm. Endovascular repair is performed by deployment of an ilio-iliac tube endograft and all required proximal and distal iliac artery extension(s), as necessary.

Description of Procedure (34707)

Deployment of this prosthesis is accomplished from one femoral access site, but intra-arterial catheterization is typically performed from both sides in order to allow imaging from one side while device deployment is performed on the opposite side. Catheter placement is bundled in this procedure and radiologic supervision and interpretation is bundled in this service. Under fluoroscopic guidance, an introducer needle is used to access the vessel. A series of graded guidewires, vascular sheaths and catheters is introduced, and angiography is performed to confirm the location of the aortic bifurcation and the iliac anatomy. The patient is then systemically anticoagulated. A rigid wire is inserted through catheters to provide secure tracking of the large introducer sheaths for the endograft. The primary component of the endograft is loaded onto the guidewire and advanced through the access vessel to correct position within the proximal common iliac artery. The main component is positioned and deployed under fluoroscopic guidance with intermittent angiographic control imaging. Additional extensions are implanted as required to obtain coverage of the iliac aneurysm. Extensions from the aortic bifurcation to the common iliac bifurcation are bundled in this service. A large compliant balloon is then placed over the wire into the endograft to perform balloon dilation at the proximal and distal seal zones of the endograft. An angiogram is performed for adequacy of the graft position, patency of outflow branches, presence or absence of endoleaks, and type of endoleak, if present. Adjunctive balloon angioplasty is performed for endoleak treatment, as necessary. When the graft is in the appropriate position and free of endoleak on angiogram, the catheters and guidewires are removed.

Clinical Example (34708)

A 75-year-old male with CAD and COPD presents with a ruptured unilateral iliac artery aneurysm. Endovascular repair is performed by deployment of an ilio-iliac tube endograft and all required proximal and distal iliac artery extension(s), as necessary.

Description of Procedure (34708)

Rapid entry is achieved with a needle and wire. A catheter is inserted into the aorta over the wire and manipulated into the abdominal aorta. A rigid wire is exchanged for the entry wire. A large sheath is placed in the entry vessel. A large sheath is placed, as needed, in the suprarenal aorta for stabilization of an aortic occlusion balloon. At any time in this process, the aortic occlusion balloon may be inflated if the patient suffers hemorrhagic shock. Fluid resuscitation and appropriate adjunct measures are performed in coordination with the anesthesia team to best stabilize the critical patient. The patient is systemically anticoagulated. Under fluoroscopic guidance, an introducer needle is used to access the vessel. A guidewire is introduced, and the needle is exchanged for a vascular sheath. A multi-sidehole catheter is placed and flush aortoiliac angiography is performed. The iliac endograft is loaded, advanced, positioned under fluoroscopic guidance, and deployed. A large compliant balloon is placed over the wire into the iliac endograft to perform balloon dilation at the proximal and distal seal zones of the endograft. An aortogram is performed for adequacy of the graft position, patency of adjacent branch vessels (hypogastric, external iliac), presence or absence of endoleaks, and type of endoleak, if present. The patency of collateral vessels (lumbar, hypogastric) that may contribute to persistent endoleaks is assessed. Any and all required proximal and distal iliac artery extensions deployed from the aortic bifurcation to the common iliac bifurcation are bundled in this service. Adjunctive balloon angioplasty is performed for endoleak treatment, as necessary. When the graft is in the appropriate position and free of endoleak on angiogram, the catheters and guidewires are removed.

Clinical Example (34709)

A 75-year-old male with CAD and COPD undergoes an endovascular repair of an infrarenal AAA performed by deployment of an aorto-bi-iliac endograft. After deployment of the endograft, completion angiography reveals an endoleak, dissection, or false aneurysm at the proximal and/or distal fixation and seal zone of the treatment area. This requires placement of a prosthesis extension proximal to the renal arteries and/or distal extension distal to the level of the iliac artery bifurcation. (Note: This add-on code only includes the additional work of nonselective catheterization and placing an additional extension endoprosthesis.)

Description of Procedure (34709)

Measurements are made from the preoperative and intraoperative imaging studies to assess the affected arterial segment and determine exactly the diameter and length of the extension required to successfully seal the endoleak, repair the dissection, or cover the false aneurysm. In this situation, the measurement work is an intraservice element because need for an extension of this type is typically unknown until the situation presents itself during the operation. The diseased arterial segment is treated but with maintenance of patency and distal perfusion. A rigid wire is inserted through the imaging catheter to provide secure tracking of the large introducer sheath necessary for the extension. The extension is loaded onto the guidewire and advanced through the access vessel. It is then positioned above the level of the renal artery and/or below the level of the iliac artery bifurcation and deployed under fluoroscopic guidance. A large compliant balloon is placed over the wire into the extension to perform balloon dilation at the proximal and/or distal seal zones. An aortogram is performed for adequacy of position, presence or absence

of endoleaks, type of endoleak, if present, dissection, or false aneurysm. Adjunctive balloon angioplasty is performed for endoleak treatment, as necessary. When the graft is in the appropriate position and free of endoleak on angiogram, the catheters and guidewires are removed.

Clinical Example (34710)

A 75-year-old male with COPD and CAD who underwent endovascular repair of 6-cm diameter AAA six months ago has preprocedural imaging that demonstrates an endoleak. Due to inadequate exclusion of the aneurysm sac, revision of the original stent graft is performed.

Description of Procedure (34710)

The prosthesis is deployed from one femoral or iliac access site, but intra-arterial catheterization is typically performed from both sides to allow imaging from one side while the device deployment occurs on the opposite side. Performance of extension graft requires special consideration of the previously placed endograft components. This is special and unique work associated with knowledge of the physical characteristics, lengths, and diameters of the prior endograft. Catheter placement is bundled in this procedure. Under fluoroscopic guidance, an introducer needle is used to access the vessel. A series of graded guidewires, vascular sheaths, and catheters is introduced, and flush aortography is performed to confirm the location in which the extension is to be placed. In a similar manner, catheterization of the aorta from the contralateral femoral or iliac artery is performed. The patient is then systemically anticoagulated. A rigid wire is inserted through the deployment side catheter to provide secure tracking of the large introducer sheaths for the main component of the endograft. The primary component is loaded onto the guidewire and advanced through the access vessel to the target site. The endograft is positioned and deployed under fluoroscopic guidance with intermittent angiographic control imaging. Additional extensions are implanted as required to obtain successful coverage of this target lesion. A large compliant balloon is placed over the wire into the endograft to perform balloon dilation at the proximal and distal seal zones of the endograft. An aortogram is performed for adequacy of the graft position, patency of adjacent branch vessels (renals and hypogastrics), presence or absence of endoleaks, and type of endoleak, if present. Adjunctive balloon angioplasty is performed for endoleak treatment, as necessary. When the graft is in the appropriate position and free of endoleak on angiogram, the catheters and guidewires are removed.

Clinical Example (34711)

A 75-year-old male with COPD and CAD who underwent endovascular repair of 6-cm diameter AAA six months ago has preprocedural imaging that demonstrates a second endoleak. Placement of an extension prosthesis for endovascular repair of the infrarenal abdominal aorta is performed. (Note: This add-on code only includes the additional work of nonselective catheterization and placing an additional extension endoprosthesis.)

Description of Procedure (34711)

A rigid wire is inserted through the imaging catheter to provide secure tracking of the large introducer sheath necessary for the extension. The extension is loaded onto the guidewire and advanced through the access vessel. It is then positioned carefully and deployed under fluoroscopic guidance. A large compliant balloon is placed over the wire into the extension to perform balloon dilation at the proximal and/or distal seal zones. An aortogram is performed for adequacy of position, presence or absence of endoleaks, type of endoleak, if present, dissection, or false aneurysm. Adjunctive balloon angioplasty is performed for endoleak treatment, as necessary. When the graft is in the appropriate position and free of endoleak on angiogram, the catheters and guidewires are removed.

Clinical Example (34712)

A 75-year-old male with COPD and CAD who previously underwent endovascular repair of 6-cm diameter AAA now presents with a proximal endoleak. Transcatheter delivery of anchors/screws to seal the endoleak is performed.

Description of Procedure (34712)

Under fluoroscopic guidance, an introducer needle is used to access the vessel. A guidewire is introduced, and the needle is exchanged for a vascular sheath. A multi-sidehole catheter is placed, and flush aortogram is performed. The patient is systemically anticoagulated. The endovascular fixation anchor delivery guide is placed in the aortic endograft over stiff wire access. Contrast imaging confirms appropriate delivery guide position within the aortic endograft. The endovascular fixation anchor delivery system is then constrained, loaded with an endovascular fixation anchor, and placed within the delivery guide into the aortic endograft. Under contrast injection and fluoroscopy, the endovascular fixation anchor position is confirmed and then deployed. Additional endovascular fixation anchors are placed, as needed, in the proximal extent of the aortic graft and aortic wall. Contrast injection to confirm endovascular fixation anchor placement and treatment of endoleak is performed. Additional wires, sheaths, and catheters are removed.

Clinical Example (34713)

A 75-year-old male with CAD and COPD presents with asymptomatic infrarenal AAA and undergoes endovascular repair by percutaneous access (reported separately). Prior to placement of a large sheath in the artery, two closure devices are inserted in preclose fashion to secure the access site hemostasis at the termination of the procedure. (Note: This add-on code only includes the additional work of ultrasound guidance to establish vascular access and placing two closure devices.)

Description of Procedure (34713)

Percutaneous access and initial catheter-based vascular assessment is performed. A guidewire is placed through the catheter, and the catheter is removed. A vascular closure device is placed into the femoral artery over the guidewire. Placement within the artery is checked and the guidewire is removed. The device is predeployed and secured at the skin surface with hemostats. The guidewire is reinserted into the first device. The first closure device is removed. A second vascular closure device is inserted over the guidewire, which is then removed. The second closure device is predeployed in a different orientation and secured at the skin surface with hemostats. A guidewire is then placed into the closure device prior to removal to ensure continued access for subsequent endovascular procedure. Once the endograft has been deployed, the skin and subcutaneous tissue are dissected with a hemostat. The delivery system, wire, and sheath are removed. The first closure device sutures are tied using the remote knot mobilizer to initially close the arteriotomy. The second closure device sutures are tied using the remote knot mobilizer to ultimately secure the arteriotomy and all excess sutures are cut. The site is inspected for hemostasis and secure closure of the artery.

Clinical Example (34714)

A 75-year-old male with CAD and COPD presents with asymptomatic infrarenal AAA. His femoral artery is too small in diameter and calcified to accommodate passage of an endovascular device. Open femoral artery exposure with placement of a femoral conduit is performed to enable endovascular aortic aneurysm repair. (Note: This add-on code only includes the additional work of open femoral artery exposure and placement of a prosthetic conduit by groin incision and closure of the wound.)

Description of Procedure (34714)

A groin incision is made with respect to anatomic landmarks. The subcutaneous tissue is dissected until the common femoral artery is located. The femoral sheath and inguinal ligament are identified. Care is taken to avoid injury to the femoral nerve and femoral vein, which lie in close proximity. The common, superficial, and deep femoral arteries in addition to the distal external iliac artery are sharply dissected and encircled with vessel loops. Retraction and/or division of the inguinal ligament are performed, if required. The vessels are assessed for caliber and suitability for introduction of the guidewires, sheaths, and endograft. The patient is systemically anticoagulated, and an appropriate-sized prosthetic graft is selected. Hemostatic clamps are placed on the vessels, and an end-to-side anastomosis between the graft and the artery is created with monofilament suture. The prosthetic conduit is then used to provide catheter, sheath, and endograft access. Once the endograft has been deployed and the wires and sheaths have been removed (reported separately), hemostatic clamps are applied to the proximal and distal vessels. The prosthetic graft is then divided and oversewn with fine monofilament suture. The vascular clamps are removed and vessel patency is assessed. After achieving hemostasis, the wound is irrigated and closed in several layers. The skin is closed with staples or suture, as appropriate.

Clinical Example (34715)

A 75-year-old male with CAD and COPD presents with asymptomatic infrarenal AAA. His iliac arteries are tortuous and too small in diameter to accommodate passage of an endovascular device. Open axillary exposure through an infraclavicular incision is performed to enable endovascular repair. (Note: This add-on code only includes the additional work of open axillary artery exposure by infraclavicular incision and closure of the wound.)

Description of Procedure (34715)

An incision is made below the clavicle. The subcutaneous tissue and fascia are divided. The axillary artery is identified, sharply dissected, and encircled with vessel loops. The large adjacent nerves and axial vein are identified and protected. Once the endograft has been deployed and the wires and sheaths have been removed (reported separately), hemostatic clamps are applied to the proximal and distal axillary artery. The arteriotomy is closed with fine monofilament suture. The vascular clamps are removed, and vessel patency is assessed. After achieving hemostasis, the wound is irrigated and closed in several layers. The skin is closed with skin staples or absorbable suture.

Clinical Example (34716)

A 75-year-old male with CAD and COPD presents with asymptomatic infrarenal AAA. His iliac arteries are tortuous and too small in diameter and calcified to accommodate passage of an endovascular device. Open axillary exposure through an infraclavicular incision with placement of a prosthetic conduit is performed to enable endovascular repair. (Note: This add-on code only includes the additional work of open axillary artery exposure by infraclavicular incision, placement of a prosthetic conduit, and closure of the wound.)

Description of Procedure (34716)

An incision is made below the clavicle. The subcutaneous tissue and fascia are divided. The axillary artery is sharply dissected and encircled with vessel loops. The adjacent veins and nerves are identified and protected. The axillary artery is very soft and friable, not suitable for endograft access. The patient is systemically anticoagulated, and an appropriate sized prosthetic graft is selected. Hemostatic clamps are placed on the artery, and an end-to-side anastomosis between the graft and the axillary artery is created with monofilament suture. The prosthetic conduit is then used to obtain catheter, sheath, and endograft access. Once the endograft has been deployed and the wires and sheaths have been removed (reported separately), hemostatic clamps are applied to the proximal and distal axillary artery. The prosthetic conduit is then divided and oversewn with fine monofilament suture. The vascular clamps are removed, and vessel patency is assessed. After achieving hemostasis, the wound is irrigated and closed in several layers. The skin is closed with skin staples or absorbable suture.

Clinical Example (34812)

A 75-year-old male with CAD and COPD presents with asymptomatic infrarenal AAA. Open femoral artery exposure for the delivery of the endovascular prosthesis by groin incision is performed. (Note: This add-on code only includes the additional work of open femoral artery exposure by groin incision and closure of the wound.)

Description of Procedure (34812)

A groin incision is made with respect to anatomic landmarks. The subcutaneous tissue is dissected until the common femoral artery is located. The femoral sheath and inguinal ligament are identified. Care is taken to avoid injury to the femoral nerve and femoral vein, which lie in close proximity. The common, superficial, and deep femoral arteries in addition to the distal external iliac artery are sharply dissected and encircled with vessel loops. Retraction and/or division of the inguinal ligament are performed, if required. The vessels are assessed for caliber and suitability for introduction of the guidewires, sheaths, and endograft. Once the endograft has been deployed and the wires and sheaths have been removed (reported separately), hemostatic clamps are applied to the proximal and distal vessels. The arteriotomy is closed with fine monofilament suture. The vascular clamps are removed, and vessel patency is assessed. After achieving hemostasis, the wound is irrigated and closed in several layers. The skin is closed with staples or suture, as appropriate.

Clinical Example (34820)

A 75-year-old male with CAD and COPD presents with asymptomatic infrarenal AAA. His bilateral distal external iliac and common femoral arteries are too small in diameter to accommodate passage of an endovascular device. Open iliac artery exposure by abdominal or retroperitoneal incision is performed to provide a suitable entry site for placement of an endoprosthesis. (Note: This add-on code only includes the additional work of open iliac artery exposure by abdominal or retroperitoneal incision and closure of the wound.)

Description of Procedure (34820)

A skin incision is made in the lower abdomen or retroperitoneum. The tissue is dissected deep into the pelvis until the iliac artery is located. A retracting system is inserted to ensure adequate exposure. The adjacent ureter, veins, and nerves are identified and protected. The iliac artery is isolated free of surrounding tissue, and circumferential vascular loops are applied. Following endograft deployment and after the wires and sheaths have been removed (reported separately), hemostatic clamps are applied to the proximal and distal vessels. The arteriotomy is closed with fine monofilament suture. The vascular clamps are removed, and vessel patency is assessed. After achieving hemostasis, the wound is irrigated and closed in several layers. The skin is closed with skin staples or absorbable suture.

Clinical Example (34833)

A 75-year-old male with CAD and COPD presents with asymptomatic infrarenal AAA. His bilateral iliac arteries are too small in diameter and calcified to accommodate passage of an endovascular device. Open iliac artery exposure with placement of an iliac conduit by abdominal or retroperitoneal incision is performed to provide a suitable entry site for placement of an endoprosthesis. (Note: This add-on code only includes the additional work of open iliac artery exposure by abdominal or retroperitoneal incision and closure of the wound.)

Description of Procedure (34833)

A skin incision is made in the lower abdomen or retroperitoneum. The tissue is dissected deep into the pelvis until the iliac artery is located. A retracting system is inserted to ensure adequate exposure. The adjacent ureter, veins, and nerves are identified and protected. The common, external, and internal iliac arteries are dissected and encircled with vessel loops. The iliac artery is found to be diseased and not suitable for endograft access. The patient is systemically anticoagulated, and an appropriate sized prosthetic graft is selected. Hemostatic clamps are placed on the iliac vessels, and an end-to-side anastomosis between the graft and the iliac artery is created with monofilament suture. The prosthetic conduit is then used to obtain catheter, sheath, and endograft access. Once the endograft has been deployed and the wires and sheaths have been removed (reported separately), hemostatic clamps are applied to the proximal and distal iliac vessels. The prosthetic conduit is then divided and oversewn with fine monofilament suture. The vascular clamps are removed, and vessel patency is assessed. After achieving hemostasis, the wound is irrigated and closed in several layers. The skin is closed with skin staples or absorbable suture.

Clinical Example (34834)

A 75-year-old male with CAD and COPD presents with asymptomatic infrarenal AAA and tortuous iliac arteries. Open brachial artery exposure is performed to enable endovascular repair. (Note: This add-on code only includes the additional work of open brachial artery exposure and closure of the wound.)

Description of Procedure (34834)

An incision is made in the arm. The subcutaneous tissue and fascia are divided. The brachial artery is identified and dissected free of surrounding tissue. The median nerve and brachial vein are identified and protected. The common, external, and internal iliac arteries are sharply dissected and encircled with vessel loops. Once the endograft has been deployed and the wires and sheaths have been removed (reported separately), hemostatic clamps are applied to the proximal and distal brachial artery. The arteriotomy is closed with fine monofilament suture. The vascular clamps are removed, and vessel patency is assessed. After achieving hemostasis, the wound is irrigated and closed in several layers. The skin is closed with skin staples or absorbable suture.

Surgery / Cardiovascular System 33010-39599

Fenestrated Endovascular Repair of the Visceral and Infrarenal Aorta

The upper abdominal aorta that contains the celiac, superior mesenteric, and renal arteries is termed the visceral aorta. For reporting purposes, the thoracic aorta extends from the aortic valve to the aortic segment just proximal to the celiac artery.

Code 34839 is used to report the physician planning and sizing for a patient-specific fenestrated visceral aortic endograft. The planning includes review of high-resolution cross-sectional images (eg, CT, CTA, MRI) and utilization of 3D software for iterative modeling of the aorta and device in multiplanar views and center line of flow analysis. Code 34839 may only be reported when the physician spends a minimum of 90 total minutes performing patient-specific fenestrated endograft planning. Physician planning time does not need to be continuous and should be clearly documented in the patient record. Code 34839 is reported on the date that planning work is complete and may not include time spent on the day before or the day of the fenestrated endovascular repair procedure (34841, 34842, 34843, 34844, 34845, 34846, 34847, 34848) nor be reported on the day before or the day of the fenestrated endovascular repair procedure.

Codes 34841, 34842, 34843, 34844, 34845, 34846, 34847, 34848 are used to report placement of a fenestrated endovascular graft in the visceral aorta, either alone or in combination with the infrarenal aorta for aneurysm, pseudoaneurysm, dissection, penetrating ulcer, intramural hematoma, or traumatic disruption. The fenestrated main body endoprosthesis is deployed within the visceral aorta. Fenestrations within the fabric allow for selective catheterization of the visceral and/or renal arteries and subsequent placement of an endoprosthesis (ie, bare metal or covered stent) to maintain flow to the visceral artery. Patient variation in the location and relative orientation of the renal and visceral artery origins requires use of a patient-specific fenestrated endograft for endovascular repair that preserves flow to essential visceral arteries and allows proximal seal and fixation to be achieved above the renal level as well as in the distal aorta or iliac vessel(s).

▶Fenestrated aortic repair is reported based on the extent of aorta treated. Codes 34841, 34842, 34843, 34844 describe repair using proximal endoprostheses that span from the visceral aortic component to one, two, three, or four visceral artery origins and distal extent limited to the infrarenal aorta. These devices do not extend into the common iliac arteries. Codes 34845, 34846, 34847, 34848 are used to report deployment of a fenestrated endograft that spans from the visceral aorta (including one, two, three, or four visceral artery origins) through the infrarenal aorta into the common iliac arteries. The infrarenal component may be a bifurcated unibody device, a modular bifurcated docking system with docking limb(s), or an aorto-uniiliac device. Codes 34845, 34846, 34847, 34848 include placement of unilateral or bilateral docking limbs (depending on the device). Any additional endograft extensions that terminate in the common iliac arteries are included in 34845, 34846, 34847, 34848. Codes 34709, 34710, 34711 may not be separately reported for proximal abdominal aortic extension prosthesis(es) or for distal extension prosthesis(es) that terminate(s) in the aorta or the common iliac arteries. However, 34709, 34710, 34711 may be reported for distal extension prosthesis(es) that terminate(s) in the internal iliac, external iliac, or common femoral artery(ies).◀

Codes 34841-34844 and 34845-34848 define the total number of visceral and/or renal arteries (ie, celiac, superior mesenteric, and/or unilateral or bilateral renal artery[s]) requiring placement of an endoprosthesis (ie, bare metal or covered stent) through an aortic endograft fenestration.

Introduction of guide wires and catheters in the aorta and visceral and/or renal arteries is included in the work of 34841-34848 and is not separately reportable. However, catheterization of the hypogastric artery(s) and/or arterial families outside the treatment zone of the graft may be separately reported. Balloon angioplasty within the target treatment zone of the endograft, either before or after endograft deployment, is not separately reportable. Fluoroscopic guidance and radiological supervision and interpretation in conjunction with fenestrated endovascular aortic repair is not separately reportable and includes angiographic diagnostic imaging of the aorta and its branches prior to deployment of the fenestrated endovascular device, fluoroscopic guidance in the delivery of the fenestrated endovascular components, and intraprocedural arterial angiography (eg, confirm position, detect endoleak, evaluate runoff) done at the time of the endovascular aortic repair.

▶Exposure of the access vessels (eg, 34713, 34714, 34715, 34716, 34812, 34820, 34833, 34834) may be reported separately. Extensive repair of an artery (eg, 35226, 35286) may be reported separately. For concomitant endovascular treatment of the descending thoracic aorta, 33880-33886 and 75956-75959 may be reported with 34841, 34842, 34843, 34844, 34845, 34846, 34847, 34848. For isolated endovascular infrarenal abdominal aortic aneurysm repair that does not require placement of a fenestrated graft to preserve flow to the visceral branch(es), see 34701, 34702, 34703, 34704, 34705, 34706.◀

Other interventional procedures performed at the time of fenestrated endovascular abdominal aortic aneurysm repair may be reported separately (eg, arterial embolization, intravascular ultrasound, balloon angioplasty or stenting of native artery[s] outside the

★ = Telemedicine   ✚ = Add-on code   ⟋ = FDA approval pending   # = Resequenced code

endoprosthesis target zone, when done before or after deployment of endoprosthesis).

34841   Endovascular repair of visceral aorta (eg, aneurysm, pseudoaneurysm, dissection, penetrating ulcer, intramural hematoma, or traumatic disruption) by deployment of a fenestrated visceral aortic endograft and all associated radiological supervision and interpretation, including target zone angioplasty, when performed; including one visceral artery endoprosthesis (superior mesenteric, celiac or renal artery)

34842   including two visceral artery endoprostheses (superior mesenteric, celiac and/or renal artery[s])

34843   including three visceral artery endoprostheses (superior mesenteric, celiac and/or renal artery[s])

34844   including four or more visceral artery endoprostheses (superior mesenteric, celiac and/or renal artery[s])

►(Do not report 34841, 34842, 34843, 34844 in conjunction with 34701, 34702, 34703, 34704, 34705, 34706, 34845, 34846, 34847, 34848)◄

(Do not report 34841, 34842, 34843, 34844 in conjunction with 34839, when planning services are performed on the day before or the day of the fenestrated endovascular repair procedure)

34845   Endovascular repair of visceral aorta and infrarenal abdominal aorta (eg, aneurysm, pseudoaneurysm, dissection, penetrating ulcer, intramural hematoma, or traumatic disruption) with a fenestrated visceral aortic endograft and concomitant unibody or modular infrarenal aortic endograft and all associated radiological supervision and interpretation, including target zone angioplasty, when performed; including one visceral artery endoprosthesis (superior mesenteric, celiac or renal artery)

34846   including two visceral artery endoprostheses (superior mesenteric, celiac and/or renal artery[s])

34847   including three visceral artery endoprostheses (superior mesenteric, celiac and/or renal artery[s])

34848   including four or more visceral artery endoprostheses (superior mesenteric, celiac and/or renal artery[s])

►(Do not report 34845, 34846, 34847, 34848 in conjunction with 34701, 34702, 34703, 34704, 34705, 34706, 34841, 34842, 34843, 34844, 35081, 35102)◄

(Do not report 34845, 34846, 34847, 34848 in conjunction with 34839, when planning services are performed on the day before or the day of the fenestrated endovascular repair procedure)

(Do not report 34841-34848 in conjunction with 37236, 37237 for bare metal or covered stents placed into the visceral branches within the endoprosthesis target zone)

►(For placement of distal extension prosthesis[es] terminating in the internal iliac, external iliac, or common femoral artery[s], see 34709, 34710, 34711, 0254T)◄

(Use 34845, 34846, 34847, 34848 in conjunction with 37220, 37221, 37222, 37223, only when 37220, 37221, 37222, 37223 are performed outside the target treatment zone of the endoprosthesis)

Rationale

In support of the changes in reporting endovascular repair of abdominal aorta and/or iliac arteries procedures, the guidelines in the Fenestrated Endovascular Repair of the Visceral and Infrarenal Aorta section have been revised by replacing deleted codes 34825 and 34826 with new codes 34709, 34710, and 34711 (extension prosthesis placement) and by making the language consistent with the language in the new endovascular repair of abdominal aorta and/or iliac arteries guidelines. The exclusionary parenthetical notes that follow codes 34841-34844 (endovascular repair of visceral aorta) and 34845-34848 (endovascular repair of visceral and infrarenal abdominal aorta) have been revised to reflect the appropriate new codes. The cross-reference parenthetical note for placement of distal extension prosthesis(es) terminating in the internal iliac, external iliac, or common femoral artery(s) that follows code 34848 has been revised with the appropriate new codes.

Refer to the codebook and the Rationale for codes 34701-34713, 34714, 34715, and 34716 for a full discussion of these changes.

Endovascular Repair of Iliac Aneurysm

►(34900 has been deleted. To report, see 34707, 34708)◄

Rationale

In support of the changes in reporting of endovascular repair of abdominal aorta and/or iliac arteries procedures, code 34900 (endovascular repair of iliac artery with tube endoprosthesis) and its associated guidelines and parenthetical notes have been deleted. An instructional parenthetical note has been added directing users to codes 34707 and 34708, which describe repair of the iliac artery with an ilio-iliac tube endograft.

Refer to the codebook and the Rationale for codes 34701-34713, 34714, 34715, and 34716 for a full discussion of these changes.

Surgery / Cardiovascular System 33010-39599

Direct Repair of Aneurysm or Excision (Partial or Total) and Graft Insertion for Aneurysm, Pseudoaneurysm, Ruptured Aneurysm, and Associated Occlusive Disease

Procedures 35001-35152 include preparation of artery for anastomosis including endarterectomy.

(For direct repairs associated with occlusive disease only, see 35201-35286)

(For intracranial aneurysm, see 61700 et seq)

▶(For endovascular repair of abdominal aortic and/or iliac artery aneurysm, see 34701-34716)◀

(For thoracic aortic aneurysm, see 33860-33875)

(For endovascular repair of descending thoracic aorta, involving coverage of left subclavian artery origin, use 33880)

35001 Direct repair of aneurysm, pseudoaneurysm, or excision (partial or total) and graft insertion, with or without patch graft; for aneurysm and associated occlusive disease, carotid, subclavian artery, by neck incision

Rationale

In support of the changes in reporting endovascular repair of abdominal aorta and/or iliac arteries procedures, cross-reference parenthetical notes in the Direct Repair of Aneurysm or Excision (Partial or Total) and Graft Insertion for Aneurysm, Pseudoaneurysm, Ruptured Aneurysm, and Associated Occlusive Disease section that directed users to deleted codes 34800-34826 (endovascular repair of abdominal aortic aneurysm) and 34900 (endovascular repair of iliac artery aneurysm) have been deleted and replaced with a new parenthetical note that directs users to the new endovascular repair of abdominal aorta and/or iliac arteries codes.

Refer to the codebook and the Rationale for codes 34701-34713, 34714, 34715, and 34716 for a full discussion of these changes.

Thromboendarterectomy

(For coronary artery, see 33510-33536 and 33572)

(35301-35372 include harvest of saphenous or upper extremity vein when performed)

35301 Thromboendarterectomy, including patch graft, if performed; carotid, vertebral, subclavian, by neck incision

35302 superficial femoral artery

35303 popliteal artery

▶(Do not report 35302, 35303 in conjunction with 37225, 37227 when performed in the same vessel)◀

35304 tibioperoneal trunk artery

35305 tibial or peroneal artery, initial vessel

+ 35306 each additional tibial or peroneal artery (List separately in addition to code for primary procedure)

(Use 35306 in conjunction with 35305)

▶(Do not report 35304, 35305, 35306 in conjunction with 37229, 37231, 37233, 37235 when performed in the same vessel)◀

Rationale

The exclusionary parenthetical note that follows code 35303 has been revised to delete code 35500, and the phrase "when performed in the same vessel" has been added. The same revision has been made to the parenthetical note that follows code 35306.

The other procedures listed in the exclusionary parenthetical note may be reported when the procedure is performed in a different vessel, per the phrase that has been added to clarify the intended use for these codes.

Refer to the codebook and the Rationale for the deletion of the exclusionary parenthetical note following code 11008 for a full discussion of these changes.

Vascular Injection Procedures

Intra-Arterial—Intra-Aortic

(For radiological supervision and interpretation, see Radiology)

36100 Introduction of needle or intracatheter, carotid or vertebral artery

(For bilateral procedure, report 36100 with modifier 50)

▶(36120 has been deleted)◀

▲ **36140** Introduction of needle or intracatheter, upper or lower extremity artery

Rationale

In support of the deletion of code 75658, code 36120, which is used to report the retrograde introduction of a

★ = Telemedicine   ✦ = Add-on code   ⊘ = FDA approval pending   # = Resequenced code

Rationale

In support of the deletion of code 75658, code 36120, which is used to report the retrograde introduction of a needle or intracatheter into the brachial artery, has been deleted because this service is more appropriately reported with other existing, upper extremity angiography codes.

As a result, code 36140 has been revised to specify upper or lower extremity artery. In addition, code 36140 has been reformatted as a stand-alone and nonparent code.

Venous

36456   Partial exchange transfusion, blood, plasma or crystalloid necessitating the skill of a physician or other qualified health care professional, newborn

(Do not report 36456 in conjunction with 36430, 36440, 36450)

▶(Do not report modifier 63 in conjunction with 36456)◀

Rationale

An exclusionary parenthetical note after code 36456 has been added. The parenthetical note provides instructions prohibiting the use of modifier 63 in conjunction with code 36456. This is consistent with other transfusion codes for patients younger than 2 years (ie, 36450, 36460) that include instruction that restricts the use of modifier 63 in conjunction with those codes.

36460   Transfusion, intrauterine, fetal

(Do not report modifier 63 in conjunction with 36460)

(For radiological supervision and interpretation, use 76941)

▶Codes 36468, 36470, 36471 describe injection(s) of a sclerosant for sclerotherapy of telangiectasia and/or incompetent vein(s). Code 36468 may only be reported once per extremity per session, regardless of the number of needle injections performed. Codes 36466, 36471 may only be reported once per extremity, regardless of the number of veins treated. Ultrasound guidance (76942), when performed, is not included in 36468, 36470, 36471 and may be reported separately.

Codes 36465, 36466 describe injection(s) of a non-compounded foam sclerosant into an extremity truncal vein (eg, great saphenous vein, accessory saphenous vein) using ultrasound-guided compression of the junction of the central vein (saphenofemoral junction or saphenopopliteal junction) to limit the dispersion of injectate. Do not report 36465, 36466 for injection of compounded foam sclerosant(s).

Compounding is a practice in which a qualified health care professional (eg, pharmacist, physician) combines, mixes, or alters ingredients of a drug to create a medication tailored to the needs of an individual patient.

When performed in the office setting, all required supplies and equipment are included in 36465, 36466, 36468, 36470, 36471 and may not be separately reported. In addition, application of compression dressing(s) (eg, compression bandages/stockings) is included in 36465, 36466, 36468, 36470, 36471, when performed, and may not be reported separately.◀

36465   Code is out of numerical sequence. See 36470-36474

36466   Code is out of numerical sequence. See 36470-36474

▲ **36468**   Injection(s) of sclerosant for spider veins (telangiectasia), limb or trunk

▶(For ultrasound imaging guidance performed in conjunction with 36468, use 76942)◀

▶(Do not report 36468 in conjunction with 29581)◀

▶(Do not report 36468 more than once per extremity)◀

(Do not report 36468 in conjunction with 37241 in the same surgical field)

▲ **36470**   Injection of sclerosant; single incompetent vein (other than telangiectasia)

▲ **36471**   multiple incompetent veins (other than telangiectasia), same leg

▶(For ultrasound imaging guidance performed in conjunction with 36470, 36471, use 76942)◀

▶(Do not report 36470, 36471 in conjunction with 29581)◀

▶(Do not report 36471 more than once per extremity)◀

▶(If the targeted vein is an extremity truncal vein and injection of non-compounded foam sclerosant with ultrasound guided compression maneuvers to guide dispersion of the injectate is performed, see 36465, 36466)◀

(Do not report 36470, 36471 in conjunction with 37241 in the same surgical field)

#● **36465**   Injection of non-compounded foam sclerosant with ultrasound compression maneuvers to guide dispersion of the injectate, inclusive of all imaging guidance and monitoring; single incompetent extremity truncal vein (eg, great saphenous vein, accessory saphenous vein)

#● **36466**   multiple incompetent truncal veins (eg, great saphenous vein, accessory saphenous vein), same leg

▶(Do not report 36465, 36466 in conjunction with 29581)◀

►(Do not report 36465, 36466 in conjunction with 37241 in the same surgical field)◄

►(For extremity truncal vein injection of compounded foam sclerosant[s], see 36470, 36471)◄

►(For injection of a sclerosant into an incompetent vein without compression maneuvers to guide dispersion of the injectate, see 36470, 36471)◄

►(For endovenous ablation therapy of incompetent vein[s] by transcatheter delivery of a chemical adhesive, see 36482, 36483)◄

►(For vascular embolization and occlusion procedures, see 37241, 37242, 37243, 37244)◄

►Codes 36473, 36474, 36475, 36476, 36478, 36479, 36482, 36483 describe endovascular ablation therapy of incompetent extremity vein(s), including all necessary imaging guidance and monitoring. Sclerosant injection(s) of vein(s) by needle or mini-catheter (36468, 36470, 36471) followed by a compression technique is not endovascular ablation therapy. Codes 36473, 36474, 36482, 36483 can be performed under local anesthesia without the need for tumescent (peri-saphenous) anesthesia. Codes 36475, 36476, 36478, 36479 are performed using adjunctive tumescent anesthesia.

Codes 36473, 36474 involve concomitant use of an intraluminal device that mechanically disrupts/abrades the venous intima and infusion of a physician-specified medication in the target vein(s).

Codes 36482, 36483 involve positioning an intravenous catheter the length of an incompetent vein, remote from the percutaneous access site, with subsequent delivery of a chemical adhesive to ablate the incompetent vein. This often includes ultrasound compression of the outflow vein to limit the dispersion of the injected solution.

Codes 36475, 36476 involve advancing a radiofrequency device the length of an incompetent vein, with subsequent delivery of radiofrequency energy to ablate the incompetent vein.

Codes 36478, 36479 involve advancing a laser device the length of an incompetent vein, with subsequent delivery of thermal energy to ablate the incompetent vein.

Codes 36474, 36476, 36479, 36483 for subsequent vein(s) treated in the same extremity may only be reported once per extremity, regardless of the number of additional vein(s) treated.

When performed in the office setting, all required supplies and equipment are included in 36473, 36474, 36475, 36476, 36478, 36479, 36482, 36483 and may not be separately reported. In addition, application of compression dressing(s) (eg, compression bandages/ stockings) is included in 36473, 36474, 36475, 36476, 36478, 36479, 36482, 36483, when performed, and may not be reported separately.◄

36473 Endovenous ablation therapy of incompetent vein, extremity, inclusive of all imaging guidance and monitoring, percutaneous, mechanochemical; first vein treated

+ 36474 subsequent vein(s) treated in a single extremity, each through separate access sites (List separately in addition to code for primary procedure)

(Use 36474 in conjunction with 36473)

(Do not report 36474 more than once per extremity)

►(Do not report 36473, 36474 in conjunction with 29581, 36000, 36002, 36005, 36410, 36425, 36475, 36476, 36478, 36479, 37241, 75894, 76000, 76001, 76937, 76942, 76998, 77022, 93970, 93971 in the same surgical field)◄

36475 Endovenous ablation therapy of incompetent vein, extremity, inclusive of all imaging guidance and monitoring, percutaneous, radiofrequency; first vein treated

+ 36476 subsequent vein(s) treated in a single extremity, each through separate access sites (List separately in addition to code for primary procedure)

(Use 36476 in conjunction with 36475)

(Do not report 36476 more than once per extremity)

►(Do not report 36475, 36476 in conjunction with 29581, 36000, 36002, 36005, 36410, 36425, 36478, 36479, 36482, 36483, 37241-37244, 75894, 76000, 76001, 76937, 76942, 76998, 77022, 93970, 93971 in the same surgical field)◄

36478 Endovenous ablation therapy of incompetent vein, extremity, inclusive of all imaging guidance and monitoring, percutaneous, laser; first vein treated

+ 36479 subsequent vein(s) treated in a single extremity, each through separate access sites (List separately in addition to code for primary procedure)

(Use 36479 in conjunction with 36478)

(Do not report 36479 more than once per extremity)

►(Do not report 36478, 36479 in conjunction with 29581, 36000, 36002, 36005, 36410, 36425, 36475, 36476, 36482, 36483, 37241, 75894, 76000, 76001, 76937, 76942, 76998, 77022, 93970, 93971 in the same surgical field)◄

#● 36482 Endovenous ablation therapy of incompetent vein, extremity, by transcatheter delivery of a chemical adhesive (eg, cyanoacrylate) remote from the access site, inclusive of all imaging guidance and monitoring, percutaneous; first vein treated

#+● 36483 subsequent vein(s) treated in a single extremity, each through separate access sites (List separately in addition to code for primary procedure)

►(Use 36483 in conjunction with 36482)◄

►(Do not report 36483 more than once per extremity)◄

★ = Telemedicine   + = Add-on code   ✎ = FDA approval pending   # = Resequenced code

Surgery / Cardiovascular System 33010-39599

▶(Do not report 36482, 36483 in conjunction with 29581, 36000, 36002, 36005, 36410, 36425, 36475, 36476, 36478, 36479, 37241, 75894, 76000, 76001, 76937, 76942, 76998, 77022, 93970, 93971 in the same surgical field)◀

36482   Code is out of numerical sequence. See 36478-36500

36483   Code is out of numerical sequence. See 36478-36500

Rationale

Four codes (36465, 36466, 36482, 36483) have been added for reporting newer treatments of incompetent veins, and three codes (36468, 36470, 36471) have been revised. Parenthetical notes and guidelines have been added, and existing parenthetical notes and guidelines have been revised to provide clear instructions on the appropriate reporting of the new and revised codes.

Prior to 2018, there were codes to report some methods of treatment for incompetent veins, specifically direct puncture sclerotherapy (36468-36471); mechanochemical endovenous ablation (36473, 36474); laser ablation (36478, 36479); radiofrequency ablation (36475, 36476); ligation/stripping (37718, 37722); and stab phlebectomy (37765, 37766). For 2018, codes 36482, 36483, 36465, and 36466 have been added to describe newer treatments that involve the use of chemical adhesive and noncompounded foam sclerosant. Prior to 2018, these treatments were reported with code 37799 (unlisted procedure, vascular surgery).

Codes 36482 and 36483 describe endovenous ablation therapy using a chemical adhesive. In this procedure, the catheter is tunneled the full length of the incompetent vein, and the adhesive is administered remotely from the access site to ablate the length of the incompetent vein, as opposed to being administered under the skin using a needle or minicatheter. Code 36482 is reported for the first vein treated. Code 36483 is an add-on code and should be reported in conjunction with code 36482 for subsequent veins that are treated in a single extremity through separate access sites. Code 36483 is reported only once per extremity, regardless of the number of subsequent veins treated. This is noted by the optional plural, ie, adding the plural form of a word in parentheses, and in this case the parentheses around the "s" in "vein(s)."

Codes 36465 and 36466 describe injection(s) of a non-compounded foam sclerosant into an extremity truncal vein. The "sclerosant" described in these codes is not compounded by a physician or other qualified health care professional. Hence, the term "non-compounded" is specified in the code descriptor. Compounding is the

process of combining, mixing, or altering the ingredients of a drug by a physician or other qualified health care professional to tailor it to an individual patient's needs. When a compounded sclerosant foam is injected for treatment of an incompetent extremity truncal vein, codes 36470 and 36471 should be reported. A definition of compounding has been included in the new guidelines to help users determine if a compounded or non-compounded sclerosant was used in the procedure. Codes 36465 and 36466 include ultrasound compression maneuvers. These compression maneuvers are performed under ultrasound guidance to control the dispersion of the foam sclerosant and to ensure that the sclerosant reaches the intended treatment area. The ultrasound guidance and monitoring are included in codes 36465 and 36466 and should not be reported separately.

Prior to 2018, the descriptor of code 36468 stated "single or multiple injections," which left room for interpretation regarding the number of times the code could be reported if multiple injections were performed. For 2018, the CPT language convention of optional plural, ie, adding the plural form of a word in parentheses, and in this case the parentheses around the "s" in "injection(s)" to clarify that code 36468 is reported once per limb or trunk, regardless of the number of injections performed. The unit of service for code 36468 is the limb or trunk, not the number of injection(s). Guidelines and parenthetical notes have been added to clarify this.

Codes 36470 and 36471 have been revised to specify the type of veins treated. Prior to 2018, these codes only described injection of sclerosing solution of a single vein (36470) or multiple veins (36471), without specifying the condition of the vein. This lack of specificity made it unclear that the codes did not include the treatment of spider veins, which made it difficult to distinguish them from code 36468, which specifies treatment of spider veins. For 2018, codes 36470 and 36471 have been revised to clarify that they describe procedures performed on incompetent veins other than spider veins, in order to make it easier to distinguish these codes from code 36468. Several clarifications on the appropriate reporting of treatment of incompetent veins codes (36468-36483) have been made to the guidelines and parenthetical notes and should be reviewed carefully.

Also, in accordance with the deletion of codes 29582 and 29583, the parenthetical note that follows code 36479 has been updated to reflect these deletions. Refer to the codebook and the Rationale for codes 29582 and 29583 for a full discussion of the changes.

Clinical Example (36465)

A female patient has painful, unilateral leg swelling that increases during the course of the day while at her job, which requires her to stand for a significant portion of the day. She was diagnosed with great saphenous vein insufficiency with resultant superficial varicosities. She chooses to undergo foam chemical ablation of the great saphenous vein under local anesthesia.

Description of Procedure (36465)

Ultrasound guidance is used to localize the primary target truncal vein (eg, great saphenous vein) as well as map and mark the entire length of the target vein. The target vein is accessed under ultrasound guidance (not separately reportable). A guidewire is introduced using the Seldinger technique. A dilator is advanced over the guidewire, and the dilator is exchanged for a sheath. The guidewire is removed, and the sheath is flushed. With the leg elevated, noncompounded foam sclerosant is injected through the sheath with ultrasound monitoring to identify arrival at the saphenofemoral junction. Manual compression is performed to prevent flow of foam sclerosant into the common femoral vein. Chemical agent administration is stopped. The treated vein is observed with ultrasound to ensure appropriate localization of noncompounded foam sclerosant. Repeat ultrasound is performed to confirm successful vein ablation. After a period of continued compression, the catheter and sheath are removed. The injected volume of noncompounded foam is recorded.

Clinical Example (36466)

A female patient has painful, unilateral leg swelling that increases during the course of the day while at her job, which requires her to stand for a significant portion of the day. She was diagnosed with great saphenous vein and small saphenous vein insufficiency with resultant superficial varicosities. She chooses to undergo foam chemical ablation of the great saphenous and anterior accessory saphenous veins under local anesthesia.

Description of Procedure (36466)

Ultrasound guidance is used to localize the primary target truncal vein (eg, great saphenous vein) as well as map and mark the entire length of target vein. The target vein is accessed under ultrasound guidance (not separately reportable). A guidewire is introduced using Seldinger technique. A dilator is advanced over the guidewire, and the dilator is exchanged for a sheath. The guidewire is removed, and the sheath is flushed. With the leg elevated, noncompounded foam sclerosant is injected through the sheath with ultrasound monitoring to identify arrival at the saphenofemoral junction. Manual compression is performed to prevent the flow of foam sclerosant into the common femoral vein. Chemical agent administration is stopped. The treated vein is observed with ultrasound to ensure successful ablation. After a period of continued compression of the outflow vein, the catheter and sheath are removed. The injected volume of noncompounded foam sclerosant is recorded. The entire process is repeated for a second truncal vein (eg, anterior accessory saphenous vein).

Clinical Example (36482)

A female patient has painful, unilateral leg swelling that increases during the course of the day while at her job, which requires her to stand for a significant portion of the day. She was diagnosed with great saphenous vein insufficiency with resultant superficial varicosities. She chooses to undergo chemical adhesive endovenous ablation therapy of the great saphenous vein under local anesthesia.

Description of Procedure (36482)

A confirmatory ultrasound is performed to identify the target vein and note tributary branches. An access point is identified, and the overlying skin is injected with local anesthetic. Using ultrasound guidance and the Seldinger technique, intravascular access is obtained in the target vein. A catheter is then introduced and guided along the vein. The ultrasound probe is used for manual pressure to compress the outflow of the vein, confirming apposition of the walls. The chemical adhesive is injected under ultrasound visualization. After a period of continued compression of the outflow vein, the catheter and sheath are removed.

Clinical Example (36483)

A female patient has painful, unilateral leg swelling that increases during the course of the day while at her job, which requires her to stand for a significant portion of the day. She was diagnosed with great and small saphenous vein insufficiency with resultant superficial varicosities. She chooses to undergo chemical adhesive endovenous ablation therapy of the great and small saphenous vein under local anesthesia.

Description of Procedure (36483)

After performing endovascular ablative therapy of a first vein with chemical adhesive (separately reported), a second target vein is identified using ultrasound, noting tributary branches. An access point is identified, and the overlying skin is injected with local anesthetic. Using ultrasound guidance and the Seldinger technique, intravascular access is obtained in the target vein. A catheter is introduced and guided along the vein. The ultrasound probe is used for manual pressure to compress the outflow of the vein, confirming apposition of the walls. The chemical adhesive is injected under ultrasound visualization. After a period of continued compression of the outflow vein, the catheter and sheath are removed.

36511	Therapeutic apheresis; for white blood cells
36512	for red blood cells
36513	for platelets

▶(Report 36513 only when platelets are removed by apheresis for treatment of the patient. Do not report 36513 for donor platelet collections)◀

Rationale

A parenthetical note to provide instruction regarding the reporting of code 36513 has been added after code 36513. During an AMA RUC review, it was found that claims data indicated that there may be misuse of code 36513. A review of the procedure determined that it was inappropriate to report code 36513 for platelets harvested for donor collection purposes. As a result, a new parenthetical note has been added to allow reporting of this code only when platelet removal by apheresis is performed as a treatment for patients from whom the platelets have been withdrawn. This code should not be reported if the procedure is performed for the treatment of a different individual.

36514	for plasma pheresis

▶(36515 has been deleted. For therapeutic apheresis with extracorporeal immunoadsorption and plasma reinfusion, use 36516)◀

▲ 36516	with extracorporeal immunoadsorption, selective adsorption or selective filtration and plasma reinfusion

(For professional evaluation, use modifier 26)

36522	Photopheresis, extracorporeal

▶(For dialysis services, see 90935-90999)◀

▶(For ultrafiltration, use 90999)◀

▶(For therapeutic apheresis for white blood cells, red blood cells, platelets and plasma pheresis, see 36511, 36512, 36513, 36514)◀

▶(For therapeutic apheresis extracorporeal adsorption procedures, use 36516)◀

Rationale

In an effort to ensure that the CPT code set reflects current clinical practice, code 36515 has been deleted due to extraordinarily low volume compared to code 36516. Code 36515 was used to report therapeutic apheresis with extracorporeal immunoadsorption and plasma reinfusion. An instructional parenthetical note directing users to code 36516 has been added for reporting therapeutic apheresis with extracorporeal immunoadsorption and plasma reinfusion.

In accordance with the deletion of code 36515, code 36516 has been revised to include immunoadsorption. Appropriate instructional parenthetical notes have been added to the Vascular Injection Procedure subsection of the Surgery section and the Dialysis subsection of the Medicine section. These changes were initiated after code 36516 appeared on the list of potentially misvalued codes.

Clinical Example (36516)

A 35-year-old male with familial hypercholesterolemia has atherosclerosis and elevated low-density lipoprotein cholesterol that has not been satisfactorily controlled with maximum medical therapy.

Description of Procedure (36516)

During the procedure, the apheresis medicine physician is responsible for the patient's well-being while on the machine. The physician periodically assesses the clinical status of the patient, paying particular attention to the vital signs flow sheet, the patient's color, urine output, mental status (if patient is awake), and other relevant parameters. The physician monitors the patient for the development of reactions to the infusion of adsorbed autologous plasma or for complaints suggestive of active coronary disease and orders supplemental treatments, as necessary. Variations in clinical status or vital signs are repeatedly evaluated to determine whether to continue the procedure to its intended extent of whole blood processing. Given the inherent level of acuity of patients undergoing this procedure, the apheresis medicine physician is the first responder in case of adverse clinical events or emergencies that arise during the procedure. Communications with other physicians and patient care providers during this phase are performed, as needed, by the apheresis medicine physician predicated on the clinical status of the patient and the need for any changes in the care plan due to clinical instability.

Dialysis Circuit

+▲ **36908** Transcatheter placement of intravascular stent(s), central dialysis segment, performed through dialysis circuit, including all imaging and radiological supervision and interpretation required to perform the stenting, and all angioplasty in the central dialysis segment (List separately in addition to code for primary procedure)

(Use 36908 in conjunction with 36818-36833, 36901, 36902, 36903, 36904, 36905, 36906)

(Do not report 36908 in conjunction with 36907)

(Report 36908 once for all stenting performed within the central dialysis segment)

Rationale

Add-on code 36908 has been editorially revised so that the terminology is consistent with the terminology of the other codes in this family. The terminology for the family of codes of 36902-36909 indicates that these services include "all imaging and radiological supervision and interpretation." Code 36908 has been revised by adding the term "and" between the phrases "all imaging" and "radiological supervision."

Endovascular Revascularization (Open or Percutaneous, Transcatheter)

37220 Revascularization, endovascular, open or percutaneous, iliac artery, unilateral, initial vessel; with transluminal angioplasty

37221 with transluminal stent placement(s), includes angioplasty within the same vessel, when performed

▶(Use 37220, 37221 in conjunction with 34701-34711, 34845, 34846, 34847, 34848, 0254T only when 37220 or 37221 are performed outside the treatment zone of the endograft)◀

+ **37222** Revascularization, endovascular, open or percutaneous, iliac artery, each additional ipsilateral iliac vessel; with transluminal angioplasty (List separately in addition to code for primary procedure)

(Use 37222 in conjunction with 37220, 37221)

+ **37223** with transluminal stent placement(s), includes angioplasty within the same vessel, when performed (List separately in addition to code for primary procedure)

(Use 37223 in conjunction with 37221)

▶(Use 37222, 37223 in conjunction with 34701-34711, 34845, 34846, 34847, 34848, 0254T only when 37222 or 37223 are performed outside the treatment zone of the endograft)◀

Rationale

In support of the changes in reporting endovascular repair of abdominal aorta and/or iliac arteries procedures, the inclusionary parenthetical notes that follow codes 37220 and 37221 (endovascular iliac artery revascularization) and add-on codes 37222 and 37223 have been revised to reflect the appropriate new codes and to make the language consistent with the language in the new guidelines.

Refer to the codebook and the Rationale for codes 34701-34713, 34714, 34715, and 34716 for a full discussion of these changes.

Intravascular Ultrasound Services

Intravascular ultrasound (IVUS) services include all transducer manipulations and repositioning within the specific vessel being examined during a diagnostic procedure or before, during, and/or after therapeutic intervention (eg, stent or stent graft placement, angioplasty, atherectomy, embolization, thrombolysis, transcatheter biopsy).

IVUS is included in the work described by codes 37191, 37192, 37193, 37197 (intravascular vena cava [IVC] filter placement, repositioning and removal, and intravascular foreign body retrieval) and should not be separately reported with those procedures. If a lesion extends across the margins of one vessel into another, this should be reported with a single code despite imaging more than one vessel.

Non-selective and/or selective vascular catheterization may be separately reportable (eg, 36005-36248).

(37250, 37251 have been deleted. To report noncoronary intravascular ultrasound during diagnostic evaluation and/or therapeutic intervention, see 37252, 37253)

+ **37252** Intravascular ultrasound (noncoronary vessel) during diagnostic evaluation and/or therapeutic intervention, including radiological supervision and interpretation; initial noncoronary vessel (List separately in addition to code for primary procedure)

+ **37253** each additional noncoronary vessel (List separately in addition to code for primary procedure)

(Use 37253 in conjunction with 37252)

▶(Report 37252, 37253 in conjunction with 33361, 33362, 33363, 33364, 33365, 33366, 33367, 33368, 33369, 33477, 33880, 33881, 33883, 33884, 33886, 34701, 34702, 34703, 34704, 34705, 34706, 34707, 34708, 34709, 34710, 34711, 34841, 34842, 34843, 34844, 34845, 34846, 34847, 34848, 36010, 36011, 36012, 36013, 36014, 36015, 36100, 36140, 36160, 36200, 36215, 36216, 36217, 36218, 36221, 36222,

36223, 36224, 36225, 36226, 36227, 36228, 36245,
36246, 36247, 36248, 36251, 36252, 36253, 36254,
36481, 36555-36571, 36578, 36580, 36581, 36582,
36583, 36584, 36585, 36595, 36901, 36902, 36903,
36904, 36905, 36906, 36907, 36908, 36909, 37184,
37185, 37186, 37187, 37188, 37200, 37211, 37212,
37213, 37214, 37215, 37216, 37218, 37220, 37221,
37222, 37223, 37224, 37225, 37226, 37227, 37228,
37229, 37230, 37231, 37232, 37233, 37234, 37235,
37236, 37237, 37238, 37239, 37241, 37242, 37243,
37244, 37246, 37247, 37248, 37249, 61623, 75600,
75605, 75625, 75630, 75635, 75705, 75710, 75716,
75726, 75731, 75733, 75736, 75741, 75743, 75746,
75756, 75774, 75805, 75807, 75810, 75820, 75822,
75825, 75827, 75831, 75833, 75860, 75870, 75872,
75885, 75887, 75889, 75891, 75893, 75894, 75898,
75901, 75902, 75956, 75957, 75958, 75959, 75970,
76000, 77001, 0075T, 0076T, 0234T, 0235T, 0236T, 0237T,
0238T, 0254T, 0338T)◄

(Do not report 37252, 37253 in conjunction with 37191,
37192, 37193, 37197)

Rationale

In 2016, codes 37252 and 37253 were established to
bundle intravascular ultrasound during venous and arterial
contrast angiography and endovascular intervention with
radiological supervision and interpretation. After these
codes were established, claims for code pairs that were
previously and appropriately allowed were being rejected.
Consequently, an instructional parenthetical note that
includes a list of codes to be reported in conjunction with
codes 37252 and 37253 has been established.

Hemic and Lymphatic Systems

General

Bone Marrow or Stem Cell Services/ Procedures

▲ **38220** Diagnostic bone marrow; aspiration(s)

►(Do not report 38220 in conjunction with 38221)◄

►(For diagnostic bone marrow biopsy[ies] and
aspiration[s] performed at the same session, use
38222)◄

►(For aspiration of bone marrow for bone graft, spine
surgery only, use 20939)◄

►(For bone marrow aspiration[s] for platelet-rich stem
cell injection, use 0232T)◄

▲ **38221** biopsy(ies)

►(Do not report 38221 in conjunction with 38220)◄

►(For diagnostic bone marrow biopsy[ies] and
aspiration[s] performed at the same session, use
38222)◄

● **38222** biopsy(ies) and aspiration(s)

►(Do not report 38222 in conjunction with 38220 and
38221)◄

►(For bilateral procedure, report 38220, 38221, 38222
with modifier 50)◄

►(For bone marrow biopsy interpretation, use 88305)◄

38230 Bone marrow harvesting for transplantation; allogeneic

38232 autologous

►(For autologous and allogeneic blood-derived
peripheral stem cell harvesting for transplantation, see
38205, 38206)◄

►(For diagnostic bone marrow aspiration[s], see 38220,
38222)◄

►(For aspiration of bone marrow for bone graft, spine
surgery only, use 20939)◄

►(For bone marrow aspiration[s] for platelet-rich stem
cell injection, use 0232T)◄

Rationale

Codes 20939 and 38222 have been added and codes
38220 and 38221 have been revised to reflect changes
made for accurate reporting of bone marrow biopsy
procedures. In addition, a number of parenthetical notes
have been added and/or revised to accommodate the
changes made.

The AMA RUC RAW recommended a review of code
38221 for high-volume growth. During the review,
consideration was given to clarify the intended use of
codes 38220 and 38221 in order to differentiate diagnostic
bone marrow aspirations from therapeutic versions of this
procedure. As a result, a decision was made to revise the
descriptors for existing codes, add new codes, and provide
guidance regarding appropriate reporting for bone
aspiration procedures.

Code 20939 has been established to report therapeutic
bone marrow aspiration procedures. This code has been
added to allow separate reporting for therapeutic bone
marrow aspirations. This code differs from other codes
(38222, 38220, 38221) added or revised to allow separate
reporting of bone marrow aspiration or biopsy performed

for diagnostic procedures. Code 20939 is specifically intended for reporting therapeutic aspiration performed for spine procedures. Code 20999 should be used if the aspiration is performed for bone grafting treatment performed for something other than the spine. Parenthetical notes provide instructions on the use of code 20939 for various procedures including reporting for bilateral therapeutic aspirations; use of code 20939 in conjunction with other spine procedures; use of code 20939 only for spine surgery; appropriate reporting for aspirations for platelet-rich stem cell injections; and appropriate codes for reporting diagnostic bone marrow aspiration procedures.

Code 38222 has been added to allow reporting of diagnostic bone marrow biopsies performed in conjunction with bone marrow aspiration procedures. This was added to the code set to simplify reporting when both procedures are performed.

To accommodate separate reporting for diagnostic bone marrow aspiration and diagnostic bone marrow biopsy, codes 38220 and 38221 have been revised to reflect that both procedures are diagnostic procedures. In addition, code 38220 now notes that any number of aspirations are included as part of the procedure. In code 38221, the phrase "needle or trocar" has been removed and the optional plural "ies" has been added to "biopsy" to indicate that any number of biopsies performed are inherently included as part of the procedure and not separately reported.

In addition, a number of parenthetical notes have been added or deleted to accommodate the change. This includes deletion of the following: parenthetical notes that restrict reporting the diagnostic bone marrow aspiration code in conjunction with the diagnostic bone marrow biopsy code (because code 38222 is intended to be reported when both procedures are performed); direction for reporting both bone marrow biopsy and aspiration; instruction for reporting marrow aspirations performed for the purpose of bone grafting for spine; direction for reporting marrow aspiration for platelet-rich stem cell injection; and instructions for reporting diagnostic aspiration performed bilaterally.

Clinical Example (38220)

A 59-year-old male with known acute myeloid leukemia with rare circulating blasts requires aspirate for assessment of relapse and clonal evolution.

Description of Procedure (38220)

The physician makes a small incision with a scalpel, inserts and advances the bone marrow aspiration needle to the periosteal bone surface position, and drills the needle into the posterior iliac crest marrow space. The trocar is then removed. The patient is questioned and warned about pain, and approximately 3 ml of bone marrow is aspirated and used to prepare microscopic slides at the bedside with a technologist's assistance after the presence of at least one spicule is confirmed. If necessary, the needle is repositioned after extraction from bone, and the process is repeated maintaining sterile techniques until adequate spicules are identified. Additional aspirates are obtained for culture, cytogenetics, flow cytometry, and molecular diagnostics. The physician reintroduces the trocar and extracts the needle. The physician places pressure on the wound site for hemostasis, and the wound is cleansed and bandaged.

Clinical Example (38221)

A 50-year-old male with newly diagnosed Hodgkins disease presents with adenopathy and fever. The patient requires a bone marrow biopsy for staging to determine bone marrow involvement.

Description of Procedure (38221)

The physician makes a small incision with a scalpel, inserts and advances the bone marrow biopsy needle to the periosteal bone surface position, and drills the needle into the posterior iliac crest marrow space. The physician removes the trochar. The patient is questioned regarding signs of pain. The physician drills the needle about 2 cm into the bone/bone marrow, replaces the trocar to make sure that the biopsy is at least 2 cm in length, and removes the trocar again. The physician rocks the needle back and forth to break off a biopsy. The biopsy is removed. The physician assesses bone marrow and biopsy length for adequacy. If adequate, the biopsy needle is removed; if necessary, a second biopsy is performed. If not, the physician places pressure on wound site for hemostasis, cleanses the wound area, and bandages it. If the first biopsy is inadequate, the physician drills the needle again about 2 cm into the bone/bone marrow. The physician replaces the trocar to make sure that the biopsy is at least 2 cm in length. The physician rocks needle back and forth to break off a biopsy. The needle is removed, and the biopsy is removed. The biopsy is assessed to make certain it is bone marrow and is measured for length and assessed for adequacy. If biopsy is less than 2 cm, another biopsy is done. The physician places pressure on the wound site for hemostasis, and the wound is cleansed and bandaged.

Clinical Example (38222)

A 59-year-old female presents with peripheral blood pancytopenia with nondiagnostic iron studies and level B12. The patient requires bone marrow biopsy and aspiration for diagnosis.

Description of Procedure (38222)

The physician makes a small incision with a scalpel, inserts and advances the bone marrow aspiration needle to the periosteal bone surface position, and drills the needle into the posterior iliac crest marrow space. The trocar is removed. The patient is questioned and warned about pain, and approximately 3 ml of bone marrow is aspirated and used to prepare microscopic slides at the bedside with a technologist's assistance after the presence of at least one spicule is confirmed. If necessary, the needle is repositioned after extraction from bone and the process is repeated maintaining sterile techniques until adequate spicules are identified. Additional aspirates are obtained for culture, cytogenetics, flow cytometry, and molecular diagnostics. The physician introduces the biopsy needle through the same skin hole but to a different spot in the bone surface. The needle is advanced to the periosteal bone surface position and drilled into the posterior iliac crest marrow space. The physician removes the trochar. The patient is questioned regarding signs of pain. The physician drills the needle about 2 cm into the bone/bone marrow of patient. The physician replaces the trocar to make sure that the biopsy is at least 2 cm in length and removes the trocar again. The physician then rocks needle back and forth to break off a biopsy. The biopsy is removed. The physician assesses the bone marrow and biopsy length for adequacy. If adequate, the biopsy needle is removed; if necessary, a second biopsy is performed. If not, the physician places pressure on wound site for hemostasis and cleanses and bandages the wound area.

Transplantation and Post-Transplantation Cellular Infusions

Hematopoietic cell transplantation (HCT) refers to the infusion of hematopoietic progenitor cells (HPC) obtained from bone marrow, peripheral blood apheresis, and/or umbilical cord blood. These procedure codes (38240-38243) include physician monitoring of multiple physiologic parameters, physician verification of cell processing, evaluation of the patient during as well as immediately before and after the HPC/lymphocyte infusion, physician presence during the HPC/lymphocyte infusion with associated direct physician supervision of clinical staff, and management of uncomplicated adverse events (eg, nausea, urticaria) during the infusion, which is not separately reportable.

HCT may be autologous (when the HPC donor and recipient are the same person) or allogeneic (when the HPC donor and recipient are not the same person). Code 38241 is used to report any autologous transplant while 38240 is used to report an allogeneic transplant. In some cases allogeneic transplants involve more than one donor and cells from each donor are infused sequentially whereby one unit of 38240 is reported for each donor infused. Code 38242 is used to report a donor lymphocyte infusion. Code 38243 is used to report a HPC boost from the original allogeneic HPC donor. A lymphocyte infusion or HPC boost can occur days, months or even years after the initial hematopoietic cell transplant. HPC boost represents an infusion of hematopoietic progenitor cells from the original donor that is being used to treat post-transplant cytopenia(s). Codes 38240, 38242, and 38243 should not be reported together on the same date of service.

If a separately identifiable evaluation and management service is performed on the same date of service, the appropriate E/M service code, including office or other outpatient services, established (99211-99215), hospital observation services (99217-99220, 99224-99226), hospital inpatient services (99221-99223, 99231-99239), and inpatient neonatal and pediatric critical care (99471, 99472, 99475, 99476) may be reported, using modifier 25, in addition to 38240, 38242 or 38243. Post-transplant infusion management of adverse reactions is reported separately using the appropriate E/M, prolonged service or critical care code(s). In accordance with place of service and facility reporting guidelines, the fluid used to administer the cells and other infusions for incidental hydration (eg, 96360, 96361) are not separately reportable. Similarly, infusion(s) of any medication(s) concurrently with the transplant infusion are not separately reportable. However, hydration or administration of medications (eg, antibiotics, narcotics) unrelated to the transplant are separately reportable using modifier 59.

38240	Hematopoietic progenitor cell (HPC); allogeneic transplantation per donor
38241	autologous transplantation
# 38243	HPC boost
38242	Allogeneic lymphocyte infusions

▶(For diagnostic bone marrow aspiration[s], see 38220, 38222)◀

▶(For aspiration of bone marrow for bone graft, spine surgery only, use 20939)◀

▶(For bone marrow aspiration[s] for platelet-rich stem cell injection, use 0232T)◀

▶(For compatibility studies, see 81379-81383, 86812, 86813, 86816, 86817, 86821)◀

Surgery / Hemic and Lymphatic Systems 38100-38999

Rationale

The parenthetical notes that follow code 38242 have been revised and new parenthetical notes have been added to address reporting of aspiration procedures. These parentheticals direct users to the appropriate codes to use when reporting diagnostic bone marrow aspiration, marrow aspiration to facilitate bone grafting for spine surgery, and marrow aspiration for stem cell injection. Refer to the codebook and the Rationale for code 38222 for a full discussion of the changes.

In support of the deletion of code 86822, the cross-reference parenthetical note for compatibility studies that follows code 38242 (allogeneic lymphocyte infusions) has been revised with the removal of code 86822. Refer to the codebook and the Rationale for the deletion of code 86822 for a full discussion of the changes.

Rationale

Code 38573 has been established in the Hemic and Lymphatic Systems, Lymph Nodes and Lymphatic Channels, Laparoscopy subsection for reporting laparoscopic total pelvic lymphadenectomy, periaortic lymph node sampling, peritoneal washings and biopsies, and omentectomy. Prior to 2018, no laparoscopic code existed that contained all of the elements of code 38573, including omentectomy. An exclusionary parenthetical note has been added to exclude the use of code 38573 with any open or laparoscopic lymphadenectomy; radical lymphadenectomy; omentectomy; surgical laparoscopy of the abdomen, peritoneum, and omentum; omentopexy; laparoscopic supracervical hysterectomy; laparoscopic radical hysterectomy; and laparoscopic vaginal hysterectomy.

Lymph Nodes and Lymphatic Channels

Laparoscopy

Surgical laparoscopy always includes diagnostic laparoscopy. To report a diagnostic laparoscopy (peritoneoscopy) (separate procedure), use 49320.

38570 Laparoscopy, surgical; with retroperitoneal lymph node sampling (biopsy), single or multiple

38571 with bilateral total pelvic lymphadenectomy

38572 with bilateral total pelvic lymphadenectomy and periaortic lymph node sampling (biopsy), single or multiple

(For drainage of lymphocele to peritoneal cavity, use 49323)

● **38573** with bilateral total pelvic lymphadenectomy and periaortic lymph node sampling, peritoneal washings, peritoneal biopsy(ies), omentectomy, and diaphragmatic washings, including diaphragmatic and other serosal biopsy(ies), when performed

▶(Do not report 38573 in conjunction with 38562, 38564, 38570, 38571, 38572, 38589, 38770, 38780, 49255, 49320, 49326, 58541, 58542, 58543, 58544, 58548, 58550, 58552, 58553, 58554)◀

Clinical Example (38573)

A 62-year-old female has undergone a laparoscopic hysterectomy and bilateral salpingo-oophorectomy for what was thought to be a benign ovarian mass. Subsequently, the final pathology showed a grade 1 ovarian cancer. The patient was counseled about her risks of recurrence and was offered a laparoscopic surgical staging of the ovarian malignancy.

Description of Procedure (38573)

A bimanual and rectovaginal exam is performed under anesthesia to assess nodularity in the cul de sac or pelvic masses. A Foley catheter is inserted into the bladder. A sponge stick is placed in the vagina. A diagnostic laparoscopy is performed, 5–6 laparoscopic ports are placed in the abdomen ranging in size from 5 to 12 mm. The patient is assessed for intra-abdominal metastases, diaphragmatic metastases, and retroperitoneal adenopathy. Biopsies of any suspicious lesions are performed. Adhesions from the prior surgery involving bowel and omentum are lysed. The bowels and bowel mesentery are systematically evaluated for the presence of metastatic disease. Peritoneal cytology is obtained. The patient is placed in steep Trendelenburg, and the bowel is mobilized and dissected out of the pelvis. The retroperitoneum is opened bilaterally to identify the ureters and paravesical and pararectal spaces. A pelvic lymphadenectomy is performed. The nodes from the external and internal iliac, lower common iliac, and obturator spaces are placed in a bag and removed separately. The peritoneum over the aorta and vena cava are opened, and ureters, inferior mesenteric artery, and renal vessels are identified. Periaortic lymph node sampling is performed. Lymph nodes are placed in a bag and removed from the abdomen. An omentectomy is performed by dissecting it free from the transverse colon and stomach. The omentum is placed in a bag and removed through a small mini-laparotomy incision. After completing the staging, hemostasis is confirmed, and the pelvis and abdomen are inspected for any injuries. The mini-laparotomy is closed. The instruments and ports are removed, and all port sites are closed.

Digestive System

Pharynx, Adenoids, and Tonsils

Excision, Destruction

42894   Resection of pharyngeal wall requiring closure with myocutaneous or fasciocutaneous flap or free muscle, skin, or fascial flap with microvascular anastomosis

(When combined with radical neck dissection, use also 38720)

(For limited pharyngectomy with radical neck dissection, use 38720 with 42890)

►(For flap used for reconstruction, see 15730, 15733, 15734, 15756, 15757, 15758)◄

Rationale

An instructional parenthetical note that follows code 42894 has been revised to remove deleted code 15732 and replaced with codes 15730 and 15733. These codes are intended to report midface flap and myocutaneous or fasciocutaneous flap procedures of the head and neck.

Refer to the codebook and the Rationale for codes 15730-15738 for a full discussion of the changes.

Esophagus

Excision

▲ **43112**   Total or near total esophagectomy, with thoracotomy; with pharyngogastrostomy or cervical esophagogastrostomy, with or without pyloroplasty (ie, McKeown esophagectomy or tri-incisional esophagectomy)

Rationale

Code 43112 has been revised to include a parenthetical reference. Addition of the phrase "(ie, McKeown esophagectomy or tri-incisional esophagectomy)" instructs the user that the noted procedures are included/intended for the procedure reported with code 43112. The use of "ie" indicates that the procedure within the parentheses is included in the procedures described by code 43112, and it is not intended as an example, which is indicated by the use of "eg." Refer to the codebook and the Rationale for codes 43286-43288 for a full discussion of the changes.

Clinical Example (43112)

A 70-year-old male presents with progressive dysphagia. Testing revealed a mid-esophageal adenocarcinoma above the level of the carina. He received neoadjuvant chemotherapy and radiation therapy. He now undergoes surgical resection.

Description of Procedure (43112)

Under general anesthesia, one lung ventilation is initiated. A right posterolateral thoracotomy is performed, dividing extrathoracic muscles with electrocautery for hemostasis and resecting a 1-cm segment of the sixth rib posteriorly to facilitate spreading of the ribs. The chest is explored. The right lung and mediastinum are carefully palpated to assess for metastatic cancer and any unsuspected pulmonary nodules. The right lung is carefully retracted anteriorly while blood pressure is monitored. The inferior pulmonary ligament is divided. The mediastinal pleura overlying the esophagus is divided and resected up to the level of the azygos vein. The azygos vein is divided, and the mediastinal pleura opened to the level of the thoracic inlet. If it will pass, an orogastric tube may be placed to decompress the stomach. A mediastinal lymphadenectomy may be performed (separately reported). Using the ultrasonic coagulating shears, electrocautery, and blunt dissection, the esophagus and periesophageal tissues are carefully circumferentially mobilized from just above the diaphragm to just below the thoracic inlet. A rubber drain placed around the esophagus may aid in esophageal traction and exposure. The vagus nerve is divided above the level of the azygos vein, with care taken to protect the right recurrent laryngeal nerve. Care is taken to avoid injury to the membranous portions of the trachea, bronchi, thoracic aorta, thoracic duct, and the recurrent laryngeal nerves. The chest is carefully evaluated for hemostasis and irrigated. Two chest tubes are placed and connected to an appropriate collection device. The right lung is reexpanded. The ribs are carefully reapproximated with pericostal sutures, and the chest incision is closed in multiple layers of absorbable suture. Sterile dressings are applied. The entire surgical field is taken down with care to maintain sterility of the surgical equipment and instrumentation for the abdominal and cervical portions of the procedure. The patient is placed in a supine position. The double lumen endotracheal tube is removed, and a single lumen endotracheal tube is placed. The surgeon completes the positioning; additional special positioning of the neck and arms is required. The skin of the neck, anterolateral chest, and abdomen is prepared from the lower ears to the pubis and laterally to each midaxillary line, after which the surgeon scrubs, gowns, and drapes the patient. A second preincision surgical pause is completed. An upper midline incision is made, and the abdomen is explored for metastatic disease and the feasibility of esophagogastric junction resection. Subcostal retractors and a liver retractor are placed to allow visualization of the esophageal hiatus. The mobilization of the stomach begins by widely resecting the gastrohepatic omentum until it reaches the right crus. The right crus is visualized and dissected, the peritoneum overlying the esophagogastric junction is incised, followed by the dissection of the left crus of the diaphragm. It is important to handle the stomach gently and with care during the procedure. Using ultrasonic coagulating shears, the greater curvature of the stomach is mobilized by dividing the gastrocolic omentum, taking great care to preserve the right gastroepiploic artery. Short gastric vessels are similarly divided, with care taken to protect the spleen. A Kocher maneuver is performed to mobilize the proximal duodenum and the hepatic flexure is mobilized again, protecting the right gastroepiploic artery. The diaphragm anterior to the esophagus is divided. A wide en bloc dissection of the esophagus, including all periesophageal tissue flush with the posterior pericardium, both parietal pleura, and the adventitia of the thoracic aorta, is carefully performed up to the level of the previously mobilized intrathoracic esophagus. Additional posterior attachments of the stomach are divided by retracting the stomach anteriorly. Celiac axis lymph nodes are resected with the specimen. The left gastric artery is divided flush with the celiac axis. A pyloromyotomy or pyloroplasty is performed. The pylorus is covered with a remnant of omentum. With mobilization of the distal and middle esophagus and stomach completed, attention is turned to the left neck. An incision is made along the anterior border of the left sternocleidomastoid muscle. The sternocleidomastoid muscle and underlying carotid sheath and its contents are retracted to the left, carefully avoiding undue compression on the carotid artery. The

neck strap muscles are divided. The trachea and thyroid gland are retracted to the right, carefully avoiding pressure on the tracheoesophageal groove and injury to the left recurrent laryngeal nerve. The middle thyroid vein and inferior thyroid artery are identified, ligated, and divided, and the underlying cervical esophagus is identified. Carefully avoiding injury to the left recurrent laryngeal nerve in the tracheoesophageal groove, the cervical esophagus is encircled with a rubber drain, and the remaining intrathoracic esophagus is carefully bluntly dissected free within the thoracic inlet. The cervical esophagus is divided with a surgical stapler. Frozen section pathology confirms that the proximal esophageal margin is free of tumor. The intrathoracic esophagus and esophagogastric junction are delivered out of the mediastinum through the diaphragmatic hiatus and placed on the anterior chest wall along with the mobilized stomach. The mediastinum is inspected for bleeding. The mediastinum is carefully packed with gauze packs, if necessary, to facilitate hemostasis. A gastric tube approximately 5 cm in diameter is created using multiple firings of the stapling device starting just proximal to the pyloroplasty. With each progressive application of the stapler toward the gastric fundus, gentle traction is placed on the tip of the greater curvature of the stomach to ensure construction of as long and straight a gastric conduit as possible. The gastroesophageal junction and juxtaposed tumor are resected with grossly free margins. The longitudinal staple line is oversewn with running suture. Frozen section pathology confirms that the gastric margin is free of tumor. The previously placed packs within the mediastinum are carefully removed, and the mediastinum inspected for bleeding. Once hemostasis has been ensured, the tip of the mobilized stomach is gently grasped with one hand, which is then inserted through the diaphragmatic hiatus and advanced superiorly through the middle mediastinum behind the trachea and beneath the aortic arch, until the tip of the stomach can be grasped by the second hand inserted downward into the superior and middle mediastinum through the neck incision. Throughout this positioning of the gastric conduit in the original esophageal bed, careful attention to the arterial blood pressure is mandatory so that prolonged hypotension is avoided. Once the tip of the stomach is grasped in the neck, gentle traction on the stomach through the neck incision along with simultaneous gentle pushing of the distal stomach from below results in an adequate length of stomach coming through the neck incision for an esophagogastric anastomosis. Care is taken to ensure that the stomach is not twisted as it is brought through the middle mediastinum and out the neck incision.

★ = Telemedicine ✚ = Add-on code ⚕ = FDA approval pending # = Resequenced code

Through the abdominal incision, several sutures between the diaphragmatic hiatus and adjacent stomach are placed to minimize the risk of subsequent herniation of intestine into the chest through the diaphragmatic hiatus. Hemostasis is carefully checked for. A feeding jejunostomy tube may be inserted (separately reported). After careful inspection for hemostasis, the abdomen is copiously irrigated. The abdominal incision is closed in multiple layers. Sterile dressings are applied to the abdominal incision. Attention is redirected to the neck. A side-to-side esophagogastric anastomosis is created using the linear stapling device for the posterior portion of the anastomosis. Prior to completing the anterior portion of the anastomosis, a nasogastric tube is placed under direct visualization. The anterior portion of the anastomosis is completed with an inner layer of running absorbable suture and an outer layer of interrupted permanent suture. After a careful inspection for hemostasis, the neck wound is irrigated, a cervical wound drain is placed, and the neck incision is closed with multiple layers of absorbable suture. Sterile dressings are applied to the neck incision. The nasogastric tube is secured in place.

Laparoscopy

43280 Laparoscopy, surgical, esophagogastric fundoplasty (eg, Nissen, Toupet procedures)

▶(Do not report 43280 in conjunction with 43279, 43281, 43282)◀

▶(For open esophagogastric fundoplasty, see 43327, 43328)◀

(For laparoscopy, surgical, esophageal sphincter augmentation procedure, placement of sphincter augmentation device, see43284, 43285)

(For esophagogastroduodenoscopy fundoplasty, partial or complete, transoral approach, use 43210)

43281 Laparoscopy, surgical, repair of paraesophageal hernia, includes fundoplasty, when performed; without implantation of mesh

43282   with implantation of mesh

▶(To report transabdominal paraesophageal hiatal hernia repair, see 43332, 43333)◀

▶(To report transthoracic diaphragmatic hernia repair, see 43334, 43335)◀

▶(Do not report 43281, 43282 in conjunction with 43280, 43450, 43453)◀

Rationale

A number of changes have been made to the existing parenthetical notes that follow codes 43280 and 43282. These include: (1) addition of codes 43281 and 43282 to the exclusionary parenthetical note that follows code 43280; (2) replacement of the term "approach" with the phrase "esophagogastric fundoplasty" in the instructional parenthetical note that follows code 43280; and (3) removal of codes 43213, 43214, 43220, 43233, 43249, and 49568 from the exclusionary parenthetical note for code 43282.

These changes were made to clarify the intended use of these codes. Codes 43281 and 43282 were not intended for use with code 43280. As a result, these codes have been added to the exclusionary parenthetical note that follows code 43280. In addition, codes 43213, 43214, 43220, 43233, 43249, and 49568 have been removed from the exclusionary parenthetical note that follows code 43282 to denote that these codes are not excluded from reporting laparoscopic mesh implantation. The procedures reported with codes 43213, 43214, 43220, 43233, and 43249 are performed via transoral endoscopy, and the procedure reported with code 49568 is performed via an open approach. Therefore, these codes are not excluded from being reported with laparoscopic procedures. Also, the cross references following code 43282 are no longer combined into one parenthetical note and have been placed into two separate parenthetical notes referencing codes for different hernia repairs. Finally, the language included in the instructional cross-reference parenthetical note for code 43280 now specifies "esophagogastric fundoplasty" to more clearly identify the open procedure that is being discussed in the parenthetical note.

● **43286** Esophagectomy, total or near total, with laparoscopic mobilization of the abdominal and mediastinal esophagus and proximal gastrectomy, with laparoscopic pyloric drainage procedure if performed, with open cervical pharyngogastrostomy or esophagogastrostomy (ie, laparoscopic transhiatal esophagectomy)

● **43287** Esophagectomy, distal two-thirds, with laparoscopic mobilization of the abdominal and lower mediastinal esophagus and proximal gastrectomy, with laparoscopic pyloric drainage procedure if performed, with separate thoracoscopic mobilization of the middle and upper mediastinal esophagus and thoracic esophagogastrostomy (ie, laparoscopic thoracoscopic esophagectomy, Ivor Lewis esophagectomy)

▶(Do not report 43287 in conjunction with 32551 for right tube thoracostomy)◀

● **43288** Esophagectomy, total or near total, with thoracoscopic mobilization of the upper, middle, and lower mediastinal esophagus, with separate laparoscopic proximal gastrectomy, with laparoscopic pyloric drainage procedure if performed, with open cervical pharyngogastrostomy or esophagogastrostomy (ie, thoracoscopic, laparoscopic and cervical incision esophagectomy, McKeown esophagectomy, tri-incisional esophagectomy)

▶(Do not report 43288 in conjunction with 32551 for right tube thoracostomy)◀

Rationale

Three new codes (43286, 43287, 43288) have been established to report esophagectomy performed via an open and laparoscopic approach (43286); via a thoracoscopic and laparoscopic approach (43287); and via a thoracoscopic, laparoscopic, and open approach (43288). A number of parenthetical notes have been added and/or revised to accommodate the addition of these new codes.

Code 43286 is intended to report a total or near total removal of the esophagus (esophagectomy). As noted in the descriptor, part of the procedure is performed via a laparoscopic approach (ie, mobilization of portions of the esophagus and proximal gastrectomy), while other portions of the procedure are accomplished via an open incision made in the neck (ie, "pharyngogastrostomy or esophagogastrostomy [ie, laparoscopic transhiatal esophagectomy]"). Code 43287 is intended to report removal of the distal two-thirds of the esophagus and includes a proximal gastrectomy as well as other services that may be necessary to complete the procedure.

Code 43287 differs from code 43286 in the amount of the esophagus that is removed and the additional work needed to mobilize the middle and upper mediastinal esophagus that is accomplished with a separate upper thoracoscopic procedure (identified in the code descriptor as "laparoscopic thoracoscopic esophagectomy" or as "Ivor Lewis esophagectomy"). This procedure requires separate preparation of the patient and separate exposure of the site via thoracoscopic access after completion of laparoscopic mobilization. Because right tube thoracostomy is inherent to this procedure, an exclusionary parenthetical note restricts the use of code 43287 in conjunction with code 32551 (tube thoracostomy). Code 43288 should be used to report a total or near total esophagectomy performed with thoracoscopic mobilization of the upper, middle, and lower mediastinal esophagus; laparoscopic proximal gastrectomy (with other services that may be necessary to facilitate completion of the removal procedure); and open cervical pharyngogastrostomy or esophagogastrostomy needed to complete the procedure. As indicated in the

descriptor, this procedure is a "tri-incisional esophagectomy" as it requires access through three locations (abdominal, thoracic, and cervical). Because right tube thoracostomy is inherent to this procedure, an exclusionary parenthetical note restricts the use of code 43288 in conjunction with code 32551 (tube thoracostomy).

Parenthetical notes that instruct the appropriate reporting of these codes in conjunction with other codes have been placed throughout the CPT code set. This includes notes that follow add-on code 32674 (thoracoscopic mediastinal and regional lymphadenectomy).

Clinical Example (43286)

A 72-year-old male presents with a history that includes gastroesophageal reflux, progressive dysphagia, and testing that revealed a distal esophageal adenocarcinoma arising within long segment Barrett's esophagus, with multifocal high-grade dysplasia. He undergoes esophageal resection and reconstruction.

Description of Procedure (43286)

If it will pass, an orogastric tube may be placed while the patient is under general anesthesia to decompress the stomach. Surgical laparoscopy is performed. Using local infiltrative anesthetic, the pneumoperitoneum is established to distend the abdomen, and the laparoscope is introduced. Gas flow and intra-abdominal pressure are carefully monitored so as not to impair ventilation or decrease venous return. Using local infiltrative anesthetic, in total, four to six 5-mm to 12-mm trocars are inserted through the anterior abdominal wall. The abdominal cavity and viscera are inspected to rule out metastatic disease. A liver retractor is inserted, and the liver is retracted to allow visualization of the esophageal hiatus. The mobilization of the stomach begins by widely resecting the gastrohepatic omentum until it reaches the right crus. The right crus is visualized, and the phrenoesophageal membrane is incised and dissected followed by the dissection of the left crus of the diaphragm. It is important to handle the stomach gently and with extreme care during the procedure. The greater curvature of the stomach is mobilized by dividing the short gastric vessels with the ultrasonic coagulating shears. Care is taken to protect the spleen. The gastrocolic omentum is divided, with care taken to preserve the right gastroepiploic artery. A Kocher maneuver is performed to mobilize the proximal duodenum. The posterior attachments of the stomach are divided by retracting the stomach anteriorly. Celiac axis lymph nodes are resected with the specimen. The left gastric artery is divided with an endovascular stapling device. An endoscopic pyloroplasty is performed in a Heineke-Mikulicz fashion. The pylorus is incised longitudinally and closed transversely with interrupted sutures. The pyloroplasty is covered with a remnant of omentum. Transhiatal dissection of the esophagus is performed. The diaphragm anterior to the esophagus is divided, and a circumferential dissection of the esophagus to above the level of the carina is performed. Care is taken to avoid opening the pleura. A gastric tube approximately 5 cm in diameter is created using multiple firings of the linear endoscopic stapler starting just proximal to the pyloroplasty. The gastroesophageal junction and juxtaposed tumor are resected with grossly free margins. The longitudinal staple line is oversewn with running suture. The tubularized gastric conduit is secured to the proximal stomach remnant with interrupted suture. A laparoscopic feeding jejunostomy tube may be inserted (separately reported). The abdomen is inspected to be sure hemostasis is adequate. The pneumoperitoneum is deflated. Attention is turned to the left neck, where an incision is made along the anterior border of the sternocleidomastoid muscle. The sternocleidomastoid muscle and underlying carotid sheath and its contents are retracted to the left, carefully avoiding undue compression on the carotid artery. The neck strap muscles are divided. The trachea and thyroid gland are retracted to the right, carefully avoiding pressure on the tracheoesophageal groove and injury to the left recurrent laryngeal nerve. The middle thyroid vein and inferior thyroid artery are identified, ligated, and divided, and the underlying cervical esophagus identified. Carefully avoiding injury to the left recurrent laryngeal nerve in the tracheoesophageal groove, the cervical esophagus is encircled with a rubber drain, and the remaining high thoracic esophagus carefully bluntly dissected free within the thoracic inlet and chest. The completely mobilized esophagus is brought into the neck wound. The cervical esophagus is divided with a surgical stapler. The pneumoperitoneum is restored. Under direct visualization so as not to twist the gastric conduit, the distal esophagus, proximal stomach, and attached gastric conduit are gently pulled up through the mediastinum and out through the cervical incision. The resected tumor is removed through the neck incision and removed from the surgical field. Frozen section pathology confirms that the proximal esophageal and distal gastric margins are free of tumor. Hemostasis within the mediastinum is checked for. Throughout this portion of the procedure, careful attention to the arterial blood pressure is mandatory. In order to perform the esophagogastric anastomosis, the tip of the stomach is grasped via the neck incision, and gentle traction on the stomach is used to deliver an adequate length of the gastric conduit out the neck incision. A side-to-side esophagogastric anastomosis is created using the linear stapling device for the posterior portion of the anastomosis. Prior to completing the anterior portion of the anastomosis, a nasogastric tube is placed under direct visualization. The anterior portion of the anastomosis is

completed with an inner layer of running absorbable suture and an outer layer of interrupted permanent suture. After a careful inspection for hemostasis, the neck wound is irrigated, a cervical wound drain is placed, and the neck incision is closed with multiple layers of absorbable suture. Attention is redirected to the abdomen where hemostasis is carefully checked. The liver retractor and trocars are removed under direct vision. All abdominal trocar sites are inspected for hemostasis, irrigated, and closed with multiple layers of absorbable suture. Sterile dressings are applied to all incisions. The nasogastric tube is secured in place.

Clinical Example (43287)

A 65-year-old female presents with a one-month history of progressive dysphagia. Testing revealed a distal esophagogastric junction adenocarcinoma. She received neoadjuvant chemotherapy and radiation therapy. She now undergoes surgical resection.

Description of Procedure (43287)

General anesthesia using a single lumen endotracheal tube is initiated. If it will pass, an orogastric tube may be placed to decompress the stomach. Surgical laparoscopy is performed. Using local infiltrative anesthetic, the pneumoperitoneum is established to distend the abdomen, and the laparoscope is introduced. Gas flow and intra-abdominal pressure are carefully monitored so as not to impair ventilation or decrease venous return. Using local infiltrative anesthetic, in total, four to six 5-mm to 12-mm trocars are inserted through the anterior abdominal wall. The abdominal cavity and viscera are inspected to rule out metastatic disease. A liver retractor is inserted, and the liver is retracted to allow visualization of the esophageal hiatus. The mobilization of the stomach begins by widely resecting the gastrohepatic omentum until it reaches the right crus. The right crus is visualized and dissected. The phrenoesophageal membrane is incised followed by the dissection of the left crus of the diaphragm. It is important to handle the stomach gently and with extreme care during the procedure. The greater curvature of the stomach is mobilized by dividing the short gastric vessels with the ultrasonic coagulating shears. Care is taken to protect the spleen. The gastrocolic omentum is divided, with care taken to preserve the right gastroepiploic artery. A Kocher maneuver is performed to mobilize the proximal duodenum. The posterior attachments of the stomach are divided by retracting the stomach anteriorly. Celiac axis lymph nodes are resected with the specimen. The left gastric artery is divided with an endovascular stapling device. An endoscopic pyloroplasty is performed in a Heineke-Mikulicz fashion. The pylorus is incised longitudinally and closed transversely with interrupted sutures. The pyloroplasty is covered with a remnant of

Surgery / Digestive System 40490-49999

omentum. Transhiatal dissection of the lower esophagus is performed. The diaphragm anterior to the esophagus is divided, and a circumferential dissection of the esophagus to about the level of the inferior pulmonary vein is performed. Care is taken to avoid opening the pleura. A gastric tube approximately 5 cm in diameter is created using multiple firings of the linear endoscopic stapler starting just proximal to the pyloroplasty. The gastroesophageal junction and juxtaposed tumor are resected with grossly free margins. The longitudinal staple line is oversewn with running suture. The tubularized gastric conduit is secured to the proximal stomach remnant with interrupted suture. A laparoscopic feeding jejunostomy tube may be inserted (separately reported). The abdomen is inspected to be sure hemostasis is adequate. Hemostasis is again checked. The liver retractor is removed under direct vision. All abdominal trocars are removed under direct vision. All abdominal trocar sites are inspected for hemostasis, irrigated, and closed with multiple layers of absorbable suture. Sterile dressings are applied to the abdominal incision. The entire surgical field is taken down with care to maintain sterility of the surgical equipment and instrumentation for the thoracic portion of the procedure. The single lumen endotracheal tube is changed to a double lumen endotracheal tube for eventual one-lung anesthesia. The patient's position is changed to the left lateral decubitus position. Correct positioning of the double-lumen endotracheal tube is ensured bronchoscopically. The skin of the right chest wall is prepared. The surgeon rescrubs, gowns, and drapes the patient. The surgeon ensures that all equipment necessary for thoracoscopy (eg, thoracoscopes, fiberoptic light cord, video camera, cautery cord) is placed in the field, assembled, and fixed to the drapes; that the ends of the camera, light, and cautery cords are passed off in sterile fashion to the circulating nurse for attachment of light and video and cautery equipment; and that the equipment is activated and the settings adjusted appropriately (focus, light settings, cautery settings). The second preincision surgical pause is completed. Single-lung ventilation is instituted. Using local infiltrative anesthetic, a total of four or five 5-mm to 10-mm trocars are used. A retracting suture is placed through the central tendon of the diaphragm and brought out through the lower chest wall through a 1-mm skin incision. This helps with downward traction on the diaphragm and exposure of the distal esophagus. The inferior pulmonary ligament of the lung is divided. The mediastinal pleura overlying the esophagus is divided and opened up to the level of the azygos vein. The azygos vein is mobilized and divided with an endovascular stapling device. A mediastinal lymphadenectomy may be performed (separately reported). Using the ultrasonic coagulating shears, electrocautery, and blunt dissection, the esophagus, periesophageal tissue, and periesophageal

lymph nodes are carefully circumferentially mobilized from the diaphragm to above the level of the azygos vein. The vagus nerve is divided above the level of the azygos vein with care taken to protect the recurrent laryngeal nerve. A rubber drain placed around the esophagus may aid in esophageal traction and exposure. Care is taken to avoid injury to the membranous portions of the trachea, bronchi, thoracic aorta, thoracic duct, and recurrent laryngeal nerves. The esophagus is divided above the level of the azygos vein. The proximal esophageal margin is sent to frozen-section pathology to confirm it is free of tumor. The distal esophagus and gastric conduit are carefully brought into the chest, maintaining proper orientation in order to avoid twisting of the gastric conduit. The eighth interspace thoracoscopic port is enlarged, a wound protector is placed, and the specimen is removed. The gastric margin is evaluated by frozen-section pathology to confirm it is free of tumor. A side-to-side esophagogastric anastomosis is created using the endoscopic linear stapling device for the posterior portion of the anastomosis. Prior to completing the anterior portion of the anastomosis, a nasogastric tube is placed under direct visualization. The anterior portion of the anastomosis is completed with an inner layer of absorbable suture and an outer layer of interrupted permanent suture. The chest is carefully evaluated for hemostasis and irrigated. Two chest tubes are placed and connected to an appropriate drainage device. A large soft drain is placed posterior to the anastomosis and brought out of the lower chest wall. All trocars are removed and hemostasis is ensured. The lung is expanded under direct vision. All trocar site wounds are irrigated and closed with multiple layers of absorbable suture. Sterile dressings are applied to the chest incision and chest tube sites. The nasogastric tube is secured in place.

Clinical Example (43288)

A 70-year-old male presents with progressive dysphagia. Testing revealed a mid-esophageal adenocarcinoma above the level of the carina. He received neoadjuvant chemotherapy and radiation therapy. He now undergoes surgical resection.

Description of Procedure (43288)

Under general anesthesia, single-lung ventilation is instituted. If it will pass, an orogastric tube may be placed to decompress the stomach. Using local infiltrative anesthetic, a total of four or five 5-mm to 10-mm trocars are used across the right chest wall. A retracting suture is placed through the central tendon of the diaphragm and brought out through the lower chest wall through a 1-mm skin incision. This helps with downward traction on the diaphragm and exposure of the distal esophagus. The inferior pulmonary ligament of the lung is divided. The mediastinal pleura overlying the esophagus is divided and opened up to the level of

★ = Telemedicine   ✚ = Add-on code   ✹ = FDA approval pending   # = Resequenced code

the azygos vein. The azygos vein is mobilized and divided with an endovascular stapling device. A mediastinal lymphadenectomy may be performed (separately reported). Using the ultrasonic coagulating sheers, electrocautery, and blunt dissection, the esophagus, periesophageal tissue, and periesophageal lymph nodes are carefully circumferentially mobilized from the diaphragm to well above the level of the azygos vein. The vagus nerve is divided above the level of the azygos vein, with care taken to protect the right recurrent laryngeal nerve. A rubber drain placed around the esophagus may aid in esophageal traction and exposure. Care is taken to avoid injury to the membranous portions of the trachea, bronchi, thoracic aorta, thoracic duct, and recurrent laryngeal nerves. The chest is carefully evaluated for hemostasis. Two chest tubes are placed and connected to an appropriate drainage device. All trocars are removed, and hemostasis is ensured. The lung is expanded under direct vision. All chest trocar site wounds are irrigated and closed with multiple layers of absorbable suture. Sterile dressings are applied to the chest incision and chest tube sites. The entire surgical field is taken down with care to maintain sterility of the surgical equipment and instrumentation for the abdominal and cervical portions of the procedure. The patient is placed in a supine position. The double lumen endotracheal tube is removed, and a single lumen endotracheal tube is placed. The surgeon places the patient in a modified lithotomy position, additional special positioning of the neck and arms is required. The skin of the neck, anterolateral chest, and abdomen is prepared and draped from the lower ears to the pubis and laterally to each midaxillary line, after which the surgeon rescrubs, gowns, and drapes the patient. The surgeon ensures that all equipment necessary for laparoscopy (laparoscopes, fiberoptic light cord, video camera, cautery cord, etc.) is placed in the field, assembled, and fixed to the drapes; that the ends of the camera, light, and cautery cords are passed off in sterile fashion to the circulating nurse for attachment of light and video and cautery equipment; and that the equipment is activated and the settings adjusted appropriately (focus, light settings, cautery settings). A second preincision surgical pause is completed. Surgical laparoscopy is performed. Using local infiltrative anesthetic, pneumoperitoneum is established to distend the abdomen, and the laparoscope is introduced. Gas flow and intra-abdominal pressure are carefully monitored so as not to impair ventilation or decrease venous return. Using local infiltrative anesthetic, in total, four to six 5-mm to 12-mm trocars are inserted through the anterior abdominal wall. The abdominal cavity and viscera are inspected to rule out metastatic disease. A liver retractor is inserted, and the liver is retracted to allow visualization of the esophageal hiatus. The mobilization of the stomach begins by widely resecting the gastrohepatic omentum until it reaches the

right crus. The right crus is visualized and dissected. The phrenoesophageal membrane is incised followed by the dissection of the left crus of the diaphragm. It is important to handle the stomach gently and with extreme care during the procedure. The greater curvature of the stomach is mobilized by dividing the short gastric vessels with the ultrasonic coagulating shears. Care is taken to protect the spleen. The gastrocolic omentum is divided, with care taken to preserve the right gastroepiploic artery. A Kocher maneuver is performed to mobilize the proximal duodenum. The posterior attachments of the stomach are divided by retracting the stomach anteriorly. Celiac axis lymph nodes are resected with the specimen. The left gastric artery is divided with an endovascular stapling device. An endoscopic pyloroplasty is performed in a Heineke-Mikulicz fashion. The pylorus is incised longitudinally and closed transversely with interrupted sutures. The pyloroplasty is covered with a remnant of omentum. Transhiatal dissection of the esophagus is performed. The diaphragm anterior to the esophagus is divided, and a circumferential dissection of the esophagus to the level of the previously thoracoscopically mobilized esophagus is performed. A gastric tube approximately 5 cm in diameter is created using multiple firings of the linear endoscopic stapler starting just proximal to the pyloroplasty. The gastroesophageal junction and juxtaposed tumor are resected with grossly free margins. The longitudinal staple line is oversewn with running suture. The tubularized gastric conduit is secured to the proximal stomach remnant with interrupted suture. A laparoscopic feeding jejunostomy tube may be inserted (separately reported). The abdomen is inspected to be sure hemostasis is adequate. The pneumoperitoneum is deflated. Attention is turned to the left neck, where an incision is made along the anterior border of the sternocleidomastoid muscle. The sternocleidomastoid muscle and underlying carotid sheath and its contents are retracted to the left, carefully avoiding undue compression on the carotid artery. The neck strap muscles are divided. The trachea and thyroid gland are retracted to the right, carefully avoiding pressure on the tracheoesophageal groove and injury to the left recurrent laryngeal nerve. The middle thyroid vein and inferior thyroid artery are identified, ligated, and divided, and the underlying cervical esophagus is identified. Carefully avoiding injury to the left recurrent laryngeal nerve in the tracheoesophageal groove, the cervical esophagus is encircled with a rubber drain, and the remaining high thoracic esophagus is carefully and bluntly dissected free within the thoracic inlet and chest. The completely mobilized esophagus is brought into the neck wound. The cervical esophagus is divided with a surgical stapler. Pneumoperitoneum is restored and, under direct visualization so as not to twist the gastric conduit, the distal esophagus, proximal stomach, and attached gastric conduit are gently pulled up through the

Surgery / Digestive System 40490-49999

mediastinum and out through the cervical incision. The resected tumor is removed through the neck incision and removed from the surgical field. Frozen-section pathology confirms that the proximal esophageal and distal gastric margins are free of tumor. Hemostasis within the mediastinum is checked for. Throughout this portion of the procedure, careful attention to the arterial blood pressure is mandatory. In order to perform the esophagogastric anastomosis, the tip of the stomach is grasped in the neck incision, and gentle traction on the stomach is used to deliver an adequate length of gastric conduit out the neck incision. A side-to-side esophagogastric anastomosis is created using the linear stapling device for the posterior portion of the anastomosis. Prior to completing the anterior portion of the anastomosis, a nasogastric tube is placed under direct visualization. The anterior portion of the anastomosis is completed with an inner layer of running absorbable suture and an outer layer of interrupted permanent suture. After a careful inspection for hemostasis, the neck wound is irrigated, a cervical wound drain is placed, and the neck incision is closed with multiple layers of absorbable suture. Attention is redirected to the abdomen where hemostasis is carefully checked. The liver retractor and abdominal trocars are removed under direct vision. All abdominal trocar sites are inspected for hemostasis, irrigated, and closed with multiple layers of absorbable suture. Sterile dressings are applied to all incisions. The nasogastric tube is secured in place.

Intestines (Except Rectum)

Excision

44120   Enterectomy, resection of small intestine; single resection and anastomosis

Rationale

The exclusionary parenthetical note that followed code 44120 restricting its use with code 45136 has been deleted. This change was made to clarify the intent for reporting code 44120 with code 45136, as these codes may be separately reported when the procedures are performed as distinct procedural services, such as in a separate area of the small intestine.

Refer to the codebook and the Rationale for code 45136 and the Rationale for the deletion of the exclusionary parenthetical note following code 11008 for a full discussion of the change.

Enterostomy—External Fistulization of Intestines

44300   Placement, enterostomy or cecostomy, tube open (eg, for feeding or decompression) (separate procedure)

▶(Do not report 44300 in conjunction with 44701 for cannulation of the colon for intraoperative colonic lavage)◀

(For percutaneous placement of duodenostomy, jejunostomy, gastro-jejunostomy or cecostomy [or other colonic] tube including fluoroscopic imaging guidance, see 49441-49442)

Rationale

An exclusionary parenthetical note has been added after code 44300, which restricts reporting code 44300 in conjunction with code 44701. The exclusionary parenthetical note that follows code 44300 has been added to identify a specific instance when placement of an enterostomy or cecostomy tube should not be separately reported, ie, when it is performed for cannulation of the colon for intraoperative colonic lavage. If the tube is placed for feeding or decompression at the same time that an intraoperative colonic lavage is performed, both codes 44300 and 44701 may be reported. The qualifier language included in the exclusionary parenthetical note that follows code 44300 provides users with the specific circumstances when it is inappropriate to use these codes together.

Other Procedures

+ 44701   Intraoperative colonic lavage (List separately in addition to code for primary procedure)

(Use 44701 in conjunction with 44140, 44145, 44150, or 44604 as appropriate)

▶(Do not report 44701 in conjunction with 44950-44960)◀

Rationale

Code 44300 has been removed from the exclusionary parenthetical note that follows add-on code 44701, which restricts the use of code 44701 in conjunction with code 44300.

This revision supports the addition of the exclusionary parenthetical note following code 44300 to identify a specific circumstance when placement of an enterostomy or cecostomy should be not be separately reported, ie, when performed for cannulation of the colon for intraoperative colonic lavage. If, instead, the placement of the tube is performed for feeding or decompression at the same time that an intraoperative colonic lavage is performed, then add-on code 44701 may be reported in conjunction with code 44300. The qualifier language included within the exclusionary parenthetical note following code 44300 provides users with the specific circumstances when it is inappropriate to use these codes together.

Colon and Rectum

Excision

45136   Excision of ileoanal reservoir with ileostomy

▶(Do not report 45136 in conjunction with 44005, 44310)◀

Rationale

Code 44120 has been deleted from the exclusionary parenthetical note that follows code 45136. This change was made to clarify the intent for reporting code 44120 with code 45136, as these codes may be separately reported when the procedures are performed as distinct services, such as in a separate area of the small intestine.

Refer to the codebook and the Rationale for code 44120 and the Rationale for the deletion of the exclusionary parenthetical note following code 11008 for a full discussion of the changes.

Abdomen, Peritoneum, and Omentum

Excision, Destruction

49203   Excision or destruction, open, intra-abdominal tumors, cysts or endometriomas, 1 or more peritoneal, mesenteric, or retroperitoneal primary or secondary tumors; largest tumor 5 cm diameter or less

49204   largest tumor 5.1-10.0 cm diameter

49205   largest tumor greater than 10.0 cm diameter

▶(Do not report 49203-49205 in conjunction with 38770, 38780, 49000, 49010, 49215, 50010, 50205, 50225, 50236, 50250, 50290, 58920, 58925, 58940, 58943, 58951, 58952, 58953, 58954, 58956, 58957, 58958, 58960)◀

(For partial or total nephrectomy, use 50220 or 50240 in conjunction with 49203-49205)

(For colectomy, use 44140 in conjunction with 49203-49205)

(For small bowel resection, use 44120 in conjunction with 49203-49205)

(For vena caval resection with reconstruction, use 49203-49205 in conjunction with 37799)

(For resection of recurrent ovarian, tubal, primary peritoneal, or uterine malignancy, see 58957, 58958)

(For cryoablation of renal tumors, see 50250, 50593)

Rationale

The exclusionary parenthetical note that follows code 49205 has been revised by the removal of codes 58900 and 58950. Other codes in the 58900-58960 code range have been specified to provide users with better instructions regarding codes that are intended for exclusion when codes 49203, 49204, and 49205 are reported.

Code 58900 should be used to report unilateral or bilateral biopsy of the ovary. This procedure is not inherently included as part of excision because reporting a biopsy of the ovary separately from excision within the abdomen would be appropriate when ovarian preservation is desired and other lesions are found in the abdomen. Similarly, for resection of ovarian, tubal, or primary peritoneal malignancy with bilateral salpingo-oophorectomy and omentectomy (58950), it would be appropriate to report resections when other lesions that require resection are found that are not related to the resection performed for the malignancy. In these instances, code 58900 or 58950 may be reported with the abdominal excision procedures (ie, 49203-49205) with the appropriate modifier appended.

Refer to the codebook and the Rationale for the deletion of the exclusionary parenthetical note following code 11008 for a full discussion of these changes.

Urinary System

Bladder

Endoscopy—Cystoscopy, Urethroscopy, Cystourethroscopy

Endoscopic descriptions are listed so that the main procedure can be identified without having to list all the minor related functions performed at the same time. For example: meatotomy, urethral calibration and/or dilation, urethroscopy, and cystoscopy prior to a transurethral resection of prostate; ureteral catheterization following extraction of ureteral calculus; internal urethrotomy and bladder neck fulguration when performing a cystourethroscopy for the female urethral syndrome. When the secondary procedure requires significant additional time and effort, it may be identified by the addition of modifier 22.

For example: urethrotomy performed for a documented pre-existing stricture or bladder neck contracture.

Because cutaneous urinary diversions utilizing ileum or colon serve as functional replacements of a native bladder, endoscopy of such bowel segments, as well as performance of secondary procedures can be captured by using the cystourethroscopy codes. For example, endoscopy of an ileal loop with removal of ureteral calculus would be coded as cystourethroscopy (including ureteral catheterization); with removal of ureteral calculus (52320).

52000   Cystourethroscopy (separate procedure)

(Do not report 52000 in conjunction with 52001, 52320, 52325, 52327, 52330, 52332, 52334, 52341, 52342, 52343, 52356)

▶(Do not report 52000 in conjunction with 57240, 57260, 57265)◀

52001   Cystourethroscopy with irrigation and evacuation of multiple obstructing clots

(Do not report 52001 in conjunction with 52000)

Rationale

In accordance with the revisions of codes 57240, 57260, and 57265, an exclusionary parenthetical note has been added after code 52000 to preclude the reporting of cystourethroscopy in conjunction with these codes.

Refer to the codebook and the Rationale for codes 57240, 57260, and 57265 for a full discussion of the changes.

Transurethral Surgery

Urethra and Bladder

52281   Cystourethroscopy, with calibration and/or dilation of urethral stricture or stenosis, with or without meatotomy, with or without injection procedure for cystography, male or female

▶(To report cystourethroscopy with urethral therapeutic drug delivery, use 0499T)◀

Rationale

An instructional parenthetical note has been added after code 52281 to direct users to the appropriate code when reporting cystourethroscopy with urethral therapeutic drug delivery. Refer to the codebook and the Rationale for code 0499T for a full discussion of the changes.

Male Genital System

Vas Deferens

Suture

▶(55450 has been deleted. To report, use 55250)◀

Rationale

Code 55450 (ligation of vas deferens) has been deleted due to low utilization and to ensure that the CPT code set reflects current clinical practice. In addition, it was determined that code 55250 more accurately describes a vasectomy procedure, therefore, a parenthetical note directing users to code 55250 has been added.

Prostate

Other Procedures

55873   Cryosurgical ablation of the prostate (includes ultrasonic guidance and monitoring)

● **55874**   Transperineal placement of biodegradable material, peri-prostatic, single or multiple injection(s), including image guidance, when performed

▶(Do not report 55874 in conjunction with 76942)◀

Rationale

Code 0438T has been deleted from Category III codes and converted to Category I code 55874 to report transperineal peri-prostatic placement of biodegradable material. An exclusionary parenthetical note has been added to accommodate the creation of the new code.

Code 55874 is intended for reporting injection of biodegradable material between the prostate and rectum, which is performed to protect viable tissue not intended for treatment during radiation of prostate cancer. Because the procedure is commonly performed using imaging, the descriptor for the procedure has been modified to inherently include imaging when it is performed for the procedure. As a result, separate reporting of imaging guidance is restricted. An exclusionary parenthetical note that follows code 55874 precludes separately reporting code 76942 (ultrasonic guidance) as image guidance for this procedure. To reflect this revision, code 55874 has been included in the exclusionary parenthetical note that follows code 76942.

Clinical Example (55874)

A 67-year-old male is discovered on digital rectal examination to have a prostate nodule that occupies more than one half of the right lobe; there is no involvement of the left side. Diagnostic workup confirms the presence of prostate cancer. To reduce rectal toxicity that results from radiation therapy, an ultrasound-guided transperineal implantation of a biodegradable material is performed to create a space between the prostate and the rectum.

Description of Procedure (55874)

The hydrogel implant is prepared by the physician. Saline is drawn into a sterile syringe, which is attached to a needle and primed. The syringe/needle assembly will be used to access and hydrodissect the periprostatic implant site. The hydrogel syringe assembly is prepared by injecting the hydrogel diluent into the powder in the vial, shaking until the powder is completely dissolved, and setting aside to allow the bubbles to dissipate. Once the bubbles dissipate, 5 mL of this precursor solution and 1 cc of air is withdrawn back into the precursor syringe. The accelerator syringe is uncapped, and the amount of accelerator liquid is prepared at 5 mL liquid/cc air. The precursor solution syringe and accelerator syringe are measured to contain the same amount of fluid and air before being assembled to the y-connector, syringe holder, and syringe plunger cap. After the physician identifies and hydrodissects the cavity as described below, the syringe assembly is ready for injecting the hydrogel. The transrectal ultrasonographic (TRUS) probe is repositioned in the rectum, and the space between the prostate (mid-gland) and rectum is identified and measured. The ultrasound probe will be repositioned to find the minimal probe pressure to maximize the visualization of the prostate without collapsing the periprostatic fat. The probe will be angled to prevent the rectum from being displaced superiorly, which would prevent the needle from being introduced without fecal contamination. After appropriate positioning is achieved, the saline syringe needle (15-cm 18-G needle) is inserted through the perineal skin under direct ultrasound guidance, through the rectourethralis muscle, and past the prostate apex to the perirectal fat

between Denonvilliers fascia at prostate mid-gland and the rectal wall. Care must be taken during needle advancement not to penetrate the rectal lumen with the needle tip to avoid potential introduction of infectious material or injury to the rectal wall. Care must also be taken not to transect the prostate. The needle position is confirmed in both the sagittal and axial ultrasound planes, and saline is injected to dissect the space between the Denonvilliers fascia and anterior rectal wall (hydrodissection). Hydrodissection confirms proper needle location and creates space for the injection of the hydrogel material. Additional axial and sagittal imaging is required to optimize needle position and bilateral saline distribution. While maintaining the desired position, aspiration is performed to ensure that the needle is not in an intravascular space. The saline syringe is removed, and the hydrogel syringe assembly is attached to the same 18-G needle with care not to displace the needle. The needle is confirmed not to have moved during assembly on ultrasound imaging. Under ultrasound guidance (sagittal plane), the hydrogel material is injected to expand the periprostatic space between the prostate and rectum. Optimal visualization of the needle during hydrogel administration is maintained at all times. Following injection, the needle is removed, and the spent applicator and needle are discarded. An axial measurement of the space between the prostate (mid-gland) and rectum is performed. The TRUS probe is removed from the patient, the stirrups are lowered, and patient is recovered.

Female Genital System

Vagina

Repair

(For urethral suspension, Marshall-Marchetti-Krantz type, abdominal approach, see 51840, 51841)

(For laparoscopic suspension, use 51990)

57200   Colporrhaphy, suture of injury of vagina (nonobstetrical)

57210   Colpoperineorrhaphy, suture of injury of vagina and/or perineum (nonobstetrical)

▲ 57240   Anterior colporrhaphy, repair of cystocele with or without repair of urethrocele, including cystourethroscopy, when performed

▶(Do not report 57240 in conjunction with 52000)◀

57250   Posterior colporrhaphy, repair of rectocele with or without perineorrhaphy

(For repair of rectocele [separate procedure] without posterior colporrhaphy, use 45560)

▲ **57260**   Combined anteroposterior colporrhaphy, including cystourethroscopy, when performed;

▶(Do not report 57260 in conjunction with 52000)◀

▲ **57265**   with enterocele repair

▶(Do not report 57265 in conjunction with 52000)◀

Rationale

Codes 57240, 57260, and 57265 have been revised to include cystourethroscopy, when performed. Related exclusionary parenthetical notes have been added to preclude the reporting of these codes with code 52000 (cystourethroscopy).

Prior to these revisions, code 52000 was used to separately report the cystourethroscopy procedure. However, when cystourethroscopy (52000) is performed, it is now included and not separately reported.

Clinical Example (57240)

A 73-year-old multigravid female presents with complaints of vaginal pressure and feeling of something protruding from the vagina. Her symptoms are worse when coughing, standing, or lifting. She denies stress urinary incontinence. In addition, she often must reduce the prolapse to complete voiding. On examination, she has an anterior compartment defect that protrudes just beyond the introitus with Valsalva maneuver. The uterus and posterior vaginal wall are well supported.

Description of Procedure (57240)

Examination under anesthesia is performed, and prolapse is appropriately staged and recorded. A Foley catheter is placed, and the urethrovesical neck and vaginal apex are identified. A weighted speculum is placed into the vagina. Hydrodissection, if performed, is completed to assist with identification and development of the true vesicovaginal space. Full-thickness incision through the vaginal mucosa is made to expose the space from the urethrovesical junction to the vaginal apex. Sharp and blunt dissection is used to mobilize the vaginal tissue laterally to the descending pubic rami bilaterally and to the vaginal apex superiorly. Identification of fascial defects is completed. Plicating sutures are placed at the level of the urethrovesical junction. Lateral, paravaginal defects, if identified, are individually repaired by suture plication to the fascia over the obturator internus muscle. Midline plication of the deep vaginal tissue is performed with interrupted sutures. Redundant vaginal epithelium is excised. Hemostasis is obtained. The vaginal incision is closed. If cystoscopy is performed, the video equipment is set up and tested, and cystoscopic instruments are assembled.

The Foley catheter is removed, and cystoscopy is performed. Mucosal integrity and bilateral ureteral patency are confirmed. The Foley catheter is replaced after cystoscopy completion. Vaginal packing, as needed, is placed. Instrument and sponge counts are confirmed.

Clinical Example (57260)

A 73-year-old multigravid female presents for evaluation of worsening vulvar pressure and a mass that protrudes from the vagina. Her symptoms are worse when she coughs or stands for a long period of time. She denies stress urinary incontinence. In addition, she complains of incomplete emptying of bowel and bladder. On examination, she has distal defects in the anterior and posterior compartments that are to the introitus with Valsalva maneuver. The uterus is well supported. An anterior and posterior colporrhaphy is recommended.

Description of Procedure (57260)

Examination under anesthesia is performed, and prolapse is appropriately staged and recorded. A Foley catheter is placed, and the urethrovesical neck and vaginal apex are identified. A weighted speculum is placed into the vagina. Hydrodissection, if performed, is completed for development of the true vesicovaginal space. A full-thickness incision through the vaginal mucosa is performed. Sharp and blunt dissection is used to mobilize the vaginal tissue laterally to the descending pubic rami on each side and superiorly to the vaginal apex superiorly. Identification of fascial defects is completed. Plicating sutures are placed at the level of the urethrovesical junction. Lateral, paravaginal defects, if identified, are individually repaired by suture plication to the fascia over the obturator internus muscle. Midline plication of the deep vaginal tissue is performed with interrupted sutures. Suture correction of vaginal defects is performed. Excessive vaginal epithelium is excised. Hemostasis is obtained. If cystoscopy is performed, the video equipment is set up and tested, and cystoscopic instruments are assembled. The Foley catheter is removed. Bladder mucosal integrity and bilateral ureteral patency are confirmed. The Foley catheter is replaced. The vaginal incision is closed. The posterior compartment defect is identified and demarcated. A triangular incision is made on the perineal body, and the overlying skin is removed. Incision is extended into the posterior vaginal epithelium, and any preexisting scar from prior obstetrical laceration is removed. Hydrodissection, if performed, is completed to develop the true rectovaginal space. Incision is extended into the posterior vaginal epithelium, and any preexisting scar from prior obstetrical laceration is removed. Full-thickness dissection of vaginal epithelium from underlying rectovaginal septum is accomplished to the vaginal apex and medial margins of the levator musculature. Rectal examination is performed to

Surgery / Female Genital System 56405–60699

identify rectovaginal fascial defects laterally, superiorly, and at the perineal body. A triangular strip of full-thickness vaginal wall is removed. Apical detachments, if present, are corrected by suture plication. Repair and plication of the perirectal and rectovaginal fascia are performed from the vaginal apex to the vaginal introitus. Puborectalis and levator ani are plicated distal to the rectovaginal space. Perineal body is reconstructed by plicating the superficial and deep perineal muscles. The distal rectovaginal septum is reattached to the perineal body. Hemostasis is obtained. Vaginal caliber is reassessed, and sutures are replaced, as needed. Posterior vaginal wall epithelium is closed. Perineal skin is closed. Rectal examination is performed. Vaginal packing, if used, is placed. Foley catheter is placed. Manipulators, retractors, and probes are removed. Instrument and sponge counts are confirmed.

Clinical Example (57265)

A 66-year-old multigravid female presents for evaluation of a mass that is protruding from the vagina. Her symptoms are worse when she coughs or stands for a long period of time. The patient had a hysterectomy 20 years ago. She denies stress incontinence. In addition, she complains of incomplete emptying of bowel and bladder. On examination, she is found to have an anterior compartment defect, a posterior compartment defect, and apical descent with ballooning of the apex extending down the upper posterior wall. She has an enterocoele on rectovaginal examination. An anterior and posterior colporrhaphy with enterocoele repair is recommended.

Description of Procedure (57265)

Examination under anesthesia is performed, and prolapse is appropriately staged and recorded. A Foley catheter is placed, and the urethrovesical neck and vaginal apex are identified. A weighted speculum is placed into the vagina. Hydrodissection, if performed, is completed with identification and development of the true vesicovaginal space. A full-thickness incision is made through the vaginal mucosa. Sharp and blunt dissection is used to mobilize the vaginal tissue laterally to the descending pubic rami bilaterally and superiorly with complete development of the vesicovaginal space to the vaginal apex. Identification of fascial defects is completed. Plicating sutures are placed at the level of the urethrovesical junction. Lateral, paravaginal defects, if identified, are individually repaired by suture plication to the fascia over the obturator internus muscle. Midline plication of the deep vaginal tissue is performed. Excessive vaginal epithelium is excised. Hemostasis is obtained. The Foley catheter is removed. Cystoscopy is performed, the video equipment is set up and tested, and cystoscopic instruments are assembled. Bladder mucosal

integrity and bilateral ureteral patency are confirmed. Vaginal incision is closed. The posterior compartment defect is identified and demarcated. A triangular incision is made on the perineal body, and the overlying skin is removed. Hydrodissection, if performed, is completed to develop the true rectovaginal space. Incision is extended into the posterior vaginal epithelium, and any preexisting scar from prior obstetrical laceration is removed. Full thickness dissection of vaginal epithelium from underlying rectovaginal septum is accomplished to the vaginal apex and medial margins of the levator musculature. Further dissection is performed above the vaginal apex to delineate the enterocele sac. The peritoneum is freed from the pubocervical tissue anteriorly and rectovaginal tissue posteriorly. The posterior vaginal wall is dissected from the enterocele sac, anterior rectal wall, and rectovaginal septum through sharp and blunt dissection. The enterocele sac is entered sharply. Small bowel and omental adhesions, if present, are dissected to the level of the neck of the enterocele. Several purse-string sutures are used to close the enterocele sac, and excessive peritoneum is excised. The cardinal-uterosacral ligaments are identified, and sutures are incorporated into the closed enterocele sac and apical vaginal tissue. Sutures are tied in sequence. Cystoscopy is again performed to confirm bilateral ureteral patency. The anterior and posterior portions of the mucosal apex are reapproximated. Rectal examination is performed to identify rectovaginal fascial defects, laterally, superiorly, and at the perineal body. Portions of full-thickness vaginal wall are removed. Repair and plication of the perirectal and rectovaginal fascia is performed from the vaginal apex to the vaginal introitus. Puborectalis and levator ani are plicated distal to the rectovaginal space. Perineal body is reconstructed by plicating the superficial and deep perineal muscles. Distal rectovaginal septum is reattached to the perineal body. Hemostasis is obtained. Vaginal caliber is reassessed, and sutures replaced, as needed. Posterior vaginal wall epithelium is closed. Perineal skin is closed. Rectal examination is performed. Vaginal packing is placed. Manipulators and retractors are removed. Instrument and sponge counts are confirmed.

Corpus Uteri

Laparoscopy/Hysteroscopy

58674   Laparoscopy, surgical, ablation of uterine fibroid(s) including intraoperative ultrasound guidance and monitoring, radiofrequency

(Do not report 58674 in conjunction with 49320, 58541-58554, 58570, 58571, 58572, 58573, 76998)

58572   Laparoscopy, surgical, with total hysterectomy, for uterus greater than 250 g;

58573 with removal of tube(s) and/or ovary(s)

(Do not report 58570-58573 in conjunction with 49320, 57000, 57180, 57410, 58140-58146, 58150, 58545, 58546, 58561, 58661, 58670, 58671)

● **58575** Laparoscopy, surgical, total hysterectomy for resection of malignancy (tumor debulking), with omentectomy including salpingo-oophorectomy, unilateral or bilateral, when performed

▶(Do not report 58575 in conjunction with 49255, 49320, 49321, 58570, 58571, 58572, 58573, 58661)◀

58578 Unlisted laparoscopy procedure, uterus

58579 Unlisted hysteroscopy procedure, uterus

Rationale

Code 58575 has been established to report laparoscopic total hysterectomy with resection of a malignancy with omentectomy and unilateral or bilateral salpingo-oophorectomy, when performed. An exclusionary parenthetical note has been added to preclude the use of this code with separate procedures that are inherently included in this new service.

Code 58575 may be used to report more extensive laparoscopic surgeries for the purpose of surgically resecting some gynecologic cancers. Other codes in the code set include components of laparoscopic resection, such as hysterectomy and salpingo-oophorectomy, but not tumor debulking or omentectomy, which are included in code 58575.

Clinical Example (58575)

A 63-year-old female presented with advanced stage ovarian cancer with a large malignant pleural effusion. She was given neoadjuvant chemotherapy. Reassessment after chemotherapy demonstrates a good partial response, with imaging tests that show an enlarged right ovarian mass, peritoneal thickening with an omental tumor, and a 3-cm mesenteric nodule. The patient is a good surgical candidate and has been offered a minimally invasive option for interval tumor debulking with a total laparoscopic hysterectomy and bilateral salpingo-oophorectomy and laparoscopic omentectomy, with resection of peritoneal, mesenteric, and diaphragmatic implants, if present.

Description of Procedure (58575)

A bimanual and rectovaginal exam is performed under anesthesia to assess uterine size, mobility, and nodularity in the cul de sac. A Foley catheter is inserted into the bladder. A speculum in placed in the vagina, and a tenaculum is placed on the cervix. The uterus is

sounded, and the cervix is dilated. An appropriate-sized uterine manipulator is chosen, placed into the uterus, and sutured in place. A diagnostic laparoscopy is performed, 5–6 laparoscopic ports are placed in the abdomen ranging in size from 5 to 12 mm. Adhesions from the ovarian cancer are systematically lysed to provide visualization of abdominal and pelvic structures. The patient is assessed for intra-abdominal metastases, diaphragmatic metastases, and retroperitoneal adenopathy. Biopsies of suspicious lesions are obtained. The bowels and bowel mesentery are systematically evaluated for the presence of metastatic disease. Peritoneal cytology is obtained. The patient is placed into steep Trendelenburg, and the bowel is mobilized and dissected out of the pelvis. The retroperitoneum is opened to identify the ureters and paravesical and pararectal spaces. The ureters are freed from pelvic and peritoneal metastases. A total laparoscopic hysterectomy with bilateral salpingo-oophorectomy is performed. The uterus and ovaries are removed through the vagina. Extra-ovarian tumor masses are resected in the pelvis, the abdomen, and from the bowel mesentery and diaphragm. Patient positioning is changed to resect disease in the upper abdomen. An omentectomy is performed by dissecting it free from the transverse colon and stomach. Specimens are removed through the vagina, and the vaginal closure is performed. After completing the resection of disease, hemostasis is confirmed and the pelvis and abdomen are inspected for any injuries. All instruments and ports are removed, and the port sites are closed.

Nervous System

Skull, Meninges, and Brain

Surgery of Skull Base

The surgical management of lesions involving the skull base (base of anterior, middle, and posterior cranial fossae) often requires the skills of several surgeons of different surgical specialties working together or in tandem during the operative session. These operations are usually not staged because of the need for definitive closure of dura, subcutaneous tissues, and skin to avoid serious infections such as osteomyelitis and/or meningitis.

The procedures are categorized according to:

(1) *approach procedure* necessary to obtain adequate exposure to the lesion (pathologic entity), (2) *definitive procedure(s)* necessary to biopsy, excise or otherwise treat the lesion, and (3) *repair/reconstruction* of the defect present following the definitive procedure(s).

★ = Telemedicine ✚ = Add-on code ✗ = FDA approval pending # = Resequenced code

The ***approach procedure*** is described according to anatomical area involved, ie, anterior cranial fossa, middle cranial fossa, posterior cranial fossa, and brain stem or upper spinal cord.

The ***definitive procedure(s)*** describes the repair, biopsy, resection, or excision of various lesions of the skull base and, when appropriate, primary closure of the dura, mucous membranes, and skin.

The ***repair/reconstruction procedure(s)*** is reported separately if extensive dural grafting, cranioplasty, local or regional myocutaneous pedicle flaps, or extensive skin grafts are required.

▶For primary closure, see the appropriate codes (ie, 15730, 15733, 15756, 15757, 15758).◀

When one surgeon performs the approach procedure, another surgeon performs the definitive procedure, and another surgeon performs the repair/reconstruction procedure, each surgeon reports only the code for the specific procedure performed.

If one surgeon performs more than one procedure (ie, approach procedure and definitive procedure), then both codes are reported, adding modifier 51 to the secondary, additional procedure(s).

Rationale

An instructional parenthetical note in the Surgery of Skull Base subsection in the Nervous System section has been revised to remove code 15732 and replaced with codes 15730 and 15733. These codes should be used to report midface flap and myocutaneous or fasciocutaneous flap procedures of the head and neck.

Refer to the codebook and the Rationale for codes 15730-15738 for a full discussion of the changes.

Spine and Spinal Cord

Anterior or Anterolateral Approach for Extradural Exploration/Decompression

For the following codes, when two surgeons work together as primary surgeons performing distinct part(s) of spinal cord exploration/decompression operation, each surgeon should report his/her distinct operative work by appending modifier 62 to the procedure code (and any associated add-on codes for that procedure code as long as both surgeons continue to work together as primary surgeons). In this situation, modifier 62 may be appended to the definitive procedure code(s) 63075, 63077, 63081, 63085, 63087, 63090 and, as appropriate, to associated additional interspace add-on code(s) 63076,

63078 or additional segment add-on code(s) 63082, 63086, 63088, 63091 as long as both surgeons continue to work together as primary surgeons.

▶For vertebral corpectomy, the term **partial** is used to describe removal of a substantial portion of the body of the vertebra. In the cervical spine, the amount of bone removed is defined as at least one-half of the vertebral body. In the thoracic and lumbar spine, the amount of bone removed is defined as at least one-third of the vertebral body.◀

63075   Discectomy, anterior, with decompression of spinal cord and/or nerve root(s), including osteophytectomy; cervical, single interspace

(Do not report 63075 in conjunction with 22554, even if performed by separate individuals. To report anterior cervical discectomy and interbody fusion at the same level during the same session, use 22551)

Rationale

A definition for partial vertebral corpectomy has been added to the anterior or anterolateral approach for extradural exploration/decompression guidelines in the Spine and Spinal Cord section.

The definition was added after the AMA RUC RAW reviewed codes 22558 (lumbar arthrodesis) and 63090 (vertebral corpectomy). It was noted that codes 22558 and 63090 may have been reported together inappropriately because partial vertebral corpectomy is not defined, which may have resulted in an overuse of code 63090.

The new definition clarifies partial corpectomy in the cervical spine, the thoracic spine, and the lumbar spine by providing a threshold of the amount of bone removed. It will now be easier for users to determine whether it is appropriate to report partial corpectomy.

Lateral Extracavitary Approach for Extradural Exploration/Decompression

▶For vertebral corpectomy, the term **partial** is used to describe removal of a substantial portion of the body of the vertebra. In the cervical spine, the amount of bone removed is defined as at least one-half of the vertebral body. In the thoracic and lumbar spine, the amount of bone removed is defined as at least one-third of the vertebral body.◀

63101   Vertebral corpectomy (vertebral body resection), partial or complete, lateral extracavitary approach with decompression of spinal cord and/or nerve root(s) (eg, for tumor or retropulsed bone fragments); thoracic, single segment

▲ = Revised code   ● = New code   ▶ ◀ = Contains new or revised text   ⊘ = Modifier 51 exempt

Rationale

A definition for partial vertebral corpectomy has been added to the lateral extracavitary approach for extradural exploration/decompression guidelines in the Spine and Spinal Cord section.

The definition was added after the AMA RUC RAW reviewed codes 22558 (lumbar arthrodesis) and 63090 (vertebral corpectomy). It was noted that codes 22558 and 63090 may have been reported together inappropriately because partial vertebral corpectomy is not defined, which may have resulted in an overuse of code 63090.

The new definition clarifies partial corpectomy in the cervical spine, the thoracic spine, and the lumbar spine by providing a threshold of the amount of bone removed. It will now be easier for users to determine whether it is appropriate to report partial corpectomy.

Rationale

A definition for partial vertebral corpectomy has been added to the excision, anterior or anterolateral approach for intraspinal lesion guidelines in the Spine and Spinal Cord section.

The definition was added after the AMA RUC RAW reviewed codes 22558 (lumbar arthrodesis) and 63090 (vertebral corpectomy). It was noted that codes 22558 and 63090 may have been reported together inappropriately because partial vertebral corpectomy is not defined, which may have resulted in an overuse of code 63090.

The new definition clarifies partial corpectomy in the cervical spine, the thoracic spine, and the lumbar spine by providing a threshold of the amount of bone removed. It will now be easier for users to determine whether it is appropriate to report partial corpectomy.

Excision, Anterior or Anterolateral Approach, Intraspinal Lesion

For the following codes, when two surgeons work together as primary surgeons performing distinct part(s) of an anterior approach for an intraspinal excision, each surgeon should report his/her distinct operative work by appending modifier 62 to the single definitive procedure code. In this situation, modifier 62 may be appended to the definitive procedure code(s) 63300-63307 and, as appropriate, to the associated additional segment add-on code 63308 as long as both surgeons continue to work together as primary surgeons.

►For vertebral corpectomy, the term **partial** is used to describe removal of a substantial portion of the body of the vertebra. In the cervical spine, the amount of bone removed is defined as at least one-half of the vertebral body. In the thoracic and lumbar spine, the amount of bone removed is defined as at least one-third of the vertebral body.◄

> (For arthrodesis, see 22548-22585)

> (For reconstruction of spine, see 20930-20938)

63300 Vertebral corpectomy (vertebral body resection), partial or complete, for excision of intraspinal lesion, single segment; extradural, cervical

Extracranial Nerves, Peripheral Nerves, and Autonomic Nervous System

Neurostimulators (Peripheral Nerve)

Codes 64553-64595 apply to both simple and complex neurostimulators. For initial or subsequent electronic analysis and programming of neurostimulator pulse generators, see codes 95970-95975. An electrode array is a catheter or other device with more than one contact. The function of each contact may be capable of being adjusted during programming services.

►Codes 64553, 64555, and 64561 may be used to report both temporary and permanent placement of percutaneous electrode arrays. Code 64550 describes application of surface (transcutaneous) neurostimulator (eg, TENS unit) at any anatomical site.◄

▲ **64550** Application of surface (transcutaneous) neurostimulator (eg, TENS unit)

64553 Percutaneous implantation of neurostimulator electrode array; cranial nerve

> ►(For percutaneous electrical stimulation of a cranial nerve using needle[s] or needle electrode[s] [eg, PENS, PNT], use 64999)◄

> (For open placement of cranial nerve (eg, vagus, trigeminal) neurostimulator pulse generator or receiver, see 61885, 61886, as appropriate)

64555   peripheral nerve (excludes sacral nerve)

> (Do not report 64555 in conjunction with 64566)

▶(For percutaneous electrical stimulation of a peripheral nerve using needle[s] or needle electrode[s] [eg, PENS, PNT], use 64999)◀

64561   sacral nerve (transforaminal placement) including image guidance, if performed

▶(64565 has been deleted)◀

▶(For percutaneous electrical neuromuscular stimulation or neuromodulation using needle[s] or needle electrode[s] [eg, PENS, PNT], use 64999)◀

Rationale

Guidelines have been added to the Neurostimulators (Peripheral Nerve) section instructing users to report codes 64553 (cranial nerve), 64555 (peripheral nerve), and 64561 (sacral nerve) for the placement of temporary or permanent percutaneous electrode arrays. It was determined that there was no difference in work and practice expense when placing a temporary or permanent electrode array, therefore, different codes to distinguish this were not necessary.

Guidelines have been added for code 64550, which is used to report the application of a surface (transcutaneous) electrical neurostimulator (TENS) unit at any anatomical site. Code 64550 has been revised to include a TENS unit as an example of a transcutaneous electrical neurostimulator.

In addition to the new guidelines and code revision, two parenthetical notes have been added after codes 64553 and 64555 to instruct users to report unlisted code 64999 for percutaneous electrical stimulation of the cranial or peripheral nerves using needle(s) or needle electrode(s).

In accordance with the establishment of these parenthetical notes to clarify the correct reporting of percutaneous electrical stimulation, code 64565 has been deleted. A parenthetical note directing users to code 64999 for reporting percutaneous electrical neuromuscular stimulation or neuromodulation using needle(s) or needle electrode(s) has been added.

64568   Incision for implantation of cranial nerve (eg, vagus nerve) neurostimulator electrode array and pulse generator

(Do not report 64568 in conjunction with 61885, 61886, 64570)

▶(For insertion of chest wall respiratory sensor electrode or electrode array, including connection to pulse generator, use 0466T)◀

64569   Revision or replacement of cranial nerve (eg, vagus nerve) neurostimulator electrode array, including connection to existing pulse generator

(Do not report 64569 in conjunction with 64570 or 61888)

(For replacement of pulse generator, use 61885)

▶(For revision or replacement of chest wall respiratory sensor electrode or electrode array, including connection to existing pulse generator, use 0467T)◀

64570   Removal of cranial nerve (eg, vagus nerve) neurostimulator electrode array and pulse generator

(Do not report 64570 in conjunction with 61888)

(For laparoscopic implantation, revision, replacement, or removal of vagus nerve blocking neurostimulator electrode array and/or pulse generator at the esophagogastric junction, see 0312T-0317T)

▶(For removal of chest wall respiratory sensor electrode or electrode array, use 0468T)◀

Rationale

In accordance with the establishment of Category III codes 0466T-0468T, parenthetical notes have been added after codes 64568, 64569, and 64570 to direct users to these Category III codes for respiratory sensor procedures.

Refer to the codebook and the Rationale for codes 0466T-0468T for a full discussion of these changes.

Neurorrhaphy With Nerve Graft, Vein Graft, or Conduit

64910   Nerve repair; with synthetic conduit or vein allograft (eg, nerve tube), each nerve

64911   with autogenous vein graft (includes harvest of vein graft), each nerve

(Do not report 69990 in addition to 64910, 64911)

● **64912**   with nerve allograft, each nerve, first strand (cable)

+● **64913**   with nerve allograft, each additional strand (List separately in addition to code for primary procedure)

▶(Use 64913 in conjunction with 64912)◀

▶(Do not report 64912, 64913 in conjunction with 69990)◀

Surgery / Auditory System 69000-69990

Rationale

Codes 64912 and 64913 have been added to describe nerve repair with nerve allograft. Prior to 2018, four types of grafts that are used for nerve repair were described in the CPT code set: nerve autograft (64885-64907); vein allograft (64910); vein autograft (64911); and synthetic conduit (64910). Nerve repair using nerve allograft was reported with code 64999 (unlisted procedure, nervous system).

Code 64912 should be reported for each nerve repaired and the first strand of nerve allograft used. Code 64913 is an add-on code that should be reported with code 64912 for each additional nerve allograft strand. Strands are part of the allograft and are sutured to the ends of the severed nerve. Nerve repair with allograft is a microsurgical procedure that includes the use of the operating microscope; therefore, code 69990 is not reported separately.

Clinical Example (64912)

A patient with a 2-cm gap in the median nerve in the forearm undergoes repair with a nerve allograft using microsurgical technique.

Description of Procedure (64912)

An incision is made over the site of the nerve injury, and dissection is carried out to expose the median nerve ends. The operating microscope is brought into position, and the ends of the median nerve are freshened. The diameter of the nerve is measured as well as the size of the gap between nerve ends. An appropriately sized nerve allograft is selected. The allograft is placed in the nerve gap. The fascicular alignment of the proximal nerve stump is evaluated and matched to that of the nerve allograft. Microsurgical technique is used to anastomose the proximal nerve stump to the proximal nerve allograft. The fascicular alignment of the distal nerve stump is evaluated and matched to that of the nerve allograft. Microsurgical technique is used to anastomose the distal proximal nerve stump to the distal nerve allograft. The wound is irrigated and closed in layers.

Clinical Example (64913)

A patient presents with a 2-cm gap in a large-diameter median nerve in the forearm. Repair with two nerve allografts is necessary due to a size mismatch between the native and allograft nerves or to separately match the sensory and motor fascicles of the native nerve. After insertion of the first nerve allograft (reported separately), a second nerve allograft is inserted using microsurgical

technique. (Note: This is an add-on code for the additional work related to insertion of an additional nerve allograft for the same nerve. The work related to the first nerve allograft is reported separately as the primary procedure and not included in the work of this add-on code.)

Description of Procedure (64913)

After insertion of the first nerve allograft (reported separately), an appropriately sized additional nerve allograft is selected. The allograft is placed in the nerve gap. The fascicular alignment of the proximal nerve stump is evaluated and matched to that of the nerve allograft. Microsurgical technique is used to anastomose the proximal nerve stump to the proximal nerve allograft. The fascicular alignment of the distal nerve stump is evaluated and matched to that of the nerve allograft. Microsurgical technique is used to anastomose the distal proximal nerve stump to the distal nerve allograft.

Auditory System

Inner Ear

Incision and/or Destruction

69801	Labyrinthotomy, with perfusion of vestibuloactive drug(s), transcanal
	(Do not report 69801 more than once per day)
	(Do not report 69801 in conjunction with 69420, 69421, 69433, 69436 when performed on the same ear)
69805	Endolymphatic sac operation; without shunt
69806	with shunt
	▶(69820, 69840 have been deleted)◀

Rationale

Codes 69820 (fenestration semicircular canal) and 69840 (revision fenestration operation) have been deleted due to low utilization and to ensure that the CPT code set reflects current clinical practice.

★ = Telemedicine   ✚ = Add-on code   ✚ = FDA approval pending   # = Resequenced code

Operating Microscope

▶The surgical microscope is employed when the surgical services are performed using the techniques of microsurgery. Code 69990 should be reported (without modifier 51 appended) in addition to the code for the primary procedure performed. Do not use 69990 for visualization with magnifying loupes or corrected vision. Do not report 69990 in addition to procedures where use of the operating microscope is an inclusive component (15756-15758, 15842, 19364, 19368, 20955-20962, 20969-20973, 22551, 22552, 22856-22861, 26551-26554, 26556, 31526, 31531, 31536, 31541, 31545, 31546, 31561, 31571, 43116, 43180, 43496, 46601, 46607, 49906, 61548, 63075-63078, 64727, 64820-64823, 64912, 64913, 65091-68850, 0184T, 0308T, 0402T).◀

+ **69990**   Microsurgical techniques, requiring use of operating microscope (List separately in addition to code for primary procedure)

Rationale

In support of the addition of codes 64912 and 64913, the guidelines on the use of code 69990 (operating microscope) have been revised to state that code 69990 should not be reported with codes 64912 and 64913.

Refer to the codebook and the Rationale for codes 64912 and 64913 for a full discussion of these changes.

Surgery / Auditory System 69000-69990

Notes

Radiology

The most substantial change to the Radiology section is the addition of new codes and reporting instructions for various X-ray services.

Changes to the Diagnostic Radiology subsection include deletion of codes 71010, 71015, 71020, 71021, 71022, 71023, 71030, 71034, and 71035 (radiologic examination) due to the addition of new codes 71045, 71046, 71047, and 71048 (for reporting radiologic examination of the chest) and deletion of codes 74000, 74010, and 74020 (radiologic examination) due to the addition of codes 74018, 74019, and 74021 (for reporting radiologic examination of the abdomen). In addition, parenthetical notes have been revised to accommodate the use of the new codes and indicate the codes that previously identified specific views used to identify the X-ray procedures.

New guidelines have been added to the Diagnostic Ultrasound subsection to clarify the appropriate use of ultrasound evaluations, including the editorial revision of code 76881 (complete ultrasound) and code 76882 (limited ultrasound) to identify specific anatomic structures for clarification purposes.

In the Radiologic Guidance subsection, many changes have been made to the exclusionary parenthetical notes and cross-references to include reporting instructions for various guidance services.

Summary of Additions, Deletions, and Revisions

The summary of changes shows the actual changes that have been made to the code descriptors.

New codes appear with a bullet (•) and are indicated as "Code added." Revised codes are preceded with a triangle (▲). Within revised codes, the deleted language appears with a ~~strikethrough~~, while new text appears underlined.

The ⁄ symbol is used to identify codes for vaccines that are pending FDA approval. The # symbol is used to identify codes that have been resequenced. CPT add-on codes are annotated by the + symbol. The ⊘ symbol is used to identify codes that are exempt from the use of modifier 51. The ★ symbol is used to identify codes that may be used for reporting telemedicine services.

Code	Description
71010	~~Radiologic examination, chest; single view, frontal~~
71015	~~stereo, frontal~~
71020	~~Radiologic examination, chest, 2 views, frontal and lateral;~~
71021	~~with apical lordotic procedure~~
71022	~~with oblique projections~~
71023	~~with fluoroscopy~~
71030	~~Radiologic examination, chest, complete, minimum of 4 views;~~
71034	~~with fluoroscopy~~
71035	~~Radiologic examination, chest, special views (eg, lateral decubitus, Bucky studies)~~
•71045	Code added

Code	Description
●71046	Code added
●71047	Code added
●71048	Code added
74000	~~Radiologic examination, abdomen; single anteroposterior view~~
74010	~~anteroposterior and additional oblique and cone views~~
74020	~~complete, including decubitus and/or erect views~~
●74018	Code added
●74019	Code added
●74021	Code added
75658	~~Angiography, brachial, retrograde, radiological supervision and interpretation~~
75952	~~Endovascular repair of infrarenal abdominal aortic aneurysm or dissection, radiological supervision and interpretation~~
75953	~~Placement of proximal or distal extension prosthesis for endovascular repair of infrarenal aortic or iliac artery aneurysm, pseudoaneurysm, or dissection, radiological supervision and interpretation~~
75954	~~Endovascular repair of iliac artery aneurysm, pseudoaneurysm, arteriovenous malformation, or trauma, using ilio-iliac tube endoprosthesis, radiological supervision and interpretation~~
▲76000	Fluoroscopy (separate procedure), up to 1 hour physician or other qualified health care professional time~~, other than 71023 or 71034 (eg, cardiac fluoroscopy)~~
▲76881	Ultrasound, ~~extremity, nonvascular,~~ <u>complete joint (ie, joint space and peri-articular soft-tissue structures)</u>, real-time with image documentation~~; complete~~
▲76882	<u>Ultrasound,</u> limited, ~~anatomic specific~~ <u>joint or other nonvascular extremity structure(s) (eg, joint space, peri-articular tendon[s], muscle[s], nerve[s], other soft-tissue structure[s], or soft-tissue mass[es]), real-time with image documentation</u>
77422	~~High energy neutron radiation treatment delivery; single treatment area using a single port or parallel-opposed ports with no blocks or simple blocking~~
78190	~~Kinetics, study of platelet survival, with or without differential organ/tissue localization~~

★ = Telemedicine   ✚ = Add-on code   ⊮ = FDA approval pending   # = Resequenced code

Radiology

Diagnostic Radiology (Diagnostic Imaging)

Chest

(For fluoroscopic or ultrasonic guidance for needle placement procedures (eg, biopsy, aspiration, injection, localization device) of the thorax, see 76942, 77002)

▶(71010 has been deleted. To report, use 71045)◀

▶(71015 has been deleted. To report, use 71045)◀

▶(71020 has been deleted. To report, use 71046)◀

▶(71021 has been deleted. To report, use 71047)◀

▶(71022 has been deleted. To report, see 71047, 71048)◀

▶(71023 has been deleted. To report, see 71046, 76000, 76001)◀

▶(71030 has been deleted. To report, use 71048)◀

▶(71034 has been deleted. To report, see 71048, 76000, 76001)◀

▶(71035 has been deleted. To report, see 71046, 71047, 71048)◀

● **71045**   Radiologic examination, chest; single view

● **71046**   2 views

● **71047**   3 views

● **71048**   4 or more views

▶(For acute abdomen series that includes a single view of the chest and one or more views of the abdomen, use 74022)◀

▶(For concurrent computer-aided detection [CAD] performed in addition to 71045, 71046, 71047, 71048, use 0174T)◀

▶(Do not report 71045, 71046, 71047, 71048 in conjunction with 0175T for computer-aided detection [CAD] performed remotely from the primary interpretation)◀

Rationale

Numerous changes for reporting chest X-ray services have been made. These include deletion of nine codes (71010, 71015, 71020, 71021, 71022, 71023, 71030, 71034, 71035); addition of four new codes (71045, 71046, 71047, 71048); and deletion, addition, and revision of parenthetical notes to accommodate the use of the new codes.

Chest radiologic examination codes 71010 and 71020 have been identified as high-expenditure services. As a result, the chest X-ray codes were reviewed, and revisions have been made to the chest radiograph codes in order to remove view-specific codes (eg, frontal, apical) and to replace them with codes that specify the number of views. This was accomplished by removing all view-specific codes included for chest radiologic examination. In their places, four new codes that specify the number of views have been added to report these services. To provide instruction regarding the appropriate codes to report for specific views, deletion cross-references and other parenthetical notes have been added to direct users to the appropriate radiology code when reporting the service. This includes instruction on how to report the specific views obtained (such as for an acute abdomen series that includes a single view of the chest with one or more views of the abdomen). Also, instruction has been provided on how to report concurrent computer-aided detection performed in addition to new chest X-ray services. (Note: The instruction, which was previously included after deleted code 71030, has been strategically relocated to follow the new codes.) The reciprocal parenthetical note that follows code 0175T includes the instruction that restricts the use of the new codes in conjunction with 0175T. Code 0175T is not to be used with the new chest X-ray codes because this code is not intended to be reported for primary interpretation. Rather, add-on code 0174T should be reported for this service. References to the deleted chest X-ray codes have been deleted and replaced throughout the code set with the new codes, including in the Critical Care guidelines and Coding Tip, Pediatric and Neonatal Critical Care guidelines, and the parenthetical notes following codes 0174T and 0175T.

Although new codes have been assigned for these chest-imaging procedures, the changes do not inherently change the efforts needed to perform the procedures (only the reporting method has changed). Revision of the reporting mechanism reflects a focus on the number of views and does not inherently change what has to be done to obtain the views and to analyze the image results (ie, eliminating the use of specific names for the views does not inherently change the work that is needed to accomplish the procedure). As a result, the intent of the revision is to simplify reporting for these services.

Clinical Example (71045)

A 65-year-old male with unstable angina underwent coronary artery bypass grafting. Immediately postoperatively, the patient was hypoxemic, with decreased breath sounds on the left. A portable anteroposterior chest radiograph is ordered.

Description of Procedure (71045)

The technologist who performs the examination is supervised. The chest radiograph is evaluated, specifically, the lung fields, heart, mediastinum, and pleural spaces. The ribs and other osseous structures, including the spine and shoulders, are assessed. Visualized soft tissues and portions of the upper abdomen are reviewed. Findings to previous studies are compared, if applicable. A report for the medical record is dictated.

Clinical Example (71046)

A 70-year-old female presents with cough and fever. Two views (posteroanterior and lateral) of the chest are ordered.

Description of Procedure (71046)

The technologist who performs the examination is supervised. The chest radiographs are interpreted. The lung fields, heart, mediastinum, and pleural spaces are evaluated. The mediastinal structures and costophrenic sulci are assessed on the second view. The ribs and other osseous structures, including the spine and shoulders, are assessed. Visualized soft tissues and portions of the upper abdomen are reviewed. Findings to previous studies are compared, if applicable. A report for the medical record is dictated.

Clinical Example (71047)

A 45-year-old male presents with a history of a possible right apical lung nodule. Three views of the chest (posteroanterior, lateral, and apical lordotic) are ordered.

Description of Procedure (71047)

The technologist who performs the examination is supervised. The chest radiographs are interpreted. The lung fields, heart, mediastinum, and pleural spaces are evaluated. The mediastinal structures and costophrenic sulci, as well as any previously identified abnormality that necessitated additional views, are assessed. The ribs and other osseous structures, including the spine and shoulders, are assessed. Visualized soft tissues and portions of the upper abdomen are reviewed. Findings to previous studies are compared, if applicable. A report for the medical record is dictated.

Clinical Example (71048)

A 70-year-old female presents with a history of malignancy and a persistent left pleural effusion. Four views of the chest (posteroanterior, lateral, and bilateral decubitus) are ordered.

Description of Procedure (71048)

The technologist who performs the examination is supervised. The chest radiographs are interpreted. The lung fields, heart, mediastinum, and pleural spaces are evaluated. The mediastinal structures and costophrenic sulci, as well as any previously identified abnormality that necessitated additional views, are assessed. The ribs and other osseous structures, including the spine and shoulders, are assessed. Visualized soft tissues and portions of the upper abdomen are reviewed. Findings to previous studies are compared, if applicable. A report for the medical record is dictated.

Spine and Pelvis

72275   Epidurography, radiological supervision and interpretation

(72275 includes 77003)

(For injection procedure, see 62280, 62281, 62282, 62320, 62321, 62322, 62323, 62324, 62325, 62326, 62327, 64479, 64480, 64483, 64484)

(Use 72275 only when an epidurogram is performed, images documented, and a formal radiologic report is issued)

▶(Do not report 72275 in conjunction with 22586, 0195T, 0196T)◀

Rationale

In accordance with the deletion of Category III code 0309T, one of the parenthetical notes that follow code 72275 has been revised.

Refer to the codebook and the Rationale for code 0309T for a full discussion of the changes.

Abdomen

▶(74000 has been deleted. To report, use 74018)◀

▶(74010 has been deleted. To report, see 74019, 74021)◀

▶(74020 has been deleted. To report, see 74019, 74021)◀

● **74018**   Radiologic examination, abdomen; 1 view

● **74019**   2 views

● **74021**   3 or more views

★ = Telemedicine   ✦ = Add-on code   ✚ = FDA approval pending   # = Resequenced code

Rationale

Three codes (74000, 74010, 74020) have been deleted and replaced by three new codes (74018, 74019, 74021) to report radiologic examination of the abdomen. In addition, deletion parenthetical notes have been added to direct users to the new codes. As part of these revisions, the parenthetical note in the Gynecological and Obstetrical subsection (listed prior to code 74710) has been revised to reflect the deletion of code 74000 and addition of codes 74018, 74019, and 74021.

Abdominal X-ray codes 74000 and 74022 have been identified as high-expenditure services. As a result, these codes were reviewed, and revisions have been made to the abdominal radiographic codes in order to remove view-specific codes (eg, anteroposterior, decubitus). In their place, three new codes that specify the number of views have been added. In addition, parenthetical notes associated with the new codes direct users to the appropriate codes for reporting services previously reported according to specific views. This includes revision of the parenthetical note in the Gynecological and Obstetrical subsection that directs users on how to report abdominal and pelvic X-ray procedures, noting the new and existing codes that should be reported. Some codes that include view-specific language, such as the complete acute abdomen series 74022, have been retained, as these codes are used to report specific services that require certain views in order to accomplish the service.

Clinical Example (74018)

An 86-year-old male presents with constipation. A single view of the abdomen is ordered.

Description of Procedure (74018)

The technologist who performs the examination is supervised. The examination is interpreted, and the findings compared to those from previous studies, if applicable. The bowel gas pattern, bowel wall, and enteric contents are assessed. Visualized portions of the lower chest, solid organs, and osseous structures, including the ribs, spine, and pelvis, are evaluated. The location of any internal tubes or catheters, if present, are determined and assessed for lithiasis. A report is dictated for the medical record.

Clinical Example (74019)

A 50-year-old female presents with acute onset abdominal pain, nausea, and vomiting. Two views of the abdomen (frontal supine and upright [erect]) are ordered.

Description of Procedure (74019)

The technologist who performs the examination is supervised. The examination is interpreted, and the findings compared to those from previous studies, if applicable. The bowel gas pattern, bowel wall, and enteric contents are assessed. The presence of lithiasis, pneumoperitoneum, or ascites is evaluated. Visualized portions of the lower chest, solid organs, and osseous structures, including the ribs, spine, and pelvis, are evaluated. A report is dictated for the medical record.

Clinical Example (74021)

A 65-year-old male with a history of renal calculi presents with flank pain. Three views of the abdomen (frontal [anteroposterior] and bilateral oblique) are ordered.

Description of Procedure (74021)

The technologist who performs the examination is supervised. The examination is interpreted, and the findings compared to those from previous studies, if applicable. The bowel gas pattern, bowel wall, and enteric contents are assessed. Visualized portions of the lower chest, solid organs, and osseous structures, including the ribs, spine, and pelvis, are evaluated. The presence or absence of lithiasis, pneumoperitoneum, or ascites is determined. A report is dictated for the medical record.

Gynecological and Obstetrical

▶(For abdomen and pelvis, see 72170-72190, 74018, 74019, 74021, 74022, 74150, 74160, 74170)◀

74710   Pelvimetry, with or without placental localization

Rationale

The instructional parenthetical note in the Gynecological and Obstetrical subsection has been revised to direct reporting of three new abdominal radiological examination procedures that specify the number of views for the procedure.

Refer to the codebook and the Rationale for codes 74018-74021 for a full discussion of these changes.

Vascular Procedures

Aorta and Arteries

▶(75658 has been deleted. To report, use 75710)◀

Rationale

Code 75658, which was used to report brachial retrograde angiography with radiological supervision and interpretation, has been deleted.

With changes in clinical practice and the addition of the Dialysis section of codes in CPT 2017, this service is more appropriately reported with existing upper extremity angiography code 75710. A deletion parenthetical note has been placed after code 75658 to direct the use of code 75710.

Transcatheter Procedures

▶(75952, 75953, 75954 have been deleted. To report, see 34701-34711, 0254T)◀

Rationale

In support of the changes in reporting endovascular aneurysm repair procedures, codes 75952, 75953, and 75954 (endovascular repair radiological supervision and interpretation) have been deleted. The services reported with these codes have been bundled into the new abdominal aorta and/or iliac arteries codes located in the Surgery section. A parenthetical note has been added directing users to the new codes.

Refer to the codebook and the Rationale for codes 34701-34713, 34714, 34715, and 34716 for a full discussion of these changes.

Other Procedures

(For computed tomography cerebral perfusion analysis, see Category III code 0042T)

(For arthrography of shoulder, use 73040; elbow, use 73085; wrist, use 73115; hip, use 73525; knee, use 73580; ankle, use 73615)

▲ **76000**   Fluoroscopy (separate procedure), up to 1 hour physician or other qualified health care professional time

Rationale

In accordance with the deletion of the chest X-ray codes, code 76000 has been revised. Code 76000 was updated by removing the reference to deleted codes 71023 and 71034, which described chest X rays with fluoroscopy. The new chest X-ray codes only specify the number of views.

Refer to the codebook and the Rationale for codes 71045-71048 for a full discussion of these changes.

Diagnostic Ultrasound

Extremities

▶Code 76881 represents a complete evaluation of a specific joint in an extremity. Code 76881 requires ultrasound examination of all of the following joint elements: joint space (eg, effusion), peri-articular soft-tissue structures that surround the joint (ie, muscles, tendons, other soft tissue structures), and any identifiable abnormality. In some circumstances, additional evaluations such as dynamic imaging or stress maneuvers may be performed as part of the complete evaluation. Code 76881 also requires permanently recorded images and a written report containing a description of each of the required elements or reason that an element(s) could not be visualized (eg, absent secondary to surgery or trauma).

When fewer than all of the required elements for a "complete" exam (76881) are performed, report the "limited" code (76882).

Code 76882 represents a limited evaluation of a joint or an evaluation of a structure(s) in an extremity other than a joint (eg, soft-tissue mass, fluid collection, or nerve[s]). Limited evaluation of a joint includes assessment of a specific anatomic structure(s) (eg, joint space only [effusion] or tendon, muscle, and/or other soft tissue structure[s] that surround the joint) that does not assess all of the required elements included in 76881. Code 76882 also requires permanently recorded images and a written report containing a description of each of the elements evaluated.◀

For spectral and color Doppler evaluation of the extremities, use 93925, 93926, 93930, 93931, 93970, or 93971 as appropriate.

▲ **76881**   Ultrasound, complete joint (ie, joint space and peri-articular soft tissue structures) real-time with image documentation

▲ **76882**   Ultrasound, limited, joint or other nonvascular extremity structure(s) (eg, joint space, peri-articular tendon[s], muscle[s], nerve[s], other soft tissue structure[s], or soft tissue mass[es]), real-time with image documentation

Rationale

Code 76881 has been revised to report a complete ultrasound examination of a joint that consists of real-time scans. Code 76882 has been revised to report a limited examination of the extremity in which a specific joint or anatomic structure(s) other than a joint is assessed. Although codes 76881 and 76882 have been editorially revised, there is no change in the intended use of these codes.

In response to a RUC analysis, it was determined that codes 76881 and 76882 and the diagnostic ultrasound extremities introductory guidelines should be revised and updated to clarify the distinction between complete and limited studies. Key terms have been added to the guidelines to distinguish between complete and limited studies.

Ultrasonic Guidance Procedures

76940   Ultrasound guidance for, and monitoring of, parenchymal tissue ablation

▶(Do not report 76940 in conjunction with 20982, 20983, 32994, 32998, 50250, 50542, 76942, 76998)◀

▶(For ablation, see 47370-47382, 47383, 50592, 50593)◀

Rationale

The parenthetical notes that follow code 76940 have been revised. This was done to accommodate the addition of a new code (32994) to the Respiratory subsection and the revision of an existing code (32998) to reflect radiofrequency ablation therapy of pulmonary tumors. This was accomplished by adding codes 32994 and 32998 to the exclusionary parenthetical note that follows 76940. In addition, the second parenthetical note that follows code 76940 has been revised by deletion of code 32998.

Refer to the codebook and the Rationale for code 32998 for a full discussion of the changes.

76941   Ultrasonic guidance for intrauterine fetal transfusion or cordocentesis, imaging supervision and interpretation

(For procedure, see 36460, 59012)

76942   Ultrasonic guidance for needle placement (eg, biopsy, aspiration, injection, localization device), imaging supervision and interpretation

▶(Do not report 76942 in conjunction with 10030, 19083, 19285, 20604, 20606, 20611, 27096, 32554, 32555, 32556, 32557, 37760, 37761, 43232, 43237, 43242, 45341, 45342, 55874, 64479, 64480, 64483, 64484, 64490, 64491, 64493, 64494, 64495, 76975, 0213T, 0214T, 0215T, 0216T, 0217T, 0218T, 0228T, 0229T, 0230T, 0231T, 0232T, 0249T, 0481T)◀

▶(For harvesting, preparation, and injection[s] of platelet-rich plasma, use 0232T)◀

Rationale

In support of establishment of codes 55874 and 0481T and the deletion of code 0301T, the exclusionary parenthetical note that follows code 76942 has been revised. In addition, numerous existing ranges in this parenthetical note have been broken up to identify the specific codes that are intended for exclusion as part of the exclusionary parenthetical listing. Refer to the codebook and the Rationale for codes 55874 and 0481T for a full discussion of the changes.

In accordance with the addition of Category III code 0481T, the second parenthetical note that follows code 76942 has been updated to specify that code 0232T is for harvesting, preparation, and injection(s) of platelet-rich plasma. Refer to the codebook and the Rationale for code 0481T for a full discussion of the changes.

Other Procedures

76998   Ultrasonic guidance, intraoperative

▶(Do not report 76998 in conjunction with 36475, 36479, 37760, 37761, 47370, 47371, 47380, 47381, 47382, 0249T)◀

(For ultrasound guidance for open and laparoscopic radiofrequency tissue ablation, use 76940)

Rationale

In accordance with the deletion of Category III code 0301T, the first instructional parenthetical note that follows code 76998 has been revised with the removal of this code.

Refer to the codebook and the Rationale for code 0301T for a full discussion of the changes.

Rationale

In support of establishment of Category I code 32994, the parenthetical notes that follow code 77013 have been updated. In addition, code 32998 has been removed from the second parenthetical note.

Refer to the codebook and the Rationale for codes 32994 and 32998 for a full discussion of the changes.

Radiologic Guidance

Computed Tomography Guidance

77011   Computed tomography guidance for stereotactic localization

77012   Computed tomography guidance for needle placement (eg, biopsy, aspiration, injection, localization device), radiological supervision and interpretation

►(Do not report 77011, 77012 in conjunction with 22586, 0195T, 0196T)◄

►(Do not report 77012 in conjunction with 10030, 27096, 32554, 32555, 32556, 32557, 64479, 64480, 64483, 64484, 64490, 64491, 64492, 64493, 64494, 64495, 64633, 64634, 64635, 64636, 0232T, 0481T)◄

►(For harvesting, preparation, and injection[s] of platelet-rich plasma, use 0232T)◄

Rationale

In support of the deletion of code 0309T and the establishment of Category III code 0481T, the parenthetical notes that follow code 77012 have been updated.

Refer to the codebook and the Rationale for codes 0309T and 0481T for a full discussion of the changes.

77013   Computed tomography guidance for, and monitoring of, parenchymal tissue ablation

►(Do not report 77013 in conjunction with 20982, 20983, 32994, 32998)◄

►(For percutaneous ablation, see 47382, 47383, 50592, 50593)◄

Magnetic Resonance Guidance

77021   Magnetic resonance guidance for needle placement (eg, for biopsy, needle aspiration, injection, or placement of localization device) radiological supervision and interpretation

(For procedure, see appropriate organ or site)

►(Do not report 77021 in conjunction with 10030, 19085, 19287, 32554, 32555, 32556, 32557, 0232T, 0481T)◄

►(For harvesting, preparation, and injection[s] of platelet-rich plasma, use 0232T)◄

Rationale

In support of establishment of Category III code 0481T, the parenthetical notes that follow code 77021 have been updated.

Refer to the codebook and the Rationale for code 0481T for a full discussion of the changes.

77022   Magnetic resonance guidance for, and monitoring of, parenchymal tissue ablation

►(Do not report 77022 in conjunction with 20982, 20983, 32994, 32998, 0071T, 0072T)◄

►(For percutaneous ablation, see 47382, 47383, 50592, 50593)◄

★ = Telemedicine   ✚ = Add-on code   ⁄ = FDA approval pending   # = Resequenced code

Rationale

The parenthetical notes that follow code 77022 have been revised. This was done to accommodate the addition of a new code (32994) to the Respiratory subsection and the revision of an existing code (32998) to reflect radiofrequency ablation therapy of pulmonary tumors. This was accomplished by adding codes 32994 and 32998 to the exclusionary parenthetical note that follows code 77022. In addition, the second parenthetical note that follows code 77022 has been revised by the deletion of code 32998 from the parenthetical note.

Refer to the codebook and the Rationale for code 32998 for a full discussion of the changes.

Radiation Oncology

Neutron Beam Treatment Delivery

►(77422 has been deleted)◄

77423   High energy neutron radiation treatment delivery, 1 or more isocenter(s) with coplanar or non-coplanar geometry with blocking and/or wedge, and/or compensator(s)

Rationale

Radiation oncology code 77422 (high energy neutron radiation treatment delivery; single treatment area using a single port or parallel-opposed ports with no blocks or simple blocking) has been deleted. This was due to low utilization and to ensure that the CPT code set reflects current clinical practice. Code 77423 was a child code under code 77422. With the deletion of code 77422, code 77423 is now a parent code; however, the meaning of code 77423 has not changed.

In support of the deletion of code 77422, the Radiation Management and Treatment Table has been revised with the removal of the reference to code 77422 and simple neutron beam treatment.

Nuclear Medicine

Diagnostic

Hematopoietic, Reticuloendothelial and Lymphatic System

78185   Spleen imaging only, with or without vascular flow

(If combined with liver study, use procedures 78215 and 78216)

►(78190 has been deleted)◄

Rationale

Nuclear medicine code 78190 (kinetics, study of platelet survival, with or without differential organ/tissue localization) has been deleted. This was due to low utilization and to ensure that the CPT code set reflects current clinical practice.

78191   Platelet survival study

▲ = Revised code   ● = New code   ►◄ = Contains new or revised text   ⊘ = Modifier 51 exempt   American Medical Association   **109**

Radiology 70010-79999

Notes

Pathology and Laboratory

In the Presumptive Drug Class Screening subsection, codes 80305, 80306, and 80307 have been revised.

Under the Molecular Pathology subsection, in the Tier 1 Molecular Pathology Procedures subsection, code 81257 has been revised to conform to the parent code structure, and 31 new Tier 1 codes 81105-81370 have been added to report gene sequencing and analysis. In addition, there have been revisions, additions, and deletions for Tier 2 codes 81400-81406.

In the Genomic Sequencing Procedures and Other Molecular Multianalyte Assays subsection, codes 81432 and 81439 have been revised.

Changes in the Multianalyte Assays with Algorithmic Analyses (MAAA) subsection include the addition of code 81520 (analysis of genes using hybrid capture), which replaces deleted code 0008M (administrative MAAA). Other changes include the addition of three new codes: 81521 for reporting the performance of analysis for measurement of risk of distant metastasis; 81541 for the MAAA test that is used to measure prostate cancer mortality risk; and 81551 for the analysis of methylation status of gene markers for detection of prostate cancer.

In the Chemistry subsection, revisions have been made to codes 82042, 82043, and 82044 to clarify quantitative urine testing.

In the Immunology subsection, revisions have been made to codes 86003 and 86005 to clarify specimen collection per current needs. In addition, new code 86008 has been added to report quantitative or semiquantitative testing of allergen-specific IgE.

Codes 87277, 87470, and 87477 have been deleted from the Microbiology subsection. In addition, two new codes have been added: 87634 for reporting nucleic acid detection of respiratory syncytial virus and 87662 to identify Zika virus detection. Parenthetical notes have also been added and revised.

Cytopathology code 88154 has been deleted and parenthetical notes have been revised.

Summary of Additions, Deletions, and Revisions

The summary of changes shows the actual changes that have been made to the code descriptors.

New codes appear with a bullet (•) and are indicated as "Code added." Revised codes are preceded with a triangle (▲). Within revised codes, the deleted language appears with a ~~strikethrough~~, while new text appears <u>underlined</u>.

The ⚡ symbol is used to identify codes for vaccines that are pending FDA approval. The # symbol is used to identify codes that have been resequenced. CPT add-on codes are annotated by the + symbol. The ⊘ symbol is used to identify codes that are exempt from the use of modifier 51. The ★ symbol is used to identify codes that may be used for reporting telemedicine services.

Pathology and Laboratory 80047-89398, 0001U-0017U

Code	Description
#▲80305	Drug test(s), presumptive, any number of drug classes, any number of devices or procedures (eg, immunoassay); capable of being read by direct optical observation only (eg, dipsticksutilizing immunoassay [eg, dipsticks, cups, cards, or cartridges]), includes sample validation when performed, per date of service
#▲80306	read by instrument assisted direct optical observation (eg, dipsticksutilizing immunoassay [eg, dipsticks, cups, cards, or cartridges]), includes sample validation when performed, per date of service
#▲80307	by instrument chemistry analyzers (eg, utilizing immunoassay [eg, EIA, ELISA, EMIT, FPIA, IA, KIMS, RIA]), chromatography (eg, GC, HPLC), and mass spectrometry either with or without chromatography, (eg, DART, DESI, GC-MS, GC-MS/MS, LC-MS, LC-MS/MS, LDTD, MALDI, TOF) includes sample validation when performed, per date of service
●81175	Code added
●81176	Code added
#●81230	Code added
#●81231	Code added
●81232	Code added
#●81238	Code added
●81247	Code added
●81248	Code added
●81249	Code added
▲81257	*HBA1/HBA2 (alpha globin 1 and alpha globin 2)* (eg, alpha thalassemia, Hb Bart hydrops fetalis syndrome, HbH disease), gene analysis; for common deletions or variant (eg, Southeast Asian, Thai, Filipino, Mediterranean, alpha3.7, alpha4.2, alpha20.5, Constant Spring)
●81258	Code added
●81259	Code added
#●81269	Code added
#●81105	Code added
#●81106	Code added
#●81107	Code added
#●81108	Code added
#●81109	Code added
#●81110	Code added
#●81111	Code added
#●81112	Code added
#●81120	Code added
#●81121	Code added
#●81283	Code added

★ = Telemedicine   ✚ = Add-on code   ✔ = FDA approval pending   # = Resequenced code

Code	Description
#●81334	Code added
●81328	Code added
●81335	Code added
●81346	Code added
●81361	Code added
●81362	Code added
●81363	Code added
●81364	Code added
▲81400	Molecular pathology procedure, Level 1 (eg, identification of single germline variant [eg, SNP] by techniques such as restriction enzyme digestion or melt curve analysis)
	~~DPYD (dihydropyrimidine dehydrogenase) (eg, 5-fluorouracil/5-FU and capecitabine drug metabolism), IVS14+1G>A variant~~
	~~Human Platelet Antigen 1 genotyping (HPA-1), ITGB3 (integrin, beta 3 [platelet glycoprotein IIIa], antigen CD61 [GPIIIa]) (eg, neonatal alloimmune thrombocytopenia [NAIT], post-transfusion purpura), HPA-1a/b (L33P)~~
	~~Human Platelet Antigen 2 genotyping (HPA-2), GP1BA (glycoprotein Ib [platelet], alpha polypeptide [GPIba]) (eg, neonatal alloimmune thrombocytopenia [NAIT], post-transfusion purpura), HPA-2a/b (T145M)~~
	~~Human Platelet Antigen 3 genotyping (HPA-3), ITGA2B (integrin, alpha 2b [platelet glycoprotein IIb of IIb/IIIa complex], antigen CD41 [GPIIb]) (eg, neonatal alloimmune thrombocytopenia [NAIT], post-transfusion purpura), HPA-3a/b (I843S)~~
	~~Human Platelet Antigen 4 genotyping (HPA-4), ITGB3 (integrin, beta 3 [platelet glycoprotein IIIa], antigen CD61 [GPIIIa]) (eg, neonatal alloimmune thrombocytopenia [NAIT], post-transfusion purpura), HPA-4a/b (R143Q)~~
	~~Human Platelet Antigen 5 genotyping (HPA-5), ITGA2 (integrin, alpha 2 [CD49B, alpha 2 subunit of VLA-2 receptor] [GPIa]) (eg, neonatal alloimmune thrombocytopenia [NAIT], post-transfusion purpura), HPA-5a/b (K505E)~~
	~~Human Platelet Antigen 6 genotyping (HPA-6w), ITGB3 (integrin, beta 3 [platelet glycoprotein IIIa, antigen CD61] [GPIIIa]) (eg, neonatal alloimmune thrombocytopenia [NAIT], post-transfusion purpura), HPA-6a/b (R489Q)~~
	~~Human Platelet Antigen 9 genotyping (HPA-9w), ITGA2B (integrin, alpha 2b [platelet glycoprotein IIb of IIb/IIIa complex, antigen CD41] [GPIIb]) (eg, neonatal alloimmune thrombocytopenia [NAIT], post-transfusion purpura), HPA-9a/b (V837M)~~
	~~Human Platelet Antigen 15 genotyping (HPA-15), CD109 (CD109 molecule) (eg, neonatal alloimmune thrombocytopenia [NAIT], post-transfusion purpura), HPA-15a/b (S682Y)~~
	~~IL28B (interleukin 28B [interferon, lambda 3]) (eg, drug response), rs12979860 variant~~
	~~SLCO1B1 (solute carrier organic anion transporter family, member 1B1) (eg, adverse drug reaction), V174A variant~~

Pathology and Laboratory 80047-89398, 0001U-0017U

Code	Description
▲81401	Molecular pathology procedure, Level 2 (eg, 2-10 SNPs, 1 methylated variant, or 1 somatic variant [typically using nonsequencing target variant analysis], or detection of a dynamic mutation disorder/triplet repeat)
	~~CYP3A4 (cytochrome P450, family 3, subfamily A, polypeptide 4) (eg, drug metabolism), common variants (eg, *2, *3, *4, *5, *6)~~
	~~CYP3A5 (cytochrome P450, family 3, subfamily A, polypeptide 5) (eg, drug metabolism), common variants (eg, *2, *3, *4, *5, *6)~~
	~~HBB (hemoglobin, beta) (eg, sickle cell anemia, hemoglobin C, hemoglobin E), common variants (eg, HbS, HbC, HbE)~~
	LINC00518 (long intergenic non-protein coding RNA 518) (eg, melanoma), expression analysis
	PRAME (preferentially expressed antigen in melanoma) (eg, melanoma), expression analysis
	~~TPMT (thiopurine S-methyltransferase) (eg, drug metabolism), common variants (eg, *2, *3)~~
	~~TYMS (thymidylate synthetase) (eg, 5-fluorouracil/5-FU drug metabolism), tandem repeat variant~~
▲81403	Molecular pathology procedure, Level 4 (eg, analysis of single exon by DNA sequence analysis, analysis of >10 amplicons using multiplex PCR in 2 or more independent reactions, mutation scanning or duplication/deletion variants of 2-5 exons)
	~~HBB (hemoglobin, beta, beta-globin) (eg, beta thalassemia), duplication/deletion analysis~~
	~~IDH1 (isocitrate dehydrogenase 1 [NADP+], soluble) (eg, glioma), common exon 4 variants (eg, R132H, R132C)~~
	~~IDH2 (isocitrate dehydrogenase 2 [NADP+], mitochondrial) (eg, glioma), common exon 4 variants (eg, R140W, R172M)~~
▲81404	Molecular pathology procedure, Level 5 (eg, analysis of 2-5 exons by DNA sequence analysis, mutation scanning or duplication/deletion variants of 6-10 exons, or characterization of a dynamic mutation disorder/triplet repeat by Southern blot analysis)
	~~HBA1/HBA2 (alpha globin 1 and alpha globin 2) (eg, alpha thalassemia), duplication/deletion analysis~~
	~~HBB (hemoglobin, beta, Beta-Globin) (eg, thalassemia), full gene sequence~~
▲81405	Molecular pathology procedure, Level 6 (eg, analysis of 6-10 exons by DNA sequence analysis, mutation scanning or duplication/deletion variants of 11-25 exons, regionally targeted cytogenomic array analysis)
	CPOX (coproporphyrinogen oxidase) (eg, hereditary coproporphyria), full gene sequence
	CTRC (chymotrypsin C) (eg, hereditary pancreatitis), full gene sequence
	~~F9 (coagulation factor IX) (eg, hemophilia B), full gene sequence~~
	~~HBA1/HBA2 (alpha globin 1 and alpha globin 2) (eg, thalassemia), full gene sequence~~
	PKLR (pyruvate kinase, liver and RBC) (eg, pyruvate kinase deficiency), full gene sequence
▲81406	Molecular pathology procedure, Level 7 (eg, analysis of 11-25 exons by DNA sequence analysis, mutation scanning or duplication/deletion variants of 26-50 exons, cytogenomic array analysis for neoplasia)
	ANOS1 (anosmin-1) (eg, Kallmann syndrome 1), full gene sequence
	HMBS (hydroxymethylbilane synthase) (eg, acute intermittent porphyria), full gene sequence
	~~KAL1 (Kallmann syndrome 1 sequence) (eg, Kallmann syndrome), full gene sequence~~
	PPOX (protoporphyrinogen oxidase) (eg, variegate porphyria), full gene sequence
▲81432	Hereditary breast cancer-related disorders (eg, hereditary breast cancer, hereditary ovarian cancer, hereditary endometrial cancer); genomic sequence analysis panel, must include sequencing of at least ~~14~~10 genes, always including ~~ATM,~~ BRCA1, BRCA2~~, BRIP1~~, CDH1, MLH1, MSH2, MSH6~~, NBN~~, PALB2, PTEN~~, RAD51C~~, STK11, and TP53
#●81448	Code added

★ = Telemedicine   ✚ = Add-on code   ✒ = FDA approval pending   # = Resequenced code

Code	Description
▲81439	~~Inherited~~Hereditary cardiomyopathy (eg, hypertrophic cardiomyopathy, dilated cardiomyopathy, arrhythmogenic right ventricular cardiomyopathy), genomic sequence analysis panel, must include sequencing of at least 5 cardiomyopathy-related genes ~~including~~(eg, DSG2, MYBPC3, MYH7, PKP2, TTN)
●81520	Code added
●81521	Code added
●81541	Code added
●81551	Code added
▲82043	urine (eg, microalbumin), quantitative
▲82044	urine (eg, microalbumin), semiquantitative (eg, reagent strip assay)
#▲82042	~~urine or~~other source, quantitative, each specimen
83499	~~Hydroxyprogesterone, 20-~~
84061	~~forensic examination~~
▲86003	Allergen specific IgE; quantitative or semiquantitative, ~~each~~crude allergen extract, each
▲86005	qualitative, multiallergen screen (~~dipstick~~eg, ~~paddle~~disk, ~~or disk~~sponge, card)
●86008	Code added
86185	~~Counterimmunoelectrophoresis, each antigen~~
86243	~~Fc receptor~~
86378	~~Migration inhibitory factor test (MIF)~~
86729	~~lymphogranuloma venereum~~
●86794	Code added
86822	~~lymphocyte culture, primed (PLC)~~
87277	~~Legionella micdadei~~
87470	~~Infectious agent detection by nucleic acid (DNA or RNA); Bartonella henselae and Bartonella quintana, direct probe technique~~
87477	~~Borrelia burgdorferi, quantification~~
87515	~~hepatitis B virus, direct probe technique~~
●87634	Code added
●87662	Code added
88154	~~with manual screening and computer-assisted rescreening using cell selection and review under physician supervision~~
●0001U	Code added
●0002U	Code added
●0003U	Code added

Code	Description
●0004U	Code added
●0005U	Code added
●0006U	Code added
●0007U	Code added
●0008U	Code added
●0009U	Code added
●0010U	Code added
●0011U	Code added
●0012U	Code added
●0013U	Code added
●0014U	Code added
●0015U	Code added
●0016U	Code added
●0017U	Code added

★ = Telemedicine   ✚ = Add-on code   ✒ = FDA approval pending   # = Resequenced code

Pathology and Laboratory

Drug Assay

Presumptive Drug Class Screening

Drugs or classes of drugs may be commonly assayed first by a presumptive screening method followed by a definitive drug identification method. The methodology is considered when coding presumptive procedures. Each code (80305, 80306, 80307) represents all drugs and drug classes performed by the respective methodology per date of service. Each code also includes all sample validation procedures performed. Examples of sample validation procedures may include, but are not limited to, pH, specific gravity, and nitrite. The codes (80305, 80306, 80307) represent three different method categories:

1. Code 80305 is used to report procedures in which the results are read by direct optical observation. The results are visually read. Examples of these procedures are dipsticks, cups, cards, and cartridges. Report 80305 once, irrespective of the number of direct observation drug class procedures performed or results on any date of service.

2. Code 80306 is used to report procedures when an instrument is used to assist in determining the result of a direct optical observation methodology. Examples of these procedures are dipsticks, cards, and cartridges inserted into an instrument that determines the final result of an optical observation methodology. Report 80306 once, irrespective of the number of drug class procedures or results on any date of service.

3. Code 80307 is used to report any number of devices or procedures by instrumented chemistry analyzers. There are many different instrumented methodologies available to perform presumptive drug assays. Examples include immunoassay (eg, EIA, ELISA, EMIT, FPIA, IA, KIMS, RIA), chromatography (eg, GC, HPLC), and mass spectrometry, either with or without chromatography (eg, DART, DESI, GC-MS, GC-MS/MS, LC-MS, LC-MS/MS, LDTD, MALDI, TOF). Some of these methodologies may be used for definitive drug testing also, but, for the purpose of presumptive drug testing; the presumptive method is insufficient to provide definitive drug identification. Report 80307 once, irrespective of the number of drug class procedures or results on any date of service.

(80300, 80301, 80302, 80303, 80304 have been deleted. To report, see 80305, 80306, 80307)

#▲ 80305   Drug test(s), presumptive, any number of drug classes, any number of devices or procedures; capable of being read by direct optical observation only (eg, utilizing immunoassay [eg, dipsticks, cups, cards, or cartridges]), includes sample validation when performed, per date of service

#▲ 80306   read by instrument assisted direct optical observation (eg, utilizing immunoassay [eg, dipsticks, cups, cards, or cartridges]), includes sample validation when performed, per date of service

#▲ 80307   by instrument chemistry analyzers (eg, utilizing immunoassay [eg, EIA, ELISA, EMIT, FPIA, IA, KIMS, RIA]), chromatography (eg, GC, HPLC), and mass spectrometry either with or without chromatography, (eg, DART, DESI, GC-MS, GC-MS/MS, LC-MS, LC-MS/MS, LDTD, MALDI, TOF) includes sample validation when performed, per date of service

Rationale

Codes 80305-80307 have been editorially revised to comply with CPT code convention regarding the display of codes with common language. The three codes include language that identifies elements that are common to the three procedures. To simplify reporting of these codes, the common language has been included before the semicolon in code 80305, and the duplicate language has been removed from child codes 80306 and 80307.

Molecular Pathology

The molecular pathology codes include all analytical services performed in the test (eg, cell lysis, nucleic acid stabilization, extraction, digestion, amplification, and detection). Any procedures required prior to cell lysis (eg, microdissection, codes 88380 and 88381) should be reported separately.

The results of the procedure may require interpretation by a physician or other qualified health care professional. When only the interpretation and report are performed, modifier 26 may be appended to the specific molecular pathology code.

All analyses are qualitative unless otherwise noted.

▶For microbial identification, see 87149-87153 and 87471-87801, and 87900-87904. For in situ hybridization analyses, see 88271-88275 and 88365-88368.◀

Rationale

In support of the deletion of code 87470, the molecular pathology guideline that directs users to microbial identification codes has been revised with the removal of code 87470.

Refer to the codebook and the Rationale for code 87470 for a full discussion of the changes.

Tier 1 Molecular Pathology Procedures

81105	Code is out of numerical sequence. See 81257-81261
81106	Code is out of numerical sequence. See 81257-81261
81107	Code is out of numerical sequence. See 81105-81383
81108	Code is out of numerical sequence. See 81257-81261
81109	Code is out of numerical sequence. See 81257-81261
81110	Code is out of numerical sequence. See 81257-81261
81111	Code is out of numerical sequence. See 81257-81261
81112	Code is out of numerical sequence. See 81257-81261
81120	Code is out of numerical sequence. See 81257-81261
81121	Code is out of numerical sequence. See 81257-81261
81170	*ABL1 (ABL proto-oncogene 1, non-receptor tyrosine kinase)* (eg, acquired imatinib tyrosine kinase inhibitor resistance), gene analysis, variants in the kinase domain
● **81175**	*ASXL1 (additional sex combs like 1, transcriptional regulator)* (eg, myelodysplastic syndrome, myeloproliferative neoplasms, chronic myelomonocytic leukemia), gene analysis; full gene sequence
● **81176**	targeted sequence analysis (eg, exon 12)

Rationale

Two new Tier 1 codes (81175 and 81176) have been added to report analysis of the ASXL1 gene. Code 81175 should be used to report the full gene sequence analysis. Code 81176 should be used to report targeted sequence analysis.

Clinical Example (81175)

A 55-year-old male presents to his physician complaining of fatigue, frequent infections, and easy bruising. The patient's complete blood count, peripheral blood smear, flow cytometry analysis, and bone marrow examination support a diagnosis of myelodysplastic syndrome. A sample of anticoagulated peripheral blood is submitted to the laboratory for ASXL1 mutation detection.

Description of Procedure (81175)

DNA is extracted from a hematologic tissue sample such as peripheral blood or bone marrow. Polymerase chain reaction (PCR) amplification is performed on DNA using bidirectional sequencing to detect the ASXL1 gene. An unrelated internal control gene is amplified to ensure adequacy of sample and assay conditions. The pathologist or other qualified health care professional analyzes appropriate laboratory control results and patient sample results to establish mutation status. The pathologist or other qualified health care professional composes a report that specifies the presence or absence of the ASXL1 gene in the patient's DNA sample and includes a comment on the implications of the test result for patient care. The report is edited and signed, and the results are communicated to appropriate caregivers.

Clinical Example (81176)

A 60-year-old male presents to his physician complaining of fatigue, frequent infections, and easy bruising. The patient's complete blood count, peripheral blood smear, flow cytometry analysis, and bone marrow examination support a diagnosis of myelodysplastic syndrome. A sample of anticoagulated peripheral blood is submitted to the laboratory for targeted ASXL1 mutation detection.

Description of Procedure (81176)

DNA is extracted from a hematologic tissue sample, such as peripheral blood or bone marrow. PCR amplification is performed on DNA using bidirectional sequencing to detect mutations in exon 12 of the ASXL1 gene. The pathologist or other qualified health care professional analyzes appropriate laboratory control results and patient sample results to establish mutation status. The pathologist or other qualified health care professional composes a report that specifies the presence or absence of a mutation in the patient's DNA sample and includes a comment on the implications of the test result for patient care. The report is edited and signed, and the results are communicated to appropriate caregivers.

81200   *ASPA (aspartoacylase)* (eg, Canavan disease) gene analysis, common variants (eg, E285A, Y231X)

\#● 81230   *CYP3A4 (cytochrome P450 family 3 subfamily A member 4)* (eg, drug metabolism), gene analysis, common variant(s) (eg, *2, *22)

\#● 81231   *CYP3A5 (cytochrome P450 family 3 subfamily A member 5)* (eg, drug metabolism), gene analysis, common variants (eg, *2, *3, *4, *5, *6, *7)

81230   Code is out of numerical sequence. See 81226-81229

81231   Code is out of numerical sequence. See 81226-81229

● 81232   *DPYD (dihydropyrimidine dehydrogenase)* (eg, 5-fluorouracil/5-FU and capecitabine drug metabolism), gene analysis, common variant(s) (eg, *2A, *4, *5, *6)

Rationale

Three new codes (81230, 81231, 81232) have been added for reporting common variant gene analysis testing. Code 81230 has been added to report common variant gene analysis testing of the CYP3A4 gene; code 81231 for common variant gene analysis testing of the CYP3A5 gene; and code 81232 for common variant gene analysis testing of the DPYD gene.

Clinical Example (81230)

A 65-year-old male presents to his physician with a history of ticagrelor use. He recently had a second myocardial infarction. An anticoagulated peripheral blood sample is submitted for mutation analysis to assess the patient's CYP3A4 metabolizer status.

Description of Procedure (81230)

High-quality genomic DNA isolated from whole blood is subjected to real-time PCR and PCR/fluorescence monitoring for the *2 and *22 variants. The pathologist or other qualified healthcare professional examines the allele calls for the *2 and *22 variants in the CYP3A4 gene. The pathologist or other qualified health care professional composes a report that specifies the patient's mutation status. The report is edited and signed, and the results are communicated to appropriate caregivers.

Clinical Example (81231)

A 65-year-old male, who recently had a kidney transplant, shows signs of acute rejection, as tacrolimus trough levels are below therapeutic range. An anticoagulated peripheral blood sample is submitted for mutation analysis to assess the patient's CYP3A5 metabolizer status.

Description of Procedure (81231)

High-quality genomic DNA isolated from whole blood is subjected to real-time PCR and PCR/fluorescence monitoring for the *3, *6, and *7 variants. The pathologist or other qualified health care professional examines the allele calls for the *3, *6, and *7 variants in the CYP3A5 gene. The pathologist or other qualified health care professional composes a report that specifies the patient's mutation status. The report is edited and signed, and the results are communicated to appropriate caregivers.

Clinical Example (81232)

A 65-year-old female is diagnosed with colon cancer. It is determined that the drug of choice for her is 5-fluorouracil (5-FU). However, after treatment with 5-FU, she exhibits toxicity. An anticoagulated peripheral blood sample is submitted for mutation analysis to assess the patient's DPYD metabolizer status.

Description of Procedure (81232)

High-quality genomic DNA isolated from whole blood is subjected to real-time PCR and PCR/fluorescence monitoring for the *2 and *13 variants. The pathologist or other qualified healthcare professional examines the allele calls for the *2 and *13 variants in the DPYD gene. The pathologist or other qualified health care professional composes a report that specifies the patient's mutation status. The report is edited and signed, and the results are communicated to appropriate caregivers.

81238   Code is out of numerical sequence. See 81240-81243

\#● 81238   *F9 (coagulation factor IX)* (eg, hemophilia B), full gene sequence

Rationale

Code 81238 has been established to report the full gene sequence of the F9 gene. This test was previously reported with Tier 2 code 81405. Since the addition of this gene analysis to the Tier 2 code set, the frequency of the test has increased to the level that is consistent with its intended clinical use. Therefore, this analysis is no longer reported with code 81405, and code 81238 has been established as a Tier 1 code.

Clinical Example (81238)

An 18-year-old male presents with prolonged and extensive bleeding following a tooth extraction. The treating physician is concerned for hemophilia. F8 testing is performed and is negative. Hemophilia B is considered, and testing is requested for factor IX full gene analysis.

Description of Procedure (81238)

High-quality genomic DNA isolated from whole blood is subjected to PCR amplification and full gene sequence analysis for F9 variants. The pathologist or other qualified healthcare professional examines the sequence results in the F9 gene. The pathologist or other qualified health care professional composes a report that specifies the patient's mutation status. The report is edited and signed, and the results are communicated to appropriate caregivers.

- ● **81247** *G6PD (glucose-6-phosphate dehydrogenase)* (eg, hemolytic anemia, jaundice), gene analysis; common variant(s) (eg, A, A-)
- ● **81248** known familial variant(s)
- ● **81249** full gene sequence

Rationale

Three new codes (81247, 81248, 81249) have been established to report identification of G6PD variants in hemolytic anemia for validation of pharmacogenomic therapy. Code 81247 should be used to report common variant analysis; code 81248 for known familial variant analysis; and code 81249 for full gene sequence analysis.

Clinical Example (81247)

A 65-year-old female, who has lymphoma and is being treated with rasburicase to prevent hyperuricemia, suddenly develops hemolytic anemia. An anticoagulated peripheral blood sample is submitted for mutation analysis to assess the patient's G6PD genotype.

Description of Procedure (81247)

High-quality genomic DNA isolated from whole blood is subjected to real-time PCR analysis for the A-variant. The pathologist or other qualified health care professional examines the allele calls for the A-variant in the G6PD gene. The pathologist or other qualified health care professional composes a report that specifies the patient's mutation status. The report is edited and signed, and the results are communicated to appropriate caregivers.

Clinical Example (81248)

A 30-year-old female has a son who was recently diagnosed with G6PD deficiency due to the A-mutation. An anticoagulated peripheral blood sample is submitted for mutation analysis to assess the patient's G6PD genotype status and risk for developing hemolytic anemia.

Description of Procedure (81248)

High-quality genomic DNA isolated from whole blood is subjected to real-time PCR analysis for the A-variant. The pathologist or other qualified health care professional examines the allele calls for the A-variant in the G6PD gene. The pathologist or other qualified health care professional composes a report that specifies the patient's mutation status. The report is edited and signed, and the results are communicated to appropriate caregivers.

Clinical Example (81249)

A 65-year-old female, who has lymphoma and is being treated with rasburicase to prevent hyperuricemia, suddenly develops hemolytic anemia. An anticoagulated peripheral blood sample is submitted for sequence analysis to assess the patient's G6PD genotype.

Description of Procedure (81249)

High-quality genomic DNA isolated from whole blood is subjected to DNA sequencing of the G6PD gene. The pathologist or other qualified health care professional examines the results. The pathologist or other qualified health care professional composes a report that specifies the patient's mutation status. The report is edited and signed, and the results are communicated to appropriate caregivers.

- ▲ **81257** *HBA1/HBA2 (alpha globin 1 and alpha globin 2)* (eg, alpha thalassemia, Hb Bart hydrops fetalis syndrome, HbH disease), gene analysis; common deletions or variant (eg, Southeast Asian, Thai, Filipino, Mediterranean, alpha3.7, alpha4.2, alpha20.5, Constant Spring)
- ● **81258** known familial variant
- ● **81259** full gene sequence
- #● **81269** duplication/deletion variants

★ = Telemedicine   ✚ = Add-on code   ✔ = FDA approval pending   # = Resequenced code

Rationale

Three new codes (81258, 81259, 81269) have been established for reporting analysis of the HBA1/HBA2 genes. HBA1/HBA2 gene analysis was previously reported with Tier 2 code 81404. Since the addition of this gene analysis to the Tier 2 code set, the frequency of the test has increased to the level that is consistent with its intended clinical use. Therefore, this analysis has been removed from code 81404 and should be reported with a Tier 1 code. Code 81257 has been revised to conform to the parent code structure and has been editorially revised to remove the word "for" from the code descriptor. Code 81258 should be used to report known familial variant analysis; code 81259 for full gene sequence analysis; and code 81269 for duplication/deletion variant analysis.

Clinical Example (81258)

A 26-year-old gravida 1, para 0 (G1P0) female presents to her obstetrician for her first prenatal visit after obtaining a positive home pregnancy test result. The patient and her partner both have a family history of alpha thalassemia with known familial variants. A blood sample is submitted to the laboratory for testing to determine if the patient is also a carrier of the familial alpha thalassemia variant.

Description of Procedure (81258)

High-quality genomic DNA is isolated from whole blood and subjected to analysis for the known familial alpha thalassemia variant. The PCR amplification products, a molecular weight marker, and an allelic ladder are separated by gel electrophoresis. The pathologist or other qualified health care professional evaluates the patterns of the PCR products on the gel in order to identify the patient's specific duplication or deletion. The pathologist or other qualified health care professional composes a report that specifies the patient's variant status and the respective chromosomal locations (eg, cis, trans). The report is edited and signed, and the results are communicated to appropriate caregivers.

Clinical Example (81259)

A 26-year-old G1P0 female presents to her obstetrician for her first prenatal visit after obtaining a positive home pregnancy test result. Both the patient and her partner have been identified as alpha thalassemia carriers by hemoglobin electrophoresis. A blood sample is submitted to the laboratory for testing to identify the specific type of alpha thalassemia mutation the patient carries.

Description of Procedure (81259)

High-quality genomic DNA is isolated from whole blood and subjected to analysis for the seven commonly occurring alpha thalassemia deletions; results are negative. Reflex analysis for sequence variants is then requested. PCR amplification products undergo bidirectional ddNTP chain termination sequencing on a capillary electrophoresis instrument. The pathologist or other qualified health care professional evaluates the results to identify nucleotide sequence variants. The pathologist or other qualified health care professional composes a report that specifies the patient's variant status and the respective chromosomal locations (eg, cis, trans). The report is edited and signed, and the results are communicated to appropriate caregivers.

Clinical Example (81269)

A 26-year-old G1P0 female presents to her obstetrician for her first prenatal visit after obtaining a positive home pregnancy test result. Both the patient and her partner have been identified as alpha thalassemia carriers by hemoglobin electrophoresis. A blood sample is submitted to the laboratory for testing to identify the specific type of alpha thalassemia variant the patient carries.

Description of Procedure (81269)

High-quality genomic DNA is isolated from whole blood and subjected to analysis for the seven commonly occurring alpha thalassemia deletions; results are negative. Reflex analysis for uncommon duplication/deletion is then requested. The multiplex PCR amplification products, a molecular weight marker, and an allelic ladder are separated by gel electrophoresis. The pathologist or other qualified health care professional evaluates the patterns of the PCR products on the gel in order to identify the patient's specific duplication or deletion. The pathologist or other qualified health care professional composes a report that specifies the patient's variant status and the respective chromosomal locations (eg, cis, trans). The report is edited and signed, and the results are communicated to appropriate caregivers.

#● **81105**   *Human Platelet Antigen 1 genotyping (HPA-1), ITGB3 (integrin, beta 3 [platelet glycoprotein IIIa], antigen CD61 [GPIIIa]) (eg, neonatal alloimmune thrombocytopenia [NAIT], post-transfusion purpura), gene analysis, common variant, HPA-1a/b (L33P)*

#● **81106**   *Human Platelet Antigen 2 genotyping (HPA-2), GP1BA (glycoprotein Ib [platelet], alpha polypeptide [GPIba]) (eg, neonatal alloimmune thrombocytopenia [NAIT], post-transfusion purpura), gene analysis, common variant, HPA-2a/b (T145M)*

#● **81107**   *Human Platelet Antigen 3 genotyping (HPA-3), ITGA2B (integrin, alpha 2b [platelet glycoprotein IIb of IIb/IIIa complex], antigen CD41 [GPIIb])* (eg, neonatal alloimmune thrombocytopenia [NAIT], post-transfusion purpura), gene analysis, common variant, HPA-3a/b (I843S)

#● **81108**   *Human Platelet Antigen 4 genotyping (HPA-4), ITGB3 (integrin, beta 3 [platelet glycoprotein IIIa], antigen CD61 [GPIIIa])* (eg, neonatal alloimmune thrombocytopenia [NAIT], post-transfusion purpura), gene analysis, common variant, HPA-4a/b (R143Q)

#● **81109**   *Human Platelet Antigen 5 genotyping (HPA-5), ITGA2 (integrin, alpha 2 [CD49B, alpha 2 subunit of VLA-2 receptor] [GPIa])* (eg, neonatal alloimmune thrombocytopenia [NAIT], post-transfusion purpura), gene analysis, common variant (eg, HPA-5a/b (K505E))

#● **81110**   *Human Platelet Antigen 6 genotyping (HPA-6w), ITGB3 (integrin, beta 3 [platelet glycoprotein IIIa, antigen CD61] [GPIIIa])* (eg, neonatal alloimmune thrombocytopenia [NAIT], post-transfusion purpura), gene analysis, common variant, HPA-6a/b (R489Q)

#● **81111**   *Human Platelet Antigen 9 genotyping (HPA-9w), ITGA2B (integrin, alpha 2b [platelet glycoprotein IIb of IIb/IIIa complex, antigen CD41] [GPIIb])* (eg, neonatal alloimmune thrombocytopenia [NAIT], post-transfusion purpura), gene analysis, common variant, HPA-9a/b (V837M)

#● **81112**   *Human Platelet Antigen 15 genotyping (HPA-15), CD109 (CD109 molecule)* (eg, neonatal alloimmune thrombocytopenia [NAIT], post-transfusion purpura), gene analysis, common variant, HPA-15a/b (S682Y)

Rationale

Eight Tier 1 codes (81105-81112) have been established to report human platelet antigen genotyping. Prior to 2018, these tests were reported with Tier 2 code 81400. Since the addition of these tests to the Tier 2 code set, the frequency of the test has increased to the level that is consistent with its intended clinical use. Therefore, these tests have been removed from code 81400 and are now reported with Tier 1 codes.

Clinical Example (81105)

A newborn male presents to the physician with severe thrombocytopenia. Otherwise, the newborn is healthy. Anticoagulated peripheral blood samples from the newborn and his parents are submitted for mutation analysis to assess the platelet antigen genotyping for possible incompatibility.

Description of Procedure (81105)

High-quality genomic DNA isolated from whole blood is subjected to real-time PCR and fluorescence monitoring (hydrolysis probes) for the HPA-1a/b (L33P) variant in the ITGB3 gene. The pathologist or other qualified healthcare professional examines the allele calls for the HPA-1a/b (L33P) variant. The pathologist or other qualified health care professional composes a report that specifies the patient's mutation status. The report is edited and signed, and the results are communicated to appropriate caregivers.

Clinical Example (81106)

A newborn male presents to the physician with severe thrombocytopenia. Otherwise, the newborn is healthy. Anticoagulated peripheral blood samples from the newborn and his parents are submitted for mutation analysis to assess the platelet antigen genotyping for possible incompatibility.

Description of Procedure (81106)

High-quality genomic DNA isolated from whole blood is subjected to real-time PCR and fluorescence monitoring (hydrolysis probes) for the HPA-2a/b (T145M) variant in the GP1BA gene. The pathologist or other qualified health care professional examines the allele calls for the HPA-2a/b (T145M) variant. The pathologist or other qualified health care professional composes a report that specifies the patient's mutation status. The report is edited and signed, and the results are communicated to appropriate caregivers.

Clinical Example (81107)

A newborn male presents to the physician with severe thrombocytopenia. Otherwise, the newborn is healthy. Anticoagulated peripheral blood samples from the newborn and his parents are submitted for mutation analysis to assess the platelet antigen genotyping for possible incompatibility.

Description of Procedure (81107)

High-quality genomic DNA isolated from whole blood is subjected to real-time PCR and fluorescence monitoring (hydrolysis probes) for the HPA-3a/b (I843S) variant in the ITGA2B gene. The pathologist or other qualified health care professional examines the allele calls for the HPA-3a/b (I843S) variant. The pathologist or other qualified health care professional composes a report that specifies the patient's mutation status. The report is edited and signed, and the results are communicated to appropriate caregivers.

Clinical Example (81108)

A newborn male presents to the physician with severe thrombocytopenia. Otherwise, the newborn is healthy. Anticoagulated peripheral blood samples from the newborn and his parents are submitted for mutation analysis to assess the platelet antigen genotyping for possible incompatibility.

Description of Procedure (81108)

High-quality genomic DNA isolated from whole blood is subjected to real-time PCR and fluorescence monitoring (hydrolysis probes) for the HPA-4a/b (R143Q) variant in the ITGB3 gene. The pathologist or other qualified health care professional examines the allele calls for the HPA-4a/b (R143Q) variant. The pathologist or other qualified health care professional composes a report that specifies the patient's mutation status. The report is edited and signed, and the results are communicated to appropriate caregivers.

Clinical Example (81109)

A newborn male presents to the physician with severe thrombocytopenia. Otherwise, the newborn is healthy. Anticoagulated peripheral blood samples from the newborn and his parents are submitted for mutation analysis to assess the platelet antigen genotyping for possible incompatibility.

Description of Procedure (81109)

High-quality genomic DNA isolated from whole blood is subjected to real-time PCR and fluorescence monitoring (hydrolysis probes) for the HPA-5a/b (K505E) variant in the ITGA2 gene. The pathologist or other qualified health care professional examines the allele calls for the HPA-5a/b (K505E) variant. The pathologist or other qualified health care professional composes a report that specifies the patient's mutation status. The report is edited and signed, and the results are communicated to appropriate caregivers.

Clinical Example (81110)

A newborn male presents to the physician with severe thrombocytopenia. Otherwise, the newborn is healthy. Anticoagulated peripheral blood samples from the newborn and his parents are submitted for mutation analysis to assess the platelet antigen genotyping for possible incompatibility.

Description of Procedure (81110)

High-quality genomic DNA isolated from whole blood is subjected to real-time PCR and fluorescence monitoring (hydrolysis probes) for the HPA-6a/b (R489Q) variant in the ITGB3 gene. The pathologist or other qualified health care professional examines the allele calls for the HPA-6a/b (R489Q) variant. The pathologist or other qualified health care professional composes a report that specifies the patient's mutation status. The report is edited and signed, and the results are communicated to appropriate caregivers.

Clinical Example (81111)

A newborn male presents to the physician with severe thrombocytopenia. Otherwise, the newborn is healthy. Anticoagulated peripheral blood samples from the newborn and his parents are submitted for mutation analysis to assess the platelet antigen genotyping for possible incompatibility.

Description of Procedure (81111)

High-quality genomic DNA isolated from whole blood is subjected to real-time PCR and fluorescence monitoring (hydrolysis probes) for the HPA-9a/b (V837M) variant in the ITGA2B gene. The pathologist or other qualified health care professional examines the allele calls for the HPA-9a/b (V837M) variant. The pathologist or other qualified health care professional composes a report that specifies the patient's mutation status. The report is edited and signed, and the results are communicated to appropriate caregivers.

Clinical Example (81112)

A newborn male presents to the physician with severe thrombocytopenia. Otherwise, the newborn is healthy. Anticoagulated peripheral blood samples from the newborn and his parents are submitted for mutation analysis to assess the platelet antigen genotyping for possible incompatibility.

Description of Procedure (81112)

High-quality genomic DNA isolated from whole blood is subjected to real-time PCR and fluorescence monitoring (hydrolysis probes) for the HPA-15a/b (S682Y) variant in the CD109 gene. The pathologist or other qualified health care professional examines the allele calls for the HPA-15a/b (S682Y) variant. The pathologist or other qualified health care professional composes a report that specifies the patient's mutation status. The report is edited and signed, and the results are communicated to appropriate caregivers.

Pathology and Laboratory 80047-89398, 0001U-0017U

#● **81120**   *IDH1 (isocitrate dehydrogenase 1 [NADP+], soluble)* (eg, glioma), common variants (eg, R132H, R132C)

#● **81121**   *IDH2 (isocitrate dehydrogenase 2 [NADP+], mitochondrial)* (eg, glioma), common variants (eg, R140W, R172M)

Rationale

Two new codes (81120, 81121) have been established to report gene analysis of the IDH1 and IDH2 genes. These tests were previously reported with Tier 2 code 81403. Since the frequency of the testing for these analytes has increased to the level that is consistent with its intended clinical use, these tests have been removed from code 81403 and are now reported with Tier 1 codes 81120 and 81121.

Clinical Example (81120)

A 50-year-old male with a history of headaches experiences a seizure. Imaging studies reveal a brain mass. A biopsy reveals glioblastoma multiforme. A formalin-fixed, paraffin-embedded tissue specimen is sent to the laboratory for testing for common mutations in IDH1.

Description of Procedure (81120)

DNA is extracted from previously microdissected tumor tissue. The DNA undergoes PCR amplification and bidirectional sequencing. A pathologist interprets the sequence data, and prepares and signs a report.

Clinical Example (81121)

A 50-year-old male with a history of headaches experiences a seizure. Imaging studies reveal a brain mass. A biopsy reveals glioblastoma multiforme. A formalin-fixed, paraffin-embedded tissue specimen is sent to the laboratory for testing for common mutations in IDH2.

Description of Procedure (81121)

DNA is extracted from previously microdissected tumor tissue. The DNA undergoes PCR amplification and bidirectional sequencing. A pathologist interprets the sequence data, and prepares and signs a report.

#● **81283**   *IFNL3 (interferon, lambda 3)* (eg, drug response), gene analysis, rs12979860 variant

Rationale

Code 81283 has been added to report rs12979860 variant gene analysis of the IFNL3 gene. This test was previously reported with Tier 2 code 81400. Since the addition of this gene analysis to the Tier 2 code set, the frequency of the test has increased to the level that is consistent with its intended clinical use. Therefore, this analysis has been removed from code 81400 and is now reported with a Tier 1 code.

Clinical Example (81283)

A 65-year-old male who has hepatitis C virus infection is not developing sustained virologic response with pegylated-interferon treatments. An anticoagulated peripheral blood sample is submitted for mutation analysis to assess the patient's IFNL3 genotype.

Description of Procedure (81283)

High-quality genomic DNA isolated from whole blood is subjected to real-time PCR and PCR/fluorescence monitoring for the rs12979860 variant. The pathologist or other qualified health care professional examines the allele calls for the rs12979860 variant in the IFNL3 gene. The pathologist or other qualified health care professional composes a report that specifies the patient's mutation status. The report is edited and signed, and the results are communicated to appropriate caregivers.

81267   Chimerism (engraftment) analysis, post transplantation specimen (eg, hematopoietic stem cell), includes comparison to previously performed baseline analyses; without cell selection

81268   with cell selection (eg, CD3, CD33), each cell type

81269   Code is out of numerical sequence. See 81257-81261

81283   Code is out of numerical sequence. See 81257-81261

#● **81334**   *RUNX1 (runt related transcription factor 1)* (eg, acute myeloid leukemia, familial platelet disorder with associated myeloid malignancy), gene analysis, targeted sequence analysis (eg, exons 3-8)

● **81328**   *SLCO1B1 (solute carrier organic anion transporter family, member 1B1)* (eg, adverse drug reaction), gene analysis, common variant(s) (eg, *5)

81334   Code is out of numerical sequence. See 81325-81328

● **81335**   *TPMT (thiopurine S-methyltransferase)* (eg, drug metabolism), gene analysis, common variants (eg, *2, *3)

● **81346**   *TYMS (thymidylate synthetase)* (eg, 5-fluorouracil/5-FU drug metabolism), gene analysis, common variant(s) (eg, tandem repeat variant)

★ = Telemedicine   ✚ = Add-on code   ✒ = FDA approval pending   # = Resequenced code

Pathology and Laboratory 80047-89398, 0001U-0017U

Rationale

Code 81334 has been added to report targeted sequence analysis of the RUNX1 gene. Code 81328 has been added for reporting common variant gene analysis of the SLCO1B1 gene. Previously, analysis of the SLCO1B1 gene was reported with Tier 2 code 81400. Since the addition of this test to the Tier 2 code set, the frequency of the test has increased to the level that is consistent with its intended clinical use. Therefore, this test has been removed from Tier 2 and is now reported with a Tier 1 code.

Code 81335 has been added to report common variant gene analysis of the TPMT gene, while code 81346 has been added to report common variant gene analysis of the TYMS gene. Previously, analyses of the TPMT and TYMS genes were reported with Tier 2 code 81401. Since the addition of these gene analyses to the Tier 2 code set, the frequency of the tests has increased to the level that is consistent with their intended clinical use. Therefore, these analyses have been removed from Tier 2 and are now reported with Tier 1 codes.

Clinical Example (81328)

A 65-year-old male presents to his physician with a history of statin use. Recently, he has had difficulty climbing stairs. Physical examination reveals myopathy. An anticoagulated peripheral blood sample is submitted for mutation analysis to assess the patient's SLCO1B1 metabolizer status.

Description of Procedure (81328)

High-quality genomic DNA isolated from whole blood is subjected to real-time PCR and PCR/fluorescence monitoring for the *5 variant. The pathologist or other qualified health care professional examines the allele calls for the *5 variant in the SLCO1B1 gene. The pathologist or other qualified health care professional composes a report that specifies the patient's mutation status. The report is edited and signed, and the results are communicated to appropriate caregivers.

Clinical Example (81334)

A 63-year-old male presenting with fatigue, weight loss, and night sweats is found to have a markedly elevated white blood cell count with myeloid blasts in the peripheral blood. Bone marrow biopsy demonstrates a predominance of myeloid precursors, including 30% myeloid blasts. Results from molecular testing are negative for FLT3 and NPM1 mutations. Mutation testing for RUNX1 is requested.

Description of Procedure (81334)

High-quality genomic DNA is isolated from the patient's specimen and subjected to targeted capture and DNA sequencing of the RUNX1 gene coding regions and intron/exon boundaries to identify mutations. The pathologist or other qualified health care professional analyzes the data and composes a report that specifies the patient's mutation status. The report is edited and signed, and the results are communicated to appropriate caregivers.

Clinical Example (81335)

A 5-year-old female is diagnosed with acute lymphoblastic leukemia. Thiopurine is determined to be a drug of choice for her. However, after treatment with thiopurines, she exhibits severe myelosuppression. An anticoagulated peripheral blood sample is submitted for mutation analysis to assess the patient's TPMT metabolizer status.

Description of Procedure (81335)

High-quality genomic DNA isolated from whole blood is subjected to real-time PCR and PCR/fluorescence monitoring for the *2 and *3 variants. The pathologist or other qualified health care professional examines the allele calls for the *2 and *3 variants in the TPMT gene. The pathologist or other qualified health care professional composes a report that specifies the patient's mutation status. The report is edited and signed, and the results are communicated to appropriate caregivers.

Clinical Example (81346)

A 65-year-old female is diagnosed with colon cancer. It is determined that the drug of choice for her is 5-FU. However, after treatment with 5-FU, she exhibits toxicity. An anticoagulated peripheral blood sample is submitted for mutation analysis to assess the patient's TYMS metabolizer status.

Description of Procedure (81346)

High-quality genomic DNA isolated from whole blood is subjected to PCR and capillary electrophoresis analysis for the tandem repeat variants. The pathologist or other qualified health care professional examines the allele calls in the TYMS gene. The pathologist or other qualified health care professional composes a report that specifies the patient's mutation status. The report is edited and signed, and the results are communicated to appropriate caregivers.

Pathology and Laboratory 80047-89398, 0001U-0017U

- **81361** *HBB (hemoglobin, subunit beta)* (eg, sickle cell anemia, beta thalassemia, hemoglobinopathy); common variant(s) (eg, HbS, HbC, HbE)
- **81362** known familial variant(s)
- **81363** duplication/deletion variant(s)
- **81364** full gene sequence

Rationale

Four codes (81361, 81362, 81363, and 81364) have been added to report analysis of the HBB gene. Analysis of the HBB gene was previously reported with Tier 2 codes 81401, 81403, and 81404. Since the addition of this test to the Tier 2 code set, the frequency of the test has increased to the level that is consistent with its intended clinical use. Therefore, this test has been removed from Tier 2 and is now reported with a Tier 1 code.

Code 81361 is used to report common variant analysis; code 81362 for known familial variant analysis; code 81363 for duplication/deletion variant analysis; and code 81364 for full gene sequence analysis.

Clinical Example (81361)

A pregnant patient at 12-weeks gestation is at risk for giving birth to a child with hemoglobin sickle cell (SC) disease. Chorionic villus biopsy is performed to test for the common variants in the HBB gene.

Description of Procedure (81361)

High-quality genomic DNA is isolated from the patient's specimen and subjected to targeted PCR amplification and DNA sequencing to test for the common variants in the HBB gene. The pathologist or other qualified health care professional analyzes the data and composes a report that specifies the patient's mutation status. The report is edited and signed, and the results are communicated to appropriate caregivers.

Clinical Example (81362)

A 32-year-old female presents to her physician based on a positive home pregnancy test result and is dated at 10 weeks gestation by ultrasound findings. She is otherwise asymptomatic but does have a family history of thalassemia in a cousin with a rare variant of the HBB gene. The patient chooses to have familial mutation testing for that beta-hemoglobin variant, and a specimen is submitted for HBB genetic analysis.

Description of Procedure (81362)

High-quality genomic DNA is isolated from the patient's specimen and subjected to targeted PCR amplification and DNA sequencing to test for the familial variant. The pathologist or other qualified health care professional analyzes the data and composes a report that specifies the patient's mutation status. The report is edited and signed, and the results are communicated to appropriate caregivers.

Clinical Example (81363)

Newborn screening results for a baby show a low mean corpuscular volume (MCV) and an abnormal hemoglobin fractionation pattern consistent with beta thalassemia. HBB full gene sequence analysis is performed on the child, but only one mutation is identified. Thus, deletion/duplication analysis is performed on the baby's blood to identify the second disease-causing variant.

Description of Procedure (81363)

High-quality genomic DNA is isolated from the patient's specimen and subjected to deletion and duplication testing of the HBB gene. The pathologist or other qualified health care professional analyzes the data and composes a report that specifies the patient's mutation status. The report is edited and signed, and the results are communicated to appropriate caregivers.

Clinical Example (81364)

A pregnant patient at 12 weeks gestation is at risk for giving birth to a child with homozygous beta-thalassemia and requests an antenatal diagnosis by direct gene analysis. Chorionic villus biopsy is performed, and the specimen is submitted for HBB full gene sequence.

Description of Procedure (81364)

High-quality genomic DNA is isolated from the patient's specimen and subjected to PCR amplification of the HBB gene. The products undergo DNA sequencing of the coding regions and intron/exon boundaries. The pathologist or other qualified health care professional evaluates the reads to identify nucleotide sequence variants. The pathologist or other qualified healthcare professional composes a report that specifies the patient's mutation status. The report is edited and signed, and the results are communicated to appropriate caregivers.

▶(For HLA antigen typing by non-molecular pathology techniques, see 86812, 86813, 86816, 86817, 86821)◀

81370 HLA Class I and II typing, low resolution (eg, antigen equivalents); *HLA-A, -B, -C, -DRB1/3/4/5,* and *-DQB1*

★ = Telemedicine   ✚ = Add-on code   ✓ = FDA approval pending   # = Resequenced code

Rationale

In support of the deletion of code 86822, the cross-reference parenthetical note before code 81370 has been revised with the removal of code 86822.

Refer to the codebook and the Rationale for code 86822 for a full discussion of the changes.

Tier 2 Molecular Pathology Procedures

▲ **81400**   Molecular pathology procedure, Level 1 (eg, identification of single germline variant [eg, SNP] by techniques such as restriction enzyme digestion or melt curve analysis)

ACADM (acyl-CoA dehydrogenase, C-4 to C-12 straight chain, MCAD) (eg, medium chain acyl dehydrogenase deficiency), K304E variant

ACE (angiotensin converting enzyme) (eg, hereditary blood pressure regulation), insertion/deletion variant

AGTR1 (angiotensin II receptor, type 1) (eg, essential hypertension), 1166A>C variant

BCKDHA (branched chain keto acid dehydrogenase E1, alpha polypeptide) (eg, maple syrup urine disease, type 1A), Y438N variant

CCR5 (chemokine C-C motif receptor 5) (eg, HIV resistance), 32-bp deletion mutation/794 825del32 deletion

CLRN1 (clarin 1) (eg, Usher syndrome, type 3), N48K variant

F2 (coagulation factor 2) (eg, hereditary hypercoagulability), 1199G>A variant

F5 (coagulation factor V) (eg, hereditary hypercoagulability), HR2 variant

F7 (coagulation factor VII [serum prothrombin conversion accelerator]) (eg, hereditary hypercoagulability), R353Q variant

F13B (coagulation factor XIII, B polypeptide) (eg, hereditary hypercoagulability), V34L variant

FGB (fibrinogen beta chain) (eg, hereditary ischemic heart disease), -455G>A variant

FGFR1 (fibroblast growth factor receptor 1) (eg, Pfeiffer syndrome type 1, craniosynostosis), P252R variant

FGFR3 (fibroblast growth factor receptor 3) (eg, Muenke syndrome), P250R variant

FKTN (fukutin) (eg, Fukuyama congenital muscular dystrophy), retrotransposon insertion variant

GNE (glucosamine [UDP-N-acetyl]-2-epimerase/N-acetylmannosamine kinase) (eg, inclusion body myopathy 2 [IBM2], Nonaka myopathy), M712T variant

IVD (isovaleryl-CoA dehydrogenase) (eg, isovaleric acidemia), A282V variant

LCT (lactase-phlorizin hydrolase) (eg, lactose intolerance), 13910 C>T variant

NEB (nebulin) (eg, nemaline myopathy 2), exon 55 deletion variant

PCDH15 (protocadherin-related 15) (eg, Usher syndrome type 1F), R245X variant

SERPINE1 (serpine peptidase inhibitor clade E, member 1, plasminogen activator inhibitor -1, PAI-1) (eg, thrombophilia), 4G variant

SHOC2 (soc-2 suppressor of clear homolog) (eg, Noonan-like syndrome with loose anagen hair), S2G variant

SMN1 (survival of motor neuron 1, telomeric) (eg, spinal muscular atrophy), exon 7 deletion

SRY (sex determining region Y) (eg, 46,XX testicular disorder of sex development, gonadal dysgenesis), gene analysis

TOR1A (torsin family 1, member A [torsin A]) (eg, early-onset primary dystonia [DYT1]), 907_909delGAG (904_906delGAG) variant

Rationale

In accordance with the establishment of Tier 1 human platelet antigen (HPA) genotyping codes 81105-81112, eight HPA tests have been removed from Tier 2 code 81400. Refer to the codebook and the Rationale for codes 81105-81112 for a full discussion of the changes.

In accordance with the establishment of Tier 1 gene analysis codes 81232, 81283, and 81328, the analyses for the DPYD, IFNL3, and SLCO1B1 genes have been removed from Tier 2 code 81400. Refer to the codebook and the Rationale for codes 81232, 81283, and 81328, for a full discussion of the changes.

▲ **81401**   Molecular pathology procedure, Level 2 (eg, 2-10 SNPs, 1 methylated variant, or 1 somatic variant [typically using nonsequencing target variant analysis], or detection of a dynamic mutation disorder/triplet repeat)

ABCC8 (ATP-binding cassette, sub-family C [CFTR/MRP], member 8) (eg, familial hyperinsulinism), common variants (eg, c.3898-9G>A [c.3992-9G>A], F1388del)

ABL1 (ABL proto-oncogene 1, non-receptor tyrosine kinase) (eg, acquired imatinib resistance), T315I variant

ACADM (acyl-CoA dehydrogenase, C-4 to C-12 straight chain, MCAD) (eg, medium chain acyl dehydrogenase deficiency), commons variants (eg, K304E, Y42H)

ADRB2 (adrenergic beta-2 receptor surface) (eg, drug metabolism), common variants (eg, G16R, Q27E)

AFF2 (AF4/FMR2 family, member 2 [FMR2]) (eg, fragile X mental retardation 2 [FRAXE]), evaluation to detect abnormal (eg, expanded) alleles

APOB (apolipoprotein B) (eg, familial hypercholesterolemia type B), common variants (eg, R3500Q, R3500W)

APOE (apolipoprotein E) (eg, hyperlipoproteinemia type III, cardiovascular disease, Alzheimer disease), common variants (eg, *2, *3, *4)

AR (androgen receptor) (eg, spinal and bulbar muscular atrophy, Kennedy disease, X chromosome inactivation), characterization of alleles (eg, expanded size or methylation status)

ATN1 (atrophin 1) (eg, dentatorubral-pallidoluysian atrophy), evaluation to detect abnormal (eg, expanded) alleles

ATXN1 (ataxin 1) (eg, spinocerebellar ataxia), evaluation to detect abnormal (eg, expanded) alleles

ATXN2 (ataxin 2) (eg, spinocerebellar ataxia), evaluation to detect abnormal (eg, expanded) alleles

ATXN3 (ataxin 3) (eg, spinocerebellar ataxia, Machado-Joseph disease), evaluation to detect abnormal (eg, expanded) alleles

ATXN7 (ataxin 7) (eg, spinocerebellar ataxia), evaluation to detect abnormal (eg, expanded) alleles

ATXN8OS (ATXN8 opposite strand [non-protein coding]) (eg, spinocerebellar ataxia), evaluation to detect abnormal (eg, expanded) alleles

ATXN10 (ataxin 10) (eg, spinocerebellar ataxia), evaluation to detect abnormal (eg, expanded) alleles

CACNA1A (calcium channel, voltage-dependent, P/Q type, alpha 1A subunit) (eg, spinocerebellar ataxia), evaluation to detect abnormal (eg, expanded) alleles

CBFB/MYH11 (inv(16)) (eg, acute myeloid leukemia), qualitative, and quantitative, if performed

CBS (cystathionine-beta-synthase) (eg, homocystinuria, cystathionine beta-synthase deficiency), common variants (eg, I278T, G307S)

CCND1/IGH (BCL1/IgH, t(11;14)) (eg, mantle cell lymphoma) translocation analysis, major breakpoint, qualitative, and quantitative, if performed

CFH/ARMS2 (complement factor H/age-related maculopathy susceptibility 2) (eg, macular degeneration), common variants (eg, Y402H [CFH], A69S [ARMS2])

CNBP (CCHC-type zinc finger, nucleic acid binding protein) (eg, myotonic dystrophy type 2), evaluation to detect abnormal (eg, expanded) alleles

CSTB (cystatin B [stefin B]) (eg, Unverricht-Lundborg disease), evaluation to detect abnormal (eg, expanded) alleles

DEK/NUP214 (t(6;9)) (eg, acute myeloid leukemia), translocation analysis, qualitative, and quantitative, if performed

DMPK (dystrophia myotonica-protein kinase) (eg, myotonic dystrophy, type 1), evaluation to detect abnormal (eg, expanded) alleles

E2A/PBX1 (t(1;19)) (eg, acute lymphocytic leukemia), translocation analysis, qualitative, and quantitative, if performed

EML4/ALK (inv(2)) (eg, non-small cell lung cancer), translocation or inversion analysis

ETV6/NTRK3 (t(12;15)) (eg, congenital/infantile fibrosarcoma), translocation analysis, qualitative, and quantitative, if performed

ETV6/RUNX1 (t(12;21)) (eg, acute lymphocytic leukemia), translocation analysis, qualitative, and quantitative, if performed

EWSR1/ATF1 (t(12;22)) (eg, clear cell sarcoma), translocation analysis, qualitative, and quantitative, if performed

EWSR1/ERG (t(21;22)) (eg, Ewing sarcoma/peripheral neuroectodermal tumor), translocation analysis, qualitative, and quantitative, if performed

EWSR1/FLI1 (t(11;22)) (eg, Ewing sarcoma/peripheral neuroectodermal tumor), translocation analysis, qualitative, and quantitative, if performed

EWSR1/WT1 (t(11;22)) (eg, desmoplastic small round cell tumor), translocation analysis, qualitative, and quantitative, if performed

F11 (coagulation factor XI) (eg, coagulation disorder), common variants (eg, E117X [Type II], F283L [Type III], IVS14del14, and IVS14+1G>A [Type I])

FGFR3 (fibroblast growth factor receptor 3) (eg, achondroplasia, hypochondroplasia), common variants (eg, 1138G>A, 1138G>C, 1620C>A, 1620C>G)

FIP1L1/PDGFRA (del[4q12]) (eg, imatinib-sensitive chronic eosinophilic leukemia), qualitative, and quantitative, if performed

FLG (filaggrin) (eg, ichthyosis vulgaris), common variants (eg, R501X, 2282del4, R2447X, S3247X, 3702delG)

FOXO1/PAX3 (t(2;13)) (eg, alveolar rhabdomyosarcoma), translocation analysis, qualitative, and quantitative, if performed

★ = Telemedicine   ✦ = Add-on code   ✗ = FDA approval pending   # = Resequenced code

FOXO1/PAX7 (t(1;13)) (eg, alveolar rhabdomyosarcoma), translocation analysis, qualitative, and quantitative, if performed

FUS/DDIT3 (t(12;16)) (eg, myxoid liposarcoma), translocation analysis, qualitative, and quantitative, if performed

FXN (frataxin) (eg, Friedreich ataxia), evaluation to detect abnormal (expanded) alleles

GALC (galactosylceramidase) (eg, Krabbe disease), common variants (eg, c.857G>A, 30-kb deletion)

GALT (galactose-1-phosphate uridylyltransferase) (eg, galactosemia), common variants (eg, Q188R, S135L, K285N, T138M, L195P, Y209C, IVS2-2A>G, P171S, del5kb, N314D, L218L/N314D)

H19 (imprinted maternally expressed transcript [non-protein coding]) (eg, Beckwith-Wiedemann syndrome), methylation analysis

HTT (huntingtin) (eg, Huntington disease), evaluation to detect abnormal (eg, expanded) alleles

IGH@/BCL2 (t(14;18)) (eg, follicular lymphoma), translocation analysis; single breakpoint (eg, major breakpoint region [MBR] or minor cluster region [mcr]), qualitative or quantitative

(When both MBR and mcr breakpoints are performed, use 81402)

KCNQ1OT1 (KCNQ1 overlapping transcript 1 [non-protein coding]) (eg, Beckwith-Wiedemann syndrome), methylation analysis

▶*LINC00518 (long intergenic non-protein coding RNA 518)* (eg, melanoma), expression analysis◀

LRRK2 (leucine-rich repeat kinase 2) (eg, Parkinson disease), common variants (eg, R1441G, G2019S, I2020T)

MED12 (mediator complex subunit 12) (eg, FG syndrome type 1, Lujan syndrome), common variants (eg, R961W, N1007S)

MEG3/DLK1 (maternally expressed 3 [non-protein coding]/delta-like 1 homolog [Drosophila]) (eg, intrauterine growth retardation), methylation analysis

MLL/AFF1 (t(4;11)) (eg, acute lymphoblastic leukemia), translocation analysis, qualitative, and quantitative, if performed

MLL/MLLT3 (t(9;11)) (eg, acute myeloid leukemia), translocation analysis, qualitative, and quantitative, if performed

MT-ATP6 (mitochondrially encoded ATP synthase 6) (eg, neuropathy with ataxia and retinitis pigmentosa [NARP], Leigh syndrome), common variants (eg, m.8993T>G, m.8993T>C)

MT-ND4, MT-ND6 (mitochondrially encoded NADH dehydrogenase 4, mitochondrially encoded NADH dehydrogenase 6) (eg, Leber hereditary optic neuropathy [LHON]), common variants (eg, m.11778G>A, m.3460G>A, m.14484T>C)

MT-ND5 (mitochondrially encoded tRNA leucine 1 [UUA/G], mitochondrially encoded NADH dehydrogenase 5) (eg, mitochondrial encephalopathy with lactic acidosis and stroke-like episodes [MELAS]), common variants (eg, m.3243A>G, m.3271T>C, m.3252A>G, m.13513G>A)

MT-RNR1 (mitochondrially encoded 12S RNA) (eg, nonsyndromic hearing loss), common variants (eg, m.1555A>G, m.1494C>T)

MT-TK (mitochondrially encoded tRNA lysine) (eg, myoclonic epilepsy with ragged-red fibers [MERRF]), common variants (eg, m.8344A>G, m.8356T>C)

MT-TL1 (mitochondrially encoded tRNA leucine 1 [UUA/G]) (eg, diabetes and hearing loss), common variants (eg, m.3243A>G, m.14709 T>C) MT-TL1

MT-TS1, MT-RNR1 (mitochondrially encoded tRNA serine 1 [UCN], mitochondrially encoded 12S RNA) (eg, nonsyndromic sensorineural deafness [including aminoglycoside-induced nonsyndromic deafness]), common variants (eg, m.7445A>G, m.1555A>G)

MUTYH (mutY homolog [E. coli]) (eg, MYH-associated polyposis), common variants (eg, Y165C, G382D)

NOD2 (nucleotide-binding oligomerization domain containing 2) (eg, Crohn's disease, Blau syndrome), common variants (eg, SNP 8, SNP 12, SNP 13)

NPM1/ALK (t(2;5)) (eg, anaplastic large cell lymphoma), translocation analysis

PABPN1 (poly[A] binding protein, nuclear 1) (eg, oculopharyngeal muscular dystrophy), evaluation to detect abnormal (eg, expanded) alleles

PAX8/PPARG (t(2;3) (q13;p25)) (eg, follicular thyroid carcinoma), translocation analysis

PPP2R2B (protein phosphatase 2, regulatory subunit B, beta) (eg, spinocerebellar ataxia), evaluation to detect abnormal (eg, expanded) alleles

▶*PRAME (preferentially expressed antigen in melanoma)* (eg, melanoma), expression analysis◀

PRSS1 (protease, serine, 1 [trypsin 1]) (eg, hereditary pancreatitis), common variants (eg, N29I, A16V, R122H)

PYGM (phosphorylase, glycogen, muscle) (eg, glycogen storage disease type V, McArdle disease), common variants (eg, R50X, G205S)

RUNX1/RUNX1T1 (t(8;21)) (eg, acute myeloid leukemia) translocation analysis, qualitative, and quantitative, if performed

---

SMN1/SMN2 (survival of motor neuron 1, telomeric/ survival of motor neuron 2, centromeric) (eg, spinal muscular atrophy), dosage analysis (eg, carrier testing)

(For duplication/deletion analysis of SMN1/SMN2, use 81401)

SS18/SSX1 (t(X;18)) (eg, synovial sarcoma), translocation analysis, qualitative, and quantitative, if performed

SS18/SSX2 (t(X;18)) (eg, synovial sarcoma), translocation analysis, qualitative, and quantitative, if performed

TBP (TATA box binding protein) (eg, spinocerebellar ataxia), evaluation to detect abnormal (eg, expanded) alleles

VWF (von Willebrand factor) (eg, von Willebrand disease type 2N), common variants (eg, T791M, R816W, R854Q)

Rationale

In accordance with the establishment of Tier 1 gene analysis codes 81230, 81231, 81335, 81346, and 81361-81364, the genes CYP3A4, CYP3A5, HBB, TPMT, and TYMS have been removed from Tier 2 code 81401. Note that code 81401 has been revised with the addition of expression analysis for LINC00518 and expression analysis of PRAME.

Refer to the codebook and the Rationale for codes 81230, 81231, 81335, 81346, 81361-81364 for a full discussion of the changes.

▲ **81403** Molecular pathology procedure, Level 4 (eg, analysis of single exon by DNA sequence analysis, analysis of >10 amplicons using multiplex PCR in 2 or more independent reactions, mutation scanning or duplication/deletion variants of 2-5 exons)

ANG (angiogenin, ribonuclease, RNase A family, 5) (eg, amyotrophic lateral sclerosis), full gene sequence

ARX (aristaless-related homeobox) (eg, X-linked lissencephaly with ambiguous genitalia, X-linked mental retardation), duplication/deletion analysis

CEL (carboxyl ester lipase [bile salt-stimulated lipase]) (eg, maturity-onset diabetes of the young [MODY]), targeted sequence analysis of exon 11 (eg, c.1785delC, c.1686delT)

CTNNB1 (catenin [cadherin-associated protein], beta 1, 88kDa) (eg, desmoid tumors), targeted sequence analysis (eg, exon 3)

DAZ/SRY (deleted in azoospermia and sex determining region Y) (eg, male infertility), common deletions (eg, AZFa, AZFb, AZFc, AZFd)

DNMT3A (DNA [cytosine-5-]-methyltransferase 3 alpha) (eg, acute myeloid leukemia), targeted sequence analysis (eg, exon 23)

EPCAM (epithelial cell adhesion molecule) (eg, Lynch syndrome), duplication/deletion analysis

F8 (coagulation factor VIII) (eg, hemophilia A), inversion analysis, intron 1 and intron 22A

F12 (coagulation factor XII [Hageman factor]) (eg, angioedema, hereditary, type III; factor XII deficiency), targeted sequence analysis of exon 9

FGFR3 (fibroblast growth factor receptor 3) (eg, isolated craniosynostosis), targeted sequence analysis (eg, exon 7)

(For targeted sequence analysis of multiple FGFR3 exons, use 81404)

GJB1 (gap junction protein, beta 1) (eg, Charcot-Marie-Tooth X-linked), full gene sequence

GNAQ (guanine nucleotide-binding protein G[q] subunit alpha) (eg, uveal melanoma), common variants (eg, R183, Q209)

Human erythrocyte antigen gene analyses (eg, SLC14A1 [Kidd blood group], BCAM [Lutheran blood group], ICAM4 [Landsteiner-Wiener blood group], SLC4A1 [Diego blood group], AQP1 [Colton blood group], ERMAP [Scianna blood group], RHCE [Rh blood group, CcEe antigens], KEL [Kell blood group], DARC [Duffy blood group], GYPA, GYPB, GYPE [MNS blood group], ART4 [Dombrock blood group]) (eg, sickle-cell disease, thalassemia, hemolytic transfusion reactions, hemolytic disease of the fetus or newborn), common variants

HRAS (v-Ha-ras Harvey rat sarcoma viral oncogene homolog) (eg, Costello syndrome), exon 2 sequence

JAK2 (Janus kinase 2) (eg, myeloproliferative disorder), exon 12 sequence and exon 13 sequence, if performed

KCNC3 (potassium voltage-gated channel, Shaw-related subfamily, member 3) (eg, spinocerebellar ataxia), targeted sequence analysis (eg, exon 2)

KCNJ2 (potassium inwardly-rectifying channel, subfamily J, member 2) (eg, Andersen-Tawil syndrome), full gene sequence

KCNJ11 (potassium inwardly-rectifying channel, subfamily J, member 11) (eg, familial hyperinsulinism), full gene sequence

Killer cell immunoglobulin-like receptor (KIR) gene family (eg, hematopoietic stem cell transplantation), genotyping of KIR family genes

Known familial variant not otherwise specified, for gene listed in Tier 1 or Tier 2, or identified during a genomic sequencing procedure, DNA sequence analysis, each variant exon

★ = Telemedicine   ✚ = Add-on code   ⟋ = FDA approval pending   # = Resequenced code

(For a known familial variant that is considered a common variant, use specific common variant Tier 1 or Tier 2 code)

MC4R (melanocortin 4 receptor) (eg, obesity), full gene sequence

MICA (MHC class I polypeptide-related sequence A) (eg, solid organ transplantation), common variants (eg, *001, *002)

MPL (myeloproliferative leukemia virus oncogene, thrombopoietin receptor, TPOR) (eg, myeloproliferative disorder), exon 10 sequence

MT-RNR1 (mitochondrially encoded 12S RNA) (eg, nonsyndromic hearing loss), full gene sequence

MT-TS1 (mitochondrially encoded tRNA serine 1) (eg, nonsyndromic hearing loss), full gene sequence

NDP (Norrie disease [pseudoglioma]) (eg, Norrie disease), duplication/deletion analysis

NHLRC1 (NHL repeat containing 1) (eg, progressive myoclonus epilepsy), full gene sequence

PHOX2B (paired-like homeobox 2b) (eg, congenital central hypoventilation syndrome), duplication/deletion analysis

PLN (phospholamban) (eg, dilated cardiomyopathy, hypertrophic cardiomyopathy), full gene sequence

RHD (Rh blood group, D antigen) (eg, hemolytic disease of the fetus and newborn, Rh maternal/fetal compatibility), deletion analysis (eg, exons 4, 5, and 7, pseudogene)

RHD (Rh blood group, D antigen) (eg, hemolytic disease of the fetus and newborn, Rh maternal/fetal compatibility), deletion analysis (eg, exons 4, 5, and 7, pseudogene), performed on cell-free fetal DNA in maternal blood

(For human erythrocyte gene analysis of RHD, use a separate unit of 81403)

SH2D1A (SH2 domain containing 1A) (eg, X-linked lymphoproliferative syndrome), duplication/deletion analysis

SMN1 (survival of motor neuron 1, telomeric) (eg, spinal muscular atrophy), known familial sequence variant(s)

TWIST1 (twist homolog 1 [Drosophila]) (eg, Saethre-Chotzen syndrome), duplication/deletion analysis

UBA1 (ubiquitin-like modifier activating enzyme 1) (eg, spinal muscular atrophy, X-linked), targeted sequence analysis (eg, exon 15)

VHL (von Hippel-Lindau tumor suppressor) (eg, von Hippel-Lindau familial cancer syndrome), deletion/duplication analysis

VWF (von Willebrand factor) (eg, von Willebrand disease types 2A, 2B, 2M), targeted sequence analysis (eg, exon 28)

Rationale

In accordance with the establishment of Tier 1 codes 81120, 81121, 81361, 81362, 81363, and 81364, the IDH1, IDH2, and HBB gene tests have been removed from code 81403.

Refer to the codebook and the Rationale for codes 81120, 81121, 81361, 81362, 81363, and 81364 for a full discussion of the changes.

▲ **81404**   Molecular pathology procedure, Level 5 (eg, analysis of 2-5 exons by DNA sequence analysis, mutation scanning or duplication/deletion variants of 6-10 exons, or characterization of a dynamic mutation disorder/triplet repeat by Southern blot analysis)

ACADS (acyl-CoA dehydrogenase, C-2 to C-3 short chain) (eg, short chain acyl-CoA dehydrogenase deficiency), targeted sequence analysis (eg, exons 5 and 6)

AFF2 (AF4/FMR2 family, member 2 [FMR2]) (eg, fragile X mental retardation 2 [FRAXE]), characterization of alleles (eg, expanded size and methylation status)

AQP2 (aquaporin 2 [collecting duct]) (eg, nephrogenic diabetes insipidus), full gene sequence

ARX (aristaless related homeobox) (eg, X-linked lissencephaly with ambiguous genitalia, X-linked mental retardation), full gene sequence

AVPR2 (arginine vasopressin receptor 2) (eg, nephrogenic diabetes insipidus), full gene sequence

BBS10 (Bardet-Biedl syndrome 10) (eg, Bardet-Biedl syndrome), full gene sequence

BTD (biotinidase) (eg, biotinidase deficiency), full gene sequence

C10orf2 (chromosome 10 open reading frame 2) (eg, mitochondrial DNA depletion syndrome), full gene sequence

CAV3 (caveolin 3) (eg, CAV3-related distal myopathy, limb-girdle muscular dystrophy type 1C), full gene sequence

CD40LG (CD40 ligand) (eg, X-linked hyper IgM syndrome), full gene sequence

CDKN2A (cyclin-dependent kinase inhibitor 2A) (eg, CDKN2A-related cutaneous malignant melanoma, familial atypical mole-malignant melanoma syndrome), full gene sequence

CLRN1 (clarin 1) (eg, Usher syndrome, type 3), full gene sequence

COX6B1 (cytochrome c oxidase subunit VIb polypeptide 1) (eg, mitochondrial respiratory chain complex IV deficiency), full gene sequence

CPT2 (carnitine palmitoyltransferase 2) (eg, carnitine palmitoyltransferase II deficiency), full gene sequence

CRX (cone-rod homeobox) (eg, cone-rod dystrophy 2, Leber congenital amaurosis), full gene sequence

CSTB (cystatin B [stefin B]) (eg, Unverricht-Lundborg disease), full gene sequence

CYP1B1 (cytochrome P450, family 1, subfamily B, polypeptide 1) (eg, primary congenital glaucoma), full gene sequence

DMPK (dystrophia myotonica-protein kinase) (eg, myotonic dystrophy type 1), characterization of abnormal (eg, expanded) alleles

EGR2 (early growth response 2) (eg, Charcot-Marie-Tooth), full gene sequence

EMD (emerin) (eg, Emery-Dreifuss muscular dystrophy), duplication/deletion analysis

EPM2A (epilepsy, progressive myoclonus type 2A, Lafora disease [laforin]) (eg, progressive myoclonus epilepsy), full gene sequence

FGF23 (fibroblast growth factor 23) (eg, hypophosphatemic rickets), full gene sequence

FGFR2 (fibroblast growth factor receptor 2) (eg, craniosynostosis, Apert syndrome, Crouzon syndrome), targeted sequence analysis (eg, exons 8, 10)

FGFR3 (fibroblast growth factor receptor 3) (eg, achondroplasia, hypochondroplasia), targeted sequence analysis (eg, exons 8, 11, 12, 13)

FHL1 (four and a half LIM domains 1) (eg, Emery-Dreifuss muscular dystrophy), full gene sequence

FKRP (fukutin related protein) (eg, congenital muscular dystrophy type 1C [MDC1C], limb-girdle muscular dystrophy [LGMD] type 2I), full gene sequence

FOXG1 (forkhead box G1) (eg, Rett syndrome), full gene sequence

FSHMD1A (facioscapulohumeral muscular dystrophy 1A) (eg, facioscapulohumeral muscular dystrophy), evaluation to detect abnormal (eg, deleted) alleles

FSHMD1A (facioscapulohumeral muscular dystrophy 1A) (eg, facioscapulohumeral muscular dystrophy), characterization of haplotype(s) (ie, chromosome 4A and 4B haplotypes)

FXN (frataxin) (eg, Friedreich ataxia), full gene sequence

GH1 (growth hormone 1) (eg, growth hormone deficiency), full gene sequence

GP1BB (glycoprotein Ib [platelet], beta polypeptide) (eg, Bernard-Soulier syndrome type B), full gene sequence

(For common deletion variants of alpha globin 1 and alpha globin 2 genes, use 81257)

HNF1B (HNF1 homeobox B) (eg, maturity-onset diabetes of the young [MODY]), duplication/deletion analysis

HRAS (v-Ha-ras Harvey rat sarcoma viral oncogene homolog) (eg, Costello syndrome), full gene sequence

HSD3B2 (hydroxy-delta-5-steroid dehydrogenase, 3 beta- and steroid delta-isomerase 2) (eg, 3-beta-hydroxysteroid dehydrogenase type II deficiency), full gene sequence

HSD11B2 (hydroxysteroid [11-beta] dehydrogenase 2) (eg, mineralocorticoid excess syndrome), full gene sequence

HSPB1 (heat shock 27kDa protein 1) (eg, Charcot-Marie-Tooth disease), full gene sequence

INS (insulin) (eg, diabetes mellitus), full gene sequence

KCNJ1 (potassium inwardly-rectifying channel, subfamily J, member 1) (eg, Bartter syndrome), full gene sequence

KCNJ10 (potassium inwardly-rectifying channel, subfamily J, member 10) (eg, SeSAME syndrome, EAST syndrome, sensorineural hearing loss), full gene sequence

LITAF (lipopolysaccharide-induced TNF factor) (eg, Charcot-Marie-Tooth), full gene sequence

MEFV (Mediterranean fever) (eg, familial Mediterranean fever), full gene sequence

MEN1 (multiple endocrine neoplasia I) (eg, multiple endocrine neoplasia type 1, Wermer syndrome), duplication/deletion analysis

MMACHC (methylmalonic aciduria [cobalamin deficiency] cblC type, with homocystinuria) (eg, methylmalonic acidemia and homocystinuria), full gene sequence

MPV17 (MpV17 mitochondrial inner membrane protein) (eg, mitochondrial DNA depletion syndrome), duplication/deletion analysis

NDP (Norrie disease [pseudoglioma]) (eg, Norrie disease), full gene sequence

NDUFA1 (NADH dehydrogenase [ubiquinone] 1 alpha subcomplex, 1, 7.5kDa) (eg, Leigh syndrome, mitochondrial complex I deficiency), full gene sequence

NDUFAF2 (NADH dehydrogenase [ubiquinone] 1 alpha subcomplex, assembly factor 2) (eg, Leigh syndrome, mitochondrial complex I deficiency), full gene sequence

NDUFS4 (NADH dehydrogenase [ubiquinone] Fe-S protein 4, 18kDa [NADH-coenzyme Q reductase]) (eg, Leigh syndrome, mitochondrial complex I deficiency), full gene sequence

NIPA1 (non-imprinted in Prader-Willi/Angelman syndrome 1) (eg, spastic paraplegia), full gene sequence

NLGN4X (neuroligin 4, X-linked) (eg, autism spectrum disorders), duplication/deletion analysis

NPC2 (Niemann-Pick disease, type C2 [epididymal secretory protein E1]) (eg, Niemann-Pick disease type C2), full gene sequence

NR0B1 (nuclear receptor subfamily 0, group B, member 1) (eg, congenital adrenal hypoplasia), full gene sequence

PDX1 (pancreatic and duodenal homeobox 1) (eg, maturity-onset diabetes of the young [MODY]), full gene sequence

PHOX2B (paired-like homeobox 2b) (eg, congenital central hypoventilation syndrome), full gene sequence

PIK3CA (phosphatidylinositol-4,5-bisphosphate 3-kinase, catalytic subunit alpha) (eg, colorectal cancer), targeted sequence analysis (eg, exons 9 and 20)

PLP1 (proteolipid protein 1) (eg, Pelizaeus-Merzbacher disease, spastic paraplegia), duplication/deletion analysis

PQBP1 (polyglutamine binding protein 1) (eg, Renpenning syndrome), duplication/deletion analysis

PRNP (prion protein) (eg, genetic prion disease), full gene sequence

PROP1 (PROP paired-like homeobox 1) (eg, combined pituitary hormone deficiency), full gene sequence

PRPH2 (peripherin 2 [retinal degeneration, slow]) (eg, retinitis pigmentosa), full gene sequence

PRSS1 (protease, serine, 1 [trypsin 1]) (eg, hereditary pancreatitis), full gene sequence

RAF1 (v-raf-1 murine leukemia viral oncogene homolog 1) (eg, LEOPARD syndrome), targeted sequence analysis (eg, exons 7, 12, 14, 17)

RET (ret proto-oncogene) (eg, multiple endocrine neoplasia, type 2B and familial medullary thyroid carcinoma), common variants (eg, M918T, 2647_2648delinsTT, A883F)

RHO (rhodopsin) (eg, retinitis pigmentosa), full gene sequence

RP1 (retinitis pigmentosa 1) (eg, retinitis pigmentosa), full gene sequence

SCN1B (sodium channel, voltage-gated, type I, beta) (eg, Brugada syndrome), full gene sequence

SCO2 (SCO cytochrome oxidase deficient homolog 2 [SCO1L]) (eg, mitochondrial respiratory chain complex IV deficiency), full gene sequence

SDHC (succinate dehydrogenase complex, subunit C, integral membrane protein, 15kDa) (eg, hereditary paraganglioma-pheochromocytoma syndrome), duplication/deletion analysis

SDHD (succinate dehydrogenase complex, subunit D, integral membrane protein) (eg, hereditary paraganglioma), full gene sequence

SGCG (sarcoglycan, gamma [35kDa dystrophin-associated glycoprotein]) (eg, limb-girdle muscular dystrophy), duplication/deletion analysis

SH2D1A (SH2 domain containing 1A) (eg, X-linked lymphoproliferative syndrome), full gene sequence

SLC16A2 (solute carrier family 16, member 2 [thyroid hormone transporter]) (eg, specific thyroid hormone cell transporter deficiency, Allan-Herndon-Dudley syndrome), duplication/deletion analysis

SLC25A20 (solute carrier family 25 [carnitine/ acylcarnitine translocase], member 20) (eg, carnitine-acylcarnitine translocase deficiency), duplication/deletion analysis

SLC25A4 (solute carrier family 25 [mitochondrial carrier; adenine nucleotide translocator], member 4) (eg, progressive external ophthalmoplegia), full gene sequence

SOD1 (superoxide dismutase 1, soluble) (eg, amyotrophic lateral sclerosis), full gene sequence

SPINK1 (serine peptidase inhibitor, Kazal type 1) (eg, hereditary pancreatitis), full gene sequence

STK11 (serine/threonine kinase 11) (eg, Peutz-Jeghers syndrome), duplication/deletion analysis

TACO1 (translational activator of mitochondrial encoded cytochrome c oxidase I) (eg, mitochondrial respiratory chain complex IV deficiency), full gene sequence

THAP1 (THAP domain containing, apoptosis associated protein 1) (eg, torsion dystonia), full gene sequence

TOR1A (torsin family 1, member A [torsin A]) (eg, torsion dystonia), full gene sequence

TP53 (tumor protein 53) (eg, tumor samples), targeted sequence analysis of 2-5 exons

TTPA (tocopherol [alpha] transfer protein) (eg, ataxia), full gene sequence

TTR (transthyretin) (eg, familial transthyretin amyloidosis), full gene sequence

TWIST1 (twist homolog 1 [Drosophila]) (eg, Saethre-Chotzen syndrome), full gene sequence

TYR (tyrosinase [oculocutaneous albinism IA]) (eg, oculocutaneous albinism IA), full gene sequence

USH1G (Usher syndrome 1G [autosomal recessive]) (eg, Usher syndrome, type 1), full gene sequence

VHL (von Hippel-Lindau tumor suppressor) (eg, von Hippel-Lindau familial cancer syndrome), full gene sequence

VWF (von Willebrand factor) (eg, von Willebrand disease type 1C), targeted sequence analysis (eg, exons 26, 27, 37)

ZEB2 (zinc finger E-box binding homeobox 2) (eg, Mowat-Wilson syndrome), duplication/deletion analysis

ZNF41 (zinc finger protein 41) (eg, X-linked mental retardation 89), full gene sequence

Pathology and Laboratory 80047-89398, 0001U-0017U

Rationale

In accordance with the establishment of Tier 1 codes 81258, 81259, 81269, 81361-81364, the HBA1/HBA2 and HBB gene tests have been removed from code 81404.

Refer to the codebook and the Rationale for codes 81257, 81258, 81259, 81269, and 81361-81364 for a full discussion of the changes.

▲ **81405**   Molecular pathology procedure, Level 6 (eg, analysis of 6-10 exons by DNA sequence analysis, mutation scanning or duplication/deletion variants of 11-25 exons, regionally targeted cytogenomic array analysis)

ABCD1 (ATP-binding cassette, sub-family D [ALD], member 1) (eg, adrenoleukodystrophy), full gene sequence

ACADS (acyl-CoA dehydrogenase, C-2 to C-3 short chain) (eg, short chain acyl-CoA dehydrogenase deficiency), full gene sequence

ACTA2 (actin, alpha 2, smooth muscle, aorta) (eg, thoracic aortic aneurysms and aortic dissections), full gene sequence

ACTC1 (actin, alpha, cardiac muscle 1) (eg, familial hypertrophic cardiomyopathy), full gene sequence

ANKRD1 (ankyrin repeat domain 1) (eg, dilated cardiomyopathy), full gene sequence

APTX (aprataxin) (eg, ataxia with oculomotor apraxia 1), full gene sequence

AR (androgen receptor) (eg, androgen insensitivity syndrome), full gene sequence

ARSA (arylsulfatase A) (eg, arylsulfatase A deficiency), full gene sequence

BCKDHA (branched chain keto acid dehydrogenase E1, alpha polypeptide) (eg, maple syrup urine disease, type 1A), full gene sequence

BCS1L (BCS1-like [S. cerevisiae]) (eg, Leigh syndrome, mitochondrial complex III deficiency, GRACILE syndrome), full gene sequence

BMPR2 (bone morphogenetic protein receptor, type II [serine/threonine kinase]) (eg, heritable pulmonary arterial hypertension), duplication/deletion analysis

CASQ2 (calsequestrin 2 [cardiac muscle]) (eg, catecholaminergic polymorphic ventricular tachycardia), full gene sequence

CASR (calcium-sensing receptor) (eg, hypocalcemia), full gene sequence

CDKL5 (cyclin-dependent kinase-like 5) (eg, early infantile epileptic encephalopathy), duplication/deletion analysis

CHRNA4 (cholinergic receptor, nicotinic, alpha 4) (eg, nocturnal frontal lobe epilepsy), full gene sequence

CHRNB2 (cholinergic receptor, nicotinic, beta 2 [neuronal]) (eg, nocturnal frontal lobe epilepsy), full gene sequence

COX10 (COX10 homolog, cytochrome c oxidase assembly protein) (eg, mitochondrial respiratory chain complex IV deficiency), full gene sequence

COX15 (COX15 homolog, cytochrome c oxidase assembly protein) (eg, mitochondrial respiratory chain complex IV deficiency), full gene sequence

▶*CPOX (coproporphyrinogen oxidase)* (eg, hereditary coproporphyria), full gene sequence◀

▶*CTRC (chymotrypsin C)* (eg, hereditary pancreatitis), full gene sequence◀

CYP11B1 (cytochrome P450, family 11, subfamily B, polypeptide 1) (eg, congenital adrenal hyperplasia), full gene sequence

CYP17A1 (cytochrome P450, family 17, subfamily A, polypeptide 1) (eg, congenital adrenal hyperplasia), full gene sequence

CYP21A2 (cytochrome P450, family 21, subfamily A, polypeptide2) (eg, steroid 21-hydroxylase isoform, congenital adrenal hyperplasia), full gene sequence

Cytogenomic constitutional targeted microarray analysis of chromosome 22q13 by interrogation of genomic regions for copy number and single nucleotide polymorphism (SNP) variants for chromosomal abnormalities

(When performing genome-wide cytogenomic constitutional microarray analysis, see 81228, 81229)

(Do not report analyte-specific molecular pathology procedures separately when the specific analytes are included as part of the microarray analysis of chromosome 22q13)

(Do not report 88271 when performing cytogenomic microarray analysis)

DBT (dihydrolipoamide branched chain transacylase E2) (eg, maple syrup urine disease, type 2), duplication/deletion analysis

DCX (doublecortin) (eg, X-linked lissencephaly), full gene sequence

DES (desmin) (eg, myofibrillar myopathy), full gene sequence

DFNB59 (deafness, autosomal recessive 59) (eg, autosomal recessive nonsyndromic hearing impairment), full gene sequence

DGUOK (deoxyguanosine kinase) (eg, hepatocerebral mitochondrial DNA depletion syndrome), full gene sequence

DHCR7 (7-dehydrocholesterol reductase) (eg, Smith-Lemli-Opitz syndrome), full gene sequence

EIF2B2 (eukaryotic translation initiation factor 2B, subunit 2 beta, 39kDa) (eg, leukoencephalopathy with vanishing white matter), full gene sequence

EMD (emerin) (eg, Emery-Dreifuss muscular dystrophy), full gene sequence

ENG (endoglin) (eg, hereditary hemorrhagic telangiectasia, type 1), duplication/deletion analysis

EYA1 (eyes absent homolog 1 [Drosophila]) (eg, branchio-oto-renal [BOR] spectrum disorders), duplication/deletion analysis

FGFR1 (fibroblast growth factor receptor 1) (eg, Kallmann syndrome 2), full gene sequence

FH (fumarate hydratase) (eg, fumarate hydratase deficiency, hereditary leiomyomatosis with renal cell cancer), full gene sequence

FKTN (fukutin) (eg, limb-girdle muscular dystrophy [LGMD] type 2M or 2L), full gene sequence

FTSJ1 (FtsJ RNA methyltransferase homolog 1 [E. coli]) (eg, X-linked mental retardation 9), duplication/deletion analysis

GABRG2 (gamma-aminobutyric acid [GABA] A receptor, gamma 2) (eg, generalized epilepsy with febrile seizures), full gene sequence

GCH1 (GTP cyclohydrolase 1) (eg, autosomal dominant dopa-responsive dystonia), full gene sequence

GDAP1 (ganglioside-induced differentiation-associated protein 1) (eg, Charcot-Marie-Tooth disease), full gene sequence

GFAP (glial fibrillary acidic protein) (eg, Alexander disease), full gene sequence

GHR (growth hormone receptor) (eg, Laron syndrome), full gene sequence

GHRHR (growth hormone releasing hormone receptor) (eg, growth hormone deficiency), full gene sequence

GLA (galactosidase, alpha) (eg, Fabry disease), full gene sequence

HNF1A (HNF1 homeobox A) (eg, maturity-onset diabetes of the young [MODY]), full gene sequence

HNF1B (HNF1 homeobox B) (eg, maturity-onset diabetes of the young [MODY]), full gene sequence

HTRA1 (HtrA serine peptidase 1) (eg, macular degeneration), full gene sequence

IDS (iduronate 2-sulfatase) (eg, mucopolysacchridosis, type II), full gene sequence

IL2RG (interleukin 2 receptor, gamma) (eg, X-linked severe combined immunodeficiency), full gene sequence

ISPD (isoprenoid synthase domain containing) (eg, muscle-eye-brain disease, Walker-Warburg syndrome), full gene sequence

KRAS (Kirsten rat sarcoma viral oncogene homolog) (eg, Noonan syndrome), full gene sequence

LAMP2 (lysosomal-associated membrane protein 2) (eg, Danon disease), full gene sequence

LDLR (low density lipoprotein receptor) (eg, familial hypercholesterolemia), duplication/deletion analysis

MEN1 (multiple endocrine neoplasia I) (eg, multiple endocrine neoplasia type 1, Wermer syndrome), full gene sequence

MMAA (methylmalonic aciduria [cobalamine deficiency] type A) (eg, MMAA-related methylmalonic acidemia), full gene sequence

MMAB (methylmalonic aciduria [cobalamine deficiency] type B) (eg, MMAB-related methylmalonic acidemia), full gene sequence

MPI (mannose phosphate isomerase) (eg, congenital disorder of glycosylation 1b), full gene sequence

MPV17 (MpV17 mitochondrial inner membrane protein) (eg, mitochondrial DNA depletion syndrome), full gene sequence

MPZ (myelin protein zero) (eg, Charcot-Marie-Tooth), full gene sequence

MTM1 (myotubularin 1) (eg, X-linked centronuclear myopathy), duplication/deletion analysis

MYL2 (myosin, light chain 2, regulatory, cardiac, slow) (eg, familial hypertrophic cardiomyopathy), full gene sequence

MYL3 (myosin, light chain 3, alkali, ventricular, skeletal, slow) (eg, familial hypertrophic cardiomyopathy), full gene sequence

MYOT (myotilin) (eg, limb-girdle muscular dystrophy), full gene sequence

NDUFS7 (NADH dehydrogenase [ubiquinone] Fe-S protein 7, 20kDa [NADH-coenzyme Q reductase]) (eg, Leigh syndrome, mitochondrial complex I deficiency), full gene sequence

NDUFS8 (NADH dehydrogenase [ubiquinone] Fe-S protein 8, 23kDa [NADH-coenzyme Q reductase]) (eg, Leigh syndrome, mitochondrial complex I deficiency), full gene sequence

NDUFV1 (NADH dehydrogenase [ubiquinone] flavoprotein 1, 51kDa) (eg, Leigh syndrome, mitochondrial complex I deficiency), full gene sequence

NEFL (neurofilament, light polypeptide) (eg, Charcot-Marie-Tooth), full gene sequence

NF2 (neurofibromin 2 [merlin]) (eg, neurofibromatosis, type 2), duplication/deletion analysis

NLGN3 (neuroligin 3) (eg, autism spectrum disorders), full gene sequence

NLGN4X (neuroligin 4, X-linked) (eg, autism spectrum disorders), full gene sequence

NPHP1 (nephronophthisis 1 [juvenile]) (eg, Joubert syndrome), deletion analysis, and duplication analysis, if performed

NPHS2 (nephrosis 2, idiopathic, steroid-resistant [podocin]) (eg, steroid-resistant nephrotic syndrome), full gene sequence

NSD1 (nuclear receptor binding SET domain protein 1) (eg, Sotos syndrome), duplication/deletion analysis

OTC (ornithine carbamoyltransferase) (eg, ornithine transcarbamylase deficiency), full gene sequence

PAFAH1B1 (platelet-activating factor acetylhydrolase 1b, regulatory subunit 1 [45kDa]) (eg, lissencephaly, Miller-Dieker syndrome), duplication/deletion analysis

PARK2 (Parkinson protein 2, E3 ubiquitin protein ligase [parkin]) (eg, Parkinson disease), duplication/deletion analysis

PCCA (propionyl CoA carboxylase, alpha polypeptide) (eg, propionic acidemia, type 1), duplication/deletion analysis

PCDH19 (protocadherin 19) (eg, epileptic encephalopathy), full gene sequence

PDHA1 (pyruvate dehydrogenase [lipoamide] alpha 1) (eg, lactic acidosis), duplication/deletion analysis

PDHB (pyruvate dehydrogenase [lipoamide] beta) (eg, lactic acidosis), full gene sequence

PINK1 (PTEN induced putative kinase 1) (eg, Parkinson disease), full gene sequence

▶ *PKLR (pyruvate kinase, liver and RBC)* (eg, pyruvate kinase deficiency), full gene sequence ◀

PLP1 (proteolipid protein 1) (eg, Pelizaeus-Merzbacher disease, spastic paraplegia), full gene sequence

POU1F1 (POU class 1 homeobox 1) (eg, combined pituitary hormone deficiency), full gene sequence

PRX (periaxin) (eg, Charcot-Marie-Tooth disease), full gene sequence

PQBP1 (polyglutamine binding protein 1) (eg, Renpenning syndrome), full gene sequence

PSEN1 (presenilin 1) (eg, Alzheimer disease), full gene sequence

RAB7A (RAB7A, member RAS oncogene family) (eg, Charcot-Marie-Tooth disease), full gene sequence

RAI1 (retinoic acid induced 1) (eg, Smith-Magenis syndrome), full gene sequence

REEP1 (receptor accessory protein 1) (eg, spastic paraplegia), full gene sequence

RET (ret proto-oncogene) (eg, multiple endocrine neoplasia, type 2A and familial medullary thyroid carcinoma), targeted sequence analysis (eg, exons 10, 11, 13-16)

RPS19 (ribosomal protein S19) (eg, Diamond-Blackfan anemia), full gene sequence

RRM2B (ribonucleotide reductase M2 B [TP53 inducible]) (eg, mitochondrial DNA depletion), full gene sequence

SCO1 (SCO cytochrome oxidase deficient homolog 1) (eg, mitochondrial respiratory chain complex IV deficiency), full gene sequence

SDHB (succinate dehydrogenase complex, subunit B, iron sulfur) (eg, hereditary paraganglioma), full gene sequence

SDHC (succinate dehydrogenase complex, subunit C, integral membrane protein, 15kDa) (eg, hereditary paraganglioma-pheochromocytoma syndrome), full gene sequence

SGCA (sarcoglycan, alpha [50kDa dystrophin-associated glycoprotein]) (eg, limb-girdle muscular dystrophy), full gene sequence

SGCB (sarcoglycan, beta [43kDa dystrophin-associated glycoprotein]) (eg, limb-girdle muscular dystrophy), full gene sequence

SGCD (sarcoglycan, delta [35kDa dystrophin-associated glycoprotein]) (eg, limb-girdle muscular dystrophy), full gene sequence

SGCE (sarcoglycan, epsilon) (eg, myoclonic dystonia), duplication/deletion analysis

SGCG (sarcoglycan, gamma [35kDa dystrophin-associated glycoprotein]) (eg, limb-girdle muscular dystrophy), full gene sequence

SHOC2 (soc-2 suppressor of clear homolog) (eg, Noonan-like syndrome with loose anagen hair), full gene sequence

SHOX (short stature homeobox) (eg, Langer mesomelic dysplasia), full gene sequence

SIL1 (SIL1 homolog, endoplasmic reticulum chaperone [S. cerevisiae]) (eg, ataxia), full gene sequence

SLC2A1 (solute carrier family 2 [facilitated glucose transporter], member 1) (eg, glucose transporter type 1 [GLUT 1] deficiency syndrome), full gene sequence

SLC16A2 (solute carrier family 16, member 2 [thyroid hormone transporter]) (eg, specific thyroid hormone cell transporter deficiency, Allan-Herndon-Dudley syndrome), full gene sequence

SLC22A5 (solute carrier family 22 [organic cation/carnitine transporter], member 5) (eg, systemic primary carnitine deficiency), full gene sequence

SLC25A20 (solute carrier family 25 [carnitine/acylcarnitine translocase], member 20) (eg, carnitine-acylcarnitine translocase deficiency), full gene sequence

★ = Telemedicine   ✛ = Add-on code   ✒ = FDA approval pending   # = Resequenced code

SMAD4 (SMAD family member 4) (eg, hemorrhagic telangiectasia syndrome, juvenile polyposis), duplication/deletion analysis

SMN1 (survival of motor neuron 1, telomeric) (eg, spinal muscular atrophy), full gene sequence

SPAST (spastin) (eg, spastic paraplegia), duplication/deletion analysis

SPG7 (spastic paraplegia 7 [pure and complicated autosomal recessive]) (eg, spastic paraplegia), duplication/deletion analysis

SPRED1 (sprouty-related, EVH1 domain containing 1) (eg, Legius syndrome), full gene sequence

STAT3 (signal transducer and activator of transcription 3 [acute-phase response factor]) (eg, autosomal dominant hyper-IgE syndrome), targeted sequence analysis (eg, exons 12, 13, 14, 16, 17, 20, 21)

STK11 (serine/threonine kinase 11) (eg, Peutz-Jeghers syndrome), full gene sequence

SURF1 (surfeit 1) (eg, mitochondrial respiratory chain complex IV deficiency), full gene sequence

TARDBP (TAR DNA binding protein) (eg, amyotrophic lateral sclerosis), full gene sequence

TBX5 (T-box 5) (eg, Holt-Oram syndrome), full gene sequence

TCF4 (transcription factor 4) (eg, Pitt-Hopkins syndrome), duplication/deletion analysis

TGFBR1 (transforming growth factor, beta receptor 1) (eg, Marfan syndrome), full gene sequence

TGFBR2 (transforming growth factor, beta receptor 2) (eg, Marfan syndrome), full gene sequence

THRB (thyroid hormone receptor, beta) (eg, thyroid hormone resistance, thyroid hormone beta receptor deficiency), full gene sequence or targeted sequence analysis of >5 exons

TK2 (thymidine kinase 2, mitochondrial) (eg, mitochondrial DNA depletion syndrome), full gene sequence

TNNC1 (troponin C type 1 [slow]) (eg, hypertrophic cardiomyopathy or dilated cardiomyopathy), full gene sequence

TNNI3 (troponin I, type 3 [cardiac]) (eg, familial hypertrophic cardiomyopathy), full gene sequence

TP53 (tumor protein 53) (eg, Li-Fraumeni syndrome, tumor samples), full gene sequence or targeted sequence analysis of >5 exons

TPM1 (tropomyosin 1 [alpha]) (eg, familial hypertrophic cardiomyopathy), full gene sequence

TSC1 (tuberous sclerosis 1) (eg, tuberous sclerosis), duplication/deletion analysis

TYMP (thymidine phosphorylase) (eg, mitochondrial DNA depletion syndrome), full gene sequence

VWF (von Willebrand factor) (eg, von Willebrand disease type 2N), targeted sequence analysis (eg, exons 18-20, 23-25)

WT1 (Wilms tumor 1) (eg, Denys-Drash syndrome, familial Wilms tumor), full gene sequence

ZEB2 (zinc finger E-box binding homeobox 2) (eg, Mowat-Wilson syndrome), full gene sequence

---

Rationale

In accordance with the establishment of Tier 1 codes 81238, 81258, 81259, and 81269, the F9 and HBA1/HBA2 gene tests have been removed from code 81405. Note that full gene sequence of the PKLR, CPOX, and CTRC genes have been added to code 81405.

Refer to codebook and the Rationale for codes 81238, 81257, 81258, 81259 for a full discussion of the changes.

▲ **81406**   Molecular pathology procedure, Level 7 (eg, analysis of 11-25 exons by DNA sequence analysis, mutation scanning or duplication/deletion variants of 26-50 exons, cytogenomic array analysis for neoplasia)

ACADVL (acyl-CoA dehydrogenase, very long chain) (eg, very long chain acyl-coenzyme A dehydrogenase deficiency), full gene sequence

ACTN4 (actinin, alpha 4) (eg, focal segmental glomerulosclerosis), full gene sequence

AFG3L2 (AFG3 ATPase family gene 3-like 2 [S. cerevisiae]) (eg, spinocerebellar ataxia), full gene sequence

AIRE (autoimmune regulator) (eg, autoimmune polyendocrinopathy syndrome type 1), full gene sequence

ALDH7A1 (aldehyde dehydrogenase 7 family, member A1) (eg, pyridoxine-dependent epilepsy), full gene sequence

ANO5 (anoctamin 5) (eg, limb-girdle muscular dystrophy), full gene sequence

►*ANOS1 (anosmin-1)* (eg, Kallmann syndrome 1), full gene sequence◄

APP (amyloid beta [A4] precursor protein) (eg, Alzheimer disease), full gene sequence

ASS1 (argininosuccinate synthase 1) (eg, citrullinemia type I), full gene sequence

ATL1 (atlastin GTPase 1) (eg, spastic paraplegia), full gene sequence

ATP1A2 (ATPase, Na+/K+ transporting, alpha 2 polypeptide) (eg, familial hemiplegic migraine), full gene sequence

Pathology and Laboratory   80047-89398, 0001U-0017U

Pathology and Laboratory   80047-89398, 0001U-0017U

ATP7B (ATPase, Cu++ transporting, beta polypeptide) (eg, Wilson disease), full gene sequence

BBS1 (Bardet-Biedl syndrome 1) (eg, Bardet-Biedl syndrome), full gene sequence

BBS2 (Bardet-Biedl syndrome 2) (eg, Bardet-Biedl syndrome), full gene sequence

BCKDHB (branched-chain keto acid dehydrogenase E1, beta polypeptide) (eg, maple syrup urine disease, type 1B), full gene sequence

BEST1 (bestrophin 1) (eg, vitelliform macular dystrophy), full gene sequence

BMPR2 (bone morphogenetic protein receptor, type II [serine/threonine kinase]) (eg, heritable pulmonary arterial hypertension), full gene sequence

BRAF (B-Raf proto-oncogene, serine/threonine kinase) (eg, Noonan syndrome), full gene sequence

BSCL2 (Berardinelli-Seip congenital lipodystrophy 2 [seipin]) (eg, Berardinelli-Seip congenital lipodystrophy), full gene sequence

BTK (Bruton agammaglobulinemia tyrosine kinase) (eg, X-linked agammaglobulinemia), full gene sequence

CACNB2 (calcium channel, voltage-dependent, beta 2 subunit) (eg, Brugada syndrome), full gene sequence

CAPN3 (calpain 3) (eg, limb-girdle muscular dystrophy [LGMD] type 2A, calpainopathy), full gene sequence

CBS (cystathionine-beta-synthase) (eg, homocystinuria, cystathionine beta-synthase deficiency), full gene sequence

CDH1 (cadherin 1, type 1, E-cadherin [epithelial]) (eg, hereditary diffuse gastric cancer), full gene sequence

CDKL5 (cyclin-dependent kinase-like 5) (eg, early infantile epileptic encephalopathy), full gene sequence

CLCN1 (chloride channel 1, skeletal muscle) (eg, myotonia congenita), full gene sequence

CLCNKB (chloride channel, voltage-sensitive Kb) (eg, Bartter syndrome 3 and 4b), full gene sequence

CNTNAP2 (contactin-associated protein-like 2) (eg, Pitt-Hopkins-like syndrome 1), full gene sequence

COL6A2 (collagen, type VI, alpha 2) (eg, collagen type VI-related disorders), duplication/deletion analysis

CPT1A (carnitine palmitoyltransferase 1A [liver]) (eg, carnitine palmitoyltransferase 1A [CPT1A] deficiency), full gene sequence

CRB1 (crumbs homolog 1 [Drosophila]) (eg, Leber congenital amaurosis), full gene sequence

CREBBP (CREB binding protein) (eg, Rubinstein-Taybi syndrome), duplication/deletion analysis

Cytogenomic microarray analysis, neoplasia (eg, interrogation of copy number, and loss-of-heterozygosity via single nucleotide polymorphism [SNP]-based comparative genomic hybridization [CGH] microarray analysis)

(Do not report analyte-specific molecular pathology procedures separately when the specific analytes are included as part of the cytogenomic microarray analysis for neoplasia)

(Do not report 88271 when performing cytogenomic microarray analysis)

DBT (dihydrolipoamide branched chain transacylase E2) (eg, maple syrup urine disease, type 2), full gene sequence

DLAT (dihydrolipoamide S-acetyltransferase) (eg, pyruvate dehydrogenase E2 deficiency), full gene sequence

DLD (dihydrolipoamide dehydrogenase) (eg, maple syrup urine disease, type III), full gene sequence

DSC2 (desmocollin) (eg, arrhythmogenic right ventricular dysplasia/cardiomyopathy 11), full gene sequence

DSG2 (desmoglein 2) (eg, arrhythmogenic right ventricular dysplasia/cardiomyopathy 10), full gene sequence

DSP (desmoplakin) (eg, arrhythmogenic right ventricular dysplasia/cardiomyopathy 8), full gene sequence

EFHC1 (EF-hand domain [C-terminal] containing 1) (eg, juvenile myoclonic epilepsy), full gene sequence

EIF2B3 (eukaryotic translation initiation factor 2B, subunit 3 gamma, 58kDa) (eg, leukoencephalopathy with vanishing white matter), full gene sequence

EIF2B4 (eukaryotic translation initiation factor 2B, subunit 4 delta, 67kDa) (eg, leukoencephalopathy with vanishing white matter), full gene sequence

EIF2B5 (eukaryotic translation initiation factor 2B, subunit 5 epsilon, 82kDa) (eg, childhood ataxia with central nervous system hypomyelination/vanishing white matter), full gene sequence

ENG (endoglin) (eg, hereditary hemorrhagic telangiectasia, type 1), full gene sequence

EYA1 (eyes absent homolog 1 [Drosophila]) (eg, branchio-oto-renal [BOR] spectrum disorders), full gene sequence

F8 (coagulation factor VIII) (eg, hemophilia A), duplication/deletion analysis

FAH (fumarylacetoacetate hydrolase [fumarylacetoacetase]) (eg, tyrosinemia, type 1), full gene sequence

FASTKD2 (FAST kinase domains 2) (eg, mitochondrial respiratory chain complex IV deficiency), full gene sequence

★ = Telemedicine   ✚ = Add-on code   ✔ = FDA approval pending   # = Resequenced code

FIG4 (FIG4 homolog, SAC1 lipid phosphatase domain containing [S. cerevisiae]) (eg, Charcot-Marie-Tooth disease), full gene sequence

FTSJ1 (FtsJ RNA methyltransferase homolog 1 [E. coli]) (eg, X-linked mental retardation 9), full gene sequence

FUS (fused in sarcoma) (eg, amyotrophic lateral sclerosis), full gene sequence

GAA (glucosidase, alpha; acid) (eg, glycogen storage disease type II [Pompe disease]), full gene sequence

GALC (galactosylceramidase) (eg, Krabbe disease), full gene sequence

GALT (galactose-1-phosphate uridylyltransferase) (eg, galactosemia), full gene sequence

GARS (glycyl-tRNA synthetase) (eg, Charcot-Marie-Tooth disease), full gene sequence

GCDH (glutaryl-CoA dehydrogenase) (eg, glutaricacidemia type 1), full gene sequence

GCK (glucokinase [hexokinase 4]) (eg, maturity-onset diabetes of the young [MODY]), full gene sequence

GLUD1 (glutamate dehydrogenase 1) (eg, familial hyperinsulinism), full gene sequence

GNE (glucosamine [UDP-N-acetyl]-2-epimerase/N-acetylmannosamine kinase) (eg, inclusion body myopathy 2 [IBM2], Nonaka myopathy), full gene sequence

GRN (granulin) (eg, frontotemporal dementia), full gene sequence

HADHA (hydroxyacyl-CoA dehydrogenase/3-ketoacyl-CoA thiolase/enoyl-CoA hydratase [trifunctional protein] alpha subunit) (eg, long chain acyl-coenzyme A dehydrogenase deficiency), full gene sequence

HADHB (hydroxyacyl-CoA dehydrogenase/3-ketoacyl-CoA thiolase/enoyl-CoA hydratase [trifunctional protein], beta subunit) (eg, trifunctional protein deficiency), full gene sequence

HEXA (hexosaminidase A, alpha polypeptide) (eg, Tay-Sachs disease), full gene sequence

HLCS (HLCS holocarboxylase synthetase) (eg, holocarboxylase synthetase deficiency), full gene sequence

▶*HMBS (hydroxymethylbilane synthase)* (eg, acute intermittent porphyria), full gene sequence◀

HNF4A (hepatocyte nuclear factor 4, alpha) (eg, maturity-onset diabetes of the young [MODY]), full gene sequence

IDUA (iduronidase, alpha-L-) (eg, mucopolysaccharidosis type I), full gene sequence

INF2 (inverted formin, FH2 and WH2 domain containing) (eg, focal segmental glomerulosclerosis), full gene sequence

IVD (isovaleryl-CoA dehydrogenase) (eg, isovaleric acidemia), full gene sequence

JAG1 (jagged 1) (eg, Alagille syndrome), duplication/deletion analysis

JUP (junction plakoglobin) (eg, arrhythmogenic right ventricular dysplasia/cardiomyopathy 11), full gene sequence

KCNH2 (potassium voltage-gated channel, subfamily H [eag-related], member 2) (eg, short QT syndrome, long QT syndrome), full gene sequence

KCNQ1 (potassium voltage-gated channel, KQT-like subfamily, member 1) (eg, short QT syndrome, long QT syndrome), full gene sequence

KCNQ2 (potassium voltage-gated channel, KQT-like subfamily, member 2) (eg, epileptic encephalopathy), full gene sequence

LDB3 (LIM domain binding 3) (eg, familial dilated cardiomyopathy, myofibrillar myopathy), full gene sequence

LDLR (low density lipoprotein receptor) (eg, familial hypercholesterolemia), full gene sequence

LEPR (leptin receptor) (eg, obesity with hypogonadism), full gene sequence

LHCGR (luteinizing hormone/choriogonadotropin receptor) (eg, precocious male puberty), full gene sequence

LMNA (lamin A/C) (eg, Emery-Dreifuss muscular dystrophy [EDMD1, 2 and 3] limb-girdle muscular dystrophy [LGMD] type 1B, dilated cardiomyopathy [CMD1A], familial partial lipodystrophy [FPLD2]), full gene sequence

LRP5 (low density lipoprotein receptor-related protein 5) (eg, osteopetrosis), full gene sequence

MAP2K1 (mitogen-activated protein kinase 1) (eg, cardiofaciocutaneous syndrome), full gene sequence

MAP2K2 (mitogen-activated protein kinase 2) (eg, cardiofaciocutaneous syndrome), full gene sequence

MAPT (microtubule-associated protein tau) (eg, frontotemporal dementia), full gene sequence

MCCC1 (methylcrotonoyl-CoA carboxylase 1 [alpha]) (eg, 3-methylcrotonyl-CoA carboxylase deficiency), full gene sequence

MCCC2 (methylcrotonoyl-CoA carboxylase 2 [beta]) (eg, 3-methylcrotonyl carboxylase deficiency), full gene sequence

MFN2 (mitofusin 2) (eg, Charcot-Marie-Tooth disease), full gene sequence

MTM1 (myotubularin 1) (eg, X-linked centronuclear myopathy), full gene sequence

MUT (methylmalonyl CoA mutase) (eg, methylmalonic acidemia), full gene sequence

MUTYH (mutY homolog [E. coli]) (eg, MYH-associated polyposis), full gene sequence

Pathology and Laboratory 80047-89398, 0001U-0017U

NDUFS1 (NADH dehydrogenase [ubiquinone] Fe-S protein 1, 75kDa [NADH-coenzyme Q reductase]) (eg, Leigh syndrome, mitochondrial complex I deficiency), full gene sequence

NF2 (neurofibromin 2 [merlin]) (eg, neurofibromatosis, type 2), full gene sequence

NOTCH3 (notch 3) (eg, cerebral autosomal dominant arteriopathy with subcortical infarcts and leukoencephalopathy [CADASIL]), targeted sequence analysis (eg, exons 1-23)

NPC1 (Niemann-Pick disease, type C1) (eg, Niemann-Pick disease), full gene sequence

NPHP1 (nephronophthisis 1 [juvenile]) (eg, Joubert syndrome), full gene sequence

NSD1 (nuclear receptor binding SET domain protein 1) (eg, Sotos syndrome), full gene sequence

OPA1 (optic atrophy 1) (eg, optic atrophy), duplication/deletion analysis

OPTN (optineurin) (eg, amyotrophic lateral sclerosis), full gene sequence

PAFAH1B1 (platelet-activating factor acetylhydrolase 1b, regulatory subunit 1 [45kDa]) (eg, lissencephaly, Miller-Dieker syndrome), full gene sequence

PAH (phenylalanine hydroxylase) (eg, phenylketonuria), full gene sequence

PALB2 (partner and localizer of BRCA2) (eg, breast and pancreatic cancer), full gene sequence

PARK2 (Parkinson protein 2, E3 ubiquitin protein ligase [parkin]) (eg, Parkinson disease), full gene sequence

PAX2 (paired box 2) (eg, renal coloboma syndrome), full gene sequence

PC (pyruvate carboxylase) (eg, pyruvate carboxylase deficiency), full gene sequence

PCCA (propionyl CoA carboxylase, alpha polypeptide) (eg, propionic acidemia, type 1), full gene sequence

PCCB (propionyl CoA carboxylase, beta polypeptide) (eg, propionic acidemia), full gene sequence

PCDH15 (protocadherin-related 15) (eg, Usher syndrome type 1F), duplication/deletion analysis

PCSK9 (proprotein convertase subtilisin/kexin type 9) (eg, familial hypercholesterolemia), full gene sequence

PDHA1 (pyruvate dehydrogenase [lipoamide] alpha 1) (eg, lactic acidosis), full gene sequence

PDHX (pyruvate dehydrogenase complex, component X) (eg, lactic acidosis), full gene sequence

PHEX (phosphate-regulating endopeptidase homolog, X-linked) (eg, hypophosphatemic rickets), full gene sequence

PKD2 (polycystic kidney disease 2 [autosomal dominant]) (eg, polycystic kidney disease), full gene sequence

PKP2 (plakophilin 2) (eg, arrhythmogenic right ventricular dysplasia/cardiomyopathy 9), full gene sequence

PNKD (paroxysmal nonkinesigenic dyskinesia) (eg, paroxysmal nonkinesigenic dyskinesia), full gene sequence

POLG (polymerase [DNA directed], gamma) (eg, Alpers-Huttenlocher syndrome, autosomal dominant progressive external ophthalmoplegia), full gene sequence

POMGNT1 (protein O-linked mannose beta1,2-N acetylglucosaminyltransferase) (eg, muscle-eye-brain disease, Walker-Warburg syndrome), full gene sequence

POMT1 (protein-O-mannosyltransferase 1) (eg, limb-girdle muscular dystrophy [LGMD] type 2K, Walker-Warburg syndrome), full gene sequence

POMT2 (protein-O-mannosyltransferase 2) (eg, limb-girdle muscular dystrophy [LGMD] type 2N, Walker-Warburg syndrome), full gene sequence

▶PPOX (protoporphyrinogen oxidase) (eg, variegate porphyria), full gene sequence◀

PRKAG2 (protein kinase, AMP-activated, gamma 2 non-catalytic subunit) (eg, familial hypertrophic cardiomyopathy with Wolff-Parkinson-White syndrome, lethal congenital glycogen storage disease of heart), full gene sequence

PRKCG (protein kinase C, gamma) (eg, spinocerebellar ataxia), full gene sequence

PSEN2 (presenilin 2 [Alzheimer disease 4]) (eg, Alzheimer disease), full gene sequence

PTPN11 (protein tyrosine phosphatase, non-receptor type 11) (eg, Noonan syndrome, LEOPARD syndrome), full gene sequence

PYGM (phosphorylase, glycogen, muscle) (eg, glycogen storage disease type V, McArdle disease), full gene sequence

RAF1 (v-raf-1 murine leukemia viral oncogene homolog 1) (eg, LEOPARD syndrome), full gene sequence

RET (ret proto-oncogene) (eg, Hirschsprung disease), full gene sequence

RPE65 (retinal pigment epithelium-specific protein 65kDa) (eg, retinitis pigmentosa, Leber congenital amaurosis), full gene sequence

RYR1 (ryanodine receptor 1, skeletal) (eg, malignant hyperthermia), targeted sequence analysis of exons with functionally-confirmed mutations

SCN4A (sodium channel, voltage-gated, type IV, alpha subunit) (eg, hyperkalemic periodic paralysis), full gene sequence

SCNN1A (sodium channel, nonvoltage-gated 1 alpha) (eg, pseudohypoaldosteronism), full gene sequence

SCNN1B (sodium channel, nonvoltage-gated 1, beta) (eg, Liddle syndrome, pseudohypoaldosteronism), full gene sequence

SCNN1G (sodium channel, nonvoltage-gated 1, gamma) (eg, Liddle syndrome, pseudohypoaldosteronism), full gene sequence

SDHA (succinate dehydrogenase complex, subunit A, flavoprotein [Fp]) (eg, Leigh syndrome, mitochondrial complex II deficiency), full gene sequence

SETX (senataxin) (eg, ataxia), full gene sequence

SGCE (sarcoglycan, epsilon) (eg, myoclonic dystonia), full gene sequence

SH3TC2 (SH3 domain and tetratricopeptide repeats 2) (eg, Charcot-Marie-Tooth disease), full gene sequence

SLC9A6 (solute carrier family 9 [sodium/hydrogen exchanger], member 6) (eg, Christianson syndrome), full gene sequence

SLC26A4 (solute carrier family 26, member 4) (eg, Pendred syndrome), full gene sequence

SLC37A4 (solute carrier family 37 [glucose-6-phosphate transporter], member 4) (eg, glycogen storage disease type Ib), full gene sequence

SMAD4 (SMAD family member 4) (eg, hemorrhagic telangiectasia syndrome, juvenile polyposis), full gene sequence

SOS1 (son of sevenless homolog 1) (eg, Noonan syndrome, gingival fibromatosis), full gene sequence

SPAST (spastin) (eg, spastic paraplegia), full gene sequence

SPG7 (spastic paraplegia 7 [pure and complicated autosomal recessive]) (eg, spastic paraplegia), full gene sequence

STXBP1 (syntaxin-binding protein 1) (eg, epileptic encephalopathy), full gene sequence

TAZ (tafazzin) (eg, methylglutaconic aciduria type 2, Barth syndrome), full gene sequence

TCF4 (transcription factor 4) (eg, Pitt-Hopkins syndrome), full gene sequence

TH (tyrosine hydroxylase) (eg, Segawa syndrome), full gene sequence

TMEM43 (transmembrane protein 43) (eg, arrhythmogenic right ventricular cardiomyopathy), full gene sequence

TNNT2 (troponin T, type 2 [cardiac]) (eg, familial hypertrophic cardiomyopathy), full gene sequence

TRPC6 (transient receptor potential cation channel, subfamily C, member 6) (eg, focal segmental glomerulosclerosis), full gene sequence

TSC1 (tuberous sclerosis 1) (eg, tuberous sclerosis), full gene sequence

TSC2 (tuberous sclerosis 2) (eg, tuberous sclerosis), duplication/deletion analysis

UBE3A (ubiquitin protein ligase E3A) (eg, Angelman syndrome), full gene sequence

UMOD (uromodulin) (eg, glomerulocystic kidney disease with hyperuricemia and isosthenuria), full gene sequence

VWF (von Willebrand factor) (von Willebrand disease type 2A), extended targeted sequence analysis (eg, exons 11-16, 24-26, 51, 52)

WAS (Wiskott-Aldrich syndrome [eczema-thrombocytopenia]) (eg, Wiskott-Aldrich syndrome), full gene sequence

Rationale

The Hugo Gene Nomenclature Committee has reassigned the KAL1 gene to the ANOS1 gene. To accommodate this reassignment, the KAL1 gene has been deleted from the CPT Molecular Pathology Gene Table and Tier 2 code 81406 has been revised to reflect that the KAL1 gene has been reassigned to the ANOS1 gene.

Molecular pathology Tier 2 code 81406 has been revised to include full gene sequencing of the HMBS and PPOX genes because no specific CPT code had been available.

Genomic Sequencing Procedures and Other Molecular Multianalyte Assays

▲ **81432**   Hereditary breast cancer-related disorders (eg, hereditary breast cancer, hereditary ovarian cancer, hereditary endometrial cancer); genomic sequence analysis panel, must include sequencing of at least 10 genes, always including *BRCA1, BRCA2, CDH1, MLH1, MSH2, MSH6, PALB2, PTEN, STK11,* and *TP53*

Rationale

Hereditary breast cancer genomic sequence procedure code 81432 has been revised by reducing the minimum number of genes included in the panel from 14 to 10 and by removing some of the genes that were previously required in order to report this code.

When code 81432 was added to the CPT code set in 2016, the evidence demonstrated that all 14 genes that were included in code 81432 were significant to the panel. Recent studies indicate that genes ATM, BRIP1, NBN, and RAD51C are not as significant as the other genes included in the panel. If laboratories remove these genes from their panels due to this lack of significance, it would not be appropriate to report code 81432 because it requires inclusion of these four genes. Therefore, genes ATM, BRIP1, NBN, and RAD51C have been removed from the list of genes that must be included in the panel in order to report code 81432. The minimum number of genes to be included is 10 rather than 14, which means that code 81432 may be reported if these four genes are included in the panel.

Clinical Example (81432)

A 36-year-old female with breast cancer and a family history of cancer is evaluated for mutations in genes known to be involved in hereditary cancer-related disorders. A whole-blood sample is submitted for hereditary cancer-related disorder panel testing, including sequence analysis of at least 10 genes that always include BRCA1, BRCA2, CDH1, MLH1, MSH2, MSH6, PALB2, PTEN, STK11, and TP53.

Description of Procedure (81432)

High-quality DNA is isolated from the patient's blood sample. DNA targets are enriched by hybrid capture for at least 10 genes always including BRCA1, BRCA2, CDH1, MLH1, MSH2, MSH6, PALB2, PTEN, STK11, and TP53. The products undergo massively parallel DNA sequencing of the coding regions and intron/exon boundaries. The pathologist or other qualified health care professional evaluates the reads to identify nucleotide sequence variants. The pathologist or other qualified health care professional composes a report that specifies the patient's mutation status. The report is edited and signed, and the results are communicated to the appropriate caregivers.

#● 81448   Hereditary peripheral neuropathies (eg, Charcot-Marie-Tooth, spastic paraplegia), genomic sequence analysis panel, must include sequencing of at least 5 peripheral neuropathy-related genes (eg, *BSCL2, GJB1, MFN2, MPZ, REEP1, SPAST, SPG11, SPTLC1*)

Rationale

In the Genomic Sequencing Procedures section, code 81448 has been established to report a peripheral neuropathy panel, which includes sequencing of at least five of the following genes: BSCL2, GJB1, MFN2, MPZ, REEP1, SPAST, SPG11, and SPTLC1. Previously, no specific CPT code was available for reporting a peripheral neuropathy panel.

Clinical Example (81448)

A 13-year-old female presents with mobility difficulties. She has impaired walking and frequent falls. Examination reveals distal weakness, sensory loss, and absent tendon reflexes. A blood sample is submitted for peripheral neuropathy genomic sequencing panel testing (eg, BSCL2, MFN2, MPZ, GJB1, and REEP1).

Description of Procedure (81448)

High-quality DNA is isolated from the patient's blood sample. DNA targets are enriched by hybrid capture for at least five peripheral neuropathic-related genes (eg, BSCL2, MFN2, MPZ, GJB1, and REEP1). The products undergo massively parallel DNA sequencing of the coding regions and intron/exon boundaries. The pathologist or other qualified health care professional evaluates the reads to identify nucleotide sequence variants. The pathologist or other qualified health care professional composes a report that specifies the patient's mutation status. The report is edited and signed, and the results are communicated to appropriate caregivers.

▲ 81439   Hereditary cardiomyopathy (eg, hypertrophic cardiomyopathy, dilated cardiomyopathy, arrhythmogenic right ventricular cardiomyopathy), genomic sequence analysis panel, must include sequencing of at least 5 cardiomyopathy-related genes (eg, *DSG2, MYBPC3, MYH7, PKP2, TTN*)

(Do not report 81439 in conjunction with 81413, 81414 when performed on the same date of service)

(For genomic sequencing panel testing for cardiac ion channelopathies, see 81413, 81414)

81448   Code is out of numerical sequence. See 81437-81440

★ = Telemedicine   ✚ = Add-on code   ✗ = FDA approval pending   # = Resequenced code

Pathology and Laboratory 80047-89398, 0001U-0017U

Rationale

In the Genomic Sequencing Procedures section, code 81439 has been revised to report targeted cardiomyopathy genomic sequence analysis. Specifically, the term "inherited" has been replaced with the term "hereditary" and the term "cardiomyopathy-related" has been added to the code descriptor.

Multianalyte Assays with Algorithmic Analyses

● **81520**   Oncology (breast), mRNA gene expression profiling by hybrid capture of 58 genes (50 content and 8 housekeeping), utilizing formalin-fixed paraffin-embedded tissue, algorithm reported as a recurrence risk score

Rationale

Code 81520 has been established to report mRNA analysis of 58 genes using hybrid capture. In addition to the establishment of a new Category I code, new code 81520 has been added to Appendix O. To accommodate the addition of the new codes, code 0008M, which is part of the administrative code for multianalyte assays with algorithmic analyses codes, has been deleted.

Clinical Example (81520)

A 58-year-old postmenopausal female patient presents with HR+, node-negative, early stage breast cancer who had breast-conserving therapy in conjunction with loco-regional treatment consistent with the standard of care.

Description of Procedure (81520)

A pathologist examines a hematoxylin and eosin (H&E) stained slide of a selected paraffin block to identify an area of invasive breast carcinoma suitable for analysis. The pathologist measures the tumor surface area in order to determine the number of required unstained slides and determines whether tumor cellularity meets test criteria (10% or greater). After macrodissection of the corresponding area on the unstained slides, RNA is extracted and purified. Gene expression is analyzed by direct mRNA hybridization with capture and fluorescent bar coded reporter probes followed by high

magnification, diffraction limited imaging to provide a "count" of fluorescent bar codes in each sample. A computational algorithm based on Pearson correlation is applied to compare the normalized expression profile of 50 genes to the prototypical expression profiles of four breast cancer intrinsic subtypes (luminal A, luminal B, HER2-enriched, or Basal-like). The patient test sample is assigned the numerical score that takes into account the patient's intrinsic subtype and tumor size.

● **81521**   Oncology (breast), mRNA, microarray gene expression profiling of 70 content genes and 465 housekeeping genes, utilizing fresh frozen or formalin-fixed paraffin-embedded tissue, algorithm reported as index related to risk of distant metastasis

Rationale

Code 81521 has been established to report analysis to measure the risk of distant metastasis. In addition to the establishment of a new Category I code, new code 81521 has been added to Appendix O.

Clinical Example (81521)

A 55-year-old female with node-negative, stage I invasive breast cancer discusses adjuvant chemotherapy with her oncologist two weeks after surgery. There are no obvious clinical features that drive the chemotherapy decision, and her oncologist orders a 70-gene mRNA expression assay on tumor tissue to determine whether the patient would benefit from chemotherapy.

Description of Procedure (81521)

A pathologist examines an H&E-stained slide of a selected paraffin block to assess tumor cell percentage. A minimum of 30% invasive tumor cells is required to qualify for the analysis. Total RNA is isolated, amplified, and labeled with a fluorescent dye. The amplified labeled cRNA is hybridized on a DNA microarray. A scanner scans the DNA microarray slide and quantifies each probe on the array. Proprietary software extracts the information from the scan. Using the 70 genes printed in 9 fold and 465 normalization genes, the scanner calculates an index related to risk of distant metastasis. The index, risk category, risk of distant metastasis in that category, and the risk of recurrence after chemotherapy and or endocrine therapy in that category are listed on the report form.

Pathology and Laboratory 80047-89398, 0001U-0017U

● **81541** Oncology (prostate), mRNA gene expression profiling by real-time RT-PCR of 46 genes (31 content and 15 housekeeping), utilizing formalin-fixed paraffin-embedded tissue, algorithm reported as a disease-specific mortality risk score

Rationale

Multianalyte assays with algorithmic analyses (MAAA) code 81541 has been added to report prostate cancer mortality-risk measure test. The test provides information regarding the aggressiveness of the prostate tumor. In addition to the establishment of a new Category I code, new code 81541 has also been added to Appendix O.

Clinical Example (81541)

A 72-year-old male presents with a prostate-specific antigen (PSA) of 4.5 ng/mL. His prostate biopsy pathology reveals two of 12 positive cores with a Gleason score of 6 for both cores. His clinical stage is T1c, and no masses were felt on digital rectal examination. Formalin-fixed paraffin-embedded biopsy tissue is submitted for a prostate cancer assay by which the expression of 46 genes is used to determine his ten-year mortality risk.

Description of Procedure (81541)

RNA is isolated from selected tumor tissue. The expression levels of the 31 cell cycle progression (CCP) genes and 15 housekeeping genes are measured using real-time PCR. The levels of expression of the CCP genes are compared to the baseline expression of the 15 housekeeping genes using a proprietary algorithm to produce a numerical score. The score is provided in the report as well as a ten-year prostate cancer–specific mortality risk.

● **81551** Oncology (prostate), promoter methylation profiling by real-time PCR of 3 genes (*GSTP1, APC, RASSF1*), utilizing formalin-fixed paraffin-embedded tissue, algorithm reported as a likelihood of prostate cancer detection on repeat biopsy

Rationale

Code 81551 has been established to report analysis of the methylation status of gene markers for detection of prostate cancer. In addition to the establishment of a new Category I code, a new code (81551) has been added to Appendix O. Previously, this procedure was not reported using a specific code; rather, it was reported as an unlisted molecular pathology procedure using code 81479.

Clinical Example (81551)

A 55-year-old male presents with a previous negative prostate biopsy, persistently elevated prostate-specific antigen, and an abnormal digital rectal examination. The urologist orders a prostate cancer test in order to analyze the promoter methylation status of three genes in biopsy tissue to determine whether the patient may benefit from a repeat biopsy.

Description of Procedure (81551)

Patient samples are derived from formalin-fixed paraffin-embedded prostate core biopsy tissues that represent all areas of the prostate. After a deparaffinization step, DNA is isolated and treated with ammonium bisulfite. GSTP1, APC, and RASSF1 gene promoter regions are amplified using methylation-specific primers and quantified using molecular beacons. Results are analyzed to determine DNA methylation status. A report to indicate methylation status is generated. In case of positive methylation, the report includes an algorithmic assessment of the likelihood of prostate cancer detection on repeat biopsy, along with prostate mapping and probability for low- or high-grade disease.

Chemistry

82030	Adenosine, 5-monophosphate, cyclic (cyclic AMP)
82040	Albumin; serum, plasma or whole blood
82042	Code is out of numerical sequence. See 82044-82085
▲ **82043**	urine (eg, microalbumin), quantitative
▲ **82044**	urine (eg, microalbumin), semiquantitative (eg, reagent strip assay)
82045	ischemia modified
#▲ **82042**	other source, quantitative, each specimen

▶(For total protein, see 84155, 84156, 84157, 84160)◀

★ = Telemedicine   ✚ = Add-on code   ✒ = FDA approval pending   # = Resequenced code

Rationale

Codes 82042, 82043, and 82044 have been editorially revised to clarify the intended use of these codes. These codes are used to differentiate the quantity of albumin being tested, not the size of the albumin molecules. To eliminate confusion, the term "eg" has been added to the descriptor of codes 82043 and 82044. This addition clarifies the intent by using the term "microalbumin" as an example of what is studied as part of this procedure and not as a type of albumin that is small in size. In addition, the phrase "urine or" has been deleted from the descriptor of code 82042 to clarify that this code may be used for any source of albumin other than serum (serum test for albumin is reported with code 82040). A parenthetical note has been included to direct users to the appropriate codes to report total protein testing.

Clinical Example (82042)

A 43-year-old female returns to her physician for a follow-up appointment after having magnetic resonance imaging (MRI) for possible multiple sclerosis. The MRI findings were inconclusive, and the doctor orders a lumbar puncture to obtain cerebrospinal fluid (CSF) for further testing. An albumin test was ordered on the CSF plus a serum albumin test to evaluate the integrity of the blood–brain barrier.

Description of Procedure (82042)

The CSF and serum specimens are submitted to the laboratory. The laboratory performs a quantitative CSF albumin assay using the immunoturbidimetric method and reports the result to the patient's physician along with the serum albumin result. The physician compares the CSF and serum results to evaluate the possibility of a breakdown of the blood–brain barrier.

83498	Hydroxyprogesterone, 17-d
	▶(83499 has been deleted)◀
83500	Hydroxyproline; free
83505	total
84035	Phenylketones, qualitative
84060	Phosphatase, acid; total
	▶(84061 has been deleted)◀
84066	prostatic

Rationale

Chemistry codes 83499 (hydroxyprogesterone, 20-) and 84061 (phosphatase, acid; forensic examination) have been deleted due to low utilization and to ensure that the CPT code set reflects current clinical practice.

Immunology

▲ **86003**	Allergen specific IgE; quantitative or semiquantitative, crude allergen extract, each
	(For total quantitative IgE, use 82785)
▲ **86005**	qualitative, multiallergen screen (eg, disk, sponge, card)
● **86008**	quantitative or semiquantitative, recombinant or purified component, each
	(For total qualitative IgE, use 83518)
	(Alpha-1 antitrypsin, see 82103, 82104)
	(Alpha-1 feto-protein, see 82105, 82106)
	(Anti-AChR [acetylcholine receptor] antibody titer, see 86255, 86256)
	(Anticardiolipin antibody, use 86147)
	(Anti-DNA, use 86225)
	(Anti-deoxyribonuclease titer, use 86215)

Rationale

Code 86008 has been established to report quantitative or semiquantitative, recombinant or purified component testing of allergen specific IgE. To accommodate the addition, codes 86003 and 86005 have been revised to accurately define current specimen collection and materials.

Clinical Example (86008)

A child with allergy history experienced a possible reaction to peanuts. Crude-extract allergen tests (ie, skin prick testing and in vitro specific IgE [sIgE] testing) for peanut were positive but equivocal; other food allergens were negative. Based on further history, component resolved diagnostics (CRD) for peanut was ordered to confirm whether a genuine peanut sensitization existed, to assess the clinical risk for a subsequent reaction, and to determine if an oral food challenge is warranted.

Description of Procedure (86008)

A quantitative, high-sensitivity fluorescent enzyme immunoassay was used to measure specific immunoglobulin E for recombinant peanut components. Ara h 8 was detected at 44.7 kU/L and Bet v 1 was detected at 59.3 kU/L. Ara h 1, 2, 3, 6, and 9 were negative. Based on the history and CRD results, a peanut challenge was performed, and there was no reaction.

86171	Complement fixation tests, each antigen
	(Coombs test, see 86880-86886)
	▶(86185 has been deleted)◀
86200	Cyclic citrullinated peptide (CCP), antibody
86235	Extractable nuclear antigen, antibody to, any method (eg, nRNP, SS-A, SS-B, Sm, RNP, Sc170, J01), each antibody
	▶(86243 has been deleted)◀
86367	Stem cells (ie, CD34), total count
	(For flow cytometric immunophenotyping for the assessment of potential hematolymphoid neoplasia, see 88184-88189)
86376	Microsomal antibodies (eg, thyroid or liver-kidney), each
	▶(86378 has been deleted)◀
86382	Neutralization test, viral
86710	Antibody; influenza virus
86711	JC (John Cunningham) virus
86713	Legionella
86717	Leishmania
86720	Leptospira
86723	Listeria monocytogenes
86727	lymphocytic choriomeningitis
	▶(86729 has been deleted)◀

Rationale

Immunology codes 86185 (counterimmunoelectrophoresis, each antigen), 86243 (Fc receptor), 86378 (migration inhibitory factor test [MIF]), and 86729 (antibody; lymphogranuloma venereum), have been deleted due to low utilization and to ensure that the CPT code set reflects current clinical practice.

86732	mucormycosis
86793	Yersinia
● 86794	Zika virus, IgM

Rationale

Two new codes (86794, 87662) have been added to the Immunology and Microbiology subsections of the Pathology section to report Zika virus detection.

Code 86794 has been established to report antibody testing for immunoglobulin M (IgM) for Zika virus. This test is performed to identify the products of an immune response in individuals who have been exposed to the virus in the past (ie, exposure of two weeks or more). The test identifies the IgM antibody in the sample to determine if exposure to the virus (and infection) has occurred.

Code 87662 has been established to report Zika virus detection performed via detection of the infectious agent itself (ie, exposure of less than two weeks). In this amplified probe technique, a probe is used to identify the virus in the sample tested as opposed to antibodies to the virus. The test may be performed when an antibody response is not detectable in the patient, but there is still a risk of exposure to the virus. The amplified probe reacts with the virus to precipitate a positive response and allows determination of the presence (or absence) of the virus in the sample.

Clinical Example (86794)

A 30-year-old pregnant female in her second trimester reports having traveled to Brazil three weeks prior to her visit where she had questionable exposure to the Zika virus via mosquito bites. Her gynecologist obtains a serum sample and orders an immunoglobulin M antibody capture enzyme-linked immunosorbent assay (MAC-ELISA). The physician uses the patient's antibody status in conjunction with other clinical data to determine appropriate clinical management.

Description of Procedure (86794)

The sample is collected in a serum-separator tube. The tube is centrifuged, and the serum is decanted prior to shipment to avoid hemolysis. The specimen is diluted and the MAC-ELISA is performed. The test result (a presumptive positive or negative) is sent to the patient's physician or other qualified health care professional.

Tissue Typing

86812	HLA typing; A, B, or C (eg, A10, B7, B27), single antigen
86813	A, B, or C, multiple antigens
86816	DR/DQ, single antigen
86817	DR/DQ, multiple antigens

★ = Telemedicine   ✚ = Add-on code   ✔ = FDA approval pending   # = Resequenced code

86821   lymphocyte culture, mixed (MLC)

▶(86822 has been deleted)◀

Rationale

Immunology code 86822 (HLA typing; lymphocyte culture, primed [PLC]) has been deleted due to low utilization and to ensure that the CPT code set reflects current clinical practice.

Transfusion Medicine

86965   Pooling of platelets or other blood products

▶(For harvesting, preparation, and injection[s] of platelet rich plasma, use 0232T)◀

▶For harvesting, preparation, and injection[s] of autologous white blood cell/autologous protein solution, use 0481T◀

Rationale

In support of establishment of Category III code 0481T, a parenthetical note has been added and another has been updated after code 86965.

Refer to the codebook and the Rationale for code 0481T for a full discussion of the changes.

Microbiology

87255   including identification by non-immunologic method, other than by cytopathic effect (eg, virus specific enzymatic activity)

▶These codes are intended for primary source only. For similar studies on culture material, refer to codes 87140-87158. Infectious agents by antigen detection, immunofluorescence microscopy, or nucleic acid probe techniques should be reported as precisely as possible. The molecular pathology procedures codes (81161, 81200-81408) are not to be used in combination with or instead of the procedures represented by 87471-87801. The most specific code possible should be reported. If there is no specific agent code, the general methodology code (eg, 87299, 87449, 87450, 87797, 87798, 87799, 87899) should be used. For identification of antibodies to many of the listed infectious agents, see 86602-86804. When separate results are reported for different species or strain of organisms, each result should be

coded separately. Use modifier 59 when separate results are reported for different species or strains that are described by the same code.◀

87260   Infectious agent antigen detection by immunofluorescent technique; adenovirus

87276   influenza A virus

▶(87277 has been deleted)◀

87278   Legionella pneumophila

87449   Infectious agent antigen detection by immunoassay technique, (eg, enzyme immunoassay [EIA], enzyme-linked immunosorbent assay [ELISA], immunochemiluminometric assay [IMCA]), qualitative or semiquantitative; multiple-step method, not otherwise specified, each organism

87450   single step method, not otherwise specified, each organism

87451   multiple step method, polyvalent for multiple organisms, each polyvalent antiserum

▶(87470 has been deleted)◀

87471   Infectious agent detection by nucleic acid (DNA or RNA); Bartonella henselae and Bartonella quintana, amplified probe technique

87476   Borrelia burgdorferi, amplified probe technique

▶(87477 has been deleted)◀

87511   Gardnerella vaginalis, amplified probe technique

87512   Gardnerella vaginalis, quantification

▶(87515 has been deleted)◀

Rationale

Microbiology codes 87277 (infectious agent antigen detection by immunofluorescent technique; Legionella micdadei); 87470 (infectious agent detection by nucleic acid [DNA or RNA]; Bartonella henselae and Bartonella quintana, direct probe technique); 87477 (infectious agent detection by nucleic acid [DNA or RNA]; Borrelia burgdorferi, quantification); and 87515 (infectious agent detection by nucleic acid [DNA or RNA]; hepatitis B virus, direct probe technique) have been deleted due to low utilization and to ensure that the CPT code set reflects current clinical practice.

87539   HIV-2, quantification, includes reverse transcription when performed

87625   Human Papillomavirus (HPV), types 16 and 18 only, includes type 45, if performed

▶(For Human Papillomavirus [HPV] detection of five or greater separately reported high-risk HPV types [ie, genotyping], use 0500T)◀

Rationale

In support of the establishment of code 0500T, cross-reference parenthetical notes have been added after code 87625 directing users to the appropriate codes to report for human papillomavirus testing.

Refer to the codebook and the Rationale for code 0500T for a full discussion of these changes.

| 87540 | Legionella pneumophila, direct probe technique |
| ● 87634 | respiratory syncytial virus, amplified probe technique |

▶(For assays that include respiratory syncytial virus with additional respiratory viruses, see 87631, 87632, 87633)◀

Rationale

A new code (87634) has been established to report nucleic acid detection of respiratory syncytial virus (RSV).

Code 87634 is used to report RSV antigen detection by nucleic acid (DNA or RNA), which also allows reporting of available RSV nucleic acid–based assays. Codes 87631, 87632, and 87633 are available for reporting nucleic acid testing for RSV, when performed as part of a panel of respiratory viruses. These codes should not be used to report RSV testing by nucleic acid technique when RSV is the only respiratory pathogen being tested for.

An instructional parenthetical note has been added after code 87634 to instruct users to separately report additional viruses, if the assays include respiratory syncytial virus.

Clinical Example (87634)

An 18-month-old child presents in the emergency room (ER) with fever, persistent cough, and difficulty breathing, evidenced by wheezing and quick, shallow breathing (50-60 breaths per minute). The physician makes a diagnosis of bronchiolitis and orders a nucleic acid–based RSV test to verify that the infection is viral, not bacterial. A nasopharyngeal swab is collected and immediately tested using a nucleic acid–based test system for RSV types A and B that reports a single result. The system reports a positive result, and the child's parents are instructed to monitor the child closely and to return to the ER if the child's symptoms worsen.

Description of Procedure (87634)

A freshly collected nasopharyngeal swab specimen is tested directly or preserved in transport media. When preserved in transport media, the swab is rotated for 10–20 seconds in 0.5–3.0 mL of transport media within one hour of collection. The sample is put into a reaction vial with reagents for the amplification reaction and mixed vigorously. Amplification occurs in the reaction vials, and the targets are detected using fluorescently labeled molecular beacons. In addition to targets that identify RSV, an internal control is used to control for functionality of the amplification/detection process and reagents. Results are reported as RSV positive, RSV negative, or invalid.

| 87661 | Trichomonas vaginalis, amplified probe technique |
| ● 87662 | Zika virus, amplified probe technique |

Rationale

Two new codes (86794, 87662) have been added to the Immunology and Microbiology subsections of the Pathology section to report Zika virus detection.

Code 87662 has been established to report Zika virus detection performed via detection of the infectious agent itself (ie, exposure of less than two weeks).

Refer to the codebook and the Rationale for code 86794 for a full discussion of these changes.

Clinical Example (87662)

A 30-year-old pregnant female traveled to Brazil six days prior to reporting symptoms of fever, rash, and joint pain. She is in her first trimester. While in Brazil, she had exposure to mosquitoes. Based on the Centers for Disease Control and Prevention guidelines, her primary care physician obtains serum and urine samples and orders a nucleic acid amplification test for the detection of RNA from the Zika virus.

Description of Procedure (87662)

The specimens are transferred into specimen-transport tubes. Target capture and selection reagents are prepared. Following reagent preparation, the laboratory confirms that specimens meet the appropriate criteria for testing and load samples onto a rack. The system is prepared according to the manufacturer's instructions. The amplification, detection, and interpretation of test signals are performed automatically by the software. The test result (positive or negative) is sent to the patient's physician or other qualified health care professional.

★ = Telemedicine   ✚ = Add-on code   ✗ = FDA approval pending   # = Resequenced code

87800 Infectious agent detection by nucleic acid (DNA or RNA), multiple organisms; direct probe(s) technique

87801 amplified probe(s) technique

(For detection of multiple infectious agents not otherwise specified which report a single result, see 87800, 87801)

(Do not use 87801 for nucleic acid assays that detect multiple respiratory viruses in a multiplex reaction [ie, single procedure with multiple results], see 87631-87633)

►(For each specific organism nucleic acid detection from a primary source, see 87471-87660. For detection of specific infectious agents not otherwise specified, see 87797, 87798, or 87799 1 time for each agent)◄

Rationale

In accordance with the deletion of code 87470, the microbiology introductory guidelines and the instructional parenthetical note that follows code 87801 have been revised by removing the reference to code 87470.

Refer to the codebook and the Rationale for code 87470 for a full discussion of these changes.

 # 87910 Infectious agent genotype analysis by nucleic acid (DNA or RNA); cytomegalovirus

►(For infectious agent drug susceptibility phenotype prediction for HIV-1, use 87900)◄

►(For Human Papillomavirus [HPV] for high-risk types [ie, genotyping], of five or greater separately reported HPV types, use 0500T)◄

Rationale

In support of the establishment of code 0500T, cross-reference parenthetical notes have been added after code 87910 directing users to the appropriate codes to report for human papillomavirus testing.

Refer to the codebook and the Rationale for code 0500T for a full discussion of these changes.

Cytopathology

88130 Sex chromatin identification; Barr bodies

88140 peripheral blood smear, polymorphonuclear drumsticks

(For Guard stain, use 88313)

►Codes 88141-88155, 88164-88167, 88174-88175 are used to report cervical or vaginal screening by various methods and to report physician interpretation services. Use codes 88150, 88152, 88153 to report conventional Pap smears that are examined using non-Bethesda reporting. Use codes 88164-88167 to report conventional Pap smears that are examined using the Bethesda System of reporting. Use codes 88142-88143 to report liquid-based specimens processed as thin-layer preparations that are examined using any system of reporting (Bethesda or non-Bethesda). Use codes 88174-88175 to report automated screening of liquid-based specimens that are examined using any system of reporting (Bethesda or non-Bethesda).Within each of these three code families choose the one code that describes the screening method(s) used. Codes 88141 and 88155 should be reported in addition to the screening code chosen when the additional services are provided. Manual rescreening requires a complete visual reassessment of the entire slide initially screened by either an automated or manual process. Manual review represents an assessment of selected cells or regions of a slide identified by initial automated review.◄

88141 Cytopathology, cervical or vaginal (any reporting system), requiring interpretation by physician

►(Use 88141 in conjunction with 88142, 88143, 88147, 88148, 88150, 88152, 88153, 88164-88167, 88174-88175)◄

88150 Cytopathology, slides, cervical or vaginal; manual screening under physician supervision

88152 with manual screening and computer-assisted rescreening under physician supervision

88153 with manual screening and rescreening under physician supervision

►(88154 has been deleted)◄

+ 88155 Cytopathology, slides, cervical or vaginal, definitive hormonal evaluation (eg, maturation index, karyopyknotic index, estrogenic index) (List separately in addition to code[s] for other technical and interpretation services)

►(Use 88155 in conjunction with 88142, 88143, 88147, 88148, 88150, 88152, 88153, 88164-88167, 88174-88175)◄

88160 Cytopathology, smears, any other source; screening and interpretation

Rationale

Code 88154 (cytopathology, slides, cervical or vaginal; with manual screening and computer-assisted rescreening using cell selection and review under physician supervision) has been deleted due to low utilization and to ensure that the CPT code set reflects current clinical practice. The guidelines regarding the cervical or vaginal cytopathology codes and the inclusionary parenthetical note that follows code 88141 have been revised by removing the reference to code 88154.

In Vivo (eg, Transcutaneous) Laboratory Procedures

▶(For transcutaneous oxyhemoglobin measurement in a lower extremity wound by near infrared spectroscopy, use 0493T)◀

Rationale

In support of the establishment of code 0493T, a new parenthetical note has been added after the In Vivo (eg, Transcutaneous) Laboratory Procedures heading.

Refer to the codebook and the Rationale for code 0493T for a full discussion of the changes.

Reproductive Medicine Procedures

89352	Thawing of cryopreserved; embryo(s)
89353	sperm/semen, each aliquot
89354	reproductive tissue, testicular/ovarian
89356	oocytes, each aliquot
89398	Unlisted reproductive medicine laboratory procedure

▶Proprietary Laboratory Analyses◀

▶Proprietary laboratory analyses (PLA) codes describe proprietary clinical laboratory analyses and can be provided either by a single ("sole-source") laboratory or licensed or marketed to multiple providing laboratories (eg, cleared or approved by the Food and Drug Administration [FDA]).

These codes include advanced diagnostic laboratory tests (ADLTs) and clinical diagnostic laboratory tests (CDLTs) as defined under the Protecting Access to Medicare Act (PAMA) of 2014.◀

- ● **0001U** Red blood cell antigen typing, DNA, human erythrocyte antigen gene analysis of 35 antigens from 11 blood groups, utilizing whole blood, common RBC alleles reported

- ● **0002U** Oncology (colorectal), quantitative assessment of three urine metabolites (ascorbic acid, succinic acid and carnitine) by liquid chromatography with tandem mass spectrometry (LC-MS/MS) using multiple reaction monitoring acquisition, algorithm reported as likelihood of adenomatous polyps

- ● **0003U** Oncology (ovarian) biochemical assays of five proteins (apolipoprotein A-1, CA 125 II, follicle stimulating hormone, human epididymis protein 4, transferrin), utilizing serum, algorithm reported as a likelihood score

- ● **0004U** Infectious disease (bacterial), DNA, 27 resistance genes, PCR amplification and probe hybridization in microarray format (molecular detection and identification of AmpC, carbapenemase and ESBL coding genes), bacterial culture colonies, report of genes detected or not detected, per isolate

- ● **0005U** Oncology (prostate) gene expression profile by real-time RT-PCR of 3 genes (ERG, PCA3, and SPDEF), urine, algorithm reported as risk score

- ● **0006U** Prescription drug monitoring, 120 or more drugs and substances, definitive tandem mass spectrometry with chromatography, urine, qualitative report of presence (including quantitative levels, when detected) or absence of each drug or substance with description and severity of potential interactions, with identified substances, per date of service

- ● **0007U** Drug test(s), presumptive, with definitive confirmation of positive results, any number of drug classes, urine, includes specimen verification including DNA authentication in comparison to buccal DNA, per date of service

★ = Telemedicine ✚ = Add-on code ✔ = FDA approval pending # = Resequenced code

- **0008U** Helicobacter pylori detection and antibiotic resistance, DNA, 16S and 23S rRNA, gyrA, pbp1, rdxA and rpoB, next generation sequencing, formalin-fixed paraffin-embedded or fresh tissue, predictive, reported as positive or negative for resistance to clarithromycin, fluoroquinolones, metronidazole, amoxicillin, tetracycline and rifabutin

- **0009U** Oncology (breast cancer), ERBB2 (HER2) copy number by FISH, tumor cells from formalin-fixed paraffin-embedded tissue isolated using image-based dielectrophoresis (DEP) sorting, reported as ERBB2 gene amplified or non-amplified

- **0010U** Infectious disease (bacterial), strain typing by whole genome sequencing, phylogenetic-based report of strain relatedness, per submitted isolate

- **0011U** Prescription drug monitoring, evaluation of drugs present by LC-MS/MS, using oral fluid, reported as a comparison to an estimated steady-state range, per date of service including all drug compounds and metabolites

- **0012U** Germline disorders, gene rearrangement detection by whole genome next-generation sequencing, DNA, whole blood, report of specific gene rearrangement(s)

- **0013U** Oncology (solid organ neoplasia), gene rearrangement detection by whole genome next-generation sequencing, DNA, fresh or frozen tissue or cells, report of specific gene rearrangement(s)

- **0014U** Hematology (hematolymphoid neoplasia), gene rearrangement detection by whole genome next-generation sequencing, DNA, whole blood or bone marrow, report of specific gene rearrangement(s)

- **0015U** Drug metabolism (adverse drug reactions), DNA, 22 drug metabolism and transporter genes, real-time PCR, blood or buccal swab, genotype and metabolizer status for therapeutic decision support

- **0016U** Oncology (hematolymphoid neoplasia), RNA, BCR/ABL1 major and minor breakpoint fusion transcripts, quantitative PCR amplification, blood or bone marrow, report of fusion not detected or detected with quantitation

- **0017U** Oncology (hematolymphoid neoplasia), JAK2 mutation, DNA, PCR amplification of exons 12-14 and sequence analysis, blood or bone marrow, report of JAK2 mutation not detected or detected

Rationale

Seventeen proprietary laboratory analyses (PLA) codes have been established.

PLA codes describe proprietary clinical laboratory analyses and can be either provided by a single ("sole-source") laboratory or licensed or marketed to multiple providing laboratories (eg, cleared or approved by the Food and Drug Administration (FDA).

This subsection includes advanced diagnostic laboratory tests (ADLTs) and clinical diagnostic laboratory tests (CDLTs), as defined under the Protecting Access to Medicare Act (PAMA) of 2014. These analyses may include a range of medical laboratory tests including, but not limited to, multianalyte assays with algorithmic analyses (MAAA) and genomic sequencing procedures (GSP). The descriptor nomenclature follows, where possible, existing code conventions (eg, MAAA, GSP).

These codes are not required to fulfill the Category I criteria. The standards for inclusion in this section are:

- The test must be commercially available in the United States for use on human specimens; and

- The clinical laboratory or manufacturer that offers the test must request the code.

For similar laboratory analyses that fulfill Category I criteria, see codes listed in the numeric 80000 series.

When a PLA code is available to report a given proprietary laboratory service, that PLA code takes precedence. The service should not be reported with any other CPT code(s) and other CPT code(s) should not be used to report services that may be reported with that specific PLA code. These codes encompass all analytical services required for the analysis (eg, cell lysis, nucleic acid stabilization, extraction, digestion, amplification, hybridization and detection). For molecular analyses, additional procedures that are required prior to cell lysis (eg, microdissection [codes 88380 and 88381]) may be reported separately.

Codes in this subsection are released on a quarterly basis to expedite dissemination for reporting. PLA codes will be published electronically on the AMA CPT website (www.ama-assn.org/practice-management/cpt-pla-codes), distributed via CPT data files on a quarterly basis, and, at a minimum, made available in print annually in the CPT codebook. Go to www.ama-assn.org/sites/default/files/media-browser/public/physicians/cpt/cpt-pla-codes-long.pdf for the most current listing.

In order to report a PLA code, the analysis performed must fulfill the code descriptor and must be the test represented by the proprietary name listed in the document published to the AMA CPT website.

Notes

Medicine

In the Vaccines, Toxoids subsection, codes 90651, 90620, and 90621 have been revised to include dosage amounts and/or the Advisory Committee on Immunization Practices (ACIP) abbreviations. In addition, four new codes have been added: 90587 for reporting a quadrivalent dengue vaccine; 90750 for Zoster vaccine; 90756 and 90682 for quadrivalent influenza virus vaccines.

The Dialysis subsection has new parenthetical notes for codes 36511-36514 with instructions to report therapeutic apheresis for blood cells and code 36516 for therapeutic apheresis extracorporeal adsorption procedures.

In the Ophthalmology subsection, new code 0469T has been added to numerous exclusionary parenthetical notes to instruct users on how to report general ophthalmological services.

In the Cardiovascular subsection, code 93462 includes the addition of new instructional parenthetical notes for catheterization and percutaneous transcatheter closure of paravalvular leak. A new subsection, Home and Outpatient International Normalized Ratio (INR) Monitoring Services, which includes guidelines, instructional parenthetical notes, and two new codes (93792 and 93793), has been added to identify home INR monitoring.

In the Pulmonary subsection, numerous changes have been made, including the addition of new and revised parenthetical notes, deletion of code 94620, and revision to code 94621 to include measurements of minute ventilation and electrocardiographic recordings. In addition, two new codes have been added: 94617 to identify exercise testing for bronchospasm and 94618 to identify pulmonary stress testing.

New guidelines have been added to the Endocrinology subsection. Two codes have been revised: 95250 includes ambulatory continuous glucose monitoring with office-provided equipment and 95251 includes the word "analysis." New code 95249 has been added to include patient-provided equipment.

In the Photodynamic Therapy subsection, guidelines have been added and parenthetical notes have been revised. Code 96567 has been revised to include the terms "with application and illumination" or activation of photosensitive drug(s) for the destruction of premalignant lesions of the skin and adjacent mucosa. In addition, two new codes (96573 and 96574) and new parenthetical notes have been added.

The previously titled subsection of "Orthotic Management and Prosthetic Management" has been revised to "Orthotic Management and Training and Prosthetic Training." In addition, one new code (97763) has been added, one code (97762) has been deleted, and two codes (97760 and 97761) have been revised to include initial encounter.

Summary of Additions, Deletions, and Revisions

The summary of changes shows the actual changes that have been made to the code descriptors.

New codes appear with a bullet (•) and are indicated as "Code added." Revised codes are preceded with a triangle (▲). Within revised codes, the deleted language appears with a ~~strikethrough~~, while new text appears <u>underlined</u>.

The ✗ symbol is used to identify codes for vaccines that are pending FDA approval. The # symbol is used to identify codes that have been resequenced. CPT add-on codes are annotated by the ✚ symbol. The ⊘ symbol is used to identify codes that are exempt from the use of modifier 51. The ★ symbol is used to identify codes that may be used for reporting telemedicine services.

Code	Description
✔●90587	Code added
▲90651	Human Papillomavirus vaccine types 6, 11, 16, 18, 31, 33, 45, 52, 58, nonavalent (9vHPV), <u>2 or </u>3 dose schedule, for intramuscular use
#●90756	Code added
●90682	Code added
#▲90620	Meningococcal recombinant protein and outer membrane vesicle vaccine, serogroup B ~~(MenB)~~<u>(MenB-4C)</u>, 2 dose schedule, for intramuscular use
#▲90621	Meningococcal recombinant lipoprotein vaccine, serogroup B ~~(MenB)~~<u>(MenB-FHbp)</u>, <u>2 or </u>3 dose schedule, for intramuscular use
#✔●90750	Code added
●93792	Code added
●93793	Code added
93982	~~Noninvasive physiologic study of implanted wireless pressure sensor in aneurysmal sac following endovascular repair, complete study including recording, analysis of pressure and waveform tracings, interpretation and report~~
●94617	Code added
●94618	Code added
94620	~~Pulmonary stress testing; simple (eg, 6-minute walk test, prolonged exercise test for bronchospasm with pre- and post-spirometry and oximetry)~~
▲94621	~~Pulmonary stress~~<u>Cardiopulmonary exercise </u>testing~~;~~<u>, including measurements of minute ventilation, CO$_2$ production, O$_2$ uptake, and electrocardiographic recordings</u> ~~complex (including measurements of CO$_2$ production, O$_2$ uptake, and electrocardiographic recordings)~~
▲95250	Ambulatory continuous glucose monitoring of interstitial tissue fluid via a subcutaneous sensor for a minimum of 72 hours; <u>physician or other qualified health care professional (office) provided equipment,</u> sensor placement, hook-up, calibration of monitor, patient training, removal of sensor, and printout of recording
#●95249	Code added
▲95251	<u>analysis,</u> interpretation and report
▲95930	Visual evoked potential (VEP) <u>checkerboard or flash </u>testing<u>,</u> central nervous system <u>except glaucoma,</u> ~~checkerboard or flash~~ with interpretation and report
▲96567	Photodynamic therapy by external application of light to destroy premalignant ~~and/or malignant~~ lesions of the skin and adjacent mucosa <u>with application and</u> ~~(eg, lip) by~~ <u>illumination/</u>activation of photosensitive drug(s), ~~each phototherapy exposure session~~ <u>per day</u>
●96573	Code added
●96574	Code added
●97127	Code added
97532	~~Development of cognitive skills to improve attention, memory, problem solving (includes compensatory training), direct (one-on-one) patient contact, each 15 minutes~~

★ = Telemedicine   ✚ = Add-on code   ✔ = FDA approval pending   # = Resequenced code

Code	Description
▲97760	Orthotic(s) management and training (including assessment and fitting when not otherwise reported), upper extremity~~(s)~~(ies), lower extremity~~(s)~~(ies) and/or trunk<u>, initial orthotic(s) encounter</u>, each 15 minutes
▲97761	Prosthetic<u>(s)</u> training, upper and/or lower extremity<u>(ies), initial prosthetic</u>(s) <u>encounter</u>, each 15 minutes
97762	~~Checkout for orthotic/prosthetic use, established patient, each 15 minutes~~
●97763	Code added

Medicine

Vaccines, Toxoids

✔● **90587** Dengue vaccine, quadrivalent, live, 3 dose schedule, for subcutaneous use

Rationale

New vaccine product code 90587 has been established in the Vaccines, Toxoids subsection to report a live quadrivalent dengue vaccine. Code 90587 describes 3-dose schedule dengue vaccine. Administration of the dengue vaccine is reported separately using codes 90460-90472 (immunization administration for vaccines/toxoids). Code 90587 carries the US Food and Drug Administration (FDA) approval pending symbol (✔); therefore, interim updates on the FDA status of this code will be reflected on the AMA CPT website at www.ama-assn.org/go/cpt-vaccine under CPT Category I Vaccine Codes on a semi-annual basis (July 1 and January 1). The Centers for Disease Control and Prevention Advisory Committee on Immunization Practices (ACIP) has not assigned a US vaccine abbreviation for this vaccine. Visit the AMA CPT website for updates on the US vaccine abbreviation status for this vaccine.

Clinical Example (90587)

A child living in a dengue endemic area presents with his mother seeking immunization against dengue virus to decrease the risk of contracting dengue fever. The patient is offered and the mother accepts for the child an initial or a subsequent dose of a three-dose regimen, intramuscular injection of dengue vaccine, which is consistent with evidence-supported guidelines for this purpose.

Description of Procedure (90587)

A dose of the dengue vaccine is selected by an appropriate health care provider for intramuscular injection. The administration of the vaccine is reported separately from the vaccine.

▲ **90651** Human Papillomavirus vaccine types 6, 11, 16, 18, 31, 33, 45, 52, 58, nonavalent (9vHPV), 2 or 3 dose schedule, for intramuscular use

Rationale

Code 90651 (vaccine product code for the human papillomavirus types 6, 11, 16, 18, 31, 33, 45, 52, 58 vaccine) has been revised by the addition of "2 or" in the code descriptor, which indicates the new alternative dosing regimen for this vaccine. The previous code descriptor did not describe a two-dose schedule; therefore, to minimize confusion and allow for accurate reporting, code 90651 has been revised to reflect the new alternative dosing regimen.

Clinical Example (90651)

A young female presents with her mother seeking immunization against human papillomavirus (HPV) to decrease the likelihood of contracting HPV-related disease. The patient is offered and the mother accepts for her an initial or a subsequent dose of either a two- or three-dose regimen, intramuscular injection of HPV vaccine (9vHPV), which is consistent with evidence-supported guidelines for this purpose.

Description of Procedure (90651)

A dose of 9vHPV is selected by an appropriate health care provider for intramuscular injection. The administration of the vaccine is reported separately from the vaccine.

#● **90756** Influenza virus vaccine, quadrivalent (ccIIV4), derived from cell cultures, subunit, antibiotic free, 0.5 mL dosage, for intramuscular use

Rationale

New vaccine product code 90756 has been established in the Vaccines, Toxoids subsection to report the intramuscular administration of an influenza vaccine.

This code differs from other influenza virus vaccine products because this code is intended to be used to identify quadrivalent (ccIIV4), a vaccine derived from cell cultures that contains preservative and is antibiotic-free. This is different from other influenza vaccine products. As a result, a separate code has been established to identify the use of the new product for vaccination against influenza virus exposure. This flu virus vaccine is intended for intramuscular use. In addition, ACIP's US vaccine abbreviation (ccIIV4) is included in this descriptor.

Clinical Example (90756)

A 33-year-old male seeks immunization against influenza to decrease the risk of contracting seasonal influenza, which is consistent with evidence-supported guidelines. He is offered and accepts an intramuscular injection of influenza vaccine for this purpose.

Description of Procedure (90756)

Influenza vaccine is selected by the appropriate health care provider for intramuscular injection. The administration of the vaccine is reported separately from the vaccine.

● **90682** Influenza virus vaccine, quadrivalent (RIV4), derived from recombinant DNA, hemagglutinin (HA) protein only, preservative and antibiotic free, for intramuscular use

Rationale

Product code 90682 has been established in the Vaccines, Toxoids subsection to report the intramuscular administration of an influenza vaccine.

This code differs from other influenza virus vaccine products because this code is intended for reporting quadrivalent (RIV4) hemagglutinin (HA) protein–only influenza vaccine product that is preservative- and antibiotic-free and derived from recombinant DNA, which is different from other influenza vaccine products. This flu virus vaccine is intended for intramuscular use. In addition, ACIP's US vaccine abbreviation (RIV4) is included in this descriptor.

Clinical Example (90682)

A 33-year-old male seeks immunization against influenza to decrease the risk of contracting seasonal influenza, which is consistent with evidence-supported guidelines. He is offered and accepts an intramuscular injection of influenza vaccine for this purpose.

Description of Procedure (90682)

Influenza vaccine is selected by the appropriate health care provider for intramuscular injection. The administration of the vaccine is reported separately from the vaccine.

\#▲ **90620** Meningococcal recombinant protein and outer membrane vesicle vaccine, serogroup B (MenB-4C), 2 dose schedule, for intramuscular use

Rationale

The maintenance of the CPT code set to incorporate ACIP's full abbreviation in the code descriptor has been continued. Code 90620 has been revised to include the full ACIP abbreviation, MenB-4C.

The AMA's Vaccine Coding Caucus (VCC) recommended that the ACIP US vaccine abbreviations be included in the vaccine code descriptions to adequately describe the vaccine product and to capture standardized vaccine.

\#▲ **90621** Meningococcal recombinant lipoprotein vaccine, serogroup B (MenB-FHbp), 2 or 3 dose schedule, for intramuscular use

Rationale

The vaccine product code for meningococcal recombinant protein and outer membrane vesicle vaccine (90621) has been revised by adding "2 or" before the 3-dose schedule in the code descriptor to include the FDA approved two-dose schedule for this vaccine. In addition, the code descriptor has been revised to include the full abbreviation, MenB-FHbp.

In 2016, the FDA added a 2-dose schedule to the package insert for the meningococcal group B vaccine. The previous code descriptor made no mention of a 2-dose schedule. To minimize confusion and allow for accurate reporting, code 90621 has been revised to reflect the approved dosing regimen when 2 or 3 doses are administered.

Clinical Example (90621)

An 18-year-old male seeks immunization to decrease the risk of meningococcal meningitis caused by serogroup B. The patient is offered and accepts an initial or a subsequent dose of either a two- or three-dose regimen, intramuscular injection of meningococcal serogroup B vaccine (MenB-FHbp), which is consistent with evidence-supported guidelines for this purpose.

Description of Procedure (90621)

A dose of MenB-FHbp is selected by an appropriate health care provider for intramuscular injection. The administration of the vaccine is reported separately from the vaccine.

#✎● 90750	Zoster (shingles) vaccine (HZV), recombinant, subunit, adjuvanted, for intramuscular use
90750	Code is out of numerical sequence. See 90717-90739
90756	Code is out of numerical sequence. See 90658-90664

Rationale

Product code 90750 has been established in the Vaccines, Toxoids subsection to report the intramuscular administration of a shingles vaccine.

This code differs from the shingles vaccination product reported with code 90736 because this code is intended for reporting nonlive, subunit adjuvanted, recombinant vaccine. The vaccine reported with code 90736 is a live vaccine that is injected subcutaneously. As a result, a separate code has been established to report the use of the new product for vaccination against Zoster virus exposure. In addition, ACIP's US vaccine abbreviation (HZV) is included in this descriptor.

Clinical Example (90750)

A 63-year-old male seeks immunization against herpes zoster to decrease the risk of shingles, which is consistent with evidence-supported guidelines. He is offered and accepts an intramuscular injection of influenza vaccine for this purpose.

Description of Procedure (90750)

Herpes zoster vaccine is selected by the appropriate health care provider for intramuscular injection. The administration of the vaccine is reported separately from the vaccine.

Dialysis

▶(For therapeutic apheresis for white blood cells, red blood cells, platelets and plasma pheresis, see 36511, 36512, 36513, 36514)◀

▶(For therapeutic apheresis extracorporeal adsorption procedures, use 36516)◀

(90918, 90922 have been deleted. To report ESRD-related services for patients younger than 2 years of age, see 90951-90953, 90963, 90967)

Rationale

In accordance with the deletion of code 36515 and the revision of code 36516, two parenthetical notes have been added following the Dialysis heading.

Refer to the codebook and the Rationale for code 36516 for a full discussion of these changes.

End-Stage Renal Disease Services

Codes 90951-90962 are reported **once** per month to distinguish age-specific services related to the patient's end-stage renal disease (ESRD) performed in an outpatient setting with three levels of service based on the number of face-to-face visits. ESRD-related services by a physician or other qualified health care professional include establishment of a dialyzing cycle, outpatient evaluation and management of the dialysis visits, telephone calls, and patient management during the dialysis provided during a full month. In the circumstances in which the patient has had a complete assessment visit during the month and services are provided over a period of less than a month, 90951-90962 may be used according to the number of visits performed.

Codes 90963-90966 are reported once per month for a full month of service to distinguish age-specific services for end-stage renal disease (ESRD) services for home dialysis patients.

For ESRD and non-ESRD dialysis services performed in an inpatient setting, and for non-ESRD dialysis services performed in an outpatient setting, see 90935-90937 and 90945-90947.

Evaluation and management services unrelated to ESRD services that cannot be performed during the dialysis session may be reported separately.

▶Codes 90967-90970 are reported to distinguish age-specific services for end-stage renal disease (ESRD) services for less than a full month of service, per day, for services provided under the following circumstances: transient patients, partial month where there was one or more face-to-face visits without the complete assessment, the patient was hospitalized before a complete assessment was furnished, dialysis was stopped due to recovery or death, or the patient received a kidney transplant. For reporting purposes, each month is considered 30 days.◄

Examples:

ESRD-related services:

ESRD-related services are initiated on July 1 for a 57-year-old male. On July 11, he is admitted to the hospital as an inpatient and is discharged on July 27. He has had a complete assessment and the physician or other qualified health care professional has performed two face-to-face visits prior to admission. Another face-to-face visit occurs after discharge during the month.

In this example, 90961 is reported for the three face-to-face outpatient visits. Report inpatient E/M services as appropriate. Dialysis procedures rendered during the hospitalization (July 11-27) should be reported as appropriate (90935-90937, 90945-90947).

If the patient did not have a complete assessment during the month or was a transient or dialysis was stopped due to recovery or death, 90970 would be used to report each day outside the inpatient hospitalization as described in the home dialysis example below.

ESRD-related services for the home dialysis patient:

Home ESRD-related services are initiated on July 1 for a 57-year-old male. On July 11, he is admitted to the hospital as an inpatient and is discharged on July 27.

▶Report inpatient E/M services as appropriate. Dialysis procedures rendered during the hospitalization (July 11-27) should be reported as appropriate (90935-90937, 90945-90947).◄

(Do not report 90951-90970 during the same month in conjunction with 99487-99489)

(Do not report 90951-90970 during the service time of 99495, 99496)

★ **90951**   End-stage renal disease (ESRD) related services monthly, for patients younger than 2 years of age to include monitoring for the adequacy of nutrition, assessment of growth and development, and counseling of parents; with 4 or more face-to-face visits by a physician or other qualified health care professional per month

Rationale

Guidelines under the End-Stage Renal Disease Services heading in the Dialysis subsection have been revised to remove requirements for reporting partial-month services for home-dialysis patients.

Guideline revisions have been made in response to part of the rulemaking for the 2015 Medicare Fee Schedule. The Centers for Medicare & Medicaid Services (CMS) revised the guidelines for reporting home-dialysis codes when a patient is hospitalized, and these guidelines allow both home-dialysis and in-center dialysis for hospitalized patients to be reported with a full-month code provided a complete assessment has occurred.

With the revision of the CMS guidelines, the dialysis guidelines in the CPT code set have been revised to remove the reference to partial-month home-dialysis patients in codes 90967-90970.

Ophthalmology

General Ophthalmological Services

New Patient

(For distinguishing between new and established patients, see **Evaluation and Management** guidelines)

92002   Ophthalmological services: medical examination and evaluation with initiation of diagnostic and treatment program; intermediate, new patient

▶(Do not report 92002 in conjunction with 99173, 99174, 99177, 0469T)◄

92004   comprehensive, new patient, 1 or more visits

▶(Do not report 92004 in conjunction with 99173, 99174, 99177, 0469T)◄

Established Patient

(For distinguishing between new and established patients, see **Evaluation and Management** guidelines)

92012   Ophthalmological services: medical examination and evaluation, with initiation or continuation of diagnostic and treatment program; intermediate, established patient

▶(Do not report 92012 in conjunction with 99173, 99174, 99177, 0469T)◀

92014   comprehensive, established patient, 1 or more visits

▶(Do not report 92014 in conjunction with 99173, 99174, 99177, 0469T)◀

(For surgical procedures, see **Surgery**, Eye and Ocular Adnexa, 65091 et seq)

Rationale

In accordance with the addition of Category III code 0469T, the instructional parenthetical notes that follow codes 92002, 92004, 92012, and 92014 have been revised.

Refer to the codebook and the Rationale for code 0469T for a full discussion of the changes

Cardiovascular

Cardiac Catheterization

+ **93462**   Left heart catheterization by transseptal puncture through intact septum or by transapical puncture (List separately in addition to code for primary procedure)

(Use 93462 in conjunction with 33477, 93452, 93453, 93458, 93459, 93460, 93461, 93582, 93653, 93654)

▶(Use 93462 in conjunction with 93590, 93591 for transapical puncture performed for left heart catheterization and percutaneous transcatheter closure of paravalvular leak)◀

▶(Do not report 93462 in conjunction with 93590 for transeptal puncture through intact septum performed for left heart catheterization and percutaneous transcatheter closure of paravalvular leak)◀

(Do not report 93462 in conjunction with 93656)

(Do not report 93462 in conjunction with 0345T unless transapical puncture is performed)

Rationale

Two new parenthetical notes have been added after code 93462. These parenthetical notes provide instructions regarding the appropriate reporting of add-on code 93462.

The instructional parenthetical note that follows code 93462 identifies a specific circumstance in which this code may be reported in conjunction with codes 93590 and 93591 for transapical puncture performed for left heart catheterization and percutaneous transcatheter closure of a paravalvular leak. This instruction is necessary because an exclusionary parenthetical note restricts reporting of most transapical punctures in conjunction with left heart catheterization code 93462. This instruction describes the specific circumstance when it is appropriate to report these two codes. In addition, a reciprocating exclusionary parenthetical note restricts reporting code 93462 in conjunction with code 93590 for the procedure that is performed for transeptal puncture, as noted in the parenthetical note.

▶Home and Outpatient International Normalized Ratio (INR) Monitoring Services ◀

▶Home and outpatient international normalized ratio (INR) monitoring services describe the management of warfarin therapy, including ordering, review, and interpretation of new INR test result(s), patient instructions, and dosage adjustments as needed.

If a significantly, separately identifiable evaluation and management (E/M) service is performed on the same day as 93792, the appropriate E/M service may be reported using modifier 25.

Do not report 93793 on the same day as an E/M service.

Do not report 93792, 93793 in conjunction with 98966, 98967, 98968, 98969, 99441, 99442, 99443, 99444, when telephone or online services address home and outpatient INR monitoring.

Do not report 93792, 93793 when performed during the service time of 99487, 99489, 99490, 99495, 99496.◀

● **93792**   Patient/caregiver training for initiation of home international normalized ratio (INR) monitoring under the direction of a physician or other qualified health care professional, face-to-face, including use and care of the INR monitor, obtaining blood sample, instructions for reporting home INR test results, and documentation of patient's/caregiver's ability to perform testing and report results

Medicine 90281-99607

►(For provision of test materials and equipment for home INR monitoring, see 99070 or the appropriate supply code)◄

● **93793** Anticoagulant management for a patient taking warfarin, must include review and interpretation of a new home, office, or lab international normalized ratio (INR) test result, patient instructions, dosage adjustment (as needed), and scheduling of additional test(s), when performed

►(Do not report 93793 in conjunction with 99201, 99202, 99203, 99204, 99205, 99211, 99212, 99213, 99214, 99215, 99241, 99242, 99243, 99244, 99245)◄

►(Report 93793 no more than once per day, regardless of the number of tests reviewed)◄

Rationale

Codes 99363 and 99364 have been deleted and replaced by codes 93792 and 93793, which have been established for reporting home international normalized ratio (INR) monitoring (of warfarin therapy). To accommodate the replacement, guidelines and parenthetical notes have been revised to reflect reporting for home and outpatient INR monitoring.

The AMA RUC Relativity Assessment Workgroup (RAW) identified warfarin therapy for high-volume growth. As a result, the descriptions previously used to describe warfarin therapy have been revised to include the deletion of codes, code section, guidelines, and other instructions regarding reporting warfarin therapy from the Evaluation and Management (E/M) section. A new section and new codes for reporting warfarin therapy services have been created and added in the Medicine section, which includes the addition of codes 93792 and 93793 to report face-to-face training provided to the patient or caregiver for initiation of the home and outpatient INR monitoring service (93792) and anticoagulation management for patients who take warfarin (93793). These services have been relocated to the Medicine section to better identify the intended use for these services.

Code 93792 should be used to report all training and instruction needed for the patient or caregiver to allow initiation of the home and outpatient INR monitoring service. This includes training on use and care of the monitoring device and on obtaining the blood sample, instructions for reporting test results, and documentation of the patient's/caregiver's ability to perform testing and report the results (93792).

Note that the provision of the test materials and equipment is reported separately from home and outpatient INR services with code 99070 or an appropriate supply code.

Code 93793 should be used to report the management services needed to treat the patient. This includes review of the home and outpatient INR test results, patient instructions, adjustment of dosages (as needed), and any additional testing or scheduling necessary for management.

Many of the services provided for home and outpatient INR management are also performed as part of E/M services. The efforts provided for home and outpatient INR management require separate focus that is not counted as effort for any other service. As a result, many of the parenthetical notes and guidelines regarding intent for reporting restricts the use of codes 93792 and 93793 with other types of management codes, including many E/M services provided. E/M services may only be reported in addition to home and outpatient INR monitoring when the efforts for the E/M services are significant enough to be separately reported and are separate from those needed to evaluate the patient for home and outpatient INR monitoring. In addition, a specific instructional parenthetical note that follows code 93793 instructs that management may not be reported more than once per day, regardless of the number of tests reviewed to allow appropriate management of the patient's warfarin status.

Clinical Example (93792)

A 75-year-old female established patient is found to have atrial fibrillation. The patient has the ability to perform home monitoring and to report results. There are no contraindications to systemic anticoagulation.

Description of Procedure (93792)

Clinical staff reviews charts and communicates results, dosage changes, etc. to patient.

Clinical Example (93793)

A 75-year-old female with a mechanical heart valve is managed for anticoagulation with warfarin.

Description of Procedure (93793)

The results are reviewed, and a determination is made regarding the need for any dosage adjustment and/or change in care plan. The dosage is adjusted and/or the care plan is changed to account for acute illness, possible drug interactions, diet changes that could affect vitamin K intake, and/or procedures that require withholding or alternative anticoagulation.

Medicine 90281-99607

Medicine 90281-99607

Noninvasive Vascular Diagnostic Studies

Extremity Arterial Studies (Including Digits)

93922 Limited bilateral noninvasive physiologic studies of upper or lower extremity arteries, (eg, for lower extremity: ankle/brachial indices at distal posterior tibial and anterior tibial/dorsalis pedis arteries plus bidirectional, Doppler waveform recording and analysis at 1-2 levels, or ankle/brachial indices at distal posterior tibial and anterior tibial/dorsalis pedis arteries plus volume plethysmography at 1-2 levels, or ankle/brachial indices at distal posterior tibial and anterior tibial/dorsalis pedis arteries with, transcutaneous oxygen tension measurement at 1-2 levels)

►(For transcutaneous oxyhemoglobin measurement in a lower extremity wound by near infrared spectroscopy, use 0493T)◄

(Do not report 93922 in conjunction with 0337T)

Rationale

In support of the establishment of code 0493T for reporting near-infrared spectroscopy studies of lower extremity wounds, a new parenthetical note has been added after code 93922.

Refer to the codebook and the Rationale for code 0493T for a full discussion of the changes.

Visceral and Penile Vascular Studies

►(93982 has been deleted)◄

Rationale

In support of the changes for reporting endovascular aneurysm repair procedures, code 93982, which was used to report noninvasive physiologic study of implanted wireless pressure sensor following endovascular surgery, has been deleted.

Refer to the codebook and the Rationale for codes 34701-34713, 34714, 34715, and 34716 for a full discussion of these changes.

Pulmonary

Pulmonary Diagnostic Testing and Therapies

94060 Bronchodilation responsiveness, spirometry as in 94010, pre- and post-bronchodilator administration

(Do not report 94060 in conjunction with 94150, 94200, 94375, 94640, 94728)

(Report bronchodilator supply separately with 99070 or appropriate supply code)

►(For exercise test for bronchospasm with pre- and post-spirometry, use 94617)◄

94250 Expired gas collection, quantitative, single procedure (separate procedure)

►(Do not report 94250 in conjunction with 94621)◄

⊘ **94610** Intrapulmonary surfactant administration by a physician or other qualified health care professional through endotracheal tube

(Do not report 94610 in conjunction with 99468-99472)

(For endotracheal intubation, use 31500)

(Report 94610 once per dosing episode)

● **94617** Exercise test for bronchospasm, including pre- and post-spirometry, electrocardiographic recording(s), and pulse oximetry

● **94618** Pulmonary stress testing (eg, 6-minute walk test), including measurement of heart rate, oximetry, and oxygen titration, when performed

►(94620 has been deleted. To report pulmonary stress testing, use 94618)◄

▲ **94621** Cardiopulmonary exercise testing, including measurements of minute ventilation, CO_2 production, O_2 uptake, and electrocardiographic recordings

►(Do not report 94617, 94621 in conjunction with 93000, 93005, 93010, 93040, 93041, 93042 for ECG monitoring performed during the same session)◄

►(Do not report 94617, 94621 in conjunction with 93015, 93016, 93017, 93018)◄

►(Do not report 94621 in conjunction with 94250, 94680, 94681, 94690)◄

►(Do not report 94617, 94618, 94621 in conjunction with 94760, 94761)◄

94680 Oxygen uptake, expired gas analysis; rest and exercise, direct, simple

94681 including CO2 output, percentage oxygen extracted

94690   rest, indirect (separate procedure)

           (For single arterial puncture, use 36600)

           ▶(Do not report 94680, 94681, 94690 in conjunction with 94621)◀

94760   Noninvasive ear or pulse oximetry for oxygen saturation; single determination

           (For blood gases, see 82803-82810)

94761   multiple determinations (eg, during exercise)

           ▶(Do not report 94760, 94761 in conjunction with 94617, 94618, 94621)◀

Rationale

In order to reflect on the changes made in reporting exercise testing, pulmonary stress testing, and cardiopulmonary testing procedures, two new codes (94617 and 94618) have been established, one code (94620) has been deleted, and one code (94621) has been revised. In addition, several parenthetical notes have been revised to clarify the reporting nature of these services.

Code 94620 was reviewed as a result of a survey requested by the AMA RUC RAW, which identified this code as part of a family of codes that were potentially misvalued. It was determined that code 94620 was being used to report two tests commonly performed for evaluation for dyspnea. These included the six-minute walk test and pre- and post-exercise spirometry. Because these are considered to be two different services, the services have been separated and should be reported with separate codes.

To accommodate this change, code 94620 was deleted to comply with the "concept permanence" rule, which dictates that a new code number(s) has to be established if a revision alters the meaning of a code(s). The separation of the services previously reported as part of code 94620 caused such a significant change that the resultant codes no longer resembled the original code.

As a result, two codes have been created to report the complete services previously identified as pulmonary stress testing.

Code 94617 should be used to report exercise testing for the purpose of identifying bronchospasm, which includes a number of pulmonary tests and electrocardiographic recordings. Conversely, code 94618 is used to report pulmonary stress testing, which includes measurements of heart rate and oxygen levels (oximetry and oxygen titration), when performed. The two new codes now appropriately represent all services that were previously included as part of deleted code 94620.

Code 94621 has been revised to reflect cardiopulmonary exercise testing. The previous language in this code descriptor that identified "complex pulmonary stress testing" has been removed. Instead, language that identifies the complete services rendered for this diagnostic testing procedure (ie, assessment for both cardiac and pulmonary elements) has been included.

To provide additional instruction regarding the intended use for these codes, parenthetical notes that direct users to appropriate codes for reporting various pulmonary- and cardiology-related testing procedures have been added. One of the instructions provided includes instructions on the appropriate reporting of exercise testing procedures for bronchospasm testing, appropriate reporting of pulmonary stress testing in place of deleted code 94620, and exclusionary instructions, which restrict reporting of various cardiography, stress testing, and pulmonary codes in conjunction with exercise testing, pulmonary stress testing, and cardiopulmonary exercise testing procedures, since these services are inherently included within the new and revised codes.

Clinical Example (94617)

A 65-year-old female is seen because of dyspnea and cough after walking several city blocks. Her physical exam is normal.

Description of Procedure (94617)

The physician is usually present for the exercise portion of the procedure. Patient data from exercise on treadmill or stationary bicycle are reviewed, including miles per hour, percent incline, exercise stage, heart rate, blood pressure, and oxygen saturation. Echocardiogram strips taken during exercise and recovery are reviewed. Baseline spirometry results before the exercise test and multiple spirometric results following exercise are reviewed. Data are analyzed and checked for irregularities. A written report, including an interpretation of test results, is prepared.

Clinical Example (94618)

A 65-year-old female with documented chronic obstructive pulmonary disease is evaluated for symptoms of dyspnea while walking.

Description of Procedure (94618)

Data on oxygen saturation, heart rate, and distance measured at 1, 2, 3, 4, 5, and 6 minutes are reviewed. Review blood pressure measured before and after exercise. The percent of distance compared to prediction

Medicine 90281-99607

is calculated. The dyspnea index is reviewed. Data are analyzed and checked for irregularities and compared to previous test results, if available. A written report is prepared, including an interpretation of test results.

94770 Carbon dioxide, expired gas determination by infrared analyzer

▶(For bronchoscopy, see 31622-31654)◄

Rationale

In accordance with the revision of code 31646, the parenthetical note in the Ventilator Management subsection has been revised with the removal of this code.

Refer to the codebook and the Rationale for codes 31645 and 31646 for a full discussion of these changes.

Endocrinology

▶Codes 95249 and 95250 are used to report the service for subcutaneous interstitial sensor placement, hook-up of the sensor to the transmitter, calibration of continuous glucose monitoring (CGM) device, patient training on CGM device functions and management, removal of the interstitial sensor, and the print-out of captured data recordings. For the CGM device owned by the physician's or other qualified health care professional's office, use 95250 for the data capture occurring over a **minimum** period of 72 hours.

Code 95249 may be reported only once during the time that a patient owns a given data receiver, including the initial episode of data collection.

Code 95249 may not be reported for subsequent episodes of data collection, unless the patient obtains a new and/or different model of data receiver. Obtaining a new sensor and/or transmitter without a change in receiver may not be reported with 95249.

Code 95249 may not be reported unless the patient brings the data receiver to the physician's or other qualified health care professional's office with the entire initial data collection procedure conducted in the physician's or other qualified health care professional's office.◄

95249 Code is out of numerical sequence. See 95199-95803

▲ **95250** Ambulatory continuous glucose monitoring of interstitial tissue fluid via a subcutaneous sensor for a minimum of 72 hours; physician or other qualified health care professional (office) provided equipment, sensor placement, hook-up, calibration of monitor, patient training, removal of sensor, and printout of recording

(Do not report 95250 more than once per month)

▶(Do not report 95250 in conjunction with 99091, 0446T)◄

#● **95249** patient-provided equipment, sensor placement, hook-up, calibration of monitor, patient training, and printout of recording

▶(Do not report 95249 more than once for the duration that the patient owns the data receiver)◄

▶(Do not report 95249 in conjunction with 99091, 0446T)◄

▲ **95251** analysis, interpretation and report

(Do not report 95251 more than once per month)

▶(Do not report 95251 in conjunction with 99091)◄

Rationale

One code has been added (95249) and two codes have been revised (95250, 95251) to report ambulatory continuous glucose monitoring. New guidelines have been included to provide specific instruction regarding the use of the codes. Code 95249 has been established for reporting ambulatory continuous glucose monitoring performed on equipment that is not owned by the physician or other qualified health care professional. In addition, a number of parenthetical notes have been included to restrict reporting based on specific circumstance that may exist for the procedure. A parenthetical note that follows code 95251 has been revised to reflect the removal of a Category III code 0446T from the parenthetical note.

Code 95250 should be used to report ambulatory continuous glucose monitoring performed when the physician or other qualified health care professional owns or is otherwise responsible for providing the equipment. This service includes a practice expense associated with the provision of the equipment, which includes sensor placement, hook-up, calibrations for the monitoring device, training the patient regarding use of the equipment (for appropriate and accurate remote monitoring), removal of the sensors, and provision of the recording printout.

★ = Telemedicine   ✚ = Add-on code   𝑵 = FDA approval pending   # = Resequenced code

Code 95249 should be used to report many of the same services reported with code 95250, as both of these codes are intended to identify practice expense. Code 95249 differs from code 95250 in that the patient is responsible for providing the device. In addition, the guidelines restrict reporting to a single time, ie, for the duration of the service that the patient owns the data receiver. It is assumed that no additional training is needed once the patient has been trained on the use of the device. If a new data receiver is necessary and additional training, sensor placement, hook-up, calibration, and similar services are provided for the patient, code 95249 may be reported to identify the additional work provided.

If the physician only interprets the analysis and provides a report, only code 95251 should be reported.

Clinical Example (95249)

A 45-year-old female with type 1 diabetes mellitus has been unable to manage her disease and has had frequent episodes of hypoglycemia symptoms and a recent hospitalization for ketoacidosis. Ambulatory continuous glucose monitoring (CGM) is ordered to assist with management of her disease. The CGM equipment is patient-provided.

Description of Procedure (95249)

Clinical staff prepares the skin site and the placement of the sensor. Transmitter is attached and sensor on receiver session is initiated. The room is cleaned. Patient is instructed on patient-specific downloading and communication requirements.

The purpose of CGM and the difference between CGM and home blood glucose testing with finger sticks are explained to the patient. In addition, explanation about the parts of the CGM device (sensor, transmitter, and receiver); the placement choices for CGM sensor; the CGM device settings (shutdown and stop sensor), button functions, menus (trend graphs and profile choices); and when and how to charge receiver are provided to the patient. Explanations of alerts (selection of choices, programming, patient responses) for the CGM device is also provided to patient.

The patient is given instructions about the precautions that should be taken during the CGM period, such as continue all medications, avoid acetaminophen, keep insulin injections at least 3 cm from sensor site, and keep receiver within 20 feet of sensor. Clinical staff also provide general patient management of CGM device, such as placement during sleep, care during shower, exercise, and other daily living activities. The necessity of continuing finger sticks during CGM period and basing treatment during CGM period on the finger-stick results, instead of the CGM readings, are explained to the patient as well. In addition, patient is advised on the importance of entering blood-glucose results into the CGM device twice daily (three times on day one), how to enter blood glucose results into CGM device, and how to ensure accuracy of blood-glucose meter (a two-hour startup period and entering startup blood-glucose results). Patient is also given instructions on how to enter events into diary and devices, as well as the importance of doing so. Clinical staff explained to the patient about the procedure if sensor site is uncomfortable or painful; if tape or dressing begins to peel off; and if sensor falls off, as well as the resources available for assistance (ie, quick-start guide, device manual, toll-free numbers, and educator's number/email).

Neurology and Neuromuscular Procedures

Evoked Potentials and Reflex Tests

▲ **95930** Visual evoked potential (VEP) checkerboard or flash testing, central nervous system except glaucoma, with interpretation and report

▶(For visual evoked potential testing for glaucoma, use 0464T)◀

(For screening of visual acuity using automated visual evoked potential devices, use 0333T)

Rationale

In support of the establishment of code 0464T for reporting visual evoked potential (VEP) testing for glaucoma, code 95930 has been revised to exclude testing for glaucoma in order to prevent duplicate mechanisms of reporting VEP testing for glaucoma. Code 95930 has been revised to include interpretation and report. A cross-reference parenthetical note directing users to code 0464T has been added after code 95930.

Refer to the codebook and the Rationale for code 0464T for a full discussion of these changes.

Clinical Example (95930)

A 30-year-old female complains of intermittent bilateral extremity weakness and past history of transient loss of vision in one eye. After physical examination, central nervous system impairment is suspected. Eye and vision examinations are normal. Visual evoked potentials are requested to evaluate the history of two weeks of diminished vision in the left eye one year ago, as possible optic neuritis.

Description of Procedure (95930)

Printed results of brain electrical activity measurements are reviewed and interpreted.

Central Nervous System Assessments/Tests (eg, Neuro-Cognitive, Mental Status, Speech Testing)

The following codes are used to report the services provided during testing of the cognitive function of the central nervous system. The testing of cognitive processes, visual motor responses, and abstractive abilities is accomplished by the combination of several types of testing procedures. It is expected that the administration of these tests will generate material that will be formulated into a report. A minimum of 31 minutes must be provided to report any per hour code. Services 96101, 96116, 96118 and 96125 report time as face-to-face time with the patient and the time spent interpreting and preparing the report.

▶(For development of cognitive skills, see 97127, 97533)◀

▶(For dementia screens, [eg, Folstein Mini-Mental State Examination, by a physician or other qualified health care professional], see **Evaluation and Management** services codes)◀

(Do not report 96101-96125 in conjunction with 0364T, 0365T, 0366T, 0367T, 0373T, 0374T)

96101　Psychological testing (includes psychodiagnostic assessment of emotionality, intellectual abilities, personality and psychopathology, eg, MMPI, Rorschach, WAIS), per hour of the psychologist's or physician's time, both face-to-face time administering tests to the patient and time interpreting these test results and preparing the report

(96101 is also used in those circumstances when additional time is necessary to integrate other sources of clinical data, including previously completed and reported technician- and computer-administered tests)

(Do not report 96101 for the interpretation and report of 96102, 96103)

Rationale

In support of the establishment of code 97127 (cognitive function intervention) and the deletion of code 97532 (cognitive skills development), the cross-reference parenthetical notes that follow the Central Nervous System Assessments/Tests (eg, Neuro-Cognitive, Mental Status, Speech Testing) guidelines have been revised.

Refer to the codebook and the Rationale for code 97127 for a full discussion of the changes.

Photodynamic Therapy

▶Codes 96573, 96574 should be used to report nonsurgical treatment of cutaneous lesions using photodynamic therapy by external application of light to destroy premalignant lesion(s) of the skin and adjacent mucosa (eg, face, scalp) by activation of photosensitizing drug(s).

A treatment session is defined as an application of photosensitizer to all lesions within an anatomic area (eg, face, scalp), with or without debridement of all premalignant hyperkeratotic lesions in that area, followed by illumination/activation with an appropriate light source to the same area.

Do not report codes for debridement (11000, 11001, 11004, 11005), lesion shaving (11300-11313), biopsy (11100, 11101), or lesion excision (11400-11471) within the treatment area(s) on the same day as photodynamic therapy (96573, 96574).◀

▲ 96567　Photodynamic therapy by external application of light to destroy premalignant lesions of the skin and adjacent mucosa with application and illumination/activation of photosensitive drug(s), per day

▶(Use 96567 for reporting photodynamic therapy when physician or other qualified health care professional is not directly involved in the delivery of the photodynamic therapy service)◀

★=Telemedicine　✚=Add-on code　✖=FDA approval pending　#=Resequenced code

+ 96570 Photodynamic therapy by endoscopic application of light to ablate abnormal tissue via activation of photosensitive drug(s); first 30 minutes (List separately in addition to code for endoscopy or bronchoscopy procedures of lung and gastrointestinal tract)

(Report 96570 with modifier 52 for service of less than 23 minutes with report)

+ 96571 each additional 15 minutes (List separately in addition to code for endoscopy or bronchoscopy procedures of lung and gastrointestinal tract)

(For 23-37 minutes of service, use 96570. For 38-52 minutes of service, use 96570 in conjunction with 96571)

(96570, 96571 are to be used in addition to bronchoscopy, endoscopy codes)

(Use 96570, 96571 in conjunction with 31641, 43229 as appropriate)

● 96573 Photodynamic therapy by external application of light to destroy premalignant lesions of the skin and adjacent mucosa with application and illumination/activation of photosensitizing drug(s) provided by a physician or other qualified health care professional, per day

▶(Do not report 96573 in conjunction with 96567, 96574 for the same anatomic area)◀

● 96574 Debridement of premalignant hyperkeratotic lesion(s) (ie, targeted curettage, abrasion) followed with photodynamic therapy by external application of light to destroy premalignant lesions of the skin and adjacent mucosa with application and illumination/activation of photosensitizing drug(s) provided by a physician or other qualified health care professional, per day

▶(Do not report 96574 in conjunction with 96567, 96573 for the same anatomic area)◀

Rationale

Two new codes (96573, 96574) have been established in the Photodynamic subsection of the Medicine section. Code 96573 describes photodynamic therapy to destroy premalignant lesions provided by a physician or other qualified health care professional. Code 96574 describes debridement of premalignant hyperkeratotic lesion(s) followed by photodynamic therapy. Exclusionary parenthetical notes have been added to preclude the use of code 96573 with 96574, and vice versa for the same anatomic area.

In support of the establishment of codes 96573 and 96574, code 96567 has been revised to report photodynamic therapy by external application of light to destroy premalignant lesions of the skin and adjacent mucosa with application and illumination/activation of photosensitive drug(s), per day. As photodynamic therapy has been more widely used and the technology and techniques evolved, it became apparent that the existing codes did not accurately reflect the procedures as performed vis-à-vis the physician-work component in that the physician identification of and debridement of hyperkeratotic lesions and physician application of a photosensitizing agent was not captured. Therefore, with the establishment of new codes 96573 and 96574, existing code 96567 needed to be revised and retained as a zero-physician work code. A parenthetical note has also been added to direct users to report code 96567 only when the physician or other qualified health care professional is not directly involved in the delivery of the photodynamic therapy service.

Clinical Example (96573)

A 65-year-old female has numerous ill-defined actinic keratoses.

Description of Procedure (96573)

Prepared photosensitizing agent in topical solution form is applied directly to individual lesions and the entire treatment field, depending on clinical characteristics. The area is allowed to dry. Topical anesthetic is applied. Occlusive dressing and photoprotective shielding are applied.

Clinical Example (96574)

A 65-year-old female patient has numerous, hyperkeratotic actinic keratoses on separate areas of her body.

Description of Procedure (96574)

Using curette, hyperkeratotic epidermis is removed from each lesion. Hemostasis with pressure, electrocautery, or application of topical hemostatic agents is achieved. Prepared photosensitizing agent in topical solution form is applied directly to individual curetted lesions, nonhyperkeratotic (noncuretted) lesions, and the entire treatment field, depending on clinical characteristics. The area is allowed to dry. Topical anesthetic is applied. Occlusive dressing and photoprotective shielding are applied.

Special Dermatological Procedures

Codes 96931, 96932, 96933, 96934, 96935, 96936 describe the acquisition and/or diagnostic interpretation of the device generated stitched image mosaics related to a single lesion. Do not report 96931, 96932, 96933, 96934, 96935, 96936 for a reflectance confocal microscopy examination that does not produce mosaic images. For services rendered using reflectance confocal microscopy not generating mosaic images, use 96999.

> ▶(For optical coherence tomography [OCT] for microstructural and morphological imaging of skin, see 0470T, 0471T)◀

96931   Reflectance confocal microscopy (RCM) for cellular and sub-cellular imaging of skin; image acquisition and interpretation and report, first lesion

96932   image acquisition only, first lesion

96933   interpretation and report only, first lesion

+ 96934   image acquisition and interpretation and report, each additional lesion (List separately in addition to code for primary procedure)

(Use 96934 in conjunction with 96931)

Rationale

In support of the establishment of codes 0471T and 0472T, a parenthetical note has been added following the Special Dermatological Procedures heading.

Refer to the codebook and the Rationale for codes 0471T, 0472T for a full discussion of the changes.

Physical Medicine and Rehabilitation

▶Codes 97010-97763 should be used to report each distinct procedure performed. Do not append modifier 51 to 97010-97763.◀

The work of the physician or other qualified health care professional consists of face-to-face time with the patient (and caregiver, if applicable) delivering skilled services. For the purpose of determining the total time of a service, incremental intervals of treatment at the same visit may be accumulated.

The meanings of terms in the Physical Medicine and Rehabilitation section are not the same as those in the Evaluation and Management Services section

(99201-99350). Do not use the Definitions of Commonly Used Terms in the Evaluation and Management (E/M) Guidelines for Physical Medicine and Rehabilitation services.

> (For muscle testing, range of joint motion, electromyography, see 95831 et seq)

> (For biofeedback training by EMG, use 90901)

> (For transcutaneous nerve stimulation (TNS), use 64550)

Therapeutic Procedures

97110   Therapeutic procedure, 1 or more areas, each 15 minutes; therapeutic exercises to develop strength and endurance, range of motion and flexibility

97112   neuromuscular reeducation of movement, balance, coordination, kinesthetic sense, posture, and/or proprioception for sitting and/or standing activities

97113   aquatic therapy with therapeutic exercises

97116   gait training (includes stair climbing)

(Use 96000-96003 to report comprehensive gait and motion analysis procedures)

97124   massage, including effleurage, petrissage and/or tapotement (stroking, compression, percussion)

● 97127   Therapeutic interventions that focus on cognitive function (eg, attention, memory, reasoning, executive function, problem solving, and/or pragmatic functioning) and compensatory strategies to manage the performance of an activity (eg, managing time or schedules, initiating, organizing and sequencing tasks), direct (one-on-one) patient contact

> ▶(Report 97127 only once per day)◀

> ▶(Do not report 97127 in conjunction with 0364T, 0365T, 0368T, 0369T)◀

> ▶(97532 has been deleted. To report, use 97127)◀

Rationale

Code 97532 (cognitive skills development) has been deleted, and code 97127 has been added to report therapeutic interventions that focus on cognitive function.

The AMA RUC RAW identified code 97532 for high-volume growth, and a recommendation was made for revision to reflect current practice. It was determined that if such extensive revisions were needed, a new code should be added and code 97532 should be deleted.

When code 97532 was initially established, it was limited to the development of cognitive skills to improve attention, memory, and problem solving only. However, current practice has evolved to address aspects beyond these three areas of cognitive function. For example,

★ = Telemedicine   ✦ = Add-on code   ✗ = FDA approval pending   # = Resequenced code

executive function, reasoning, and pragmatic functioning are also addressed. Current practice also includes the use of compensatory strategies for managing the performance of activities. New code 97127 clarifies that this service involves therapeutic interventions and lists examples of cognitive functions to avoid, thus limiting use of the code to specific areas of cognitive function. It also includes the use of compensatory strategies. Code 97127 is not time based as opposed to code 97532, which was based on each 15 minutes of service. Exclusionary and instructional parenthetical notes have been added following the code and throughout the code set regarding the appropriate reporting of code 97127.

Clinical Example (97127)

A 30-year-old male presents with traumatic brain injury sustained in a vehicular accident resulting in memory problems, distractibility, depression, inappropriate social interaction, inability to self-monitor, and impaired organizational skills for executive function. He is seen for treatment.

Description of Procedure (97127)

The clinician implemented therapeutic activities that may include: attention tasks (eg, gradually increasing levels of distracting background noise); memory tasks (eg, visualization, mnemonics, environmental adaptations); problem solving activities (eg, techniques to define a problem, set a goal, and organize an action); and pragmatic activities to improve social communication skills and increase self-awareness of limitations and disabilities (eg, use of internal dialogue). Tools (eg, technology-assisted activities, role-playing activities) and compensatory strategies (eg, memory log) may be used to accomplish functional outcomes.

Active Wound Care Management

►Active wound care procedures are performed to remove devitalized and/or necrotic tissue and promote healing. Chemical cauterization (17250) to achieve wound hemostasis is included in active wound care procedures (97597, 97598, 97602) and should not be separately reported for the same lesion. Services require direct (one-on-one) contact with the patient.◄

(Do not report 97597-97602 in conjunction with 11042-11047 for the same wound)

(For debridement of burn wounds, see 16020-16030)

97597 Debridement (eg, high pressure waterjet with/without suction, sharp selective debridement with scissors, scalpel and forceps), open wound, (eg, fibrin, devitalized epidermis and/or dermis, exudate, debris, biofilm), including topical application(s), wound assessment, use of a whirlpool, when performed and instruction(s) for ongoing care, per session, total wound(s) surface area; first 20 sq cm or less

Rationale

The guidelines for active wound care management have been revised. Language that restricts reporting code 17250 (chemical cauterization) in conjunction with the active wound care procedures, when performed for the same lesion, has been added.

Refer to the codebook and the Rationale for code 17250 for a full discussion of the changes.

►Orthotic Management and Training and Prosthetic Training ◄

▲ **97760** Orthotic(s) management and training (including assessment and fitting when not otherwise reported), upper extremity(ies), lower extremity(ies) and/or trunk, initial orthotic(s) encounter, each 15 minutes

►(Code 97760 should not be reported with 97116 for the same extremity[ies])◄

▲ **97761** Prosthetic(s) training, upper and/or lower extremity(ies), initial prosthetic(s) encounter, each 15 minutes

►(97762 has been deleted. To report, use 97763)◄

● **97763** Orthotic(s)/prosthetic(s) management and/or training, upper extremity(ies), lower extremity(ies), and/or trunk, subsequent orthotic(s)/prosthetic(s) encounter, each 15 minutes

►(Do not report 97763 in conjunction with 97760, 97761)◄

Medicine 90281-99607

Rationale

The Orthotic Management and Prosthetic Management section title has been revised to Orthotic Management and Training and Prosthetic Training.

Physical medicine and rehabilitation services reported with codes 97760, 97761, and 97762 were identified in a screen for high-volume growth services by the AMA RUC and subsequently by the CMS in a high-expenditure screen for codes reported together 75% of the time. After further review of the code language and vignettes, it was determined that the code descriptor language needed to be updated to reflect current practice and correct coding.

Codes 97760 and 97761 have been revised to include the initial encounter. Per the concept of the permanence principle, which dictates that a new code number(s) has to be established if a revision alters the meaning of a code(s), code 97762 has been deleted. A deletion parenthetical note has been added to clarify reporting of this service.

New code 97763 has been established to report orthotic and prosthetic management and/or training for the upper or lower extremities and/or trunk for each 15 minutes during a subsequent encounter.

Clinical Example (97760)

A patient presents with a median nerve injury. Direct one-on-one services are provided to design, fit, and instruct in the use of an orthosis.

Description of Procedure (97760)

Status check of skin integrity, sensation, fit of orthotic, and observation of movement are performed. Using direct contact (one on one) techniques, patient is assessed for proper orthotic fit and function (optimal components/position); necessary modifications to orthotic are completed; patient is trained on proper use of orthotic, wearing schedule, care, and precautions; how orthotic is tolerated is assessed and necessary modifications are made; and patient is instructed in adaptive functional activities while wearing orthotic to assure safety and competence. Patient is given instructions in the performance of skin checking for pressure points at regular intervals, wearing schedule, and exercises to be performed at home.

Clinical Example (97761)

A patient presents for prosthetic training, following a below-knee amputation, for use and care of a below-knee prosthesis with molded socket and solid ankle cushion heel (SACH) foot.

Description of Procedure (97761)

Status check of skin integrity, wound changes or abnormalities of incision, sensation, fit of prosthetic, and observation of movement are performed. The clinician may focus the intervention on instructing on the use and purpose of the components of the prosthetic and checking prosthetic fit; instructing patient in care of prosthetic characteristics, precautions and durations of wear; assessing level of function, posture, and gait while wearing prosthetic; instructing in-home program based on education and functional task training techniques learned in clinic. Patient is given instructions in the performance of skin checks and skin care; residual limb shrinkage causing pistoning, wearing schedule, care for prosthetic components, exercises for muscle strengthening and flexibility.

Clinical Example (97763)

A patient presents following a metacarpal phalangeal (MP) flexible implant arthroplasty with increased edema. The postoperative orthosis causes pressure on the ulnar styloid. Direct one-on-one services are provided to make adjustments to the previously fitted orthosis.

Description of Procedure (97763)

Status check of skin integrity and wound changes or abnormalities of incision, sensation, fit of prosthetic/orthotic, observation of movement, and edema observation are performed. The clinician may focus the intervention on assessing upper and/or lower quadrant for any potential problems; integumentary concerns, assistive range of motion; sensation; pain; assessing orthotic for alignment and fit; modifying/adjusting/repairing components of orthotic/prosthetic; adding/deleting/padding; reinstruct patient regarding wearing schedule, application, and care of orthotic/prosthetic; and ensuring patient practices proper technique. Patient is given instructions in performance of skin checks and skin care; proper care of orthotic and exercises to perform at home throughout the day.

Non-Face-to-Face Nonphysician Services

Telephone Services

98966   Telephone assessment and management service provided by a qualified nonphysician health care professional to an established patient, parent, or guardian not originating from a related assessment and management service provided within the previous 7 days nor leading to an assessment and management service or procedure within the next 24 hours or soonest available appointment; 5-10 minutes of medical discussion

98967   11-20 minutes of medical discussion

98968   21-30 minutes of medical discussion

(Do not report 98966-98968 during the same month with 99487-99489)

(Do not report 98966-98968 when performed during the service time of codes 99495, 99496)

▶(Do not report 98966, 98967, 98968 in conjunction with 93792, 93793)◀

On-line Medical Evaluation

98969   Online assessment and management service provided by a qualified nonphysician health care professional to an established patient or guardian, not originating from a related assessment and management service provided within the previous 7 days, using the Internet or similar electronic communications network

(Do not report 98969 when using 99339-99340, 99374-99380 for the same communication[s])

▶(Do not report 98969 for home and outpatient INR monitoring when reporting 93792, 93793)◀

Rationale

A parenthetical note has been added after code 98969 to restrict reporting of code 98969 in conjunction with anticoagulation management (home and outpatient INR monitoring) services.

Refer to the codebook and the Rationale for codes 93792 and 93793 for a full discussion of the changes.

Other Services and Procedures

99170   Anogenital examination, magnified, in childhood for suspected trauma, including image recording when performed

(For moderate sedation, see 99151, 99152, 99153, 99155, 99156, 99157)

99172   Visual function screening, automated or semi-automated bilateral quantitative determination of visual acuity, ocular alignment, color vision by pseudoisochromatic plates, and field of vision (may include all or some screening of the determination[s] for contrast sensitivity, vision under glare)

(This service must employ graduated visual acuity stimuli that allow a quantitative determination of visual acuity [eg, Snellen chart]. This service may not be used in addition to a general ophthalmological service or an E/M service)

▶(Do not report 99172 in conjunction with 99173, 99174, 99177, 0469T)◀

99173   Screening test of visual acuity, quantitative, bilateral

(The screening test used must employ graduated visual acuity stimuli that allow a quantitative estimate of visual acuity [eg, Snellen chart]. Other identifiable services unrelated to this screening test provided at the same time may be reported separately [eg, preventive medicine services]. When acuity is measured as part of a general ophthalmological service or of an E/M service of the eye, it is a diagnostic examination and not a screening test.)

(Do not report 99173 in conjunction with 99172, 99174, 99177)

99174   Instrument-based ocular screening (eg, photoscreening, automated-refraction), bilateral; with remote analysis and report

(Do not report 99174 in conjunction with 92002-92014, 99172, 99173, 99177)

 # 99177   with on-site analysis

(Do not report 99177 in conjunction with 92002-92014, 99172, 99173, 99174)

▶(For retinal polarization scan, use 0469T)◀

Rationale

In accordance with the addition of Category III code 0469T, an instructional parenthetical note after code 99177 has been created.

Refer to the codebook and the Rationale for code 0469T for a full discussion of the changes.

Notes

Category II Codes

In the Category II section, the guidelines have been editorially revised to reflect the current review practice of developing new Category II codes. The criteria for developing Category II codes is included in this section as well.

Category II Codes

The following section of *Current Procedural Terminology* (CPT) contains a set of supplemental tracking codes that can be used for performance measurement. It is anticipated that the use of Category II codes for performance measurement will decrease the need for record abstraction and chart review, and thereby minimize administrative burden on physicians, other health care professionals, hospitals, and entities seeking to measure the quality of patient care. These codes are intended to facilitate data collection about the quality of care rendered by coding certain services and test results that support nationally established performance measures and that have an evidence base as contributing to quality patient care.

The use of these codes is optional. The codes are not required for correct coding and may not be used as a substitute for Category I codes.

These codes describe clinical components that may be typically included in evaluation and management services or clinical services and, therefore, do not have a relative value associated with them. Category II codes may also describe results from clinical laboratory or radiology tests and other procedures, identified processes intended to address patient safety practices, or services reflecting compliance with state or federal law.

Category II codes described in this section make use of alphabetical characters as the 5th character in the string (ie, 4 digits followed by the letter **F**). These digits are not intended to reflect the placement of the code in the regular (Category I) part of the CPT code set. To promote understanding of these codes and their associated measures, users are referred to the Alphabetical Clinical Topics Listing, which contains information about performance measurement exclusion modifiers, measures, and the measure's source.

Cross-references to the measures associated with each Category II code and their source are included for reference in the Alphabetical Clinical Topics Listing. In addition, acronyms for the related diseases or clinical condition(s) have been added at the end of each code descriptor to identify the topic or clinical category in which that code is included. A complete listing of the diseases/clinical conditions, and their acronyms are provided in alphabetical order in the Alphabetical Clinical Topics Listing. The Alphabetical Clinical Topics Listing can be accessed on the website at www. ama-assn.org, under the Category II link. Users should review the complete measure(s) associated with each code prior to implementation.

▶Requests for Category II CPT codes will be reviewed by the CPT/HCPAC Advisory Committee just as requests for Category I CPT codes are reviewed. In developing new and revised performance measurement codes, requests for codes are considered from:

■ measurements that were developed and tested by a national organization;

■ evidenced-based measurements with established ties to health outcomes;

■ measurements that address clinical conditions of high prevalence, high risk, or high cost; and

■ well-established measurements that are currently being used by large segments of the health care industry across the country.

In addition, all of the following are required:

■ Definition or purpose of the measure is consistent with its intended use (quality improvement and accountability, or solely quality improvement)

■ Aspect of care measured is substantially influenced by the physician (or other qualified health care professional or entity for which the code may be relevant)

■ Reduces data collection burden on physicians (or other qualified health care professional or entities)

■ Significant

   • Affects a large segment of health care community

   • Tied to health outcomes

   • Addresses clinical conditions of high prevalence, high costs, high risks

■ Evidence-based

   • Agreed upon

   • Definable

   • Measurable

■ Risk-adjustment specifications and instructions for all outcome measures submitted or compelling evidence as to why risk adjustment is not relevant

■ Sufficiently detailed to make it useful for multiple purposes

■ Facilitates reporting of performance measure(s)

■ Inclusion of select patient history, testing (eg, glycohemoglobin), other process measures, cognitive or procedure services within CPT, or physiologic measures (eg, blood pressure) to support performance measurements

Category II 0001F-9007F

■ Performance measure–development process that
includes

- Nationally recognized expert panel

- Multidisciplinary

- Vetting process◄

Rationale

The guidelines section for Category II codes has been
editorially revised to reflect the current review process
used to develop Category II codes, which includes
removing the reference to the Performance Measures
Advisory Group, as they are no longer the reviewing body
for these codes. Rather, language has been added that
details the review of proposals by the CPT Advisory
Committee and the CPT Editorial Panel. In addition,
criteria for developing Category II codes have been
included in the Category II code section to clarify the
requirements and elements that are necessary when
developing Category II codes.

Notes

Category III Codes

Forty-one new Category III codes (0464T-0504T) have been added to cover emerging technology and services, two codes (0254T and 0333T) have been revised, and 22 codes (0051T-0053T, 0178T-0180T, 0255T, 0293T-0294T, 0299T-0310T, 0340T, 0340T, 0438T) have been deleted and/or converted to Category I codes.

New guidelines, parenthetical notes, and two codes (0483T, 0484T) have been added for reporting transcatheter mitral valve implantation procedures in order to differentiate the types of approach.

Code 0488T has been added for reporting an online/electronic structured intensive program for prevention of diabetes. In addition, this code has been resequenced to follow existing code 0403T, which uses a standardized curriculum in a group setting, for the prevention of diabetes through preventive behavior change. Three codes (0466T, 0467T, and 0468T) have been added to report implantation, replacement, and removal of respiratory sensor electrodes or electrode arrays.

Codes 0475T, 0476T, 0477T, and 0478T have been added for reporting fetal magnetic cardiac signals in order to differentiate arrhythmias from normal rhythm.

Two codes (0489T and 0490T) have been added for reporting autologous adipose-derived regenerative cell therapy. Code 0493T has been added for reporting near-infrared spectroscopy studies of lower extremity wounds. Three codes (0494T, 0495T, and 0496T) have been added for reporting ex vivo assessment procedures of marginal donor lungs prior to transplantation. Two codes (0497T and 0498T) have been added for reporting external patient-activated prescribed electrocardiographic rhythms.

Codes 0470T and 0471T have been added for optical coherence tomography for imaging of the skin. Add-on code 0471T has been added for reporting each additional lesion.

New parenthetical notes and codes 0501T, 0502T, 0503T, and 0504T have been added for noninvasive estimated coronary fractional flow reserve.

Summary of Additions, Deletions, and Revisions

The summary of changes shows the actual changes that have been made to the code descriptors.

New codes appear with a bullet (•) and are indicated as "Code added." Revised codes are preceded with a triangle (▲). Within revised codes, the deleted language appears with a ~~strikethrough~~, while new text appears <u>underlined</u>.

The ✗ symbol is used to identify codes for vaccines that are pending FDA approval. The # symbol is used to identify codes that have been resequenced. CPT add-on codes are annotated by the + symbol. The ⊘ symbol is used to identify codes that are exempt from the use of modifier 51. The ★ symbol is used to identify codes that may be used for reporting telemedicine services.

Code	Description
0051T	Implantation of a total replacement heart system (artificial heart) with recipient cardiectomy
0052T	Replacement or repair of thoracic unit of a total replacement heart system (artificial heart)
0053T	Replacement or repair of implantable component or components of total replacement heart system (artificial heart), excluding thoracic unit
0178T	Electrocardiogram, 64 leads or greater, with graphic presentation and analysis; with interpretation and report
0179T	tracing and graphics only, without interpretation and report
0180T	interpretation and report only
▲0254T	Endovascular repair of iliac artery bifurcation (eg, aneurysm, pseudoaneurysm, arteriovenous malformation, trauma, dissection) using bifurcated ~~endoprosthesis~~endograft from the common iliac artery into both the external and internal iliac artery, including all selective and/or nonselective catheterization(s) required for device placement and all associated radiological supervision and interpretation, unilateral
0255T	radiological supervision and interpretation
0293T	Insertion of left atrial hemodynamic monitor; complete system, includes implanted communication module and pressure sensor lead in left atrium including transseptal access, radiological supervision and interpretation, and associated injection procedures, when performed
0294T	pressure sensor lead at time of insertion of pacing cardioverter-defibrillator pulse generator including radiological supervision and interpretation and associated injection procedures, when performed (List separately in addition to code for primary procedure)
0299T	Extracorporeal shock wave for integumentary wound healing, high energy, including topical application and dressing care; initial wound
0300T	each additional wound (List separately in addition to code for primary procedure)
0301T	Destruction/reduction of malignant breast tumor with externally applied focused microwave, including interstitial placement of disposable catheter with combined temperature monitoring probe and microwave focusing sensocatheter under ultrasound thermotherapy guidance
0302T	Insertion or removal and replacement of intracardiac ischemia monitoring system including imaging supervision and interpretation when performed and intra-operative interrogation and programming when performed; complete system (includes device and electrode)
0303T	electrode only
0304T	device only
0305T	Programming device evaluation (in person) of intracardiac ischemia monitoring system with iterative adjustment of programmed values, with analysis, review, and report
0306T	Interrogation device evaluation (in person) of intracardiac ischemia monitoring system with analysis, review, and report
0307T	Removal of intracardiac ischemia monitoring device
0309T	Arthrodesis, pre-sacral interbody technique, including disc space preparation, discectomy, with posterior instrumentation, with image guidance, includes bone graft, when performed, lumbar, L4-L5 interspace (List separately in addition to code for primary procedure)
0310T	Motor function mapping using non-invasive navigated transcranial magnetic stimulation (nTMS) for therapeutic treatment planning, upper and lower extremity
▲0333T	Visual evoked potential, screening of visual acuity, automated, with report

★ = Telemedicine   + = Add-on code   ⚡ = FDA approval pending   # = Resequenced code

Category III 0042T-0504T

Code	Description
#●0464T	Code added
0340T	~~Ablation, pulmonary tumor(s), including pleura or chest wall when involved by tumor extension, percutaneous, cryoablation, unilateral, includes imaging guidance~~
#●0488T	Code added
0438T	~~Transperineal placement of biodegradable material, peri-prostatic (via needle), single or multiple, includes image guidance~~
●0465T	Code added
+●0466T	Code added
●0467T	Code added
●0468T	Code added
●0469T	Code added
●0470T	Code added
+●0471T	Code added
●0472T	Code added
●0473T	Code added
●0474T	Code added
●0475T	Code added
●0476T	Code added
●0477T	Code added
●0478T	Code added
●0479T	Code added
+●0480T	Code added
●0481T	Code added
+●0482T	Code added
●0483T	Code added
●0484T	Code added
●0485T	Code added
●0486T	Code added
●0487T	Code added
●0489T	Code added
●0490T	Code added
●0491T	Code added
+●0492T	Code added

Code	Description
●0493T	Code added
●0494T	Code added
●0495T	Code added
✚●0496T	Code added
●0497T	Code added
●0498T	Code added
●0499T	Code added
●0500T	Code added
●0501T	Code added
●0502T	Code added
●0503T	Code added
●0504T	Code added

★ = Telemedicine ✚ = Add-on code ✔ = FDA approval pending # = Resequenced code

Category III

►(0051T, 0052T, 0053T have been deleted. To report, see 33927, 33928, 33929)◄

Rationale

In accordance with the addition of Category I codes 33927, 33928, and 33929, Category III codes 0051T, 0052T, and 0053T, which described artificial heart system procedures, have been deleted.

Refer to the codebook and the Rationale for codes 33927, 33928, and 33929 for a full discussion of these changes.

0100T   Placement of a subconjunctival retinal prosthesis receiver and pulse generator, and implantation of intraocular retinal electrode array, with vitrectomy

►(For initial programming of implantable intraocular retinal electrode array device, use 0472T)◄

0101T   Extracorporeal shock wave involving musculoskeletal system, not otherwise specified, high energy

Rationale

In accordance with the addition of Category III code 0472T, a cross-reference parenthetical note has been added after code 0100T to direct users to the new code for initial programming of implantable intraocular retinal electrode array device.

Refer to the codebook and the Rationale for code 0472T for a full discussion of these changes.

+ 0174T   Computer-aided detection (CAD) (computer algorithm analysis of digital image data for lesion detection) with further physician review for interpretation and report, with or without digitization of film radiographic images, chest radiograph(s), performed concurrent with primary interpretation (List separately in addition to code for primary procedure)

►(Use 0174T in conjunction with 71045, 71046, 71047, 71048)◄

0175T   Computer-aided detection (CAD) (computer algorithm analysis of digital image data for lesion detection) with further physician review for interpretation and report, with or without digitization of film radiographic images, chest radiograph(s), performed remote from primary interpretation

►(Do not report 0175T in conjunction with 71045, 71046, 71047, 71048)◄

Rationale

In accordance with the deletion of codes 71010, 71020, 71021, 71022, and 71030 (chest X ray) and the addition of codes 71045-71048, the inclusionary parenthetical note following code 0174T and the exclusionary parenthetical note following code 0175T have been revised with the addition of the new codes and the removal of the deleted codes.

Refer to the codebook and the Rationale for codes 71045-71048 for a full discussion of these changes.

►(0178T, 0179T, 0180T have been deleted)◄

►(For electrocardiogram, 64 leads or greater, with graphic presentation and analysis, use 93799)◄

(For electrocardiogram routine, with at least 12 leads separately performed, see 93000-93010)

Rationale

In accordance with the CPT guidelines for archiving Category III codes, codes 0178T, 0179T, 0180T (64-lead or greater electrocardiogram) have been deleted. To reflect the change, the appropriate parenthetical notes in this section have been revised as well. Similarly, the guidelines and parenthetical notes in the Cardiovascular/Cardiography subsection in the Medicine section that are affected by this deletion have been revised accordingly.

A cross-reference parenthetical note has been added to direct users to code 93799 (unlisted cardiovascular service or procedure) for 64-lead or greater electrocardiogram with graphic presentation and analysis.

0184T   Excision of rectal tumor, transanal endoscopic microsurgical approach (ie, TEMS), including muscularis propria (ie, full thickness)

(For non-endoscopic excision of rectal tumor, see 45160, 45171, 45172)

►(Do not report 0184T in conjunction with 45300, 45308, 45309, 45315, 45317, 45320, 69990)◄

Rationale

The exclusionary parenthetical note following transanal rectal tumor excision code 0184T has been revised. Prior to 2018, this parenthetical note included proctosigmoidoscopy codes for dilation; biopsy; removal of foreign body; decompression of volvulus; and stent placement, and they could not be reported separately. However, these listed procedures are not inherent to the transanal tumor excision procedure, as described by code 0184T. Therefore, in 2018, codes 45303, 45305, 45307, 45321, and 45327, which describe these procedures, have been removed from the exclusionary parenthetical note following code 0184T.

Refer to the codebook and the Rationale for the deletion of the exclusionary parenthetical note following code 11008 for a full discussion of the change.

0232T	Injection(s), platelet rich plasma, any site, including image guidance, harvesting and preparation when performed

▶(Do not report 0232T in conjunction with 20550, 20551, 20600, 20604, 20605, 20606, 20610, 20611, 20926, 36415, 36592, 76942, 77002, 77012, 77021, 86965, 0481T)◀

(Do not report 38220-38230 for bone marrow aspiration for platelet rich stem cell injection. For bone marrow aspiration for platelet rich stem cell injection, use 0232T)

Rationale

In support of the establishment of code 0481T (autologous white blood cell concentration injection), the exclusionary parenthetical note following code 0232T has been revised with the addition of codes 20611 (arthrocentesis); 36415 (venipuncture blood collection); 36592 (central/peripheral catheter blood collection), and 0481T.

Refer to the codebook and the Rationale for code 0481T for a full discussion of these changes.

▲ **0254T**	Endovascular repair of iliac artery bifurcation (eg, aneurysm, pseudoaneurysm, arteriovenous malformation, trauma, dissection) using bifurcated endograft from the common iliac artery into both the external and internal iliac artery, including all selective and/or nonselective catheterization(s) required for device placement and all associated radiological supervision and interpretation, unilateral

▶(0255T has been deleted. To report, use 0254T)◀

Rationale

Code 0254T (endovascular aneurysm repair) has been revised, and code 0255T (radiological supervision and interpretation) has been deleted.

These changes were prompted by the identification of codes 34800-34806, 34825, and 34826 as services frequently billed together on the AMA/Specialty Society Relative Value Scale (RVS) Update Committee (RUC) Relativity Assessment Workgroup (RAW) screen. It was subsequently determined that all of the endovascular aneurysm repair codes should be revised by bundling the services with which they are frequently performed.

Because codes 0254T and 0255T are used to report endovascular aneurysm repair services, they have been bundled with their associated services. For 2018, code 0254T includes selective and/or nonselective catheterization(s) required for device placement and all associated radiological supervision and interpretation. Because radiological supervision and interpretation services have been bundled into code 0254T, code 0255T has been deleted.

Refer to the codebook and the Rationale for codes 34701-34713, 34714, 34715, and 34716 for a full discussion of these changes.

Clinical Example (0254T)

A 73-year-old male with a history of hypertension and computer-assisted detection (CAD) presents with a 6.5-cm abdominal aortic aneurysm (AAA), as well as bilateral common iliac aneurysms, that involve the distal left common iliac artery and the origin of the left internal iliac artery. The right internal iliac artery is chronically occluded. Medical comorbidities make him an increased-risk for open surgical repair. Endovascular aortic aneurysm repair is undertaken using a modular bifurcated prosthesis with two docking limbs, via bilateral open femoral artery exposures. A branch endovascular iliac artery stent graft is placed in the left common external and internal iliac arteries with a second covered stent deployed in the left internal iliac artery to achieve a seal-and-maintain pelvic perfusion through the left internal iliac artery.

Description of Procedure (0254T)

Bilateral open femoral artery exposure by groin incision for delivery of endovascular prosthesis is performed. For anticoagulation, patient is given IV heparin. Entry needles, guidewires, and sheaths are inserted into bilateral femoral arteries. Marker catheter is inserted and angiogram is performed to assess anatomy for endovascular aneurysm repair the location of internal iliac artery, and to exchange wire for stiffer lower esophageal sphincter (LES) guidewire. Branch iliac delivery device is inserted. The branch endovascular graft device is opened and prepared on the back table with appropriate flushing. The orientation of branch marker with fluoroscopy is checked, sheath is removed, and branch iliac delivery system is inserted through appropriate femoral artery over the stiff wire. Hydrophilic 0.018 nitinol wire is inserted through the device into the aorta. The snare is inserted through the contralateral sheath. The tip of the nitinol wire is snared and pulled through to form a through-and-through guidewire. The 8-French contralateral sheath is advanced over the 0.018 guidewire to the bifurcation, and angiogram is performed. The location of internal iliac artery is confirmed and proper orientation of branch iliac device is ensured. Branch iliac stent graft is deployed until side branch is exposed. Contralateral up-and-over sheath is advanced through the side branch and the targeted internal iliac artery is cannulated with another wire and guide catheter. After cannulation of internal iliac artery, the wire is exchanged for a supported wire. Balloon expandable covered peripheral stent is inserted up, over and into the internal iliac artery. The introducer sheath is withdrawn to deploy the external iliac component of the branch iliac device. The balloon expandable covered stent is deployed with a suitable overlap in the internal iliac artery. The covered stent is expanded with appropriate balloons to seat the internal iliac endograft. Completion angiography is performed, as appropriate. Activated clotting times (ACTs) are rechecked and monitored, as appropriate, during the procedure to ensure adequate anticoagulation. The remaining modular bifurcated prosthesis is deployed with two docking limbs. As appropriate, "balloon" is performed and completion angiography is performed to assess patency of limbs and presence or absence of endoleak. Bilateral femoral arteries are repaired after bilateral wires, catheters, and sheaths are removed from both femoral arteries, which is followed by closure of incisions in multiple layers.

▶(0293T, 0294T have been deleted)◀

Rationale

In accordance with CPT guidelines for archiving Category III codes, codes 0293T and 0294T (insertion of left atrial hemodynamic monitor) have been deleted to reflect current clinical practice.

0295T   External electrocardiographic recording for more than 48 hours up to 21 days by continuous rhythm recording and storage; includes recording, scanning analysis with report, review and interpretation

0296T   recording (includes connection and initial recording)

0297T   scanning analysis with report

0298T   review and interpretation

▶(0299T, 0300T have been deleted)◀

▶(For extracorporeal shock wave for integumentary wound healing, high energy, use 28899)◀

Rationale

In accordance with CPT guidelines for archiving Category III codes, codes 0299T and 0300T (extracorporeal shockwave) and all related parenthetical notes have been deleted. Unlisted code 28899 may be reported for extracorporeal shock wave for integumentary wound healing with high energy, if performed.

▶(0301T has been deleted)◀

▶(For focused microwave thermotherapy of the breast, use 19499)◀

Rationale

In accordance with CPT guidelines for archiving Category III codes, code 0301T (focused breast microwave therapy) has been deleted. Report code 19499 (unlisted procedure, breast) if focused microwave therapy of the breast is performed. To reflect the change, all related parenthetical notes have been revised as well.

▶(0302T, 0303T, 0304T, 0305T, 0306T, 0307T have been deleted)◀

Rationale

In accordance with CPT guidelines for archiving Category III codes, codes 0302T, 0303T, 0304T, 0305T, 0306T, and 0307T (insertion, removal, replacement, programming, and interrogation of an intracardiac ischemia monitoring system) have been deleted to reflect current clinical practice.

▶(0309T has been deleted)◀

▶(For arthrodesis, pre-sacral interbody technique, including disc space preparation, discectomy, with posterior instrumentation, with image guidance, including bone graft, when performed, lumbar, L4-L5 interspace, use 22899)◀

Rationale

In accordance with CPT guidelines for archiving Category III codes, code 0309T (pre-sacral interbody arthrodesis) has been deleted. Report code 22899 (unlisted procedure, spine) if pre-sacral interbody arthrodesis, including disc space preparation, discectomy, with posterior instrumentation, with image guidance, including bone graft, when performed, on the lumbar, L4-L5 interspace is performed.

To reflect the change, all related parenthetical notes have been revised as well. Similarly, the guidelines and parenthetical notes in the Diagnostic Radiology (Diagnostic Imaging) subsection in the Radiology section that are affected by this deletion have been revised accordingly.

▶(0310T has been deleted)◀

▶(For motor function mapping using non-invasive navigated transcranial magnetic stimulation [nTMS] for therapeutic treatment planning, upper and lower extremity, use 64999)◀

Rationale

In accordance with CPT guidelines for archiving Category III codes, code 0310T (non-invasive navigated transcranial magnetic stimulation [nTMS]) has been deleted. Report code 64999 (unlisted, nervous system) if motor function mapping using nTMS for therapeutic planning for the upper and lower extremity is performed.

To reflect the change, all related parenthetical notes have been revised as well. Similarly, the guidelines and parenthetical notes in the Psychiatry subsection in the Medicine section that are affected by this deletion have been revised accordingly.

0312T	Vagus nerve blocking therapy (morbid obesity); laparoscopic implantation of neurostimulator electrode array, anterior and posterior vagal trunks adjacent to esophagogastric junction (EGJ), with implantation of pulse generator, includes programming
0313T	laparoscopic revision or replacement of vagal trunk neurostimulator electrode array, including connection to existing pulse generator
0314T	laparoscopic removal of vagal trunk neurostimulator electrode array and pulse generator

0315T	removal of pulse generator
0316T	replacement of pulse generator
0317T	neurostimulator pulse generator electronic analysis, includes reprogramming when performed
▲ **0333T**	Visual evoked potential, screening of visual acuity, automated, with report

▶(For visual evoked potential testing for glaucoma, use 0464T)◀

#● **0464T**	Visual evoked potential, testing for glaucoma, with interpretation and report

▶(For visual evoked potential screening of visual acuity, use 0333T)◀

Rationale

Code 0333T (visual evoked potential [VEP]) has been revised to include the term "report" in the descriptor, in order to clarify that it includes documentation of the study result. New code 0464T has been added to describe VEP testing for glaucoma. Code 0464T is different from code 0333T in that it describes testing specifically for glaucoma and it includes interpretation and report. Code 0333T describes an automated test to screen for visual acuity. Cross-reference parenthetical notes to assist in appropriate code selection have been added following codes 0333T and 0464T.

Clinical Example (0333T)

A 3-year-old child presents for a well-child check. In addition, vision screening using an automated VEP machine is performed.

Description of Procedure (0333T)

The technician places three VEP electrodes on the child's head. The nurse turns on the machine and initiates the test. Music and graphics play on a computer screen while a series of six black-and-white stimuli alternate on a video display. The testing sequence lasts about five minutes. When this is completed, the nurse repeats the process for the other eye. When testing sequences for both eyes are completed, the output is saved for physician review.

Clinical Example (0464T)

A 66-year-old female presents with elevated intraocular pressure and possible glaucomatous changes in the optic nerve.

★ = Telemedicine   ✚ = Add-on code   ✗ = FDA approval pending   # = Resequenced code

Description of Procedure (0464T)

The patient has electrodes placed on the head and scalp. The patient is placed in front of a checkerboard for low-contrast testing to evaluate latencies in the magnocellular pathways, commonly damaged in glaucoma. The output is evaluated by the physician, and a report is prepared.

▶(0340T has been deleted. To report, use 32994)◀

Rationale

In support of the addition of code 32994 (pulmonary tumor cryoablation), Category III code 0340T (pulmonary tumor cryoablation) has been deleted.

Refer to the codebook and the Rationale for code 32994 for a full discussion of these changes.

0345T Transcatheter mitral valve repair percutaneous approach via the coronary sinus

(For transcatheter mitral valve repair percutaneous approach including transseptal puncture when performed, see 33418, 33419)

(Do not report 0345T in conjunction with 93451, 93452, 93453, 93456, 93457, 93458, 93459, 93460, 93461 for diagnostic left and right heart catheterization procedures intrinsic to the valve repair procedure)

(Do not report 0345T in conjunction with 93453, 93454, 93563, 93564 for coronary angiography intrinsic to the valve repair procedure)

▶(For transcatheter mitral valve implantation/replacement [TMVI], see 0483T, 0484T)◀

+ 0346T Ultrasound, elastography (List separately in addition to code for primary procedure)

Rationale

In support of the addition of codes 0483T and 0484T, a cross-reference parenthetical note has been added following code 0345T to direct users to report these new codes for transcatheter mitral valve implantation/replacement [TMVI].

Refer to the codebook and the Rationale for codes 0483T and 0484T for a full discussion of these changes.

Adaptive Behavior Treatment

0364T Adaptive behavior treatment by protocol, administered by technician, face-to-face with one patient; first 30 minutes of technician time

+ 0365T each additional 30 minutes of technician time (List separately in addition to code for primary procedure)

(Use 0365T in conjunction with 0364T)

▶(Do not report 0364T, 0365T in conjunction with 90785-90899, 92507, 96101-96155, 97127)◀

0368T Adaptive behavior treatment with protocol modification administered by physician or other qualified health care professional with one patient; first 30 minutes of patient face-to-face time

+ 0369T each additional 30 minutes of patient face-to-face time (List separately in addition to code for primary procedure)

(Use 0369T in conjunction with 0368T)

▶(Do not report 0368T, 0369T in conjunction with 90791, 90792, 90846, 90847, 90887, 92507, 97127)◀

Rationale

In support of the establishment of code 97127 (cognitive function intervention) and the deletion of code 97532 (cognitive skills development), the exclusionary parenthetical notes following codes 0365T and 0369T (adaptive behavior) have been revised to reflect the new code, 97127.

Refer to the codebook and the Rationale for code 97127 for a full discussion of the changes.

0402T Collagen cross-linking of cornea (including removal of the corneal epithelium and intraoperative pachymetry when performed)

(Do not report 0402T in conjunction with 65435, 69990, 76514)

▶A diabetes prevention program consists of intensive behavioral counseling that is provided in person, online, or via electronic technology, or a combination of both modalities.

Intensive behavioral counseling consists of care management, lifestyle coaching, facilitation of a peer-support group, and provision of clinically validated educational lessons based on a standardized curriculum that is focused on nutrition, exercise, stress, and weight management. Lifestyle coaches must complete a nationally recognized training program. The lifestyle coach is available to interact with the participants.

Codes 0403T and 0488T describe diabetes prevention programs that use a standardized diabetes prevention curriculum. For educational services that use a standardized curriculum provided to patients with an established illness/disease, see 98960, 98961, 98962. Use 0403T for diabetes prevention programs that are provided only in-person. Use 0488T for programs that are provided online or via electronic technology. Code 0488T includes in person components, if provided.◄

0403T   Preventive behavior change, intensive program of prevention of diabetes using a standardized diabetes prevention program curriculum, provided to individuals in a group setting, minimum 60 minutes, per day

►(Do not report 0403T in conjunction with 98960, 98961, 98962, 0488T)◄

#● 0488T   Preventive behavior change, online/electronic structured intensive program for prevention of diabetes using a standardized diabetes prevention program curriculum, provided to an individual, per 30 days

►(Do not report 0488T in conjunction with 98960, 98961, 98962, 0403T)◄

Rationale

Code 0488T has been established to report intense behavioral counseling through provision of online diabetes prevention program curriculum. In addition, new guidelines have been added to define the types of prevention programs and modalities that apply to the diabetes prevention codes.

Code 0488T describes an online/electronic delivery of behavior change intervention for the purpose of preventing diabetes. This code should be reported when following an online/electronic structured program for prevention.

New code 0488T has been resequenced to follow the existing code 0403T, which describes the delivery of a diabetes prevention program that uses a standardized curriculum in a group format with the intention of preventing the onset of diabetes. The difference between codes 0403T and 0488T is that code 0403T requires patients to be seen in an in-person setting, while code 0488T is intended for patients using an online/electronic program. Code 0488T also includes in-person components, if provided. Exclusionary parenthetical notes have been added following both diabetes prevention codes, precluding their use with each other and codes 98960-98962, which are used for educational services using a standardized curriculum provided to patients with an established illness or disease.

Clinical Example (0488T)

A 55-year-old female has a body mass index (BMI) of 30 and an elevated glucose level on her recent fasting plasma glucose test, indicating she is in the prediabetes range (between 100 and 125 mg/dL). Upon learning of the diabetes prevention program that is provided online or via electronic technology, she is enrolled.

Description of Procedure (0488T)

The patient is enrolled in the diabetes prevention program. After training, she receives educational lessons each week via online or electronic technology that is based on a standardized curriculum for education on lifestyle change; this is provided in combination with lifestyle health coaching. The trained lifestyle health coach facilitates interaction with a peer group, including guided discussion of lesson topics. The trained lifestyle health coach also answers questions related to the program, such as physical activity, meal planning, motivation, and avoiding triggers, and initiates intervention or troubleshooting based on the participant's remotely monitored weight and behavior tracking.

+ 0437T   Implantation of non-biologic or synthetic implant (eg, polypropylene) for fascial reinforcement of the abdominal wall (List separately in addition to code for primary procedure)

(For implantation of mesh or other prosthesis for open incisional or ventral hernia repair, use 49568 in conjunction with 49560, 49561, 49565, 49566)

(For insertion of mesh or other prosthesis for closure of a necrotizing soft tissue infection wound, use 49568 in conjunction with 11004, 11005, 11006)

►(0438T has been deleted. To report, use 55874)◄

0464T   Code is out of numerical sequence. See 0332T-0337T

● 0465T   Suprachoroidal injection of a pharmacologic agent (does not include supply of medication)

►(To report intravitreal injection/implantation, see 67025, 67027, 67028)◄

+● 0466T   Insertion of chest wall respiratory sensor electrode or electrode array, including connection to pulse generator (List separately in addition to code for primary procedure)

►(Use 0466T in conjunction with 64568)◄

● 0467T   Revision or replacement of chest wall respiratory sensor electrode or electrode array, including connection to existing pulse generator

►(Do not report 0467T in conjunction with 0466T, 0468T)◄

★ = Telemedicine   + = Add-on code   ✓ = FDA approval pending   # = Resequenced code

►(For revision or replacement of cranial nerve [eg, vagus nerve] neurostimulator electrode array, including connection to existing pulse generator, use 64569)◄

● **0468T**   Removal of chest wall respiratory sensor electrode or electrode array

►(Do not report 0468T in conjunction with 0466T, 0467T)◄

►(For removal of cranial nerve [eg, vagus nerve] neurostimulator electrode array and pulse generator, use 64570)◄

Rationale

Three Category III codes have been established to report insertion (0466T), revision or replacement (0467T), and removal (0468T) of respiratory sensor electrode or electrode array. Implantation of electrode or electrode array and pulse generator for some cranial nerves (eg, hypoglossal nerve) involves the insertion of a respiratory sensor into the chest wall to monitor breathing. Code 64568 is reported for the cranial nerve stimulator electrode or electrode array and the pulse generator, but it does not include the work of inserting the respiratory sensor electrode or electrode array into the chest wall. Therefore, add-on code 0466T has been established to reflect the insertion of the respiratory sensor electrode or electrode array into the chest wall, and is reported in conjunction with code 64568. Connection of the respiratory sensor to the pulse generator is included in code 0466T. The revision and removal codes 0467T and 0468T are stand-alone codes because the revision and removal of the respiratory sensor electrode or array may be performed independently. Parenthetical notes have been added to provide guidance on the appropriate reporting of these services.

Clinical Example (0465T)

A 45-year-old male with macular edema associated with noninfectious uveitis in the right eye is treated with a suprachoroidal injection of a drug into the right eye.

Description of Procedure (0465T)

During the eye examination, visual acuity and intraocular pressure are reviewed. The eye to be treated is confirmed. Informed consent is obtained, and any questions are answered. Any imaging studies such as optical coherence tomography, fluorescein angiography, and indocyanine green angiography are reviewed. The eye to be treated is reconfirmed and examined with slit lamp biomicroscopy and indirect ophthalmoscopy. The patient is placed in supine position.

Topical anesthetic is applied prior to subconjunctival injection of local anesthetic. Topical antiseptic with povidone iodine solution is applied to the injection site and lid margins. Using a proprietary vial adapter, the drug is drawn up and then transferred to a 1-cc microinjector that has an option of a 900-μm or 1100-μm microneedle. A lid speculum is placed. The injection location is measured with calipers at 4.0–5.0 mm from the corneal limbus, preferably temporal. The microinjector is primed, and the presence of 100 μL of drug in the syringe for injection is confirmed. With the microinjector held perpendicular to the ocular surface, the needle is inserted into the sclera.

Once the microneedle is inserted into the sclera, the hub of the needle is in firm contact with the conjunctiva and remains perpendicular to the ocular surface. The dimple is maintained with perpendicular positioning throughout the injection procedure. The plunger handle is gently pressed until loss of resistance to flow is observed, noted by plunger movement, and the drug is injected slowly over 5–10 seconds. The hub is maintained against the eye for 5–10 seconds after the injection is complete.

The needle is slowly removed from the eye while the injection site is simultaneously covered with a cotton swab. The cotton swab is held over the injection site with light pressure for a few seconds, and the lid speculum is removed. Optic nerve perfusion is confirmed with indirect ophthalmoscopy and/or visual acuity. Intraocular pressure is measured, when necessary. Eye and lid margins are irrigated with balanced salt solution to remove residual povidone iodine.

The patient is instructed in postoperative care with topical medications. Symptoms of potential complications are reviewed. Operative notes are completed.

Clinical Example (0466T)

A 46-year-old male presents with obstructive sleep apnea after failing positive airway pressure therapy. Examination shows airway collapse at the base of the tongue.

Description of Procedure (0466T)

The planned incision site is prepared and draped in a sterile fashion and injected with local anesthetic with epinephrine. A horizontal incision is made in the lateral chest wall. The incision is taken through the skin and subcutaneous tissue until the serratus anterior and pectoralis major muscles are identified. Dissection proceeds between these structures to the sixth intercostal space; external and internal intercostal muscles are identified. Blunt dissection extends between the intercostal muscles, avoiding the neurovascular bundle.

Category III 0042T-0504T

A sensor lead is placed between the intercostal muscles and secured with multiple permanent sutures to the fascia overlying the chest wall.

A subcutaneous tunnel is created to connect the sensor lead incision to the generator pocket. The sensor lead is attached to the generator, and respiratory sensing is verified. The sensor lead is repositioned if the sensor waveform is not adequate.

The sensor lead incision is irrigated with antibacterial solution and closed in multiple layers. A pressure dressing is applied at the conclusion of the surgery.

Clinical Example (0467T)

A 48-year-old male, who underwent placement of hypoglossal nerve, neuroelectrode array, pulse generator, and chest-wall sensor electrode, develops a malfunctioning sensor electrode. He undergoes replacement of chest-wall sensor electrode, including connection to the existing pulse generator.

Description of Procedure (0467T)

Incisions are made to access the chest-wall sensor and generator sites. Dissection proceeds to the sensor lead placed between the intercostal muscles. Once identified, the sensor is removed, and its lead is dissected from its subcutaneous tunnel to the generator pocket. The old sensor lead is removed, and a new sensor is placed to the chest wall, with its lead threaded to the generator and attached to it. Respiratory sensing is verified. The incision is closed, and a dressing applied, as needed.

Clinical Example (0468T)

A 48-year-old male, who underwent placement of hypoglossal nerve, neuroelectrode array, pulse generator, and chest wall sensor electrode, develops a malfunctioning sensor and/or electrode. He undergoes removal of the chest wall sensor electrode.

Description of Procedure (0468T)

Incisions are made to access the chest-wall sensor and generator, if needed. Dissection proceeds to the sensor, and a lead is placed between the intercostal muscles. Once identified, the sensor is removed, and its lead dissected from its subcutaneous tunnel to the generator pocket. They are removed. The incision is closed, and a dressing is applied, as needed.

● **0469T**   Retinal polarization scan, ocular screening with on-site automated results, bilateral

▶(Do not report 0469T in conjunction with 92002, 92004, 92012, 92014)◀

▶(For ocular photoscreening, see 99174, 99177)◀

Rationale

Code 0469T has been established to identify the use of a retinal polarization scan for ocular screening with automated results. Two parenthetical notes have been added following code 0469T. The first parenthetical note indicates that code 0469T should not be reported in conjunction with codes 92002, 92004, 92012, and 92014. The second parenthetical note indicates that codes 99174 and 99177 should be reported for ocular photoscreening. Similarly, the parenthetical note following codes 92002, 92004, 92012, 92014, and 99172 have been updated as well as a result of new code 0469T. In addition, a new parenthetical note has been added following codes 99174 and 99177 to instruct that code 0469T should be reported for retinal polarization scan.

Clinical Example (0469T)

A 3-year-old child presents to the pediatrician for an annual well-child visit. The pediatrician performs a vision screening. A retinal birefringence scanning test is ordered.

A 2-year-old child presents for an examination. There is a family history of amblyopia, and the parents report possible crossing of the eyes. Ocular examination is normal, but refraction indicates the presence of borderline amblyopia risk factors. The specialist orders a retinal birefringence scanning test.

Description of Procedure (0469T)

The child is positioned in front of the instrument. The retinal birefringence scanning is performed with the child looking at the instrument. The readout is a binocularity score of 40% with reduced fixation of the right eye. The physician considers referral threshold in the context of patient age, cooperation, and risk factors and makes a decision to refer.

● **0470T**   Optical coherence tomography (OCT) for microstructural and morphological imaging of skin, image acquisition, interpretation, and report; first lesion

★ = Telemedicine   ✚ = Add-on code   ✐ = FDA approval pending   # = Resequenced code

+● 0471T   each additional lesion (List separately in addition to code for primary procedure)

▶(Use 0471T in conjunction with 0470T)◀

▶(For optical coherence tomography for coronary vessel or graft, see 92978, 92979)◀

▶(For reflectance confocal microscopy [RCM] of the skin, see 96931, 96932, 96933, 96934, 96935, 96936)◀

Rationale

Codes 0470T and 0471T have been established to report optical coherence tomography (OCT) for microstructural and morphological imaging of the skin with image acquisition and interpretation and report. A parenthetical note has also been added to the Special Dermatological Procedures subsection to direct users to the correct codes to report OCT for microstructural and morphological imaging of the skin.

Currently, no specific code exists for OCT of the skin. Existing codes 0351T, 0352T, 0353T, 0354T describe OCT of the breast and/or axillary lymph nodes. In addition, codes 92978, 92979 describe OCT for a coronary vessel or graft. There are also codes (eg, 96931-96936) to report skin optical imaging technology, reflectance confocal microscopy (RCM), which are different from OCT because they consist of cellular and sub-cellular imaging of skin, rather than imaging of the microstructure and morphology of the skin. Instructional parenthetical notes that include this guidance have been added to help clarify the appropriate reporting of OCT services.

Because code 0471T is an add-on code that should be reported for each additional lesion, it is not intended to be reported as a stand-alone code. Therefore, an instructional parenthetical note has been added to identify the primary code (0470T) that should first be reported when this procedure is performed on each additional lesion.

Clinical Example (0470T)

A 63-year-old male with a history of actinic keratosis (AK) and nonmelanoma skin cancer (NMSC) is found to have nonpigmented lesions suggestive of NMSC on the head and neck. Optical coherence tomography (OCT) is ordered by the examining dermatologist.

Description of Procedure (0470T)

The physician reviews the clinical history and referral information. The OCT device is prepared for use by the technician. The technician uses the OCT device probe to scan the lesion. The lesion image record is selected for interpretation by the physician. The physician reviews

the set of OCT images associated with the lesion. A diagnostic report is completed. The report includes a list of the specific features observed in the OCT images that are diagnostic. On completion, a report that contains the physician's narrative description of the diagnosis is produced, and the relevant OCT images are labeled with the key diagnostically relevant features.

Clinical Example (0471T)

A 67-year-old female with a history of AK and NMSC is found to have five nonpigmented lesions suggestive of NMSC on the head and neck. OCT is ordered by the examining dermatologist.

Description of Procedure (0471T)

After scanning the first lesion, the technician uses the OCT device probe to scan each additional lesion, creating a lesion record on the OCT device for each lesion. The technician uses an alcohol swab to disinfect the OCT device probe.

After completing the interpretation and diagnostic report of the first lesion, the physician selects the next lesion record for interpretation. The physician reviews the set of OCT images associated with the lesion. A diagnostic report is completed for each lesion. The report includes a list of the specific features observed in the OCT images that are diagnostic. For each additional lesion, a report is produced that contains the physician's narrative description of the diagnosis, and the relevant OCT images are labeled with the key diagnostically relevant features.

● 0472T   Device evaluation, interrogation, and initial programming of intraocular retinal electrode array (eg, retinal prosthesis), in person, with iterative adjustment of the implantable device to test functionality, select optimal permanent programmed values with analysis, including visual training, with review and report by a qualified health care professional

● 0473T   Device evaluation and interrogation of intraocular retinal electrode array (eg, retinal prosthesis), in person, including reprogramming and visual training, when performed, with review and report by a qualified health care professional

▶(For implantation of intraocular electrode array, use 0100T)◀

▶(For reprogramming of implantable intraocular retinal electrode array device, use 0473T)◀

Rationale

Two new codes (0472T and 0473T) have been established to report the postoperative analysis and programming of a subconjunctival retinal prosthesis system.

Codes 0472T and 0473T describe the evaluation and interrogation of an intra-ocular retinal electrode array and may be used to treat patients with severe retinitis pigmentosa (RP) with bare light perception (BLP) or no light perception (NLP). These codes are distinguished by the type of programming of the intra-ocular retinal electrode array. Code 0472T describes the initial programming with interative adjustment of the implantable device to test functionality, while code 0473T includes reprogramming and visual training, when performed.

Codes 0472T and 0473T are different from the existing code 0100T (retinal prosthesis), which only includes the surgical procedure and not subsequent programming and reprogramming that are required to make the system operational. An instructional parenthetical note follows code 0100T has been added to identify the code that should be reported with code 0472T. In addition, two instructional parenthetical notes after code 0473T have been added to identify the code that should be reported with code 0473T.

Clinical Example (0472T)

A 67-year-old blind male with end-stage retinitis pigmentosa had an intraocular electrode array surgically implanted. This included placement of a subconjunctival retinal prosthesis receiver and pulse generator that requires visits with clinical staff to interrogate, evaluate, and perform customized programming of the retinal prosthesis system. Visual training is provided after completion of each programming session.

Description of Procedure (0472T)

After the retinal prosthesis is surgically implanted, it is custom programmed by trained clinical staff. The patient uses the retinal prosthesis to aid in the various functions and activities of daily living that can benefit from vision. Programming involves customizing the implant's stimulation levels to the patient's perceptual ability in order to achieve optimal device performance. After the patient has adequately healed from the implantation procedure, trained clinical staff analyze and program the equipment and provide extensive patient education on use and maintenance of the equipment. Clinical staff provide training to the patient and collect sensitivity threshold measurements on each electrode. Threshold levels are tested, verified, and adjusted, as necessary. Clinical staff create patient-specific stimulation parameters and programs based on

the thresholds. Clinical staff use the newly created stimulation program and special video filters to custom program the retinal prosthesis for the patient. Clinical staff adjust the camera angle and radiofrequency coil on the glasses to achieve optimal communication between the glasses and the implant. The clinical staff initiates a prolonged conversation about at home use and maintenance with the patient and caregivers.

Clinical Example (0473T)

A 67-year-old blind male with end-stage retinitis pigmentosa had an intraocular electrode array surgically implanted. This involved placement of a subconjunctival retinal prosthesis receiver and pulse generator. Initial programming of the retinal prosthesis system was performed and requires subsequent reprogramming. Visual training is provided after completion of each reprogramming session.

Description of Procedure (0473T)

After the initial postoperative programming sessions, follow-up reprogramming may be needed as the patient's perceptual levels change. In addition, after the patient gains home use and community experience, programming adjustments may be made so that the patient can use the system more effectively. The frequency of reprogramming varies from patient to patient, and it is typically conducted at three months, six months, and 12 months and annually, thereafter. The reprograming may include some of the procedures and steps included in the initial postoperative programming sessions as well as ongoing education on home use and maintenance.

● **0474T**   Insertion of anterior segment aqueous drainage device, with creation of intraocular reservoir, internal approach, into the supraciliary space

Rationale

New code (0474T) has been established to report the insertion of anterior segment aqueous drainage device into the supraciliary space via internal approach.

Code 0474T describes the internal approach of an anterior segment aqueous drainage device into the supraciliary space. The establishment of this code enables the availability of a separate code to report the procedure that is performed after cataract surgery is complete. Code 0474T differs from the insertion of anterior segment aqueous drainage device codes 0191T and 0376T in how the procedure is performed. Codes 0191T and 0376T are used to describe stent placement without guidewire placement or dissection in the extraocular reservoir.

Clinical Example (0474T)

A 68-year-old female with progressive visual field loss presents for surgery due to comorbid conditions of progressive cataract and open angle glaucoma, confirmed by prior optic nerve exam. The patient has consistent high measurements of intraocular pressure in spite of her pharmacologic regimen. She experiences significant disability due to visual field loss, contrast sensitivity, and diminished visual acuity, which prevents her from driving and maintaining her independence. She presents for cataract surgery with a microstent implant.

Description of Procedure (0474T)

The microstent procedure is performed after completion of cataract surgery but during the same surgical event for the treatment of mild to moderate primary open angle glaucoma. The physician injects a myotic agent and viscoelastic to ensure patency of the anterior chamber during the procedure. Visualization is confirmed by gonioscopy. A guidewire with a loaded stent is inserted through the cataract incision, with careful attention to avoid the highly vascularized 3, 6, and 9 o'clock positions. The preloaded guidewire is inserted into the supraciliary space, creating a deliberate cyclodialysis area for aqueous humor outflow. The 6-mm stent is placed into the supraciliary space, and the guidewire is retracted. The gonia lens is placed on the cornea to ensure appropriate stent placement. The patient is brought into recovery where intraocular pressure is monitored prior to discharge the same day.

- **0475T**   Recording of fetal magnetic cardiac signal using at least 3 channels; patient recording and storage, data scanning with signal extraction, technical analysis and result, as well as supervision, review, and interpretation of report by a physician or other qualified health care professional

- **0476T**   patient recording, data scanning, with raw electronic signal transfer of data and storage

- **0477T**   signal extraction, technical analysis, and result

- **0478T**   review, interpretation, report by physician or other qualified health care professional

Rationale

Four new Category III codes (0475T, 0476T, 0477T, 0478T) have been established to report recording of a fetal magnetic cardiac signal. Prior to 2018, no code specifically described this procedure. These four new codes enable the reporting of fetal magnetic cardiac signal recording; patient recording; data scanning; signal extraction; and review and interpretation.

Clinical Example (0475T)

A 25-year-old healthy gravida 4 para 3 (G4P3) pregnant female at 27 weeks gestational age presents for fetal magnetocardiography (fMCG) to evaluate fetal bradycardia (sustained regular fetal heart rate [FHR] of 110 beats/min, normal is >135/min). Fetal echocardiogram shows normal cardiac anatomy and function and confirms the low FHR.

Description of Procedure (0475T)

The fMCG procedure is performed inside a magnetically shielded room that attenuates electric and magnetic noise. Unlike magnetic resonance imaging, fMCG does not emit magnetic energy. The patient lies supine on a padded table, and a limited ultrasound is performed, followed by positioning of the superconducting quantum interference device over the patient's abdomen in close approximation to the fetal heart. Four or more 10-minute segments of fetal rhythm are recorded.

The data are processed to remove noise and the patient's MCG signal. A report is provided within hours to the patient's physician. The report contains a full-disclosure rhythm analysis, beat-to-beat heart rate trends, signal-averaged cardiac time intervals, and 3-lead rhythm strip with any identified arrhythmias. Based on fMCG, the fetal cardiologist determines that the fetus likely has congenital long QT syndrome (LQTS) and proceeds with cascade assessment of the family (ECGs in all first-degree relatives and genetic testing of the fetus prior to or at birth). The obstetrician determines that the patient's vitamin D and magnesium levels are low, and these are corrected. The patient's hospital chart is marked regarding risk of QT-prolonging drugs during pregnancy. The fetus is observed closely for LQTS arrhythmias (heart block, ventricular tachycardia) throughout the pregnancy. Perinatal coordination of care is completed.

Clinical Example (0476T)

A 25-year-old healthy G4P3 pregnant female at 27 weeks gestational age presents for fMCG to evaluate fetal bradycardia (sustained regular FHR110 beats/min, normal is >135/min). Fetal echocardiogram shows normal cardiac anatomy and function and confirms the low FHR.

Description of Procedure (0476T)

The fMCG procedure is performed inside a mobile truck-based unit equipped with the magnetically shielded room that attenuates electric and magnetic noise and the superconducting quantum interference device (SQUID) recorder. The patient lies supine on a padded table, and a limited ultrasound is performed, followed by positioning of the SQUID device over the patient's abdomen in close approximation to the fetal heart. Four or more 10-minute segments of fetal rhythm are recorded.

The electronic signal is encrypted and transmitted to a medical physics laboratory for further analysis by the company that provides the acquisition, a mobile MCG truck-based unit.

Clinical Example (0477T)

A 25-year-old healthy G4P3 pregnant female at 27 weeks gestational age presents for fMCG to evaluate fetal bradycardia (sustained regular FHR110 beats/min, normal is >135/min). Fetal echocardiogram shows normal cardiac anatomy and function and confirms the low FHR.

Description of Procedure (0477T)

The staff at the medical physics laboratory received the encrypted file. Signal separation, processing, and analysis are performed, and a report is generated. Because they are not physicians, the results are provided to a fetal cardiologist for interpretation and clinical decision making.

Clinical Example (0478T)

A 25-year-old healthy G4P3 pregnant female at 27 weeks gestational age presents for fMCG to evaluate fetal bradycardia (sustained regular FHR110 beats/min, normal is >135/min). Fetal echocardiogram shows normal cardiac anatomy and function and confirms the low FHR.

Description of Procedure (0478T)

The patient is seen in consultation by the fetal cardiologist at the referring hospital. The uninterpreted results provided to him or her by the medical physics laboratory is evaluated by the cardiologist. Measurements are made and the rhythm is analyzed, and a report is generated.

● **0479T**   Fractional ablative laser fenestration of burn and traumatic scars for functional improvement; first 100 cm2 or part thereof, or 1% of body surface area of infants and children

+● **0480T**   each additional 100 cm², or each additional 1% of body surface area of infants and children, or part thereof (List separately in addition to code for primary procedure)

▶(Use 0480T in conjunction with 0479T)◀

▶(Report 0479T, 0480T only once per day)◀

▶(Do not report 0479T, 0480T in conjunction with 0492T)◀

▶(For excision of cicatricial lesion[s] [eg, full thickness excision, through the dermis], see 11400-11446)◀

Rationale

Two new codes (0479T, 0480T) and three parenthetical notes have been established to report ablative treatment of burn and traumatic scars. For consistency throughout the CPT code set, several new parenthetical notes have been added in the Surgery section to support accurate reporting.

Ablative treatment of burn and traumatic scars procedure, which is new procedure in the CPT code set, may increase the functionality of contracted burn and traumatic scars using lasers and other energy devices. Code 0479T has been established to report fractional ablative laser fenestration of burn and traumatic scars for functional improvement for the first 100 cm² or part thereof, or 1% of body surface area. Add-on code 0480T has been established to report fractional ablative laser fenestration of burn and traumatic scars for each additional 100 cm², or each additional 1% of body surface.

Four parenthetical notes have been added to assist in the appropriate reporting of these new codes. The first parenthetical note indicates that code 0480T should be reported in conjunction with code 0479T because add-on code 0480T must never be reported as a stand-alone code. The second parenthetical note indicates that codes 0479T and 0480T should be reported only once per day. The third parenthetical note precludes reporting codes 0479T and 0480T with code 0492T. The fourth parenthetical note indicates that codes 11400-11446 should be reported for excision of cicatricial lesion(s).

Clinical Example (0479T)

A 45-year-old male burned in a house fire presents with hypertrophic scars and restriction of motion of his right forearm and hand. In spite of extensive skin grafting and physical therapy, the patient still has chronic discomfort and restricted range of motion of his elbow and wrist. He is unable to approximate his index finger and thumb sufficiently to hold a pen or handle household appliances with his dominant hand. The skin surface with scar and restricted motion is 30 cm² on his dorsal right hand and 50 cm² on his volar forearm including the antecubital area and elbow.

★ = Telemedicine   ✛ = Add-on code   ✗ = FDA approval pending   # = Resequenced code

Description of Procedure (0479T)

Scar areas associated with functional restriction are identified and confirmed. The patient is asked to perform range of motion exercises in order to document the degree of restriction at various body sites. Intralesional anesthesia is infiltrated into the dermis and subcutis, with topical anesthesia additionally applied under occlusion to the treatment sites.

Treatment fluence (or energy level) and the percentage of skin surface ablation (for fractional lasers, the distance between laser holes being drilled can be varied) are selected. Each scar section is sequentially treated with the laser. As needed, the spot size is adjusted and each targeted area treated with various fluences, which depends on the thickness and previous treatment response(s) of the individual scar(s). Care is taken to avoid inadvertent overlapping by checking sequential positioning and parameters of the treatment plan. If overlap is required, appropriate blocking templates are used to avoid treatment of uninvolved areas and to deal with geometric scar configurations that would preclude overlap avoidance.

The patient is monitored for pain as well as for skin surface reaction throughout the process. Treatment is modified based on observed tissue effects such as immediate ulceration, blistering, necrosis, or unremitting pain. The process is repeated and modified for each subsequent lesion that is treated. Once laser treatment is complete, topical corticosteroid is applied.

Multilayer occlusive and mildly compressive, nonstick dressings are applied. Slings or other appliances to restrict range of motion during healing are fitted.

Pain management and implementation of an appropriate plan are discussed with the patient. Care of the treated areas and gentle cleansing are discussed with patient. A one-week follow-up assessment is scheduled to ensure appropriate wound care and wound healing.

Clinical Example (0480T)

A 45-year-old male burned in a house fire presents with hypertrophic scars and restriction of motion of his right forearm and hand. He sustained similar burns to left shoulder and forearm including the antecubital space.

In spite of extensive skin grafting and physical therapy, the patient still has chronic discomfort and restricted range of motion of his shoulder and left elbow. He is unable to flex his elbow or raise his left arm to bath or shave. The initial 100 cm^2 of elbow and dorsal right hand has already been fractionally ablated. The procedure continues for a planned 170 cm^2 total fractional ablation.

Description of Procedure (0480T)

Additional treatment areas with functional restriction are identified prior to the initial fractional ablation. Intralesional anesthesia is injected into the dermis and subcutis, with any additional application of topical anesthesia. Treatment fluence (or energy level) and the percentage of skin surface ablation (for a fractional laser) is selected. The additional 70 cm^2 of scarred skin surface is treated.

● **0481T**　Injection(s), autologous white blood cell concentrate (autologous protein solution), any site, including image guidance, harvesting and preparation, when performed

▶(Do not report 0481T in conjunction with 20550, 20551, 20600, 20604, 20605, 20606, 20610, 20611, 20926, 36415, 36592, 76942, 77002, 77012, 77021, 86965, 0232T)◀

▶(Do not report 38220, 38221, 38222, 38230 for bone marrow aspiration for autologous white blood cell concentrate [autologous protein solution] injection. For bone marrow aspiration for autologous white blood cell concentrate [autologous protein solution] injection, use 0481T)◀

Rationale

New code 0481T has been established to report injections of autologous white blood cell concentrate/autologous protein solution. To support accurate reporting, two exclusionary parenthetical notes following code 0481T have been added: one to indicate the procedures that should not be reported with new code 0481T; and the other to indicate that codes 38220-38230 should not be reported for bone marrow aspiration for autologous white blood cell concentrate/autologous protein solution injection; however, code 0481T should be reported for bone marrow aspiration for autologous white blood cell concentrate/autologous protein solution injection.

Injections of autologous white blood cell concentrate/ autologous protein solution, which is a new procedure in the CPT code set, that involves a different component, ie, white blood cell concentrate, than what is currently reported with code 0232T (injection(s), platelet-rich plasma, any site, including image guidance, harvesting and preparation when performed).

Code 0481T describes injection(s), autologous white blood cell concentrate, which could assist in the treatment of diagnoses or conditions, such as osteoarthrosis and other similar disorders. For consistency throughout the CPT code set, numerous existing parenthetical notes in the Surgery, Radiology, and Pathology and Laboratory subsections have been updated to include reference to code 0481T. Similarly, existing parenthetical notes have been updated as well. The existing exclusionary parenthetical note following code 20551 has been revised to include code 0481T. A second instructional parenthetical note has been updated to specify that code 0232T is for harvesting, preparation, and injections of platelet-rich plasma. Similarly, the instructional parenthetical note following code 20926 has been updated.

The existing exclusionary parenthetical notes following codes 76942, 77012, and 77021 in the Radiology section have been revised to include code 0481T. Similarly, the instructional parenthetical notes following these codes have been updated to specify that code 0232T should be reported for harvesting, preparation, and injections of platelet-rich plasma.

The existing exclusionary parenthetical note following code 86965 in the Pathology and Laboratory section has been updated to specify that code 0232T should be reported for harvesting, preparation, and injections of platelet-rich plasma. Similarly, an instructional parenthetical note has been added to indicate that code 0481T should be reported for harvesting, preparation, and injections of autologous white blood cell /autologous protein solution.

Clinical Example (0481T)

A 57-year-old female presents with a ten-year history of osteoarthritis. Her pain has gradually increased in severity and duration, and she no longer achieves satisfactory pain relief with rest, ice, or acetaminophen. She tried a hyaluronic acid injection one year ago but did not achieve satisfactory results. She has visited her orthopedic surgeon. Her X rays show that she is Kellgren-Lawrence grade III and is not yet a candidate for a total joint arthroplasty.

Description of Procedure (0481T)

A total of 55 mL of blood is drawn from the patient and spun down to separate and concentrate the white blood cells. The autologous white blood cell concentrate is drawn up into a syringe and injected into the patient under image guidance (ultrasonic, fluoroscopic, computed tomography, or magnetic resonance guidance), which is not reported separately.

+● **0482T** Absolute quantitation of myocardial blood flow, positron emission tomography (PET), rest and stress (List separately in addition to code for primary procedure)

▶(Use 0482T in conjunction with 78491, 78492)◀

▶(For myocardial imaging metabolic evaluation, use 78459)◀

▶(For positron emission tomography [PET] myocardial perfusion study, see 78491, 78492)◀

Rationale

New add-on code 0482T has been established to report absolute quantitation of myocardial blood flow positron emission tomography at rest and stress. The new procedure is distinct from myocardial profusion imaging (78491, 78492) in that the new procedure includes a time domain and uses separate computer processing to generate measures of global and regional absolute myocardial blood flow. This procedure requires separate technologist's work, usually on a separate computer system and separate physician interpretive work. Absolute quantification of myocardial blood flow would only be performed in conjunction with procedures described in either code 78491 or 78492. Therefore, an inclusionary parenthetical note has been added to identify the primary codes that should be reported when this procedure is performed.

Two instructional parenthetical notes have been added to direct the user to refer to code 78459 (myocardial imaging metabolic evaluation) and to report either code 78491 or 78492 (positron emission tomography myocardial perfusion study).

Clinical Example (0482T)

A 65-year-old male with known coronary artery disease presents with symptoms suspicious for myocardial ischemia. He is not able to exercise. Pharmacologic stress/rest positron emission tomography (PET) myocardial perfusion imaging is recommended. Absolute quantitation myocardial blood flow (AQMBF) is also requested because more specific physiological assessment is desired.

Description of Procedure (0482T)

Images or PET myocardial perfusion imaging are acquired by the nuclear medicine/nuclear cardiology technologist in a manner that will allow quantitation of AQMBF (eg, images are acquired in three-dimension and list mode). The data are rebinned to allow AQMBF, and the dataset is exported to a dedicated computer/software program for AQMBF. In addition to the usual myocardial perfusion imaging processing, the rebinned data is processed by the technologist for AQMBF using a separate software program (and usually using a separate computer). The data are imported by the technologist into a computerized quality control software program for analysis of data quality. The processed dataset and quality control information are transferred to the interpreting physician. The quality control for AQMBF (eg, the bolus duration, peak, and plateau waveforms) are reviewed by the physician and, if quality is acceptable,

★ = Telemedicine   + = Add-on code   ✎ = FDA approval pending   # = Resequenced code

the numeric output of AQMBF in mL/g/min for rest, stress, and indexed/reserve flow for each coronary bed and for the global left ventricular are reviewed. The interactive polar map display is also reviewed by the physician. The AQMBF data are integrated with the static perfusion image data, attenuation maps, and clinical data, and a report is generated.

▶Codes 0483T, 0484T include vascular access, catheterization, balloon valvuloplasty, deploying the valve, repositioning the valve as needed, temporary pacemaker insertion for rapid pacing, and access site closure, when performed.

Angiography, radiological supervision and interpretation, intraprocedural roadmapping (eg, contrast injections, fluoroscopy) to guide the TMVI, left ventriculography (eg, to assess mitral regurgitation for guidance of TMVI), and completion angiography are included in codes 0483T,0484T.

Diagnostic right and left heart catheterization codes (93451, 93452, 93453, 93456, 93457, 93458, 93459, 93460, 93461, 93530, 93531, 93532, 93533) should **not** be used with 0483T, 0484T to report:

1. contrast injections, angiography, road-mapping, and/ or fluoroscopic guidance for the transcatheter mitral valve implantation (TMVI),

2. left ventricular angiography to assess or confirm valve positioning and function,

3. right and left heart catheterization for hemodynamic measurements before, during, and after TMVI for guidance of TMVI.

Diagnostic right and left heart catheterization codes (93451, 93452, 93453, 93456, 93457, 93458, 93459, 93460, 93461, 93530, 93531, 93532, 93533) and diagnostic coronary angiography codes (93454, 93455, 93456, 93457, 93458, 93459, 93460, 93461, 93563, 93564) performed at the time of TMVI may be separately reportable, if:

1. no prior study is available and a full diagnostic study is performed, or

2. a prior study is available, but as documented in the medical record:

   a. there is inadequate visualization of the anatomy and/or pathology, or

   b. the patient's condition with respect to the clinical indication has changed since the prior study, or

   c. there is a clinical change during the procedure that requires new evaluation.

For same session/same day diagnostic cardiac catheterization services, report the appropriate diagnostic cardiac catheterization code(s) appended with modifier 59, indicating separate and distinct procedural service from TMVI.

When cardiopulmonary bypass is performed in conjunction with TMVI, 0483T, 0484T may be reported with the appropriate add-on code for percutaneous peripheral bypass (33367), open peripheral bypass (33368), or central bypass (33369).◀

● **0483T** Transcatheter mitral valve implantation/replacement (TMVI) with prosthetic valve; percutaneous approach, including transseptal puncture, when performed

● **0484T** transthoracic exposure (eg, thoracotomy, transapical)

Rationale

Two Category III codes (0483T, 0484T) have been added for reporting transcatheter mitral valve implantation (TMVI)/replacement with prosthetic valve placement. Guidelines have also been added to explain the procedure and provide instruction on the appropriate reporting of these codes.

Prior to 2018, there were no codes for implantation/ replacement of the mitral valve. Codes 33418 and 33419 describe transcatheter repair of the mitral valve using prosthesis to supplement the mitral valve leaflets; while code 0345T describes mitral valve repair with placement of a device in the coronary sinus. Codes 0483T and 0484T describe transcatheter implantation or replacement of the mitral valve including the mitral valve leaflets. Code 0483T should be reported when the procedure is performed via percutaneous approach and code 0484T should be reported via transcatheter exposure.

The new guidelines state the services that are included in codes 0483T and 0484T. The guidelines regarding diagnostic right and left heart catheterization should be reviewed carefully, as there are criteria for when this service may be reported separately and criteria for when it may not be reported separately.

Clinical Example (0483T)

A 72-year-old male presents with severe, symptomatic mitral regurgitation. Prior diagnostic transesophageal echocardiography demonstrated mitral regurgitation with papillary muscle dysfunction and dilated left ventricle. He is evaluated by the valve team comprised of a cardiac surgeon and an interventional cardiologist who agree that the patient is high risk for open valve surgery. The team recommends transcatheter mitral valve implantation.

Description of Procedure (0483T)

After initiation of general anesthesia, femoral vein access is obtained. Under fluoroscopic guidance, a guidewire is inserted into the vein, and a sheath is inserted over the guidewire. Baseline right heart catheterization is performed through the sheath to obtain and assess intracardiac hemodynamics.

A catheter is placed over the wire through the sheath and advanced to the superior vena cava. The guidewire is removed, and a transseptal puncture needle is advanced through the catheter with entry into the right atrium confirmed using transesophageal echocardiographic guidance (coded separately when performed by a different physician or other qualified health care professional). After proper positioning is confirmed, the needle is advanced from the right atrium across the interatrial septum and into the left atrium. This may require multiple attempts. Entry and positioning in the left atrium is confirmed by fluoroscopy and transesophageal echocardiography. A dilator is placed through the transseptal puncture to prepare it for the valve delivery catheter.

After dilating the femoral venous access site and upsizing the venous sheath as needed, the valve delivery catheter is advanced via the vena cava to the right atrium and through the transseptal opening into the left atrium. The appropriate position for deployment of the valve within the mitral plane is determined by left ventriculography and transesophageal echocardiography. Under transesophageal echocardiography visualization to minimize the risk of entanglement in the chordae, the mitral valve may be crossed with the guidewire to aid in positioning the valve. The delivery catheter is positioned within the mitral valve. Under rapid pacing by a temporary transvenous pacemaker electrode, the transcatheter mitral valve prosthesis is expanded and deployed.

After deployment of the new valve prosthesis, the degree of regurgitation and resultant gradients are measured and evaluated. Right heart catheterization may be repeated to assess intracardiac hemodynamics. After confirmation of proper position and function of the valve by left ventriculography and transesophageal echocardiography, the delivery catheter is withdrawn. The atrial septal defect that was created is assessed with transesophageal echocardiography and, as needed, closed using an occluder device. Guidewires and sheaths are removed, and venous access is closed.

Clinical Example (0484T)

A 78-year-old female with multiple medical problems, including dialysis-dependent chronic renal failure, severe chronic obstructive pulmonary disease, and significant coronary artery disease, presents with severe,

symptomatic mitral regurgitation. Prior diagnostic transesophageal echocardiography demonstrated mitral regurgitation in the setting of class III–IV heart failure. In addition, she is noted to have severe mitral annular calcification and thrombus in her left atrial appendage. The patient is referred for transcatheter mitral valve implantation. The heart valve team comprised of a cardiac surgeon and an interventional cardiologist agree that the patient is high risk for open valve surgery. The team recommends transcatheter mitral valve implantation via thoracotomy with a transapical exposure.

Description of Procedure (0484T)

After initiation of general anesthesia, arterial access (eg, femoral) is obtained for reference pigtail catheter placement to obtain left ventriculography, as needed.

The heart is exposed through a thoracotomy (eg, fourth, fifth, or sixth intercostal space), and a pericardotomy is performed. Two circumferential pledgeted purse-string sutures are placed in the apex of the left ventricle, carefully avoiding the coronary vasculature. Anticoagulant therapy is administered to achieve therapeutic anticoagulation levels. A sheath may be introduced into the left ventricle. The pigtail catheter is advanced over a guidewire to inject contrast and obtain a fluoroscopic view of the mitral valve.

As situated by the purse-string sutures, a needle is inserted at the apex of the left ventricle followed by a guidewire. The apical dilator and sheath are advanced over the wire and through the left ventricular wall, with small cuts being made as necessary to facilitate insertion. The purse-string sutures are tightened to hold the sheath in place, and the guidewire and apical dilator are removed.

The pigtail catheter may be advanced into the left ventricle and contrast injected to obtain a left ventriculogram, noting the position of the native mitral valve. Using wires affixed to the ventricle, rapid ventricular pacing is performed during the ventriculogram. The pigtail catheter may then be withdrawn into the aorta.

While managing the apical sheath and under transesophageal echocardiography guidance (coded separately when performed by a different physician or other qualified health care professional), the mitral valve delivery catheter is advanced through the sheath and into the left ventricle. The delivery catheter is advanced up through the ventricle and across the mitral valve into the left atrium. The mitral valve prosthesis is positioned in the mitral plane, taking care to minimize the risk to the chordae. Under rapid pacing by a temporary transvenous pacemaker electrode, the transcatheter

★ = Telemedicine   ✚ = Add-on code   ✚ = FDA approval pending   # = Resequenced code

mitral valve prosthesis is expanded and seated. Fluoroscopy and transesophageal echocardiography are used continuously during deployment to monitor positioning.

After deployment of the new valve prosthesis, the degree of regurgitation and resultant gradients are measured and evaluated. After confirmation of proper position and function of the valve by fluoroscopy and transesophageal echocardiography, the delivery catheter is withdrawn and the purse-string sutures are tied to close the apical access. Guidewires and sheaths are removed. A chest tube is placed in the left pleural space and brought out below the wound. The subcutaneous tissues are closed in layers, and the skin incision is closed with a running intracuticular stitch.

● **0485T**   Optical coherence tomography (OCT) of middle ear, with interpretation and report; unilateral

● **0486T**   bilateral

Rationale

Two Category III codes (0485T, 0486T) have been established to report optical coherence tomography (OCT) of the middle ear. There are existing CPT codes for audiologic function testing in the Medicine section and for therapeutic procedures in the Surgery section, however, there was no codes to report OCT imaging of the middle ear. OCT is a method of imaging that generates cross-sectional, high resolution images. OCT is used to detect and assess the contents of the middle ear.

Codes 0485T and 0486T include interpretation of the images and report. Code 0485T should be reported when OCT is performed for one ear. Code 0486T should be reported when OCT is performed bilaterally.

Clinical Example (0485T)

A 3-year-old male presents with acute otitis media under standard otoscopic examination and recent history of repeat cases of otitis media. OCT is indicated to visualize through the eardrum and evaluate the presence and purulence of effusion in the middle ear and to determine appropriateness of antibiotic use or surgical intervention with tympanostomy tubes.

Description of Procedure (0485T)

A disposable tip is placed on the OCT imaging device, and the device is placed in the patient's ear canal. Near-infrared and standard video otoscopic images of the tympanic membrane (TM) and the underlying middle ear space are collected. A capture button is pressed at

multiple locations of interest in the ear, using the TM surface video for orientation and positioning. Once sufficient data have been collected, a subset of the images is chosen and areas of interest are indicated. A printout of selected data is obtained and reviewed by the physician or other qualified health care professional, who later dictates a report.

Clinical Example (0486T)

A 9-year-old male is referred by his pediatrician following recent, progressive unilateral hearing loss and recurring, foul-smelling otorrhea that is characterized as a scant but purulent discharge. Under standard otoscopic examination, the child presents with a retraction pocket of the attic; the tympanic membrane appears diffusely thickened. OCT is indicated to visualize through the eardrum and evaluate the presence of cholesteatoma and/or effusion in the middle ear and to determine appropriateness of surgical intervention.

Description of Procedure (0486T)

A disposable tip is placed on the OCT imaging device, and the device is placed in the patient's ear canal. Near-infrared and standard video otoscopy images of the tympanic membrane (TM) and the underlying middle ear space are collected. A capture button is pressed at multiple locations of interest in the ear, using the TM surface video for orientation and positioning. Once sufficient data have been collected, the imaging procedure is repeated for the other ear. A subset of the images is chosen and areas of interest are indicated. A printout of selected data from both ears is obtained and reviewed by the physician or other qualified health care professional, who later dictates a report.

● **0487T**   Biomechanical mapping, transvaginal, with report

0488T   Code is out of numerical sequence. See 0402T-0405T

Rationale

Code 0487T has been established for reporting transvaginal biomechanical mapping. Previously, code 58999 (unlisted procedure, female genital system) was used to report this procedure. Biomechanical mapping differs from an ultrasound procedure, as it uses a pressure-sensor probe to collect data, such as pelvic muscle strength, elasticity, tissue integrity and tone. These data produce images in real time, which are mapped to produce a report for physician review, interpretation, and report.

Clinical Example (0487T)

A 59-year-old G2P2 female patient presents complaining of increasing vaginal pressure, discomfort, backache, and bulging exacerbated by lifting and straining. The physician performs transvaginal biomechanical mapping to assess her pelvic floor support status, tissue elasticity, and muscle function and uses the information to determine the best course of treatment.

Description of Procedure (0487T)

The physician performs biomechanical mapping using a vaginal probe. Multiple (up to eight) subprocedures are completed to collect comprehensive biomechanical data for characterization of the vaginal and pelvic floor conditions. The procedure images are visualized in real time on a display to provide feedback to an operator. The information is mapped to produce an examination report in the form of a computer file and hard copy record, so that the physician can review and interpret the results.

The measurements include pressure response distribution along the anterior and posterior compartments of the vagina at probe insertion; pressure response pattern of pelvic floor support structures and ligaments at probe elevation; circumferential pressure mapping of the vaginal walls to assess irregularities along the entire vagina due to implants, hypertonic muscles, or scar tissue; pattern of involuntary muscle contractions along the entire vagina while performing the Valsalva maneuver; pattern of voluntary muscle contractions for anterior vs posterior and for left vs right sides; and pattern for involuntary muscle contraction (cough) and involuntary relaxation by assessing the muscles' resting tone and contraction strength distributions of the anterior and posterior compartments. The physician interprets the results, dictates a report, and discusses the results with the patient.

● **0489T**   Autologous adipose-derived regenerative cell therapy for scleroderma in the hands; adipose tissue harvesting, isolation and preparation of harvested cells including incubation with cell dissociation enzymes, removal of non-viable cells and debris, determination of concentration and dilution of regenerative cells

▶(Do not report 0489T in conjunction with 15876, 15877, 15878, 15879, 20600, 20604, 20926)◀

● **0490T**   multiple injections in one or both hands

▶(Do not report 0490T in conjunction with 15876, 15877, 15878, 15879, 20600, 20604, 20926)◀

▶(Do not report 0490T for a single injection)◀

▶(For complete procedure, use 0490T in conjunction with 0489T)◀

Rationale

Two new codes (0489T and 0490T) have been established to report autologous adipose-derived regenerative cell therapy. Autologous adipose-derived regenerative cell therapy assists in the treatment of diagnoses for conditions, such as sclerodactyly, progressive systemic sclerosis, CREST syndrome, and systemic sclerosis induced by drug and chemical.

The structure of codes 0489T and 0490T identifies tissue harvesting, isolation, and preparation of harvested cells, including incubation with cell dissociation enzymes, removal of non-viable cells and debris, determination of concentration, and dilution of regenerative cells.

Autologous adipose-derived regenerative cell therapy should not be reported with codes 15876, 15877, 15878, and 15879 (suction-assisted lipectomy), 20926 (tissue graft), or 20600 and 20604 (arthrocentesis, aspiration and/ or injection). Parenthetical notes have been added to provide instruction on the appropriate reporting of these services.

Clinical Example (0489T)

A 45-year-old female presents with a ten-year history of limited scleroderma with hand manifestations. She is experiencing sclerodactyly, Raynaud's phenomenon, and calcinosis of the fingers. Her hand symptoms are no longer adequately controlled with medications. She has significant impairment of hand function and is unable to perform many activities of daily living.

Description of Procedure (0489T)

Medical documentation is reviewed. The patient's abdomen or thighs are marked to delineate the area where adipose tissue is to be extracted. The patient is prepared and draped in a sterile manner. Tumescent fluid is used to infiltrate the targeted area of adipose tissue. Local anesthesia is administered. Using a scalpel, several 0.5-cm puncture incisions are made in the perimeter of the targeted area for the introduction of the infiltrating cannula. Tumescent fluid is injected evenly throughout the subcutaneous adipose tissue. After waiting approximately 10–15 minutes for the skin to appear visibly blanched from vasoconstriction, the tip of the collection cannula is placed through the same incision used for infiltration of the tumescent fluid. The plunger of the syringe is pulled back and locked in place in order to maintain negative pressure in the syringe.

Once negative pressure has been achieved in the syringe, the patient's skin and subcutaneous fat in the area to be extracted are grabbed with one hand, and the tissue is lifted away from the patient. With the other hand on the syringe, the cannula in the subcutaneous space is advanced and withdrawn in a fanning motion. The cannula that is passing between the fingers into the subcutaneous fat is monitored to avoid unintended penetration into the abdominal cavity and risk of visceral injury. Once the syringe is full of tissue, the cannula is removed from the patient, and the specimen is handed off. This is repeated with additional syringes until adequate tissue volume has been obtained for cell processing. Once extraction is complete, a dry sterile dressing is placed over the incisions, and a pressure garment is applied to the area to minimize postoperative edema and ecchymosis. With the extracted tissue sample, the autologous adipose-derived regenerative cell suspension is prepared according to manufacturer's instructions for adipose-derived regenerative cell processing, including incubation with cell dissociation enzymes and removal of nonviable cells and debris. The appropriate concentration and dilution of regenerative cells is determined for syringe preparation.

Clinical Example (0490T)

A 45-year-old female presents with a ten-year history of limited scleroderma with hand manifestations and is experiencing sclerodactyly, Raynaud's phenomenon, and calcinosis of the fingers. Her hand symptoms are no longer adequately controlled with medications. She has significant impairment of hand function and is unable to perform many activities of daily living.

Description of Procedure (0490T)

Moderate sedation is administered. Using aseptic technique and a 25-gauge needle, the lateral and medial areas of the proximal interphalangeal region and of the metacarpal-phalangeal joint of the thumb are punctured, and two subcutaneous injections are administered per digit. Per injection, the needle is inserted and placed approximately 5–10 mm away from the neurovascular bundle. When the needle is in the proper position, 0.5 mL of cell is delivered per site such that per digit, the injection volume of 1.0 mL is divided equally proximally and distally. After cell delivery is completed, a dry dressing is placed on each punctured area.

● **0491T**   Ablative laser treatment, non-contact, full field and fractional ablation, open wound, per day, total treatment surface area; first 20 sq cm or less

+● **0492T**   each additional 20 sq cm, or part thereof (List separately in addition to code for primary procedure)

▶(Use 0492T in conjunction with 0491T)◀

▶(Do not report 0492T in conjunction with 0479T, 0480T)◀

Rationale

Codes 0491T and 0492T have been added to report ablative laser treatment, non-contact, full field, and fractional ablation for treatment of open wounds. This is a new procedure that was not in the CPT code set. These codes are reported per day of wound treatment. Code 0491T should be reported for the first 20 square centimeters or less. Add-on code 0492T should be reported for each additional 20 square centimeters or part thereof.

Codes 0491T and 0492T should not be reported with new codes 0479T and 0480T (fractional ablative laser fenestration of burn and traumatic scar). Parenthetical notes have been added to provide instruction on the appropriate reporting of these services.

Clinical Example (0491T)

A 62-year-old smoker with clinical obesity presents with a venous leg ulcer. The patient has undergone treatment for venous stasis, including compression and endovenous thermal ablation. Despite these treatments, the ulcer has persisted. The ulcer is being treated with weekly debridement and antibiotics; 20 cm^2 is identified for ablative laser treatment.

Description of Procedure (0491T)

Topical anesthesia, such as lidocaine gel (2%–5%), is used prior to any sharp debridement. Sufficient analgesia is provided to perform the laser procedure without the addition of further anesthetic (Debridement is a separate procedure and is reported separately under existing debridement codes.) If a sharp debridement is not performed, topical anesthesia is still used prior to the laser procedure.

Full-field ablative scan: The full-field scanning handpiece is attached to the laser arm. Appropriate settings are entered into the laser for the full-field ablative scan. The handpiece is positioned over a portion of the wound, and the laser is activated with a foot switch. A 4-mm laser spot moves automatically in a serpentine pattern to cover 100% of the area targeted. The scan stops automatically when the area targeted under the handpiece has been scanned or when the foot switch is released. The handpiece is moved to the next section of the wound being treated, and the process is repeated until the entire wound bed overlapping the wound edge 2–3 mm has been treated. The resulting tissue effect is the removal of material (residual biofilm and senescent cells) from the entire surface area of the wound. Material is removed to a precise depth that is variable and determined by the health care professional. Current standard depth for full-field ablation is 100 μm.

The full-field handpiece is removed from the laser arm and replaced with a different handpiece that is used to provide the fractional treatment.

Fractional ablative scan: With the fractional handpiece attached to the laser, the health care professional enters the appropriate settings into the laser. The handpiece is positioned over a portion of the wound, and the laser is activated with a foot switch. A very small-diameter laser spot (430 μm) moves in a serpentine pattern, creating holes as it goes, but only in a portion of the area targeted under the handpiece. The scan stops automatically when the area targeted under the handpiece has been scanned or when the foot switch is released. The handpiece is moved to the next section of the wound being treated, and the process is repeated until the entire wound bed overlapping the wound edge 2–3 mm has been treated. The resulting tissue effect is the creation of extremely small-diameter holes. The holes are created in only a portion of the surface area of the wound. The health care professional determines what percentage of the surface area of the wound will be covered by these holes and how deep the holes will be. These settings are entered into the laser prior to activation. The current standard for fractional ablation is to create holes that cover 22% of the wound surface, with the holes being 500-μm deep. These tiny holes reach below the wound bed to bring up punctate bleeding that is stimulatory to wound healing.

Completion of both scans on larger wounds takes 20 minutes. The exact amount of time will vary based on the size of the wound.

Clinical Example (0492T)

A 62-year-old smoker with clinical obesity presents with a venous leg ulcer. The patient has undergone treatment for venous stasis, including compression and endovenous thermal ablation. Despite these treatments, the ulcer has persisted. The ulcer is being treated with weekly debridement and antibiotics. An additional 20 cm² requires ablative laser treatment.

Description of Procedure (0492T)

Topical anesthesia, such as lidocaine gel (2%–5%), is used prior to any sharp debridement. Sufficient analgesia is provided to perform the laser procedure without the addition of further anesthetic (Debridement is a separate procedure and is reported separately under existing debridement codes.) If a sharp debridement is not done, topical anesthesia is still used prior to the laser procedure.

Full-field ablative scan: The full-field scanning handpiece is attached to the laser arm. Appropriate settings are entered into the laser for the full-field ablative scan. The handpiece is positioned over a portion of the wound, and the laser is activated with a foot switch. A 4-mm laser spot moves automatically in a serpentine pattern to cover 100% of the area targeted. The scan stops automatically when the area targeted under the handpiece has been scanned or when the foot switch is released. The handpiece is moved to the next section of the wound to be treated, and the process is repeated until the entire wound bed overlapping the wound edge 2–3 mm has been treated. The resulting tissue effect is the removal of material (residual biofilm and senescent cells) from the entire surface area of the wound. Material is removed to a precise depth that is variable and determined by the health care professional. Current standard depth for full field ablation is 100 μm.

The full-field handpiece is removed from the laser arm and replaced with a different handpiece that is used to provide the fractional treatment.

Fractional ablative scan: With the fractional handpiece attached to the laser. The health care professional enters the appropriate settings into the laser. The handpiece is positioned over a portion of the wound, and the laser is activated with a foot switch. A very small-diameter laser spot (430 μm) moves in a serpentine pattern, creating holes as it goes, but only in a portion of the area targeted under the handpiece. The scan stops automatically when the area targeted under the handpiece has been scanned or when the footswitch is released. The handpiece is moved to the next section of the wound being treated, and the process is repeated until the entire wound bed overlapping the wound edge 2–3 mm has been treated. The resulting tissue effect is the creation of extremely small-diameter holes. The holes are created in only a portion of the surface area of the wound. The health care professional determines what percent of the surface area of the wound will be covered by these holes and how deep the holes will be. These settings are entered into the laser prior to activation. The current standard for fractional ablation is to create holes that cover 22% of the wound surface, with the holes being 500-μm deep. These tiny holes reach below the wound bed to bring up punctate bleeding that is stimulatory to wound healing.

Completion of both scans on larger wounds takes 20 minutes. The exact amount of time will vary based on the size of the wound.

● **0493T**   Near-infrared spectroscopy studies of lower extremity wounds (eg, for oxyhemoglobin measurement)

★ = Telemedicine   ✚ = Add-on code   ⅄ = FDA approval pending   # = Resequenced code

Rationale

Code 0493T has been established to report near-infrared spectroscopy studies of lower extremity wounds.

In 2012, code 0286T was created to report near-infrared spectroscopy studies of lower extremity wounds. Category III codes have an archive date of 5 years following their creation. As such, code 0286T was archived in January 2017. Due to an interest to continue tracking this procedure, it was reinstated as code 0493T.

Near-infrared spectroscopy is used to measure the oxy-hemoglobin and total hemoglobin levels from blood vessels in wound tissue. It is a non-invasive physiological study, which assists in the treatment of diagnoses or conditions, such as ulcers of lower limbs, gangrene, and diabetes mellitus with an ulcer. Data outputs are generated in the form of concentrations of oxygenated hemoglobin and total hemoglobin in the blood vessels in the wound, which are evaluated by the clinician to assess the wound.

Clinical Example (0493T)

A 65-year-old female presents with a heel ulcer that is approximately 10 cm^2 and has not progressed to healing in the past 3–4 weeks. The patient has a history of diabetes mellitus (type 2) with related complications, including diabetic neuropathy. The patient is seen by the clinician on a regular basis for evaluation and treatment. Near-infrared spectroscopy is used to assess tissue beneath the surface in order to guide treatment.

Description of Procedure (0493T)

A noninvasive near-infrared spectroscopy is performed. The near-infrared spectroscopy device is turned on, warmed, and calibrated prior to patient measurement. The patient is placed on the examination table with the foot at the distal end of the table. Any existing wound dressings are removed. The clinician cleans the wound and assesses it visually, including surrounding tissue. Size measurements and pictures are taken. Patient data are entered into the device computer. A sterile single-use cover is placed on the device (to prevent cross contamination), and the patient's wound is interrogated with the device in up to 10 locations. Data output is in the form of concentrations of oxygenated hemoglobin and total hemoglobin in the blood vessels in the wound. The clinician evaluates these outputs to assess wound healing progression, comparing results on a weekly or biweekly basis, to determine the need for changes in clinical approach.

● **0494T** Surgical preparation and cannulation of marginal (extended) cadaver donor lung(s) to ex vivo organ perfusion system, including decannulation, separation from the perfusion system, and cold preservation of the allograft prior to implantation, when performed

● **0495T** Initiation and monitoring marginal (extended) cadaver donor lung(s) organ perfusion system by physician or qualified health care professional, including physiological and laboratory assessment (eg, pulmonary artery flow, pulmonary artery pressure, left atrial pressure, pulmonary vascular resistance, mean/peak and plateau airway pressure, dynamic compliance and perfusate gas analysis), including bronchoscopy and X ray when performed; first two hours in sterile field

+● **0496T** each additional hour (List separately in addition to code for primary procedure)

▶(Report 0496T in conjunction with 0495T)◀

Rationale

Codes 0494T, 0495T, and 0496T have been established to report ex-vivo assessment procedures of marginal donor lungs prior to transplantation.

There are existing codes to describe the backbench preparation of cadaver donor lung allografts (32855, 32856), which includes dissection of the allograft from surrounding soft tissues to prepare the pulmonary venous/atrial cuff, pulmonary artery, and bronchus. Ex-vivo function assessment is performed prior to the backbench work and transplantation to observe and evaluate the organ's function to determine whether the lung(s) is viable for transplant. Prior to 2018, these services were reported using code 32999 (unlisted procedure, lungs and pleura).

Code 0494T describes the surgical preparation of the marginal cadaver donor lung and cannulation to the ex-vivo perfusion system. Code 0495T describes the initiation and the first two hours of monitoring of the donor lung on the perfusion system. Add-on code 0496T should be reported for each additional hour of monitoring, and it should be reported in conjunction with code 0495T.

Clinical Example (0494T)

A cadaver donor lung(s) allograft is determined to not meet the standard criteria for lung transplantation. However, it may be transplantable if there is more time to observe and evaluate the organ's function and to determine whether the lung(s) is viable for transplant.

Description of Procedure (0494T)

The lung allograft is received by the transplant hospital in a sterile container and is maintained in cold preservation solution. The surgeon requests and confirms that a sterile field is set up in the operating room, with appropriate instruments for cannulation and perfusion of the allograft. An appropriate recipient has been identified. The correct identification process is carried out to make sure that the allograft is being allocated to the correct recipient. The surgeon makes the appropriate arrangements with the operating room staff to allow for sterile dissection, cannulation, and perfusion of the organ in coordination with the recipient procedure. The surgeon scrubs and gowns. The allograft is removed from the sterile container and placed on a sterile table, on ice, while being bathed in cold preservation solution. The allograft is inspected to be certain that it is grossly intact and that its appearance is acceptable for ex vivo lung perfusion.

On ice, with continuous bathing in cold preservation solution, the left atrium and pulmonary artery are cannulated to allow for perfusion of the Steen solution and other necessary critical components (eg, antibiotics). The cannulated allograft is placed in a sterile organ chamber retrograde perfused to de-air and then antegrade perfused for evaluation. The allograft is warmed to normothermia. At 32°C (89.6°F), the trachea is cannulated and lung protective ventilation is initiated.

Clinical Example (0495T)

A cadaver donor lung(s) allograft that has been determined to not meet the standard criteria for lung transplantation was cannulated for further evaluation of suitability for transplant.

Description of Procedure (0495T)

The ex vivo function of the lung is physiologically assessed hourly for up to two hours for pulmonary artery flow, pulmonary artery pressure, left atrial pressure, pulmonary vascular resistance, mean/peak and plateau airway pressure, dynamic compliance, and perfusate gas analysis. A bronchoscopy and/or X ray may also be performed.

Clinical Example (0496T)

A cadaver donor lung(s) allograft that has been determined to not meet the standard criteria for lung transplantation was cannulated to an ex vivo organ perfusion system and evaluated for two hours. It now requires additional monitoring on the system for further evaluation of suitability for transplant.

Description of Procedure (0496T)

The ex vivo function of the cadaver donor lung(s) is physiologically assessed hourly for pulmonary artery flow, pulmonary artery pressure, left atrial pressure, pulmonary vascular resistance, mean/peak and plateau airway pressure, dynamic compliance, and perfusate gas analysis. A bronchoscopy and/or X ray may also be performed. Code 0496T is used to describe each additional hour of the ongoing physiologic assessment.

● **0497T**   External patient-activated, physician- or other qualified health care professional-prescribed, electrocardiographic rhythm derived event recorder without 24 hour attended monitoring; in-office connection

● **0498T**   review and interpretation by a physician or other qualified health care professional per 30 days with at least one patient-generated triggered event

▶(Do not report 0497T, 0498T in conjunction with 93040, 93041, 93042, 93228, 93229, 93268, 93271, 93272, 0295T, 0296T, 0297T, 0298T)◀

Rationale

Codes 0497T and 0498T have been established to report external patient-activated prescribed electrocardiographic (EKG) rhythm-derived event recording without 24-hour attended monitoring.

Existing code 93268 describes external patient-activated or auto-activated EKG rhythm-derived event recording with 24-hour attended monitoring. However, there was no mechanism to report services without the 24-hour attended monitoring. Codes 0497T and 0498T should be reported when the services are provided without 24-hour monitoring. Code 0497T describes the in-office connection of the device and code 0498T describes the review and interpretation per 30 days, with at least one patient-generated triggered event.

An exclusionary parenthetical note has been added listing the codes with which codes 0497T and 0498T should not be reported.

Clinical Example (0497T)

A 66-year-old female with a history of hypertension has intermittent palpitations. Several Holter monitors have been performed but are unrevealing. She is referred to a cardiologist who suspects she may have paroxysmal atrial fibrillation.

★ = Telemedicine   ✦ = Add-on code   ✔ = FDA approval pending   # = Resequenced code

Description of Procedure (0497T)

A physician or other qualified health care professional performs in-office teaching for the patient on the activation and use of an external, patient-activated electrocardiographic event recorder that transmits data via the patient's smartphone to a remote site.

Clinical Example (0498T)

A 66-year-old female with a history of hypertension has intermittent palpitations. Several Holter monitors have been performed but are unrevealing. She is referred to a cardiologist who suspects she may have paroxysmal atrial fibrillation. She is now using an external, patient-activated electrocardiographic event recorder to record her cardiac activity.

Description of Procedure (0498T)

A physician or other qualified health care professional reviews and interprets the summary report of the patient's electrocardiogram (EKG) recordings that were submitted via the patient's smartphone to the online application. Every 30 days, the summary report is created automatically in the online application. To facilitate review, the EKG recordings in the report are labeled by an automated algorithm into three categories: possible atrial fibrillation, normal sinus rhythm, or unclassified (all other EKGs other than atrial fibrillation and normal sinus rhythm). The physician or other qualified health care professional report includes assessment of heart rate trends (minimum, maximum, and average heart rates), review and interpretation of EKG recordings, and review of symptoms reported with EKG recordings to determine if a correlative symptomatic arrhythmia exists. At least one EKG recording/submission is required per 30 days. The report is edited, reviewed, and signed by a physician or other qualified health care professional, and the report is transmitted to the patient's medical record.

● **0499T**   Cystourethroscopy, with mechanical dilation and urethral therapeutic drug delivery for urethral stricture or stenosis, including fluoroscopy, when performed

   ►(Do not report 0499T in conjunction with 52281, 52283)◄

Rationale

Code 0499T has been established for reporting urethral therapeutic drug delivery via cystourethroscopy including fluoroscopy. Code 0499T describes cystourethroscopy with mechanical dilation including fluoroscopy to treat urethral stricture disease. Fluoroscopy is included in code 0499T and should not be reported separately.

Code 0499T is different from the existing code 52281 (cystourethroscopy), as code 52281 does not include delivery of a therapeutic drug. In addition, code 0499T is different from existing code 52283, in that code 52283 describes injection of a steroid but does not include dilation. Code 0499T should not be reported with either code 52281 or 52283.

Clinical Example (0499T)

A 60-year-old male who underwent transurethral resection of the prostate two years ago for benign prostatic hyperplasia presents with daytime frequency, nocturia, and decreased stream. A cystoscopy is performed, and a urethral stricture is found and treated with therapeutic drug delivery.

Description of Procedure (0499T)

The patient is placed in the lithotomy position. A cystoscope is passed through the urethra toward the bladder. A guidewire is placed through the urethra and through the working channel of the cystoscope until the tip reaches the bladder. A predilation catheter is tracked over the guidewire. Using fluoroscopy, the position of the balloon radiopaque markers are checked to ensure their correct position. The stricture is predilated using a standard 20F uncoated balloon. The physician ensures that the urethra is flushed with saline and that the bladder is filled with saline before introduction of the drug-coated balloon. The drug-coated balloon is placed across the predilated stricture with the cystoscope proximal to the balloon to visualize proper placement. The balloon is left in position without inflation. Using fluoroscopy, the balloon radiopaque markers are checked to ensure they are in the correct position. The balloon is inflated with a 50:50 contrast solution. Pressure is maintained while drug delivery takes place. The rated burst pressure of 14 ATM is not exceeded. The device and cystoscope are removed. A urinary catheter is inserted, if required.

● **0500T**   Infectious agent detection by nucleic acid (DNA or RNA), Human Papillomavirus (HPV) for five or more separately reported high-risk HPV types (eg, 16, 18, 31, 33, 35, 39, 45, 51, 52, 56, 58, 59, 68) (ie, genotyping)

▶(For reporting four or fewer separately reported high-risk HPV types, see 87624, 87625)◀

▶(For reporting of separately reported high-risk Human Papillomavirus [HPV] types 16, 18 and 45, if performed, use 87625)◀

▶(Do not report 0500T in conjunction with 87624 or 87625 for the same procedure)◀

Rationale

Code 0500T has been added to report human papillomavirus (HPV) detection by nucleic acid (DNA or RNA) detection of high-risk HPV types. Existing codes 87624 and 87625 describe testing for four or fewer separately reported results of high-risk HPV types. Code 87625 describes testing for types 16, 18, and 45 only. Code 0500T has been added to report five or more separately reported results of high-risk HPV types. Parenthetical notes have been added to provide instruction on the appropriate reporting of HPV testing.

Clinical Example (0500T)

A 34-year-old female is screened for cervical cancer using Papanicolaou (Pap) smear. A test for human papillomavirus (HPV) detection and genotyping for high-risk HPV (hrHPV) is requested.

Description of Procedure (0500T)

An aliquot from the liquid-based Pap vial is subjected to real-time polymerase chain reaction HPV detection and genotyping. A result of positive for hrHPV type 31 is obtained and separately reported.

● **0501T**   Noninvasive estimated coronary fractional flow reserve (FFR) derived from coronary computed tomography angiography data using computation fluid dynamics physiologic simulation software analysis of functional data to assess the severity of coronary artery disease; data preparation and transmission, analysis of fluid dynamics and simulated maximal coronary hyperemia, generation of estimated FFR model, with anatomical data review in comparison with estimated FFR model to reconcile discordant data, interpretation and report

● **0502T**   data preparation and transmission

● **0503T**   analysis of fluid dynamics and simulated maximal coronary hyperemia, and generation of estimated FFR model

● **0504T**   anatomical data review in comparison with estimated FFR model to reconcile discordant data, interpretation and report

▶(Report 0501T, 0502T, 0503T, 0504T one time per coronary CT angiogram)◀

▶(Do not report 0501T in conjunction with 0502T, 0503T, 0504T)◀

Rationale

Codes 0501T, 0502T, 0503T, and 0504T have been added to report non-invasive estimated coronary fractional flow reserve (FFR). FFR uses computational fluid dynamics and simulated maximal coronary hyperemia to compute fractional flow reserve measurements from data obtained from an existing imaging service. Previously, either code 76497 (computed tomography procedure, unlisted) or 93799 or (cardiovascular procedure or service, unlisted) were used to report this procedure. Code 0501T contains all of the components within codes 0502T, 0503T, and 0504T. Code 0502T describes the data preparation and transmission; code 0503T describes the analysis and generation of the FFR model; and code 0504T describes the anatomical data review. Two parenthetical notes have been added to provide instruction on the appropriate reporting of these services.

Clinical Example (0501T)

A 67-year-old patient with chest pain had a coronary computed tomographic angiography performed that showed coronary artery plaque and lumen narrowing of moderate severity (60% of the diameter narrowed) in the left anterior descending and right coronary arteries. An estimated coronary fractional flow reserve (FFR) analysis is indicated.

Description of Procedure (0501T)

The technician extracts the necessary biometric and demographic data on the patient from the medical records system and locates and transmits the necessary images after deidentification. The data are processed through an algorithm that analyzes anatomy, topology, pathology, lumen extraction, myocardial mass, and modeling. The system calculates computational fluid dynamics, which apply physiologic data unique to the patient and simulate hyperemia. The computed noninvasive estimated coronary FFR values are displayed in a color-coded report. The report provides the noninvasive estimated coronary FFR values at specific points along each artery/system; an interactive Web-based viewer allows the physician to further interrogate specific areas of interest at each point along the coronary arteries and system.

Once the data are processed and returned to the physician, the physician accesses the Web-based interactive viewer. This allows the physician to examine and query the entire model and capture noninvasive estimated coronary FFR values anywhere within the coronary tree. The physician reviews the anatomical data and compares it with the estimated FFR model to reconcile discordant data, evaluate multiple and sequential lesions, and determine likely false-positive and false-negative results. This approach allows the imager and the interventional cardiologist to determine the location of the disease burden and the lesion with the most hemodynamic significance, allowing for a targeted interventional approach that yields the most benefit to the patient. A final report is prepared, notated, and documented in the patient's record. The study results are communicated to the patient and the referring physician to facilitate appropriate patient management.

Clinical Example (0502T)

A 67-year-old patient with chest pain had a coronary computed tomographic angiography study performed that showed coronary artery plaque and lumen narrowing of moderate severity (60% of the diameter narrowed) in the left anterior descending and right coronary arteries.

Description of Procedure (0502T)

The necessary biometric and demographic data on the patient are extracted by the technician from the medical records system. The necessary images are located and transmitted after deidentification.

Clinical Example (0503T)

A 67-year-old patient with chest pain had a coronary computed tomographic angiography performed that showed coronary artery plaque and lumen narrowing of moderate severity (60% of the diameter narrowed) in the left anterior descending and right coronary arteries. An estimated coronary FFR analysis is indicated.

Description of Procedure (0503T)

The necessary biometric and demographic data on the patient are extracted by the technician from the medical records system. The necessary images are located and transmitted after deidentification. Upon receipt, the data are processed through an algorithm that analyzes anatomy, topology, pathology, lumen extraction, myocardial mass, and modeling. The system computes computational fluid dynamics, which apply physiologic data unique to the patient and simulate hyperemia. The computed noninvasive estimated coronary FFR values are displayed in a color-coded report. The report provides the noninvasive estimated coronary FFR values at specific points along each artery/system; a Web-based interactive viewer allows the physician to further interrogate specific areas of interest at each point along the coronary arteries and system.

Clinical Example (0504T)

A 67-year-old patient with chest pain had a coronary computed tomographic angiography performed that showed coronary artery plaque and lumen narrowing of moderate severity (60% of the diameter narrowed) in the left anterior descending and right coronary arteries. An estimated coronary FFR analysis is indicated.

Description of Procedure (0504T)

Once the data are processed and returned to the physician, the physician accesses the Web-based interactive viewer. This allows the physician to examine and query the entire model and capture noninvasive estimated coronary FFR values anywhere within the coronary tree. The physician reviews the anatomy and compares it with the estimated FFR model to reconcile discordant data, evaluate multiple and sequential lesions, and determine possible false-positive and false-negative result. This approach allows the imager and the interventional cardiologist to determine the location of the disease burden and the lesion with the most hemodynamic significance, allowing for a targeted interventional approach that yields the most benefit to the patient. A final report is prepared, notated, and documented in patient's record. The study results are communicated to the patient and the referring physician to facilitate appropriate patient management.

Notes

Appendix A

Appendix A has been updated to include two new modifiers: modifier 96 to allow reporting of habilitative services to help an individual keep, learn, or improve skills and functioning for daily living; and modifier 97 to allow reporting of rehabilitative services to help an individual keep, get back, or improve skills and functioning for daily living that have been lost or impaired because the individual was sick, hurt, or disabled.

Summary of Additions, Deletions, and Revisions

The summary of changes shows the actual changes that have been made to the code descriptors.

New codes appear with a bullet (•) and are indicated as "Code added." Revised codes are preceded with a triangle (▲). Within revised codes, the deleted language appears with a ~~strikethrough~~, while new text appears underlined.

The ✔ symbol is used to identify codes for vaccines that are pending FDA approval. The # symbol is used to identify codes that have been resequenced. CPT add-on codes are annotated by the + symbol. The ⊘ symbol is used to identify codes that are exempt from the use of modifier 51. The ★ symbol is used to identify codes that may be used for reporting telemedicine services.

Modifier	Modifier Descriptor
96	▶**Habilitative Services:** When a service or procedure that may be either habilitative or rehabilitative in nature is provided for habilitative purposes, the physician or other qualified health care professional may add modifier 96 to the service or procedure code to indicate that the service or procedure provided was a habilitative service. Habilitative services help an individual learn skills and functioning for daily living that the individual has not yet developed, and then keep and/or improve those learned skills. Habilitative services also help an individual keep, learn, or improve skills and functioning for daily living.◀
97	▶**Rehabilitative Services:** When a service or procedure that may be either habilitative or rehabilitative in nature is provided for rehabilitative purposes, the physician or other qualified health care professional may add modifier 97 to the service or procedure code to indicate that the service or procedure provided was a rehabilitative service. Rehabilitative services help an individual keep, get back, or improve skills and functioning for daily living that have been lost or impaired because the individual was sick, hurt, or disabled.◀

Appendix A

Modifiers

96 ▶**Habilitative Services**: When a service or procedure that may be either habilitative or rehabilitative in nature is provided for habilitative purposes, the physician or other qualified health care professional may add modifier 96 to the service or procedure code to indicate that the service or procedure provided was a habilitative service. Habilitative services help an individual learn skills and functioning for daily living that the individual has not yet developed, and then keep and/or improve those learned skills. Habilitative services also help an individual keep, learn, or improve skills and functioning for daily living.◀

97 ▶**Rehabilitative Services**: When a service or procedure that may be either habilitative or rehabilitative in nature is provided for rehabilitative purposes, the physician or other qualified health care professional may add modifier 97 to the service or procedure code to indicate that the service or procedure provided was a rehabilitative service. Rehabilitative services help an individual keep, get back, or improve skills and functioning for daily living that have been lost or impaired because the individual was sick, hurt, or disabled.◀

Rationale

Modifiers 96 and 97 have been established for reporting either habilitative or rehabilitative services and procedures. These modifiers are meant to be reported with procedure or service codes that are identified as either habilitative or rehabilitative in nature (eg, physical medicine and rehabilitation codes). Appending either modifier informs the payer that the service provided was for habilitative (to learn new skills) or for rehabilitative (to keep, get back, or improve skills) purposes.

These modifiers enable the payer to differentiate between habilitative and rehabilitative services. Because CPT codes for habilititative and rehabilitative procedures and services are not differentiated, ie, a code may be used to report the provided procedures or services for either purpose, a method to differentiate the purpose, or intent, for providing the service or procedure is needed. The requirements are related to benefit allotment according to the requirements of the Affordable Care Act.

Appendix M

Appendix M has been revised to remove deleted codes from the list of codes. The deleted codes and citations appear with a strikethrough in the summary table below.

Summary of Additions, Deletions, and Revisions

The summary of changes shows the actual changes that have been made to the content in Appendix M. New code numbers appear <u>underlined</u>, while deleted codes and content appear with a ~~strikethrough~~.

Current Code(s)	Deleted/Former Code	Year Code Deleted	Citations Referencing Former Code— Applicable to Current Code(s)
~~77785, 77786~~	~~77781~~	~~2009~~	~~Winter 90:10, Winter 91:23, Mar 99:3, Feb 02:7, Mar 02:2, Sep 05:1, Nov 05:15~~
~~77785-77787~~	~~77782~~	~~2009~~	~~Winter 90:10, Winter 91:23, Mar 99:3, Feb 02:7, Mar 02:2, Sep 05:1, Nov 05:15~~
~~77785-77787~~	~~77783~~	~~2009~~	~~Winter 90:10, Winter 91:23, Mar 99:3, Feb 02:7, Mar 02:2, Sep 05:1, Nov 05:15~~
~~77785-77787~~	~~77784~~	~~2009~~	~~Winter 90:10, Winter 91:23, Mar 99:3, Feb 02:7, Mar 02:2, Sep 05:1, Nov 05:15~~
20985-20987	0054T	2008	May 04:14, Jun 04:8 CPT Changes: An Insider's View 2004
20985-20987	0055T	2008	May 04:14, Jun 04:8 CPT Changes: An Insider's View 2004, 2005
20985-20987	0056T	2008	May 04:14, Jun 04:8 CPT Changes: An Insider's View 2004
75557-75563	75552	2008	Fall 95:2
34806	~~0153T~~	~~2008~~	~~CPT Changes: An Insider's View 2007, Clinical Examples in Radiology Winter 06:19~~
93982	~~0154T~~	~~2008~~	~~CPT Changes: An Insider's View 2007, Clinical Examples in Radiology Winter 06:19~~
32421	~~32000~~	~~2008~~	~~Spring 91:4, Winter 92:20~~
32422	~~32002~~	~~2008~~	~~Nov 03:14~~
75557-75563<u>4</u>	75553	2008	Fall 95:2
75557-75563<u>4</u>	75554	2008	Fall 95:2
75557-75563<u>4</u>	75555	2008	Fall 95:2
75557-75563<u>4</u>	75556	2008	Fall 95:2
~~0160T, 0161T~~	~~0018T~~	~~2007~~	~~CPT Changes: An Insider's View 2002~~
47719	47716	~~2007~~	
72291	~~76012~~	~~2007~~	~~Mar 01:2 CPT Changes: An Insider's View 2001, 2006~~
72292	~~76013~~	~~2007~~	~~Mar 01:2 CPT Changes: An Insider's View 2001~~
77079	~~76071~~	~~2007~~	~~CPT Changes: An Insider's View 2003~~
77082	~~76077~~	~~2007~~	~~CPT Changes: An Insider's View 2005~~
77083	~~76078~~	~~2007~~	~~Nov 97:24 CPT Changes: An Insider's View 2002~~
77051	~~76082~~	~~2007~~	~~CPT Changes: An Insider's View 2004~~
77052	~~76083~~	~~2007~~	~~CPT Changes: An Insider's View 2004~~
77055	~~76090~~	~~2007~~	~~Jul 96:6, Jun 99:10 CPT Changes: An Insider's View 2004~~
77056	~~76091~~	~~2007~~	~~Jul 96:6 CPT Changes: An Insider's View 2004~~
77057	~~76092~~	~~2007~~	~~Jul 96:6, Jun 99:10 CPT Changes: An Insider's View 2004~~
77031	~~76095~~	~~2007~~	~~April 96:9, Nov 97:24, Jan 01:9 CPT Changes: An Insider's View 2001~~
77032	~~76096~~	~~2007~~	~~Jan 01:10 CPT Changes: An Insider's View 2001~~

Appendix M

Renumbered CPT Codes–Citations Crosswalk

This listing is a summary of crosswalked deleted and renumbered codes and descriptors with the associated *CPT Assistant* references for the deleted codes. This listing includes codes deleted and renumbered from 2007 to 2009. Additional codes will not be added, since the principle of deleting and renumbering is no longer being utilized in the CPT code set.

Current Code(s)	Deleted/Former Code	Year Code Deleted	Citations Referencing Former Code— Applicable to Current Code(s)
89240	0058T	2009	Jun 04:8 CPT Changes: An Insider's View 2004
89240	0059T	2009	CPT Changes: An Insider's View 2004
41530	0088T	2009	May 05:7, Sep 05:9 CPT Changes: An Insider's View 2005
95803	0089T	2009	Jun 05:6, Feb 06:1 CPT Changes: An Insider's View 2006
22856	0090T	2009	Jun 05:6, Feb 06:1 CPT Changes: An Insider's View 2006, 2007
22864	0093T	2009	Jun 05:6, Feb 06:1 CPT Changes: An Insider's View 2006, 2007
22861	0096T	2009	Jun 05:6, Feb 06:1 CPT Changes: An Insider's View 2006, 2007
55706	0137T	2009	CPT Changes: An Insider's View 2006
95980-95982	0162T	2009	CPT Changes: An Insider's View 2007
1123F, 1124F	1080F	2009	CPT Changes: An Insider's View 2008
0054T, 0055T	20986	2009	CPT Changes: An Insider's View 2008
0054T, 0055T	20987	2009	CPT Changes: An Insider's View 2008
4177F	4007F	2009	CPT Changes: An Insider's View 2008
52214	52606	2009	Apr 01:4
52601	52612	2009	Apr 01:4
52601	52614	2009	Apr 01:4
52630	52620	2009	Apr 01:4
61796-61800, 63620, 63621	61793	2009	Nov 97:23, May 03:19, Apr 04:15, Jan 06:46
88720	88400	2009	Aug 05:9
96360	90760	2009	Nov 05:1, Jul 06:4, Sep 06:14, Dec 06:14 CPT Changes: An Insider's View 2006, 2008
96361	90761	2009	Nov 05:1, Jul 06:4, Sep 06:14, Dec 06:14, Mar 07:10 CPT Changes: An Insider's View 2006, 2007
96365	90765	2009	Nov 05:1, Sep 06:14, Nov 06:22, Dec 06:14 CPT Changes: An Insider's View 2006
96366	90766	2009	Nov 05:1, Sep 06:14, Dec 06:14, Mar 07:10 CPT Changes: An Insider's View 2006, 2007
96367	90767	2009	Nov 05:1, Sep 06:14, Nov 06:22, Dec 06:14 CPT Changes: An Insider's View 2006
96368	90768	2009	Nov 05:1, Aug 06:11, Sep 06:14, Nov 06:22, Dec 06:14 CPT Changes: An Insider's View2006
96369	90769	2009	CPT Changes: An Insider's View 2008
96370	90770	2009	CPT Changes: An Insider's View 2008
96371	90771	2009	CPT Changes: An Insider's View 2008
96372	90772	2009	Nov 05:1, Sep 06:14, Dec 06:14 CPT Changes: An Insider's View 2006
96373	90773	2009	Nov 05:1, Sep 06:14, Dec 06:14 CPT Changes: An Insider's View 2006
96374	90774	2009	Nov 05:1, Sep 06:14, Dec 06:14 CPT Changes: An Insider's View 2006
96375	90775	2009	Nov 05:1, Sep 06:14, Dec 06:14 CPT Changes: An Insider's View 2006

★ = Telemedicine   ✚ = Add-on code   ✔ = FDA approval pending   # = Resequenced code

Current Code(s)	Deleted/Former Code	Year Code Deleted	Citations Referencing Former Code— Applicable to Current Code(s)
96376	90776	2009	CPT Changes: An Insider's View 2008
96379	90779	2009	Nov 05:1, Sep 06:14, Dec 06:14 CPT Changes: An Insider's View 2006
90951-90953, 90963, 90967	90918	2009	Fall 93:5, May 96:4, May 02:17, Jan 03:22
90954-90956, 90964, 90968	90919	2009	Fall 93:5, May 96:5, May 02:17, Jan 03:22
90957-90959, 90965, 90969	90920	2009	Fall 93:5, May 96:5, May 02:17, Jan 03:22
90960-90962, 90966, 90970	90921	2009	Fall 93:5, May 96:5, May 02:17, Jan 03:22
90951-90953, 90963, 90967	90922	2009	Fall 93:5, May 96:5, May 02:17, Jan 03:22
90954-90956, 90964, 90968	90923	2009	May 96:5, May 02:17, Jan 03:22
90957-90959, 90965, 90969	90924	2009	May 96:5, May 02:17, Jan 03:22
90960-90962, 90966, 90970	90925	2009	May 96:5, May 02:17, Jan 03:22
93285, 93291, 93298	93727	2009	Nov 99:50, Jul 00:5, CPT Changes: An Insider's View 2000
93280, 93288, 93294	93731	2009	Summer 94:23, Feb 98:11
93280, 93288, 93294	93732	2009	Summer 94:23, Feb 98:11, Mar 00:10
93293	93733	2009	Summer 94:23
93279, 93288, 93294	93734	2009	Summer 94:23, Feb 98:11
93279, 93288, 93294	93735	2009	Summer 94:23, Feb 98:11
93293	93736	2009	Summer 94:23
93282, 93289, 93292, 93295	93741	2009	Nov 99:50-51, Jul 00:5, Nov 00:9, Sep 05:8 CPT Changes: An Insider's View 2000, 2005
93282, 93289, 93292, 93295	93742	2009	Nov 99:50-51, Jul 00:5, Nov 00:9 CPT Changes: An Insider's View 2000, 2005
93283, 93289, 93295	93743	2009	Nov 99:50-51, Jul 00:5, Nov 00:9, Sep 05:8 CPT Changes: An Insider's View 2000
93283, 93289, 93295	93744	2009	Nov 99:50-51, Jul 00:5, Nov 00:9 CPT Changes: An Insider's View 2000
99466	99289	2009	May 05:1, Jul 06:4 CPT Changes: An Insider's View 2002, 2003
99467	99290	2009	CPT Changes: An Insider's View 2002
99468	99295	2009	Summer 93:1, Nov 97:4-5, Mar 98:11, Nov 99:5-6, Dec 00:14, Feb 03:15, Oct 03:1, May 05:1, Nov 05:10, CPT Changes: An Insider's View 2000, 2003, 2004, 2005
99469	99296	2009	Summer 93:1, Nov 97:4-5, Mar 98:11, Nov 99:5-6, Dec 00:14, Feb 03:15, Oct 03:1, Nov 05:10, CPT Changes: An Insider's View 2000, 2003, 2004, 2005, 2008
99471	99293	2009	Feb 03:15, Oct 03:2, Aug 04:7, 10, May 05:1, Nov 05:10, Jul 06:4, Apr 07:3 CPT Changes: An Insider's View 2003, 2004, 2005
99472	99294	2009	Feb 03:15, Oct 03:2, Aug 04:7, Nov 05:10, Jul 06:4, Apr 07:3 CPT Changes: An Insider's View 2003, 2004, 2005

Appendix M

Current Code(s)	Deleted/Former Code	Year Code Deleted	Citations Referencing Former Code— Applicable to Current Code(s)
99478	99298	2009	Nov 98:2-3, Nov 99: 5-6, Aug 00:4, Dec 00:15, Oct 03:2, May 05:1, Nov 05:10; CPTChanges: An Insider's View 2000, 2003
99479	99299	2009	Oct 03:2, Nov 05:10; CPT Changes: An Insider's View 2003
99480	99300	2009	CPT Changes: An Insider's View 2006
99460	99431	2009	Apr 97:10, Nov 97:9, Sep 98:5, Apr 04:14, May 05:1
99461	99432	2009	Sep 98:5, May 99:11, Apr 04:14
99462	99433	2009	Sep 98:5, Apr 03:27
99463	99435	2009	Sep 98:5, Apr 04:14
99464	99436	2009	Nov 97:9-10, Sep 98:5, Nov 99:5-6, Aug 00:3, Aug 04:9, Nov 05:15
99465	99440	2009	Summer 93:3, Mar 96:10, Nov 97:9, Sep 98:5, Nov 99:5-6, Aug 00:3, Oct 03:3, Aug04:9, Apr 07:3
20985	0054T	2008	May 04:14, Jun 04:8 CPT Changes: An Insider's View 2004
20985	0055T	2008	May 04:14, Jun 04:8 CPT Changes: An Insider's View 2004, 2005
20985-	0056T	2008	May 04:14, Jun 04:8 CPT Changes: An Insider's View 2004
99174	0065T	2008	Mar 05:1, 3-4 CPT Changes: An Insider's View 2005
99444	0074T	2008	May 05:7, Sep 05:6 CPT Changes: An Insider's View 2005
99605-99607	0115T	2008	CPT Changes: An Insider's View 2006
99605-99607	0116T	2008	CPT Changes: An Insider's View 2006
99605-99607	0117T	2008	CPT Changes: An Insider's View 2006
50593	0135T	2008	CPT Changes: An Insider's View 2006, Clinical Examples in Radiology Winter 06:18
01935, 01936	01905	2008	Mar 06:15 CPT Changes: An Insider's View 2002
24357-24359	24350	2008	
24357-24359	24351	2008	
24357-24359	24352	2008	
24357-24359	24354	2008	
24357-24359	24356	2008	
3044F-3045F	3047F	2008	CPT Changes: An Insider's View 2007
3074F-3075F	3076F	2008	CPT Changes: An Insider's View 2007
32560	32005	2008	
32550	32019	2008	CPT Changes: An Insider's View 2005
32551	32020	2008	Fall 92:13, Nov 03:14
36591	36540	2008	Jan 02:11, Nov 02:3, Apr 03:26, Nov 05:1 CPT Changes: An Insider's View 2001, 2003
36593	36550	2008	Nov 99:20, Nov 05:1 CPT Changes: An Insider's View 2000
49203-49205, 58957, 58958	49200	2008	CPT Changes: An Insider's View 2003
49203-49205, 58957, 58958	49201	2008	
51100	51000	2008	Nov 99:32-33, Aug 00:3, Oct 03:2
51101	51005	2008	
51102	51010	2008	
60300	60001	2008	
67041, 67042, 67043	67038	2008	Aug 03:15, Sep 05:12

★ = Telemedicine   ✚ = Add-on code   ✐ = FDA approval pending   # = Resequenced code

Current Code(s)	Deleted/Former Code	Year Code Deleted	Citations Referencing Former Code— Applicable to Current Code(s)
75557, 75559, 75561, 75563	75552	2008	Fall 95:2
75557, 75559, 75561, 75563	75553	2008	Fall 95:2
75557, 75559, 75561, 75563	75554	2008	Fall 95:2
75557, 75559, 75561, 75563	75555	2008	Fall 95:2
75557, 75559, 75561, 75563	75556	2008	Fall 95:2
78610	78615	2008	CPT Changes: An Insider's View 2002
86356, 86486	86586	2008	Jul 98:11
99366-99368	99361	2008	May 05:1
99366-99368	99362	2008	
99441-99443	99371	2008	Spring 94:34, May 00:11, May 05:1, Nov 05:10
99441-99443	99372	2008	Spring 94:34, May 00:11, Nov 05:10
99441-99443	99373	2008	Spring 94:34, May 00:11, Nov 05:10
96904	0044T	2007	CPT Changes: An Insider's View 2003, 2004
96904	0045T	2007	Jul 04:7 CPT Changes: An Insider's View 2004
77371-77373	0082T	2007	CPT Changes: An Insider's View 2005
77371-77373	0083T	2007	CPT Changes: An Insider's View 2005
22857	0091T	2007	CPT Changes: An Insider's View 2006
22865	0094T	2007	CPT Changes: An Insider's View 2006
22862	0097T	2007	CPT Changes: An Insider's View 2006
19105	0120T	2007	CPT Changes: An Insider's View 2006
15002, 15004	15000	2007	Fall 93:7, Apr 97:4, Aug 97:6, Sep 97:2, Nov 98:5, Jan 99:4, Apr 99:10, May 99:10, Nov 02:7, Aug 03:14 CPT Changes: An Insider's View 2001, 2006
15003, 15005	15001	2007	Nov 98:5-6, Jan 99:4, May 99:10, Aug 03:14
15830, 15847, 17999	15831	2007	May 01:11 CPT Changes: An Insider's View 2007
17311	17304	2007	Winter 94:19, Mar 99:11, Jun 99:10, Nov 02:7, Nov 03:15, Feb 04:11, Jul 04:2 CPT Changes: An Insider's View 2003
17312, 17314	17305	2007	Winter 94:19, Mar 99:11, Jun 99:10, Nov 02:7, Feb 04:11, Jul 04:3
17312, 17314	17306	2007	Winter 94:19, Mar 99:11, Jun 99:10, Nov 02:7, Feb 04:11, Jul 04:4
17312, 17314	17307	2007	Winter 94:19, Mar 99:11, Jun 99:10, Nov 02:7, Nov 03:15, Feb 04:11, Jul 04:4
17315	17310	2007	Winter 94:19, Mar 99:11, Jun 99:10, Nov 02:7, Feb 04:11, May 04:14, Jul 04:4 CPT Changes: An Insider's View 2003
19300	19140	2007	Feb 96:9, Apr 05:13
19301	19160	2007	Apr 05:7 CPT Changes: An Insider's View 2005
19302	19162	2007	Jun 00:11, Apr 05:7
19303	19180	2007	Apr 05:7
19304	19182	2007	Apr 05:7
19305	19200	2007	Apr 05:7
19306	19220	2007	Apr 05:7
19307	19240	2007	Apr 05:7
25606	25611	2007	Fall 93:23, Oct 99:5

▲ =Revised code   ● =New code   ▶ ◀ =Contains new or revised text   ⊘ =Modifier 51 exempt

Appendix M

Current Code(s)	Deleted/Former Code	Year Code Deleted	Citations Referencing Former Code— Applicable to Current Code(s)
25607-25609	25620	2007	
26390	26504	2007	
27325	27315	2007	
27326	27320	2007	
28055	28030	2007	
33254-33256	33253	2007	
35302-35306	35381	2007	
35506	35507	2007	
35537, 35538	35541	2007	
35539, 35540	35546	2007	
35637, 35638	35641	2007	Dec 01:7
44799	44152	2007	
44799	44153	2007	
48105	48005	2007	
48548	48180	2007	
49402	49085	2007	
54150	54152	2007	Sep 96:11, Dec 96:10, May 98:11, Apr 03:27 CPT Changes: An Insider's View 2007
54865	54820	2007	Oct 01:8
55875	55859	2007	Apr 04:6
56442	56720	2007	
57558	57820	2007	
67346	67350	2007	
77001	75998	2007	Dec 04:12-13 CPT Changes: An Insider's View 2004 Clinical Examples in Radiology Inaugural 04:1-2, Winter 05:9
77002	76003	2007	Fall 93:14, Jul 01:7 CPT Changes: An Insider's View 2001 Clinical Examples in Radiology Spring 05:5-6
77003	76005	2007	Nov 99:32, 34, 41, Jan 00:2, Feb 00:6, Aug 00:8, Sep 02:11, Sep 04:5 CPT Changes: An Insider's View 2000
77071	76006	2007	Nov 98:21 CPT Changes: An Insider's View 2003
77072	76020	2007	
77073	76040	2007	
77074	76061	2007	
77075	76062	2007	
77076	76065	2007	
77077	76066	2007	CPT Changes: An Insider's View 2002
77078	76070	2007	Nov 97:24 CPT Changes: An Insider's View 2002, 2003
77080	76075	2007	Nov 97:24, Jun 03:11 CPT Changes: An Insider's View 2005
77081	76076	2007	Nov 97:24
77053	76086	2007	
77054	76088	2007	
77058	76093	2007	
77059	76094	2007	
77011	76355	2007	CPT Changes: An Insider's View 2002, 2003
77012	76360	2007	Fall 93:12, Fall 94:2, Jan 01:9-10, Mar 05:2 CPT Changes: An Insider's View 2001, 2002, 2003

★ = Telemedicine   ✚ = Add-on code   ✗ = FDA approval pending   # = Resequenced code

Current Code(s)	Deleted/Former Code	Year Code Deleted	Citations Referencing Former Code— Applicable to Current Code(s)
77013	76362	2007	Oct 02:4 CPT Changes: An Insider's View 2002, 2004
77014	76370	2007	Fall 91:12 CPT Changes: An Insider's View 2002, 2003
77021	76393	2007	Jan 01:10, Mar 05:2 CPT Changes: An Insider's View 2001, 2002
77022	76394	2007	Oct 02:4, Mar 05:5 CPT Changes: An Insider's View 2002, 2004
77084	76400	2007	
76775, 76776	76778	2007	CPT Changes: An Insider's View 2002
76998	76986	2007	CPT Changes: An Insider's View 2001
78707-78709	78704	2007	
78701-78709	78715	2007	
78761	78760	2007	
92700	92573	2007	
94002, 94004	94656	2007	Fall 92:30, Spring 95:4, Summer 95:4, Feb 96:9, Aug 00:2, Oct 03:2
94003, 94004	94657	2007	Fall 92:30, Spring 95:4, Summer 95:4, Feb 96:9, Aug 00:2, Oct 03:2

Rationale

Appendix M has been updated with the removal of deleted codes. Although additional codes are no longer added to this table because the principle of deleting and renumbering is no longer being utilized in the CPT code set, it was determined to be beneficial to remove deleted codes to assist users referencing this table. Therefore, in an effort to keep the information in the CPT code set current, the table in Appendix M has been updated to remove any code that has been deleted from the CPT code set.

Appendix N

Appendix N has been editorially revised to include a table of resequenced codes with their corresponding ranges. These ranges provide a more efficient way of locating resequenced codes within the codebook.

Appendix N

Summary of Resequenced CPT Codes

▶This is a table of CPT codes that do not appear in numeric sequence in the listing of CPT codes and the code ranges with their corresponding locations. Rather than deleting and renumbering, resequencing allows existing codes to be relocated to an appropriate location for the code concept, regardless of the numeric sequence. The codes listed below are identified in the CPT 2018 code set with a # symbol for the location of the resequenced number within the family of related concepts. Numerically placed references (eg, **Code is out of numerical sequence. See...**) are used as navigational alerts to direct the user to the location of an out-of-sequence code.◀

Resequenced Code	Corresponding Locations of Resequenced Code	Resequenced Code	Corresponding Locations of Resequenced Code	Resequenced Code	Corresponding Locations of Resequenced Code	Resequenced Code	Corresponding Locations of Resequenced Code
11045	11012-11047	31552	31579-31587	33989	33958-33968	44401	44391-44402
11046	11012-11047	31553	31579-31587	34812	34712-34716	45346	45337-45341
21552	21550-21558	31554	31579-31587	34820	34712-34716	45388	45381-45385
21554	21550-21558	31572	31577-31580	34833	34712-34716	45390	45391-45397
22858	22853-22861	31573	31577-31580	34834	34712-34716	45398	45391-45397
22859	22853-22861	31574	31577-31580	36465	36470-36474	45399	45910-45999
23071	23066-23078	31651	31646-31649	36466	36470-36474	46220	46200-46255
23073	23066-23078	32994	32997-32999	36482	36478-36500	46320	46200-46255
24071	24066-24079	33221	33212-33215	36483	36478-36500	46945	46200-46255
24073	24066-24079	33227	33226-33244	37211	37197-37216	46946	46200-46255
25071	25066-25078	33228	33226-33244	37212	37197-37216	46947	46761-46910
25073	25066-25078	33229	33226-33244	37213	37197-37216	50430	50395-50405
26111	26110-26118	33230	33226-33244	37214	37197-37216	50431	50395-50405
26113	26110-26118	33231	33226-33244	37246	37234-37237	50432	50395-50405
27043	27041-27052	33262	33226-33244	37247	37234-37237	50433	50395-50405
27045	27041-27052	33263	33226-33244	37248	37234-37237	50434	50395-50405
27059	27041-27052	33264	33226-33244	37249	37234-37237	50435	50395-50405
27329	27358-27365	33270	33244-33251	38243	38240-38300	51797	51728-51741
27337	27326-27331	33271	33244-33251	43210	43254-43261	52356	52352-52355
27339	27326-27331	33272	33244-33251	43211	43216-43227	58674	58520-58542
27632	27616-27625	33273	33244-33251	43212	43216-43227	64461	64483-64487
27634	27616-27625	33962	33958-33968	43213	43216-43227	64462	64483-64487
28039	28035-28047	33963	33958-33968	43214	43216-43227	64463	64483-64487
28041	28035-28047	33964	33958-33968	43233	43248-43251	64633	64617-64632
28295	28292-28298	33965	33958-33968	43266	43254-43261	64634	64617-64632
29914	29862-29867	33966	33958-33968	43270	43254-43261	64635	64617-64632
29915	29862-29867	33969	33958-33968	43274	43264-43279	64636	64617-64632
29916	29862-29867	33984	33958-33968	43275	43264-43279	67810	67710-67801
31253	31254-31267	33985	33958-33968	43276	43264-43279	77085	77080-77261
31257	31254-31267	33986	33958-33968	43277	43264-43279	77086	77080-77261
31259	31254-31267	33987	33958-33968	43278	43264-43279	77295	77293-77301
31551	31579-31587	33988	33958-33968	44381	44380-44385	77385	77412-77427

Appendix N

Resequenced Code	Corresponding Locations of Resequenced Code	Resequenced Code	Corresponding Locations of Resequenced Code	Resequenced Code	Corresponding Locations of Resequenced Code	Resequenced Code	Corresponding Locations of Resequenced Code
77386	77412-77427	80329	See Definitive Drug Testing subsection	80346	See Definitive Drug Testing subsection	80363	See Definitive Drug Testing subsection
77387	77412-77427						
77424	77412-77427	80330	See Definitive Drug Testing subsection	80347	See Definitive Drug Testing subsection	80364	See Definitive Drug Testing subsection
77425	77412-77427						
80081	80053-80069						
80164	80200-80203	80331	See Definitive Drug Testing subsection	80348	See Definitive Drug Testing subsection	80365	See Definitive Drug Testing subsection
80165	80200-80203						
80171	80168-80173						
80305	See Presumptive Drug Class Screening subsection	80332	See Definitive Drug Testing subsection	80349	See Definitive Drug Testing subsection	80366	See Definitive Drug Testing subsection
		80333	See Definitive Drug Testing subsection	80350	See Definitive Drug Testing subsection	80367	See Definitive Drug Testing subsection
80306	See Presumptive Drug Class Screening subsection	80334	See Definitive Drug Testing subsection	80351	See Definitive Drug Testing subsection	80368	See Definitive Drug Testing subsection
80307	See Presumptive Drug Class Screening subsection	80335	See Definitive Drug Testing subsection	80352	See Definitive Drug Testing subsection	80369	See Definitive Drug Testing subsection
		80336	See Definitive Drug Testing subsection	80353	See Definitive Drug Testing subsection	80370	See Definitive Drug Testing subsection
80320	See Definitive Drug Testing subsection	80337	See Definitive Drug Testing subsection	80354	See Definitive Drug Testing subsection	80371	See Definitive Drug Testing subsection
80321	See Definitive Drug Testing subsection	80338	See Definitive Drug Testing subsection	80355	See Definitive Drug Testing subsection	80372	See Definitive Drug Testing subsection
80322	See Definitive Drug Testing subsection	80339	See Definitive Drug Testing subsection	80356	See Definitive Drug Testing subsection	80373	See Definitive Drug Testing subsection
80323	See Definitive Drug Testing subsection	80340	See Definitive Drug Testing subsection	80357	See Definitive Drug Testing subsection	80374	See Definitive Drug Testing subsection
80324	See Definitive Drug Testing subsection	80341	See Definitive Drug Testing subsection	80358	See Definitive Drug Testing subsection	80375	See Definitive Drug Testing subsection
80325	See Definitive Drug Testing subsection	80342	See Definitive Drug Testing subsection	80359	See Definitive Drug Testing subsection	80376	See Definitive Drug Testing subsection
80326	See Definitive Drug Testing subsection	80343	See Definitive Drug Testing subsection	80360	See Definitive Drug Testing subsection	80377	See Definitive Drug Testing subsection
80327	See Definitive Drug Testing subsection	80344	See Definitive Drug Testing subsection	80361	See Definitive Drug Testing subsection	81105	81257-81261
						81106	81257-81261
						81107	81257-81261
80328	See Definitive Drug Testing subsection	80345	See Definitive Drug Testing subsection	80362	See Definitive Drug Testing subsection	81108	81257-81261
						81109	81257-81261

★ = Telemedicine   ✚ = Add-on code   ✗ = FDA approval pending   # = Resequenced code

Resequenced Code	Corresponding Locations of Resequenced Code	Resequenced Code	Corresponding Locations of Resequenced Code	Resequenced Code	Corresponding Locations of Resequenced Code	Resequenced Code	Corresponding Locations of Resequenced Code
81110	81257-81261	90672	90658-90664	97161	See Physical Therapy Evaluations subsection	99177	99173-99183
81111	81257-81261	90673	90658-90664			99224	99219-99222
81112	81257-81261	90674	90658-90664			99225	99219-99222
81120	81257-81261	90750	90717-90739	97162	See Physical Therapy Evaluations subsection	99226	99219-99222
81121	81257-81261	90756	90658-90664			99415	99358-99366
81161	81210-81235	92558	92585-92607			99416	99358-99366
81162	81210-81235	92597	92585-92607	97163	See Physical Therapy Evaluations subsection	99484	99497-99499
81230	81226-81229	92618	92585-92607			99485	99466-99469
81231	81226-81229	92920	92997-93005			99486	99466-99469
81238	81240-81243	92921	92997-93005	97164	See Physical Therapy Evaluations subsection	99490	99480-99489
81269	81257-81261	92924	92997-93005			0253T	0191T-0196T
81283	81257-81261	92925	92997-93005			0357T	0055T-0072T
81287	81276-81294	92928	92997-93005	97165	See Occupational Therapy Evaluations subsection	0376T	0190T-0195T
81288	81276-81294	92929	92997-93005			0464T	0332T-0337T
81334	81325-81328	92933	92997-93005			0488T	0402T-0405T
81448	81437-81440	92934	92997-93005	97166	See Occupational Therapy Evaluations subsection		
81479	81407-81411	92937	92997-93005				
82042	82044-82085	92938	92997-93005				
82652	82300-82310	92941	92997-93005	97167	See Occupational Therapy Evaluations subsection		
83992	See Definitive Drug Testing subsection	92943	92997-93005				
		92944	92997-93005				
86152	86146-86155	92973	92997-93005	97168	See Occupational Therapy Evaluations subsection		
86153	86146-86155	92974	92997-93005				
87623	87538-87541	92975	92997-93005				
87624	87538-87541	92977	92997-93005				
87625	87538-87541	92978	92997-93005	97169	See Athletic Training Evaluations subsection		
87806	87802-87903	92979	92997-93005				
87906	87802-87903	93260	93283-93291				
87910	87802-87903	93261	93283-93291	97170	See Athletic Training Evaluations subsection		
87912	87802-87903	95249	95199-95803				
88177	88172-88175	95782	95805-95813				
88341	88334-88372	95783	95805-95813	97171	See Athletic Training Evaluations subsection		
88350	88334-88372	95800	95805-95813				
88364	88334-88372	95801	95805-95813				
88373	88334-88372	95885	95870-95874	97172	See Athletic Training Evaluations subsection		
88374	88334-88372	95886	95870-95874				
88377	88334-88372	95887	95870-95874				
90620	90717-90739	95938	95912-95933				
90621	90717-90739	95939	95912-95933				
90625	90717-90739	95940	95912-95933				
90630	90653-90656	95941	95912-95933				
90644	90717-90739	95943	95912-95933				

Rationale

Appendix N has been revised to include the resequenced code ranges in the appendix. Also, all code ranges in the reference parenthetical notes for resequenced codes throughout the code set have been revised to provide more accurate cross-referenced ranges. These editorially revised code ranges are now listed in Appendix N to further assist in locating the resequenced code. Similarly, the introductory text for Appendix N has been revised to indicate the inclusion of the new ranges.

These changes have been made in response to concerns that previous code ranges were too large or too vague, making it difficult to locate the resequenced codes in the code set.

Resequenced codes that are not placed numerically are identified with the # symbol as a navigational alert to direct users to the location of the out-of-sequence code. Resequencing is used to enable related concepts to be placed in appropriate locations within families of codes, regardless of sequential numerical placement. The revised resequenced code ranges in the code set have been condensed by reducing the size of the ranges, ie, to make the code ranges smaller, making it possible to more efficiently locate the resequenced codes. For example, in CPT 2017, the resequenced code range for 81479 was 81400-81479, while in CPT 2018, the revised resequenced range is 81407-81411.

Appendix O

In Appendix O, four new Category I codes (81520, 81521, 81541, 81551) have been added to the Multianalyte Assay with Algorithmic Analyses (MAAA) codes. In addition, code 0008M (administrative MAAA) has been deleted.

Summary of Additions, Deletions, and Revisions

The summary of changes shows the actual changes that have been made to the code descriptors.

New codes appear with a bullet (•) and are indicated as "Code added." Revised codes are preceded with a triangle (▲). Within revised codes, the deleted language appears with a ~~strikethrough~~, while new text appears <u>underlined</u>.

The ⁄ symbol is used to identify codes for vaccines that are pending FDA approval. The # symbol is used to identify codes that have been resequenced. CPT add-on codes are annotated by the + symbol. The ⊘ symbol is used to identify codes that are exempt from the use of modifier 51. The ★ symbol is used to identify codes that may be used for reporting telemedicine services.

Proprietary Name and Clinical Laboratory or Manufacturer	Alpha-Numeric Code	Code Descriptor
Administrative Codes for Multianalyte Assays with Algorithmic Analyses (MAAA)		
~~Prosigna Breast Cancer Assay, NanoString Technologies~~	~~0008M~~	~~Oncology (breast), mRNA analysis of 58 genes using hybrid capture, on formalin-fixed paraffin-embedded (FFPE) tissue, prognostic algorithm reported as a risk score~~
Category I Codes for Multianalyte Assays with Algorithmic Analyses (MAAA)		
►Prosigna® Breast Cancer Assay, NanoString Technologies, Inc.◄	•81520	►Oncology (breast), mRNA gene expression profiling by hybrid capture of 58 genes (50 content and 8 housekeeping), utilizing formalin-fixed paraffin-embedded tissue, algorithm reported as a recurrence risk score◄
►MammaPrint®, Agendia, Inc.◄	•81521	►Oncology (breast), mRNA, microarray gene expression profiling of 70 content genes and 465 housekeeping genes, utilizing fresh frozen or formalin-fixed paraffin-embedded tissue, algorithm reported as index related to risk of distant metastasis◄
►Prolaris®, Myriad Genetic Laboratories, Inc.◄	•81541	►Oncology (prostate), mRNA gene expression profiling by real-time RT-PCR of 46 genes (31 content and 15 housekeeping), utilizing formalin-fixed paraffin-embedded tissue, algorithm reported as a disease-specific mortality risk score◄
►ConfirmMDx® for Prostate Cancer, MDxHealth, Inc.◄	•81551	►Oncology (prostate), promoter methylation profiling by real-time PCR of 3 genes (GSTP1, APC, RASSF1), utilizing formalin-fixed paraffin-embedded tissue, algorithm reported as a likelihood of prostate cancer detection on repeat biopsy◄

Appendix O

Multianalyte Assays with Algorithmic Analyses

The following list includes a set of administrative codes for Multianalyte Assays with Algorithmic Analyses (MAAA) procedures that by their nature are typically unique to a single clinical laboratory or manufacturer.

Multianalyte Assays with Algorithmic Analyses (MAAAs) are procedures that utilize multiple results derived from assays of various types, including molecular pathology assays, fluorescent in situ hybridization assays and non-nucleic acid based assays (eg, proteins, polypeptides, lipids, carbohydrates). Algorithmic analysis using the results of these assays as well as other patient information (if used) is then performed and reported typically as a numeric score(s) or as a probability. MAAAs are typically unique to a single clinical laboratory or manufacturer. The results of individual component procedure(s) that are inputs to the MAAAs may be provided on the associated laboratory report, however these assays are not reported separately using additional codes.

The list includes a proprietary name and clinical laboratory or manufacturer in the first column, an alpha-numeric code in the second column and code descriptor in the third column. The format for the code descriptor usually includes (in order):

- Disease type (eg, oncology, autoimmune, tissue rejection),

- Chemical(s) analyzed (eg, DNA, RNA, protein, antibody),

- Number of markers (eg, number of genes, number of proteins),

- Methodology(s) (eg, microarray, real-time [RT]-PCR, in situ hybridization [ISH], enzyme linked immunosorbent assays [ELISA]),

- Number of functional domains (if indicated),

- Specimen type (eg, blood, fresh tissue, formalin-fixed paraffin-embedded),

- Algorithm result type (eg, prognostic, diagnostic),

- Report (eg, probability index, risk score).

MAAA procedures that have been assigned a Category I code are noted in the list below and additionally listed in the Category I MAAA section (81500-81599). The Category I MAAA section introductory language and associated parenthetical instruction(s) should be used to govern the appropriate use for Category I MAAA codes. If a specific MAAA procedure has not been assigned a Category I code, it is indicated as a four-digit number followed by the letter M.

When a specific MAAA procedure is not included in either the list below or in the Category I MAAA section, report the analysis using the Category I MAAA unlisted code (81599). The codes below are specific to the assays identified in Appendix O by proprietary name. In order to report an MAAA code, the analysis performed must fulfill the code descriptor **and**, if proprietary, must be the test represented by the proprietary name listed in Appendix O. When an analysis is performed that may potentially fall within a specific descriptor, however the proprietary name is not included in the list below, the MAAA unlisted code (81599) should be used.

Additions in this section may be released tri-annually via the AMA CPT website to expedite dissemination for reporting. The list will be published annually in the CPT codebook. Go to www.ama-assn.org/go/cpt for the most current listing.

These administrative codes encompass all analytical services required for the algorithmic analysis (eg, cell lysis, nucleic acid stabilization, extraction, digestion, amplification, hybridization and detection) in addition to the algorithmic analysis itself. Procedures that are required prior to cell lysis (eg, microdissection, codes 88380 and 88381) should be reported separately.

The codes in this list are provided as an administrative coding set to facilitate accurate reporting of MAAA services. The minimum standard for inclusion in this list is that an analysis is generally available for patient care. The AMA has not reviewed procedures in the administrative coding set for clinical utility. The list is not a complete list of all MAAA procedures.

★ = Telemedicine   ✚ = Add-on code   ✔ = FDA approval pending   # = Resequenced code

Proprietary Name and Clinical Laboratory or Manufacturer	Alpha-Numeric Code	Code Descriptor
Administrative Codes for Multianalyte Assays with Algorithmic Analyses (MAAA)		
HCV FibroSURE™, LabCorp FibroTest™, Quest Diagnostics/BioPredictive	0001M	Infectious disease, HCV, six biochemical assays (ALT, A2-macroglobulin, apolipoprotein A-1, total bilirubin, GGT, and haptoglobin) utilizing serum, prognostic algorithm reported as scores for fibrosis and necroinflammatory activity in liver
ASH FibroSURE™, LabCorp	0002M	Liver disease, ten biochemical assays (ALT, A2-macroglobulin, apolipoprotein A-1, total bilirubin, GGT, haptoglobin, AST, glucose, total cholesterol and triglycerides) utilizing serum, prognostic algorithm reported as quantitative scores for fibrosis, steatosis and alcoholic steatohepatitis (ASH)
NASH FibroSURE™, LabCorp	0003M	Liver disease, ten biochemical assays (ALT, A2-macroglobulin, apolipoprotein A-1, total bilirubin, GGT, haptoglobin, AST, glucose, total cholesterol and triglycerides) utilizing serum, prognostic algorithm reported as quantitative scores for fibrosis, steatosis and nonalcoholic steatohepatitis (NASH)
ScoliScore™ Transgenomic	0004M	Scoliosis, DNA analysis of 53 single nucleotide polymorphisms (SNPs), using saliva, prognostic algorithm reported as a risk score
—	(0005M has been deleted, use 81507)	—
HeproDX™, GoPath Laboratories, LLC	0006M	Oncology (hepatic), mRNA expression levels of 161 genes, utilizing fresh hepatocellular carcinoma tumor tissue, with alpha-fetoprotein level, algorithm reported as a risk classifier
NETest, Wren Laboratories, LLC	0007M	Oncology (gastrointestinal neuroendocrine tumors), real-time PCR expression analysis of 51 genes, utilizing whole peripheral blood, algorithm reported as a nomogram of tumor disease index
—	▶(0008M has been deleted, use 81520)◀	—
VisibiliT test, Sequenom Center for Molecular Medicine, LLC	0009M	Fetal aneuploidy (trisomy 21, and 18) DNA sequence analysis of selected regions using maternal plasma, algorithm reported as a risk score for each trisomy
—	(0010M has been deleted, use 81539)	—
Category I Codes for Multianalyte Assays with Algorithmic Analyses (MAAA)		
Vectra® DA, Crescendo Bioscience, Inc.	81490	Autoimmune (rheumatoid arthritis), analysis of 12 biomarkers using immunoassays, utilizing serum, prognostic algorithm reported as a disease activity score (Do not report 81490 in conjunction with 86140)

Corus® CAD, CardioDx, Inc.	81493	Coronary artery disease, mRNA, gene expression profiling by real-time RT-PCR of 23 genes, utilizing whole peripheral blood, algorithm reported as a risk score
AlloMap®, CareDx, Inc.	81595	Cardiology (heart transplant), mRNA, gene expression profiling by real-time quantitative PCR of 20 genes (11 content and 9 housekeeping), utilizing subfraction of peripheral blood, algorithm reported as a rejection risk score
Risk of Ovarian Malignancy Algorithm (ROMA)™, Fujirebio Diagnostics	81500	Oncology (ovarian), biochemical assays of two proteins (CA-125 and HE4), utilizing serum, with menopausal status, algorithm reported as a risk score
OVA1™, Vermillion, Inc.	81503	Oncology (ovarian), biochemical assays of five proteins (CA-125, apolipoprotein A1, beta-2 microglobulin, transferrin, and pre-albumin), utilizing serum, algorithm reported as a risk score
Pathwork® Tissue of Origin Test, Pathwork Diagnostics	81504	Oncology (tissue of origin), microarray gene expression profiling of >2000 genes, utilizing formalin-fixed paraffin-embedded tissue, algorithm reported as tissue similarity scores
PreDx Diabetes Risk Score™, Tethys Clinical Laboratory	81506	Endocrinology (type 2 diabetes), biochemical assays of seven analytes (glucose, HbA1c, insulin, hs-CRP, adiponectin, ferritin, interleukin 2-receptor alpha), utilizing serum or plasma, algorithm reporting a risk score
Harmony™ Prenatal Test, Ariosa Diagnostics	81507	Fetal aneuploidy (trisomy 21, 18, and 13) DNA sequence analysis of selected regions using maternal plasma, algorithm reported as a risk score for each trisomy
No proprietary name and clinical laboratory or manufacturer. Maternal serum screening procedures are well-established procedures and are performed by many laboratories throughout the country. The concept of prenatal screens has existed and evolved for over 10 years and is not exclusive to any one facility.	81508	Fetal congenital abnormalities, biochemical assays of two proteins (PAPP-A, hCG [any form]), utilizing maternal serum, algorithm reported as a risk score
	81509	Fetal congenital abnormalities, biochemical assays of three proteins (PAPP-A, hCG [any form], DIA), utilizing maternal serum, algorithm reported as a risk score
	81510	Fetal congenital abnormalities, biochemical assays of three analytes (AFP, uE3, hCG [any form]), utilizing maternal serum, algorithm reported as a risk score
	81511	Fetal congenital abnormalities, biochemical assays of four analytes (AFP, uE3, hCG [any form], DIA) utilizing maternal serum, algorithm reported as a risk score (may include additional results from previous biochemical testing)
	81512	Fetal congenital abnormalities, biochemical assays of five analytes (AFP, uE3, total hCG, hyperglycosylated hCG, DIA) utilizing maternal serum, algorithm reported as a risk score

★ = Telemedicine   ✦ = Add-on code   ✗ = FDA approval pending   # = Resequenced code

Oncotype DX®, Genomic Health	81519	Oncology (breast), mRNA, gene expression profiling by real-time RT-PCR of 21 genes, utilizing formalin-fixed paraffin-embedded tissue, algorithm reported as recurrence score
▶Prosigna® Breast Cancer Assay, NanoString Technologies, Inc.◀	●81520	▶Oncology (breast), mRNA gene expression profiling by hybrid capture of 58 genes (50 content and 8 housekeeping), utilizing formalin-fixed paraffin-embedded tissue, algorithm reported as a recurrence risk score◀
▶MammaPrint®, Agendia, Inc.◀	●81521	▶Oncology (breast), mRNA, microarray gene expression profiling of 70 content genes and 465 housekeeping genes, utilizing fresh frozen or formalin-fixed paraffin-embedded tissue, algorithm reported as index related to risk of distant metastasis◀
Oncotype DX® Colon Cancer Assay, Genomic Health	81525	Oncology (colon), mRNA, gene expression profiling by real-time RT-PCR of 12 genes (7 content and 5 housekeeping), utilizing formalin-fixed paraffin-embedded tissue, algorithm reported as a recurrence score
Cologuard™, Exact Sciences, Inc.	81528	Oncology (colorectal) screening, quantitative real-time target and signal amplification of 10 DNA markers (KRAS mutations, promoter methylation of NDRG4 and BMP3) and fecal hemoglobin, utilizing stool, algorithm reported as a positive or negative result (Do not report 81528 in conjunction with 81275, 82274)
ChemoFX®, Helomics, Corp.	81535 +81536	Oncology (gynecologic), live tumor cell culture and chemotherapeutic response by DAPI stain and mor-phology, predictive algorithm reported as a drug response score; first single drug or drug combination each additional single drug or drug combination (List separately in addition to code for primary procedure) (Use 81536 in conjunction with 81535)
VeriStrat, Biodesix, Inc.	81538	Oncology (lung), mass spectrometric 8-protein signature, including amyloid A, utilizing serum, prog-nostic and predictive algorithm reported as good versus poor overall survival
4Kscore test, OPKO Health, Inc.	81539	Oncology (high-grade prostate cancer), biochemical assay of four proteins (Total PSA, Free PSA, Intact PSA and human kallikrein-2 [hK2]), utilizing plasma or serum, prognostic algorithm reported as a probability score
CancerTYPE ID, bioTheranostics, Inc.	81540	Oncology (tumor of unknown origin), mRNA, gene expression profiling by real-time RT-PCR of 92 genes (87 content and 5 housekeeping) to classify tumor into main cancer type and subtype, utilizing formalin-fixed paraffin-embedded tissue, algorithm reported as a probability of a predicted main cancer type and subtype

▶Prolaris®, Myriad Genetic Laboratories, Inc.◀	●81541	▶Oncology (prostate), mRNA gene expression profiling by real-time RT-PCR of 46 genes (31 content and 15 housekeeping), utilizing formalin-fixed paraffin-embedded tissue, algorithm reported as a disease-specific mortality risk score◀
Afirma® Gene Expression Classifier, Veracyte, Inc.	81545	Oncology (thyroid), gene expression analysis of 142 genes, utilizing fine needle aspirate, algorithm reported as a categorical result (eg, benign or suspicious)
▶ConfirmMDx® for Prostate Cancer, MDxHealth, Inc.◀	●81551	▶Oncology (prostate), promoter methylation profiling by real-time PCR of 3 genes (GSTP1, APC, RASSF1), utilizing formalin-fixed paraffin-embedded tissue, algorithm reported as a likelihood of prostate cancer detection on repeat biopsy◀
	81599	Unlisted multianalyte assay with algorithmic analysis

Rationale

Multianalyte assay with algorithmic analysis (MAAA) administrative code 0008M has been deleted. This is in accordance with the establishment of MAAA Category I code 81520. A parenthetical note has been added to indicate that code 81520 should be reported for the same breast cancer MAAA test that was represented by deleted code 0008M. Refer to the codebook and the Rationale for code 81520 for a full discussion of the changes.

Category I MAAA codes 81521, 81541, and 81551 have also been added to Appendix O. Refer to the codebook and the Rationale for codes 81521, 81541, and 81551 for a full discussion of the changes.

Refer to the introductory guidelines in Appendix O for specific guidance on how to accurately report or assign new codes, as well as the specific requirements for inclusion in the Administrative Code List or as a Category I code.

★ = Telemedicine   ✚ = Add-on code   ✗ = FDA approval pending   # = Resequenced code

Indexes

Instructions for the Use of the Changes Indexes

The Changes Indexes are **not** a substitute for the main text of *CPT Changes 2018* or the main text of the CPT codebook. The changes indexes consist of two types of content—coding changes and modifiers—all of which are intended to assist users in searching and locating information quickly within *CPT Changes 2018*.

Index of Coding Changes

The Index of Coding Changes does not list existing codes unless they are new, revised, or deleted, or if the code may be affected by revised and/or new guidelines and parenthetical notes. Also included are codes described in the Rationales. This index enables users to quickly search and locate the codes within a page(s), in addition to discerning the status of a code (new, revised, deleted, or textually changed) because the status of each new, revised, or deleted code is noted in parentheses next to the code number:

Index of Modifiers

A limited Index of Modifiers, ie, limited to only the modifiers that are in new and/or revised parenthetical notes and guidelines in this book, as well as limited to only those modifiers that appear in the Rationales, is provided to help users quickly locate these modifiers and to know where in the book these modifiers are listed or mentioned.

Index of Coding Changes

Indexes

★ = Telemedicine   ✚ = Add-on code   ✗ = FDA approval pending   # = Resequenced code

★ = Telemedicine   ✚ = Add-on code   𝗡 = FDA approval pending   # = Resequenced code

Indexes

★ = Telemedicine   ✚ = Add-on code   ✅ = FDA approval pending   # = Resequenced code

Indexes

▲ = Revised code   ● = New code   ▶ ◀ = Contains new or revised text   ⊘ = Modifier 51 exempt

Indexes

★ = Telemedicine   ✚ = Add-on code   ✗ = FDA approval pending   # = Resequenced code

Indexes

★ = Telemedicine   ✚ = Add-on code   ✒ = FDA approval pending   # = Resequenced code

Indexes

★ = Telemedicine   ✚ = Add-on code   ✗ = FDA approval pending   # = Resequenced code

▲ =Revised code   ● =New code   ▶ ◀ =Contains new or revised text   ⃠ =Modifier 51 exempt

Indexes

Indexes

★ = Telemedicine   ✚ = Add-on code   ⟋ = FDA approval pending   # = Resequenced code

Indexes

Index of Modifiers

Modifier, Descriptor

Page Numbers

★ = Telemedicine   ✚ = Add-on code   ◢ = FDA approval pending   # = Resequenced code